Playing the Identity Card

National identity cards are in the news. While paper ID documents have been used in some countries for a long time, today's rapid growth features high-tech IDs with built-in biometrics and RFID chips. Both long-term trends towards e-Government and the more recent responses to 9/11 have prompted the quest for more stable identity systems. Commercial pressures mix with security rationales to catalyse ID development, aimed at accuracy, efficiency and speed. New ID systems also depend on computerized national registries. Many questions are raised about new IDs but they are often limited by focusing on the cards themselves or on 'privacy'.

Playing the Identity Card shows not only the benefits of how the state can 'see' citizens better using these instruments but also the challenges this raises for civil liberties and human rights. ID cards are part of a broader trend towards intensified surveillance and as such are understood very differently according to the history and cultures of the countries concerned.

This collection addresses a variety of issues in international and comparative perspective, bringing together articles on existing and proposed identity systems in countries around the globe as well as from the European Union and the International Aviation Authority (ICAO). The articles in the collection explore not only the technical and administrative dimensions but also the historical, international sociological and political economy perspective as well.

Colin J. Bennett is a Professor in the Department of Political Science at the University of Victoria, Canada. His research has focused on the comparative analysis of surveillance technologies and privacy protection policies at the domestic and international levels.

David Lyon is the Director of the Surveillance Project and Research Chair in Sociology at Queen's University, Canada. He has been working on surveillance issues since the 1980s, and has particular research interests in national ID cards, aviation security and surveillance and in promoting the cross-disciplinary and international study of surveillance.

Playing the Identity Card

Surveillance, security and
identification in global perspective

**Edited by Colin J. Bennett
and David Lyon**

Routledge
Taylor & Francis Group

LONDON AND NEW YORK

First published 2008
by Routledge
2 Park Square, Milton Park, Abingdon, Oxon OX14 4RN

Simultaneously published in the USA and Canada
by Routledge
270 Madison Ave, New York, NY 10016

*Routledge is an imprint of the Taylor & Francis Group,
an informa business*

© 2008 Colin J. Bennett and David Lyon for editorial matter and selection;
individual chapters, the contributors

Typeset in Times New Roman
by Swales and Willis Ltd, Exeter, Devon
Printed and bound in Great Britain by CPI Antony Rowe,
Chippenham, Wiltshire

British Library Cataloguing in Publication Data
A catalogue record for this book is available
from the British Library

Library of Congress Cataloging in Publication Data
A catalog record has been requested for this book

ISBN 10: 0–415–46563–X (hbk)
ISBN 10: 0–415–46564–8 (pbk)
ISBN 10: 0–203–92713–3 (ebk)

ISBN 13: 978–0–415–46563–2 (hbk)
ISBN 13: 978–0–415–46564–9 (pbk)
ISBN 13: 978– 0–203–92713–7 (ebk)

Contents

Contributors

Louise Amoore specializes in the geopolitics of risk and security in the Department of Geography, Durham University, UK. She is currently leading two Economic and Social Research Council (ESRC) projects on risk and the technologies of the War on Terror: 'Contested Borders' and 'Data Wars'. She is co-editor (with Marieke deGoede) of *Risk and the War on Terror* (London: Routledge, 2008), and has published some of her recent work in *Security Dialogue, Political Geography, Antipode* and *Transactions*.

Colin J. Bennett is a Professor in the Department of Political Science at the University of Victoria, Canada. His research is focused on the comparative analysis of surveillance technologies and privacy protection policies at the domestic and international levels. He has published three books on the topic: *Regulating Privacy: Data Protection and Public Policy in Europe and the United States* (Cornell University Press, 1992); *Visions of Privacy: Policy Choices for the Digital Age* (University of Toronto Press, 1999, with Rebecca Grant); and *The Governance of Privacy: Policy Instruments in the Digital Age* (Ashgate Press, 2003; with Charles Raab, MIT Press, 2006).

Krista Boa is a PhD candidate at the Faculty of Information Studies, University of Toronto, Canada. Her research focuses on the development of technology-based identification systems, such as machine-readable travel documents and national ID cards, by examining the ways in which technologies are framed discursively. She is interested in how these discourses influence the design of the system and transform conceptions of identity, anonymity and privacy. Other related areas of interest which inform her research include: surveillance, access to information, and conceptualizations of privacy, particularly legal and theoretical arguments about reasonable expectations of privacy in public.

Keith Breckenridge is an Associate Professor of History and Internet Studies at the University of KwaZulu-Natal, South Africa. His current research is focused on a history of biometric registration in South Africa, and he has recently published in *History Workshop* and the *Journal of Southern African Studies* on this subject.

Cheryl L. Brown, an Associate Professor of Political Science, teaches Internet Law and Policy, Cyberspace and Politics, Digital Forensics and Policy, and Politics of

China at the University of North Carolina at Charlotte in the USA. She received a National Science Foundation Award to study the formation of networks in cyberspace in the age of electronic government. Brown has conducted extensive research on information and communication technology in the Asia Pacific and published an article on smart card technology for e-government.

Andrew Clement is a Professor in the Faculty of Information Studies at the University of Toronto, Canada where he has coordinated the Information Policy Research Programme since 1995. He is a co-founder of the Identity Privacy and Security Initiative. His recent research has focused on public information policy, Internet use in everyday life, digital identity, information rights, public participation in information/communication infrastructure development and community networking. Clement is the principal investigator of the Digital Identities Construction project, as well as the Office of the Privacy Commissioner funded CAN-ID – Visions for Canada's Identity Policy, research project.

Simon Davies is Founder and Director of the watchdog group Privacy International and is also a Visiting Fellow in the Department of Information Systems of the London School of Economics and Political Science, UK. He works on privacy, data protection, consumer rights, policy analysis and technology assessment, and his expertise is in identity and identity systems. His publications include *Privacy and Human Rights 1998: An International Survey of Privacy Laws and Developments* (with David Banisar, 1998) and *Big Brother: Britain's Web of Surveillance and the New Technological Order* (Pan Books, 1997).

Kelly Gates is an Assistant Professor of Communication at the University of California, San Diego in the USA. She teaches courses on media law and policy, the history of media technologies, and theories of the information society. She has published several articles on biometrics, and is currently writing a book on the politics of facial recognition technology.

Graham Greenleaf is a Professor of Law at the University of New South Wales, and formerly Distinguished Visiting Professor (2001–2002) at the University of Hong Kong. His research interests include privacy law and policy, commons in intellectual property, and free access to law. He is Asia-Pacific Editor of the bimonthly *Privacy Laws & Business International*.

Gus Hosein is a Visiting Senior Fellow at the London School of Economics and Political Science. At the LSE, he co-mentored its research into the UK Identity Card Bill. Subsequently, he co-founded the Policy Engagement Network that continues to bring academic research to policy fora. He is a Senior Fellow at Privacy International and Visiting Scholar at the American Civil Liberties Union. For more information, see http://personal.lse.ac.uk/hosein.

Zeinab Karake-Shalhoub is the Director of Research at the Dubai International Financial Center (DIFC), the United Arab Emirates. Before that Zeinab was a

Professor of Business in the School of Business and Management (SBM) at the American University in Sharjah, UAE; she also served as the Associate Dean of SBM for five years. She is the author of five books: *Technology and Developing Economies* (Praeger Publishers, New York, 1990), *Information Technology and Managerial Control* (Praeger Publishers, New York, 1992), *Organizational Downsizing, Discrimination, and Corporate Social Responsibility* (Quorum Publishers, New York, 1999), *Trust and Loyalty in Electronic Commerce: An Agency Theory Perspective* (Quorum, New York, 2002), and *The Diffusion of Electronic Commerce in Developing Economies*, coauthored with Sheikha Lubna Al Qasimi, UAE Minister of Economy (Edward Elgar, November 2006).

Laurent Laniel is a sociologist of international relations and a Research Fellow at the Institut National des Hautes Etudes de Sécurité (INHES) near Paris, France. His research interests are international trade of illicit drugs, policing, and identification. He was a member of UNESCO's MOST-Drugs network between 1997 and 2002 and co-author of the MOST-Drugs final report, *Drugs, Globalization and Criminalization*. He is the author of many papers and translations on the international drug problem and law enforcement. Most of his writings and photographs are available at http://laniel.free.fr.

David Lyon is the Director of the Surveillance Project and Research Chair in Sociology at Queen's University, Canada. Professor Lyon has been working on surveillance issues since the 1980s, and has particular research interests in national ID cards, aviation security and surveillance and in promoting the cross-disciplinary and international study of surveillance. His most recent books are the edited collection *Theorizing Surveillance: The Panopticon and Beyond* (Willan, 2006) and *Surveillance Studies: An Overview* (Polity, 2007). He is currently preparing *Identifying Citizens: Software, Social Sorting and the State* for Polity Press (2008).

Willem Maas is Associate Professor and Chair of Political Science at Glendon College, York University, Canada and was previously Assistant Professor of Politics and European Studies at NYU. He has been a Parliamentary Intern and also worked at the Privy Council Office in Ottawa and the European Commission in Brussels. Professor Maas' teaching and research focus on comparative politics, European integration, citizenship and migration, sovereignty, nationalism, democratic theory and federalism. He is the author of *Creating European Citizens* (Rowman & Littlefield, 2007) and many chapters and articles.

Taha Mehmood is trained as a media practitioner. His areas of interest include the history of surveillance, work practices of new economy labour, urban studies and film. His chapter stems out of his research with the Information Society Project at SARAI CSDS, Delhi, India. He is currently pursuing his Master's in City Design at London School of Economics.

Midori Ogasawara worked for Japan's national newspaper, *Asahi Shimbun*, from 1994–2004. As a reporter, she covered surveillance issues including national identification card systems, CCTV in public spaces, war compensation between Japan and Asian countries, especially sex slavery on behalf of the Japanese army, and other human rights issues. She is also the author of four books including a children's picture storybook, *Princess Sunflower*, which is based on the Convention on the Elimination of All Forms of Discrimination against Women. She has been an MA student in Sociology at Queen's University in Canada since 2005.

Pierre Piazza is a lecturer in political science at Cergy-Pontoise University near Paris, France. He is a specialist of the social history of state identification systems and techniques and has published several papers on the Bertillon system (anthropometry), finger printing (dactyloscopy), identity cards and biometrics. Piazza is author or editor of *Histoire de la carte nationale d'identité* (*A History of the French National ID Card*) (Paris, Odile Jacob, March 2004), 'Police et identification. Enjeux, pratiques, techniques' ('Policing and Identification: Issues, Practices and Techniques'), and *Du papier à la biométrie. Identifier les individus* (*From Paper to Biometrics: Identifying Individuals*) (Paris, Presses de science, June 2006).

Jeffrey M. Stanton (PhD, University of Connecticut, 1997) is Associate Dean for Research and Doctoral Programs in the School of Information Studies at Syracuse University. Dr Stanton's research focuses on organizational behavior and technology, with his most recent projects examining how behavior affects information security and privacy in organizations. He is the author with Dr Kathryn Stam of the book *The Visible Employee: Using Workplace Monitoring and Surveillance to Protect Information Assets – Without Compromising Employee Privacy or Trust* (*Information Today,* 2006).

Scott Thompson is a PhD candidate in sociology at the University of Victoria and is currently engaged in research concerning surveillance, classification and its consequences during the pre-electronic period. He has published several papers on surveillance and liquor control in Ontario, Canada and is currently writing a book with Dr Gary Genosko tentatively entitled *Punched Drunk: Alcohol, Identity and Surveillance in Ontario 1927–1975* (forthcoming).

David Wills is a final year doctoral student at the University of Nottingham, and will be taking up a Research Fellowship at POLSIS, University of Birmingham, UK. His research interests include political theory, social movements, and the politics of information technology. He has taught political theory at Nottingham and wrote the POSTnote on Computer Crime for the Parliamentary Office of Science and Technology in 2006.

Dean Wilson is a Senior Lecturer in Criminology in the School of Political and Social Inquiry, Monash University, Melbourne, Australia. His research interests include the impact of biometrics on border control, police interactions with victims of crime, and the role of surveillance in the structuring of security. He has published widely on policing, CCTV in Australian public spaces and biometrics. He is the Oceania editor for the online journal *Surveillance & Society* and the editor (with Clive Norris) of *Surveillance, Crime and Social Control* (2006).

Preface and acknowledgments

All modern societies have developed systems to establish that their citizens 'are who they say they are'. Those systems have evolved over time as new technologies and the demands of a complex, mobile and interconnected world have provided more sophisticated identity management systems. Forms of personal identification might vary from something you own (such as a passport), to something you know (such as a password), to something you do (such as signing a document or speaking in a typical voice pattern), to something you are (the most modern forms of 'biometric' identifiers, such as a fingerprint, a retinal scan, a hand geometry and so on). The pocket-sized card remains, however, an enduring symbol of the process of self-identification in our many interactions with different state and private agencies.

Identity cards are not just technologies; they are also contemporary tools of governance which may be used to address a multiple and shifting set of social and political problems. They may facilitate travel and hence help control illegal immigration. They may provide a more reliable method of establishing the age of the bearer (both for young and old). They may incorporate medical information for use in an emergency (e.g. blood type, allergies, diabetes etc.). They may assist in crime detection. They may improve access to a range of public services (social benefits, health, education, libraries, employment services) and facilitate the prevention of fraud and identity theft. More recently, they are seen as tools to assist border management and thus contribute to the 'War on Terror'. Advanced card technologies are often seen as solutions that need to be linked to corresponding problems. How that linkage takes place will determine the choices made in different countries and the opposition encountered, raising questions of profound interest to social scientists.

Identity cards vary in terms of their compulsory nature, their contents, their security features, the database support, as well as in terms of the accompanying rules concerning which authorities, under what circumstances, may request their production and access their contents. Most card systems are now designed with sophisticated biometric identifiers. The extraordinary capacity and processing power of advanced card technology now offers a realistic vision that one card cannot only provide more reliable methods of identification and authentication, but can also help the individual engage in a variety of verifiable and anonymous transactions. Cards are now not only forms of identification and transaction; they are also fully integrated 'smart agents' of data processing. They are, therefore, instruments of power, which might discriminate, infringe civil liberties and contribute to the spread of surveillance. The fact that the manifestation of this policy instrument is confined to the individual's pocket does not alter the larger set of relationships that still tend to be politically determined and that raise a complex range of social, economic, political, legal and technological issues.

This collection addresses these various issues in international and comparative perspective. It brings together papers on existing and proposed identity card systems in 11 different countries (Australia, Britain, Canada, China, France, Hong Kong, India, Japan, South Africa, the United Arab Emirates and the USA), as well as from two international organizations, the European Union and the International Civil Aviation Organization (ICAO). The chapters in this collection explore not only the technical and administrative dimensions but also the historical, international, sociological and political economy aspects. In particular, the book aims to understand how new identification processes contribute to surveillance practices, through the classification of citizens and residents according to varying criteria, thus affecting their life-chances, status and prospects.

Although some countries have inevitably been omitted, the majority of the world's population is potentially covered within these chapters. We have deliberately gone outside the realm of the 'usual suspects' of North America and Western Europe, also including case studies of identification card systems in Japan, China, India, South Africa and the United Arab Emirates (UAE). We also wanted to look at countries both within and outside the common law tradition, because that distinction has in times past worked as a divider between states with or without such systems. Although we would have liked to have included one or two Latin or Central American countries, or to discuss Malaysia along with Hong Kong, we are confident that this is the most international scholarly treatment of the subject to date.

The authors come from several disciplines: sociology, political science, criminology, communications, law, business and management, and information studies. They were asked to address three questions about the development of identity card systems in their respective countries. What were/are the drivers (both domestic and international)? How is the system designed to work, both administratively and technologically? And what are the lessons? Some chapters emphasize law, others technology, information, politics or policy. Most chapters also give at least a nod – some considerably more – towards the historical background of the ID system discussed. Some chapters lean towards the factual and descriptive; others are explicit in their commendation or critique. Collectively, the chapters allow us to distinguish the more generic and transnational processes from the more specific cultural and institutional features of individual countries. They permit us to understand the impact of post-9/11 security measures in contrast to the historical legacies. They offer an opportunity to understand and compare the opposition and resistance in different countries. They allow a thorough examination of the nature of contemporary surveillance practices.

The collection is based on a research workshop, held under the auspices of the Surveillance Project at Queen's University, Kingston, Ontario in June 2007. It was funded through the 'Globalization of Personal Data' project from the Social Sciences and Humanities Research Council's Initiative on the New Economy (INE) programme. The editors are extremely grateful to the authors who contributed to this volume for their research and for their diligent and timely submission of drafts. We are also grateful to those who presented papers at the workshop, whose work could not be included, and especially to Charles Raab and Ben Muller. We also appreciate the careful and diligent research assistance from Emily Smith, as well as the Project Manager, Joan Sharpe.

Colin J. Bennett and David Lyon

Section One

Setting the scene

1 Playing the ID card

Understanding the significance of identity card systems

David Lyon and Colin J. Bennett

Introduction: Identity cards and identity card systems

Identification systems have become a key mode of governance in the early years of the twenty-first century. People cannot get on with their daily lives without constant demands for identification, usually provided within automated systems dependent on complex relations of plastic cards and networked databases. This is particularly true of the nation-state. National identification systems have been proliferating in recent years as part of a concerted drive to find common identifiers for populations around the world. Whether the driving force is immigration control, anti-terrorism, electronic government or rising rates of identity theft, identity card systems are being developed, proposed or debated in most countries.

The identity 'card' provides the symbolic starting-point for the chapters presented in this volume. In popular consciousness, the average citizen regards the 'card' as the overt manifestation of authority, the carrying and presentation of which defines a host of relations between the individual and organizations. But the card is only the visible evidence of complex and more latent systems of identification. National identity policy comprises a whole administrative and technological regime, and hence a complicated series of social and policy choices. The question is not a binary one; whether to institute a national identity card or not. Rather a range of political, administrative and technical questions require careful analysis and debate. As an influential report from the UK put it:

> All identity systems carry consequential dangers as well as potential benefits. Depending on the model used, identity systems may create a range of new and unforeseen problems. These include the failure of systems, unforeseen financial costs, increased security threats and unacceptable imposition on citizens. The success of a national identity system depends on a sensitive, cautious and cooperative approach involving all key stakeholder groups including an independent and rolling risk assessment and a regular review of management practices.
>
> (LSE 2005: 5)

When individuals identify themselves, they are making a claim about who they are. This claim might be based on a variety of different identifiers – a name, a number, an address, a date of birth and so on. But these claims do not prove that they are indeed who they say they are. Organizations also, therefore, need to *authenticate*, to establish confidence in individual claims. This is an important distinction. In many of our interactions with authority, the authentication that an agency needs is simply evidence of that individual's entitlement, and not necessarily evidence of identity. New encryption technologies offer some promise of authentication without identification (Privacy Commissioner of Canada 2007).

Many states are seriously developing comprehensive 'identity management' policies to govern peoples' identities through their entire life cycle in order to authenticate their interactions with many agencies, public and private. Identity cards often form an important part of these strategies. Yet some key questions and choices emerge about the roles of identity card systems as identifiers and authenticators. For what purposes will the identity card systems be developed – for a single purpose or multiple purposes? Will the technology permit further functions and uses to be added down the road? Will the ownership and/or carrying of the card be voluntary or compulsory? If the former, will citizens be expected to pay for the privilege? If the latter, what legal restrictions will control the circumstances under which the card might be demanded, and the agents who might demand it? What mechanisms will be introduced to prevent forgery? What are the systems of data storage and how will back-up databases be secured from malicious attack, technical error and human fallibility? What administrative arrangements will be established for the accessing and sharing of personal data? What personal identifiers will be used and how will these be assigned or obtained? What are the costs in terms of human resources, financial expenditures, security risks, as well as social relations? Even for the most basic systems, the choices are complex and the answers have varied.

At the same time, these choices are socially-shaped by powerful interests. In particular, as one of us has noted (Lyon 2007), a 'Card Cartel' involving the state, corporations and technical standards appears to be involved in the production of new identity card systems. Not only is there a close mutual constitutive process between the technologies and the social processes, but also national identity card systems already evince a particular way of seeing the world – indeed, of *being* in the world – and they speak to some specific circumstances and situations in which they appear to 'fit' (see Introna 2007: 325). The world is already framed in the twenty-first century in ways that seem to call for identity cards. For many, they make sense as an idea whose time has come. An identity card is not, therefore, just 'another piece of plastic' in the wallet or the purse (Clarke 1988). The card is just the overt manifestation of complex system of identity control and management.

Identity cards around the world

The diffusion of identity card systems is revealed in Table 1.1. Once, the use of identity card systems by national governments was taken to relate to authoritarian conditions – colonial or communist, perhaps – such as in South Africa or the old Soviet Union, or to the exigencies of war, such as in Britain or Canada, or to a centralized state or a lack of a common law tradition, such as in France. But those simple guides no longer hold true.

Various groups have attempted to catalogue the spread of ID card systems, but the estimates do vary and the global situation is extremely fluid (see Privacy International 1996; Prevent Genocide International 2001). The more complex the table, the more difficult it is to find and present equivalent information. Table 1.1 presents a basic list of well over 100 countries with information on whether they have an identity card system; whether the card is mandatory or voluntary; and whether or not it is supported by a biometric identifier.[1]

We tried to be as comprehensive as possible, and countries were chosen primarily because they are OECD countries, major countries in the developing world and those with significant ID card initiatives. We attempted to ensure that the information is as correct as possible, but it is by definition a volatile and emergent field. Among the most useful sources are United Nations documents and the research findings of Prevent Genocide International and the Electronic Privacy Information Center in association with Privacy International.

Table 1.1 does shield some important features of identity card systems, which can only be unearthed through the kind of contextual analysis of the individual case study. Four questions are particularly pertinent. One, what are the reasons for introducing ID card systems? These vary considerably, and only overlap to a limited extent. When we review the cases in this volume, a number of multiple, shifting and unclear purposes are put forward to justify their introduction: identity theft; the provision of services through e-government; law enforcement; the detection and prevention of terrorism; border control; financial criminality; the monitoring of internet usage; even obtaining food during periods of rationing. Many countries also seem to desire technological enhancement of their national systems as a point of prestige, to indicate their being up-to-date with other countries, even though ironically, some of the most advanced and richest states have yet to go down this path.

A second question has to do with what reception identity cards have when proposed or introduced. Major controversies have arisen over card systems in Australia, the UK, Japan and France, and the relative success of oppositional movements is crucial to the success or otherwise of card systems. Those movements may be generated by privacy, civil liberties or primarily historical and religious concerns. Other proposals have been reconsidered, in the light of careful reflections about financial costs or political liabilities. The fact that there is strong evidence of a trend, both technological and political, towards establishing national identification systems, does not mean that the outcomes are similar everywhere. Indeed, the cultural and political conditions in which identity card systems grow differ vastly, and have a major impact on how well the systems work and are accepted by the populace. Part of the present task, then, is a careful comparison and contrast of different situations with a view to making measured judgements about the actual and likely consequences of what, in many cases, appears to be fundamental recalibration of the relation between state and citizen.

Third, it is not always clear from the name given to the system that it is in fact a national identification card system. The American Real ID programme, still in

Table 1.1 National ID Cards: December 2007

Country	National ID Card	Voluntary or Mandatory	Biometric
Afghanistan	Yes	Mandatory	No
Algeria	Yes	Mandatory	No
Angola	Yes	Mandatory	No
Argentina	Yes	Mandatory	Yes: right thumbprint
Australia	Yes (see Ch. 11)	Voluntary	Yes: smart card (digital photograph)
Austria	Yes	Mandatory	No
Bahamas	Yes	Mandatory	No
Bahrain	Yes	Mandatory	No
Bangladesh	Yes	Voluntary	No
Barbados	Yes	Voluntary	No
Belarus	Yes	Mandatory	No
Belgium	Yes	Mandatory	No
Bhutan	Yes	Mandatory	No
Bolivia	Yes	Mandatory	No
Bosnia and Herzegovina	Yes	Mandatory	Yes: fingerprint
Botswana	Yes	Mandatory	Yes: thumbprint
Brazil	Yes	Mandatory	Yes: right thumbprint
Brunei	Yes	Mandatory	Yes: 2 thumbprints
Brunei Darussalam	Yes	Mandatory	Yes: 2 thumbprints
Bulgaria	Yes	Mandatory	No
Burundi	Yes	Mandatory	No
Cambodia	Yes	Mandatory	Yes: fingerprint
Cameroon	Yes	Voluntary	No
Canada	No (see Ch. 14)	N/A	N/A
Chile	Yes	Mandatory	Yes: right thumbprint
China	Yes (see Ch. 4)	Mandatory	No
Colombia	Yes	Mandatory	Yes: right index print
Costa Rica	Yes	Mandatory	No
Croatia	Yes	Mandatory	No
Cuba	Yes	Mandatory	Yes: fingerprint
Cyprus	Yes	Voluntary	No
Czech Republic	Yes	Mandatory	No
Democratic Republic of Congo	Discontinued in 1960	N/A	N/A
Denmark	Yes	Voluntary	No
Ecuador	Yes	Mandatory	Yes: fingerprint
Egypt	Yes	Mandatory	Yes: fingerprint
El Salvador	Yes	Mandatory	No
Estonia	Yes	Mandatory	No
Ethiopia	Yes	Voluntary	No
Finland	Yes	Voluntary	No
France	Yes (see Ch. 12)	Voluntary (plans to make mandatory)	Proposed: fingerprint
Gabon	Yes	Mandatory	No
Germany	Yes	Mandatory	Yes: thumbprint
Ghana	Yes	Mandatory	No

Country	National ID Card	Voluntary or Mandatory	Biometric
Greece	Yes	Mandatory	No: fingerprint removed 11-08-07
Grenada	Yes	Mandatory	No
Guatemala	Yes	Mandatory	No
Guyana	Yes	Mandatory	No
Haiti	Yes	Mandatory	No
Honduras	Yes	Mandatory	Yes: fingerprint
Hong Kong	Yes (see Ch. 5)	Mandatory	Yes: thumbprint
Hungary	Yes	Mandatory	No
India	Pilot project begun (see Ch. 7)	N/A	Yes: fingerprint
Indonesia	Yes	Mandatory	No
Iran	Yes	Voluntary (plans to make mandatory)	No
Iraq	Yes	Mandatory	No
Israel/ Palestine	Yes	Mandatory	Yes: facial recognition and fingerprint
Italy	Yes	Voluntary (plans to make mandatory)	Proposed: fingerprint
Jamaica	Yes	Mandatory	No
Japan	No (Alien registration cards for foreigners) (see Ch. 6)	N/A	Yes: fingerprint
Jordan	Yes	Mandatory	Yes: retinal scan and fingerprint
Kenya	Yes	Mandatory	No
Kuwait	Yes	Mandatory	No
Latvia	Yes	Voluntary	No
Lebanon	Yes	Mandatory	No
Lithuania	Yes	Mandatory	No
Luxembourg	Yes	Voluntary	No
Macedonia	Yes	Mandatory	No
Madagascar	Yes	Mandatory	No
Malawi	Yes	Mandatory	
Malaysia	Yes	Mandatory	Yes: thumbprint
Mali	Yes	Mandatory	Yes: fingerprint
Mauritania	Yes	Mandatory	Yes: fingerprint
Mauritius	Yes	Mandatory	No
Mexico	Yes	Voluntary	Yes: fingerprint
Mongolia	Yes	Mandatory	Proposed fingerprint in future
Morocco	Yes	Mandatory	No
Myanmar (Burma)	Yes	Mandatory	No
Netherlands	Yes	Mandatory	Yes: iris scan
Nigeria	Yes	Mandatory	Yes: fingerprint
Norway	Yes	Voluntary	Yes: fingerprints and facial recognition

Table 1.1 (cont.)

Country	National ID Card	Voluntary or Mandatory	Biometric
Oman	Yes	Mandatory for men, optional for women	Yes: fingerprint
Pakistan	Yes	Mandatory	Yes: fingerprint
Panama	Yes	Mandatory	Yes: thumbprint
Paraguay	Yes	Mandatory	Yes: fingerprint
Peru	Yes	Mandatory	Yes: fingerprint
Poland	Yes	Mandatory	No
Portugal	Yes	Mandatory	Yes: right index fingerprint
Romania	Yes	Mandatory	No
Russia	Yes	Mandatory	Yes: facial recognition
Rwanda	Discontinued in 1996	N/A	N/A
Saudi Arabia	Yes	Mandatory	No
Senegal	Yes	Mandatory	No
Serbia and Montenegro	Yes	Mandatory	No
Singapore	Yes	Mandatory	No
Slovakia	Yes	Mandatory	No
Slovenia	Yes	Mandatory	No
South Africa	Yes (see Ch. 3)	Mandatory	No
South Korea	Yes	Mandatory	Yes: both thumbprints
Spain	Yes	Mandatory	Yes: fingerprint
Sri Lanka	Yes	Mandatory	No
Sudan	Yes	Mandatory	No
Sweden	Yes	Voluntary	Yes: fingerprint (2008) and facial recognition
Switzerland	Yes	Voluntary	No
Syria	Yes	Mandatory	Yes: fingerprint
Taiwan	Yes	Mandatory	No
Thailand	Yes	Mandatory	Yes: fingerprint
Trinidad and Tobago	Yes	Mandatory	No
Tunisia	Yes	Mandatory	Yes: fingerprint
Turkey	Yes	Mandatory	No
Ukraine	Yes	Mandatory	No
United Arab Emirates	Yes (see Ch. 8)	Mandatory	Yes: fingerprint
UK	No (ID Cards Act passed 2006, see Ch. 10; see also Ch. 9)	N/A	N/A
USA	No (see Ch. 13)	N/A	N/A
Uruguay	Yes	Mandatory	Yes: thumbprint
Venezuela	Yes	Mandatory	No
Vietnam	Yes	Mandatory	Yes: fingerprint
Zimbabwe	Yes	Mandatory	Yes: fingerprint

development, is a federal scheme based on the (state-run) drivers' licence system and although it was initiated by the Department of Homeland Security, its association with licensing drivers deflects attention from its actual purpose (this is further discussed by Kelly Gates in Chapter 13). The now abandoned 2006 Australian 'Access Card' scheme, likewise, takes its name from the e-government aspect of its emergence, even though, as Dean Wilson (Chapter 11) demonstrates, the familiar targets of welfare cheats, criminals, illegal immigrants and terrorists explain its logic more directly. Other schemes originate from the supranational level, such as the 'European Health Card' (explored by Willem Maas in Chapter 16) or the biometric 'RFID passport' (discussed by Jeffrey Stanton in Chapter 15).

Fourth, the notion of 'voluntariness' requires critical scrutiny. In some countries, such as France (see Piazza and Laniel's Chapter 12), mandatory identity cards have been in existence for many decades; in others, such as Canada (see Chapter 14), they have been debated but never introduced. In some countries, the systems are mandatory; in others they are voluntary. But even this distinction, as Graham Greenleaf (Chapter 5) shows in the case of Hong Kong, may be moot. What is presented as a 'voluntary' system may in practice be hard for an individual citizen to live without. If cards are 'voluntary' (and especially if there is a charge levied), it is not hard to predict the kinds of people who would be unlikely to cope with the complex administrative procedures to take-up the voluntary offer: the old, the unemployed, the mentally ill and so on. Indeed, for certain social assistance and health applications, these might be precisely the people whom these schemes are designed to help. However 'voluntary' a card might be at the outset, there is always the probability that it would become a *de facto* universal card, as those without this 'voluntary' card would find it increasingly difficult to operate in certain social contexts and to gain access to certain services. Moreover, it is difficult to construct a case for the effectiveness of voluntary cards as a means of combating crime or illegal immigration because those at risk of detection would be the least likely to obtain such a card. Once cards are mandatory, then they may be used to single out or even to harass visible minorities and those with alternative lifestyles. Thus, identity cards contribute to the process of surveillance as 'social sorting'.

Some card systems are supported by sophisticated biometrics, such as multiple fingerprints or iris scans; others are more prosaic. Some card systems are multi-purpose and support several social and political functions; others are designed and implemented for a single purpose. Some systems apply to the entire population; others are designed for a single target population. Table 1.1 clearly depicts a diffusion of identity card systems as a result of some common and broad transnational trends. At the same time, it also suggests that these trends may be mediated, diffracted or obstructed by the quite distinctive institutions and cultures of specific states. These policy instruments have to be selected and adapted by public and private sector agents influenced by a myriad of historical, cultural and institutional constraints. 'How the cards fall' in each jurisdiction is therefore dependent on the interplay between the larger forces and distinctive contextual factors.

The title of this work, *Playing the Identity Card*, also suggests through the analogy of a game that ID cards may be both provocative and decisive. 'Playing a card' may be a gamble with power or even with technological potential. If public opinion turned decisively against the identity card proposals, might this contribute to bringing down a government, or to the loss of major contracts? Technologically, no one knows if some proposed systems will work and historical evidence – for instance in countries like South Africa, as Keith Breckenridge shows (Chapter 3) – does not always support optimism. But playing a card may also be decisive, as in the production of an ace that changes how the game will be played.

This aspect of the trope works for the contents of the book too. Although in some cases the significance of new ID systems may be overplayed, it is nevertheless the case that unique identifiers connected with powerful searchable and networked databases may be the means of undemocratic and unaccountable surveillance, just as much as they may be the means of greater efficiency and convenience promised by their proponents. The following suggests a theoretical framework which might assist the interpretation of the larger pattern of global ID production, as well as the individual case studies.

Common drivers and theoretical claims

Systems of identification have a long history in the modern world. Indeed, part of what is meant by 'the modern world' is that government administration becomes more complex and touches ordinary citizens' lives in more profound ways. The civil identity of the individual had to be clearly recognized after the French revolution for example, in ways that would supersede the old confusions associated with 'religious and civil' records of births, marriages and deaths (Noiriel 2001). 'Individuation' is basic to this process, as individuals are treated as such, rather than as members of families or clans, and acquire government records that apply uniquely to them and not to others (Abercrombie and Urry 1982). Names are vital to this task, but as administered populations grow, and administrative tasks proliferate, so identification numbers are added in an attempt to increase accuracy, particularly imperative in China where, for example, 93 million people have the surname Wang (see Cheryl Brown's Chapter 4). In some countries, a card was also issued to citizens in order to indicate that they had rights as people enrolled in the system, as well as responsibilities to the nation-state and entitlements as citizens. This was the case in France, and was proposed several times during the twentieth century in the UK (Higgs 2004).

The real pressure to create new ID card systems, however, came from several sources towards the end of the twentieth century. They were part of a supposed logic of administrative efficiency that encouraged the growth of 'electronic government' (e-government). They answered a felt need for reliable identification and authentication systems outside the strictly governmental realm of administration, that is, in commercial spheres, such as banking and credit. And their development was catalyzed, especially by the 'security' imperatives that had been for decades making their presence felt within contemporary nation-states but that were propelled into prominence, above all by the events of 9/11 and its reverberations in a number of other countries with sympathies to the USA.

Anticipating the later argument of this introductory chapter, as well as the main body of this book, it should be noted that these general trends work themselves out in specific ways in different countries, even though there is often shared knowledge about identity card schemes between different countries. For instance, Chapter 14 notes that it was precisely information about the experiences of other (European) countries that halted deliberations about the desirability and viability of identity cards in Canada. Yet, the general trends are nonetheless present and visible in Canada. Enthusiasm for e-government is a steady factor in many countries with advanced information infrastructures, as in the case of the Gulf States, as Zeinab Karake-Shalhoub shows in Chapter 8. But in countries where there may be resistance to national ID systems, it may take a perceived crisis of national security to bring about change. The very fact that a national ID could be discussed in the UK, or the 'Real ID' programme initiated in the USA evidences this, as David Wills (Chapter 10) and Kelly Gates (Chapter 13) demonstrate. It is clear from several chapters in this book that 9/11 was a tipping point that inclined some countries to look seriously at establishing national ID systems. For others, such as India (see Chapter 7) and China (see Chapter 4), 9/11 scarcely registered in this respect.

Reference was made earlier to the 'Card Cartel' and it is worth elaborating on this theory here, at least briefly. Writing of passports in the modern world, John Torpey made the now widely accepted proposal that they represent a 'monopoly on the means of movement' (Torpey 2000). That is, following Marx's claim about the capitalist monopoly on the means of production and Weber's rejoinder about the state's monopoly of the means of violence, Torpey asserts a further dimension of modern monopolization on the part of the state; regulating movement. This is made visible in the international passport system that grew from nineteenth century origins to its complex global development today.

Within his work on the passport, Torpey notes that other identifiers are in use at various times and in various places, including internal passports (used widely in the old Soviet Union, for example) and identification cards. While he notes that identity cards point both inwards to citizenship rights and outwards to who may count as a citizen, he does not pay attention either to the range of reasons for adopting identification systems or to the fact that it is identification itself, not just movement, that is regulated by identity cards. As Louise Amoore indicates in Chapter 2, it is the politics of identification *per se* that has now moved front and centre, such that it makes sense to speak of 'governing by identity.'

Building on Torpey's work, however, it may be said that today we are witnessing the growth, not of a monopoly, but an oligopoly of the means of identification. This, put more simply, is the 'Card Cartel'. While Torpey's insightful analysis focuses on the role of the nation-state, we have to recognize that today's identity cards are the product, not merely of formally constituted governing bodies, but of corporate entities competing for contracts to use their 'solutions', and also of technical standards which shape the very architecture and the peculiar characteristics of the identity card scheme in question (Jones 2007). In criminological terms, such architectures in today's national security climate would tend the system towards 'crime control' rather than 'due process'.

Three key components of the Card Cartel, then, are the nation-state, whose work in galvanizing the development of identity card systems is clear from many chapters in this book, the corporation and technical standards including protocols. Not a lot of attention has been paid, as yet, to the role of the last, although the work of Lawrence Lessig (1999) is highly suggestive. In this book, Jeffrey Stanton's (Chapter 15) examination of the role of standards in steering biometric RFID passports within the International Civil Aviation Organization (ICAO) also shows how significant is the role of standards for software and hardware development. But that the corporate sector plays a major role in determining the direction of ID schemes is clear in cases as far apart as France (Chapter 12), Hong Kong (Chapter 5) and of course the USA. Kelly Gates in Chapter 13 draws specific attention to this in her political economy of 'Real ID', citing the role of the Digimarc Corporation in particular.

The point of discussing oligopoly, however, is that it is a system of rule and indicates how 'digital rule' has become centrally significant (Jones 2000). If this argument is correct, the protocols of identity management are rising to a prominent position within the triangulated forces fostering ID card systems today. The securitized identities are indeed manifold and, yes, citizenship is realized through other means, such as consumption and employment. But the state is still involved as an enabler and as a coordinator of planning. Moreover, as we have seen, the role of competing corporations is also vital in providing the means and the model for ID systems. Political economy is still present and must be considered as indispensable to the overall explanation.

If there is a system of rule, however, there are also subjects, but these too alter within the oligopoly of identity. The consequences for citizenship, at least as conceived in ways that are inclusive and based on the extension of rights and obligations, are profound. The nature of the rule is through social sorting; classification for differential treatment based on varying profiles as written into identity card systems. At the very least, analyses of these systems should explore the consequences, and thus also policy alternatives, for those likely to be most negatively affected – visible minorities (often 'Arab', 'Muslim' ones), welfare recipients and refugees and asylum seekers (see Amoore and De Goede 2005). In the Australian 'Access Card' case discussed by Wilson (Chapter 11), familiar folk devils including aboriginal people are lumped together with terrorists to receive the 'high risk' label that serves to separate 'undesirables' from the Australian majority population. These are the ones for whom 'cumulative disadvantage' (see Gandy 2006) is a reality and who are easily rendered invisible by the same system that states use to *increase* legibility (Scott 1998).

Identity cards as policy instruments

The theory of the 'Card Cartel' helps us understand the broad patterns, but it gives us the view as if from a high-flying aircraft, identifying the contours of the landscape but glossing over much of the detail. If we are observing nothing less than a new system of governance, it is one that has been embraced more readily by some states than by others. There is nothing deterministic in this theory. The Card Cartel can be diverted and obstructed by agents who have to make choices according to the particular historical, cultural and institutional conditions of their specific jurisdictions. The reality, expressed in Table 1.1, is messy and contingent and any theoretical framework must also take account of the variations and complexities. How the forces behind the Card Cartel are mediated, resisted, diverted, refracted then determines the nature and level of adoption of ID card systems.

At this level of analysis, we view identity cards as policy instruments, tools of governance, chosen to advance particular social goals. Hood (1983, 2007) for example, makes a basic distinction between 'effecting' tools (the means by which government can impact on the outside world) and 'detecting' tools (the instruments that government uses for taking in information). Historically, identity cards have been regarded as 'tools of detection': 'a set of tools for examination, inspection, monitoring, watching and detecting, tools which must be applicable to a wide range of objects' (Hood 1983: 91). More recently, however, they are seen as 'effecting tools' or ways by which a range of services can be delivered. Instruments are chosen not only according to the instrumental pursuit of goals, but in response to constraints. A particular policy instrument must 'fit' with dominant social and political attitudes, with institutional arrangements, as well as with the legacies from the past.

Identity cards and political culture

Hypothetically we might expect ID card systems to be developed more readily within cultures that have historically exhibited higher levels of trust toward state authority, especially where comprehensive identification schemes are proposed which mandate individuals to carry their cards with them at all times and to submit them on demand from state authorities. Attitudes to identity cards should be closely related to broader attitudes about participation in public affairs and about trust in the authority of governmental agencies; these issues have attracted considerable attention from students of comparative politics (e.g. Almond and Verba 1965, 1980), as well as from more anthropological perspectives on social and cultural history (Moore 1984).

It is interesting to hypothesize that the way the balance between privacy and community obligations and duties is struck within different democratic societies will vary according to their cultural traditions. Unfortunately, we have little systematic cross-national survey evidence with which to investigate the nature and influence of wider cultural attributes. Most of this argument tends, therefore, to rest on anecdotal and impressionistic evidence, such as this editorial from the *The Times* in 1995: 'Britons may be happy to produce a driving license for the purposes of driving a car, or a credit card in order to buy goods, but they are likely to recoil from having to carry a piece of plastic merely in order to exist within the law' (*The Times* 1995). This construction of British culture is counterpoised against more interventionist practices supposedly prevalent in other parts of Europe. Indeed Clement, Boa, Davies and Hosein report, in Chapter 14, a recent comment by the US Secretary of the Department of Homeland Security, that if ever they tried to introduce a national identity card in the USA, Americans' 'heads would explode'. So there are attitudes towards identity cards, as well as the construction of those attitudes by elites.

There is, however, evidence throughout this volume that identity cards settle more easily within some cultures than others. At one end of the scale, they may be seen as a desired reward. In India, for example (see Taha Mehmood's Chapter 7), the MNIC card has been embraced by many citizens as a symbolic reward of citizenship, as a desired designation of belonging. Ogasawara (Chapter 6) reports similar reactions to the original Koseki system in Japan. In other countries, such as the United Arab Emirates, they designate a status as a citizen, in distinction from large numbers of residents who do not have, and maybe aspire to, that status. Thus, cultural homogeneity is a very important factor. Where there is a 'problem' population that is deemed necessary for regulation/surveillance, then not only are identity card systems regarded with greater approval by government, they are also more readily embraced by those citizens who are entitled to that benefit. Some citizens in some states, therefore, regard it as an advantage to be rendered 'legible'.

Whereas in some jurisdictions, identity cards might be regarded as symbolic of status, in others they are considered a reflection of an intrusive and heavy-handed state. Such perceptions have generated resistance through civil society actors, bolstered by the benefits of Internet networking, who make the argument that ID cards represent an unacceptable extension of state surveillance and a denial of the inalienable right not to transact with the state and its agents. The civil liberties tradition in the USA certainly asserted its muscle with respect to the proposals for Real ID, as documented in Chapter 13. The extensive network of the American Civil Liberties Union (ACLU) activists throughout the USA successfully convinced a number of states to opt-out of the system. The opposition to the first 'Australia Card' proposal in the late 1980s was led and coordinated through the Australian Privacy Foundation (Clarke 1988), and that opposition has been carried through to the contemporary debates about the Access Card, as Dean Wilson shows in Chapter 11. Similar opposition to the new biometric identification system in France is documented in Chapter 12. Resistance to identification systems has also emerged in societies which have not historically manifested such traditions; the strong opposition to JukiNet in Japan, for example, is evidence of how a poorly devised system can generate resistance from within a culture often regarded as highly deferential.

The broader civil libertarian position is also supplemented by the more precise and technical critique of the arrangements for the collection, storage, processing and distribution of the data within the many back-up systems. In most societies, this advocacy role is institutionalized within a data protection authority, such as the Privacy Commissioners of Canada, Hong Kong or Australia, the Information Commissioner in the UK, or the Commission Nationale de L'Informatique et Libertés (CNIL) in France. Typically, these agencies do not have the political and financial resources to prevent the introduction of comprehensive identity card schemes, but they can and do raise the necessary questions about the administrative and technical specifications – and it should be remembered that these systems typically have to conform to pre-existing privacy or data protection laws and thus be constructed with due regard to standard information privacy principles (Bennett and Raab 2006). The work of these agencies is probably a lot easier when there is a population more sceptical of comprehensive governmental surveillance schemes, and aware of the dangers to privacy and other civil liberties.

However, political culture is a problematic and slippery concept. It is always difficult to separate the intrinsic and perennial orientations to government and authority, from the more temporary set of attitudes about the government-of-the-day. Opposition to identity card schemes may just as easily be explained by a desire to resist a prominent governmental scheme by an unpopular administration, as by deeper traits concerning trust in government *per se*. In several countries discussed below, the politics of identity cards became intertwined with a range of related, and unrelated, questions about the competence and trustworthiness of those in power at the time. In some countries, Britain, France and Australia being the prominent examples, these schemes are not just technical administrative arrangements; they reached the level of high electoral politics and threatened the popularity and even legitimacy of those in power.

Identity cards and the structural configuration of the state

The patterns of adoption of identity card systems are also likely to vary according to various structural factors. A distinction is often made between weak states and strong states (Migdal 1988). The latter have the institutions and resources to penetrate and regulate society; they possess a full range of 'detecting' and 'effecting' tools of government. At this basic level, we would expect national and comprehensive identification schemes to be the product of strong states. Perhaps they might also be a reflection of the efforts by weaker states to render society legible and thus to become strong. Following these propositions, we can identify three further attributes of the strong state model which might help us understand the patterns of adoption and non-adoption. The structural configuration of states influences the ways that issues are defined, debated and resolved (Skocpol 1985). Some configurations are more conducive to the development of these tools of government than others.

The first factor relates to the hierarchical integration of state bureaucracy. Identity cards, especially those of a multi-functional nature, require continuous bureaucratic cooperation over the sharing and processing of existing personal information systems. That cooperation will be more forthcoming in societies in which horizontal linkages are institutionalized across the bureaucratic divide. In some states, strong lines of hierarchical integration, bolstered by a departmental *esprit de corps*, foster secrecy both *vis-à-vis* the general public, and in relation to other administrative departments. Strong institutional jealousies militate against the sharing of personal data for dataveillance purposes (Bennett 1996), and probably also for the development of multifunctional 'smart' identity cards. It is no accident therefore that British proposals for identity cards went hand in hand with other proposals for 'joined-up government' and efforts to break down the traditional 'silos' of the UK civil service.

The need for inter-agency cooperation is not only a matter of administrative culture, but also one of technical inter-operability. Agencies must want to share the personal data within their custody, but they must also be able to. The legacies of information system design as well as technical standards sometimes impose significant constraints on the building of the databases necessary to support multipurpose identification card systems. Certainly the South African HANIS system was hampered by a lack of technical interoperability as demonstrated by Keith Breckenridge in Chapter 3. The built-in technical standards and protocols might impose a bias in favour of single purpose identification systems.

The second structural hypothesis relates to the centralization of state functions. The more the delivery of services is shared between central and peripheral governments, the greater the difficulty of cooperation in developing the information systems necessary in support of the technology. Where law enforcement, social service delivery, immigration control and so on, are responsibilities of both central and local governments, cooperative agreements over the major policy choices outlined above, as well as over the sharing of costs for upgrading and consolidating dispersed information systems, will be more difficult than in countries where policy-making is more centralized, such as South Africa where the HANIS project was coordinated completely through the government in Pretoria. In Canada, on the other hand, the degree of federal/provincial cooperation necessary to establish any common identity management policy is extraordinary. In the USA, the 'Real ID' programme has suffered considerable setbacks because of the reluctance of many states to upgrade their driving licences to the new federal biometric standard without the necessary funds to do so. Federalism, and associated tensions over the financing of national identification schemes, can be significant hurdles.

Third, cards may be more prevalent in states that are more permeable to private sector influence. Card technology is produced by businesses that now constitute a significant and growing portion of the high technology market. In most societies, they are now represented by trade associations. Perhaps those states, traditionally defined as 'weak' rather than 'strong' may be more permeable to such influence and to the lure of technological solutions to solve social problems. The distinction is, of course, further eroded the more private organizations use public data to perform public functions. To the extent that a privatization agenda is part of political discourse, we will see for instance, the use of automatic teller machines for the dispensing of benefits, the matching of government data with those of financial institutions, the use of consumer credit reports for security checks and so on.

There is much evidence in the case studies within this volume of extraordinary private sector influence over identification card policy. For example, Gates documents the role of Digimarc over Real ID policy in the United States, a country whose pluralistic and fragmented political system is perhaps the most permeable to influence from the corporate sector (Chapter 13). Companies stand to make enormous amounts of money from certain identity card schemes. But they also want to be associated with successful schemes, and may just as easily voice opposition and criticism if they lack confidence in the legal and administrative infrastructures.

Identity cards and policy legacies

Finally, all identification systems must be built upon the pre-existing legacies of past policies. This suggests that identity cards are less likely to be developed in societies that have not used such forms of identification before. Where the citizenry is used to carrying such a card and where existing information systems support such cards, the incremental costs of upgrading and extension are going to be lower than in those countries which are establishing national identification systems *de novo*. Historical policy legacies, which have produced inefficient but less intrusive systems of state surveillance in these countries, not only create customs for bureaucracies and citizens alike, but are also extremely expensive to replace.

In some of the case studies in this volume, we see strong historical trajectories which reach way back into that country's past. Contemporary debates in France, for instance, are profoundly influenced by elite thinking that has its roots in the Bertillon system and the Vichy regime during the Second World War. In South Africa, it has taken a century to create the largest fingerprinting project in the world through HANIS. An understanding of Japanese policy must also be based on the legacies of the Koseki Act of 1871. The 'second-generation' Chinese identity card is founded on the traditional household registration system (*hukou*). There are few examples where comprehensive national registration schemes, supported by identity cards, have been introduced and then disbanded. Scott Thompson (Chapter 9) reports one case, the identity card system in Britain during the Second World War, disbanded in the 1950s when the need for food rationing disappeared. Even here, this system produced legacies in the form of the National Health Insurance Number, still used in the UK today. In the UAE, on the other hand, one gets the impression that the new database structure for the identity card was planned and implemented from scratch, and a new government agency was expressly created to administer the system.

This argument about legacies also suggests that the simultaneous appearance of national ID card systems in many countries around the world cannot be explained merely in terms of the post-9/11 panics. The cultures of fear generated in the wake of 9/11 may well have been decisive in giving them their chance in some countries. It was at most a triggering event. In others, it has been a monumental irrelevance.

Conclusion

In an era when policy-making in advanced industrial states is characterized by new governance arrangements, by innovative ways to use institutions in civil society to co-regulate society, and by a conventional wisdom that many tools are necessary for the delivery of public goods, identity cards do perhaps stand out as a classic, authority-based model of government based on command and sanction. As Dean Wilson suggests (Chapter 11), identity cards are one reflection of the resurgence of the state's attempt to reassert its sovereignty and perhaps a reversal of the transnational, complex, and multilevel aspects of policy-making that characterized the political science and international relations of the 1990s (Grande and Pauly 2005).

We suggest, however, that ID card systems also represent an 'oligopoly of identity'. This builds on but transcends Rose's work on the securitizing of identity, which shows that citizenship is achieved today through consuming and working as much as through relations with the state and which highlights the importance of being able to demonstrate legitimate identity in order to exercise freedom (Rose 1999). It also builds on but transcends Torpey's work, acknowledging the power and the embrace of the state. Rather than seeing only 'state control', we add corporations and technical standards to the narrative and rather than focusing on the 'means of movement' that passports regulate, we contend that it is identity itself that is regulated by ID cards, for both travel *and* transactions.

How this process occurs however, is heavily contingent upon policy choices, influenced by culture, institutions and history. These various forces are not necessarily mutually reinforcing, reconcilable or consistent. They may tug in different directions, with unpredictable results. It should also be noted that these policy choices are never made within the tightly sealed unit of analysis of the 'nation-state'. Identity management policy in one country is nearly always influenced by events elsewhere: by the attempts to harmonize standards through international bodies, such as the ICAO and the European Union, as the respective chapters by Stanton and Maas (Chapters 15 and 16) demonstrate; by more informal 'epistemic communities' (Haas 1992), which coalesce at the international level and provide their expertise to governments and corporations alike; by the externalities of policies pursued by a dominant neighbour with unintended consequences across borders, a pattern particularly evident in Canada; by more intended strategies of 'policy laundering', whereby governments try to achieve through international regimes, what they cannot attain domestically (Hosein 2004); as well as by genuine attempts to learn from and emulate the perceived pioneers in identity management and control.

But who are the pioneers from this story? Tony Blair (2006) asserted that to have an identity card system is part and parcel of being a 'modern' state: 'The case for ID cards is a case not about liberty but about the modern world'. This construction is, however, inconsistent with the patterns of adoption described in this volume. Some of the richest and most 'modern' states have not embarked on the path of national identity card systems (yet). But this is just one contradiction among many. The oligopoly of the means of identity is a factor of 'modern life'. But that force finds expression through different laws, standards, technologies and practices, which in turn are contingent upon domestic cultures and institutions. Advanced card technologies are solutions that need to be linked to corresponding problems. How that linkage takes place in different societies will determine 'how the cards fall'. How different states with different institutional features, historical legacies and cultural orientations adopt these instruments can say much about their capacities to manage new technological change and to shape the application of this 'Card Cartel' to desirable or undesirable ends.

Note

1 What is meant here by a 'biometric identifier' is authentication techniques that rely on measurable physical characteristics that can be automatically checked, including, primarily, fingerprint or face.

Bibliography

Abercrombie, N. and Urry, J. (1982) *Sovereign Individuals of Capitalism*, London: Allen and Unwin.

Almond, G.A. and Verba, S. (1965) *The Civic Culture,* Boston: Little Brown.

Almond, G.A. and Verba, S. (1980) *The Civic Culture Revisited*, Boston: Little Brown.

Amoore, L. and De Goede, M. (2005) 'Governance, risk and dataveillance in the war on terror', *Crime, Law and Social Change* 43: 149–73.

Bennett, C.J. (1996) 'The public surveillance of personal data: a cross-national analysis', in D. Lyon and E. Zureik (eds) *Computers, Surveillance and Privacy*, Minneapolis: University of Minnesota Press.

Bennett, C.J. and Raab, C.D. (2006) *The Governance of Privacy: Policy Instruments in Global Perspective,* Cambridge: MIT Press.

Blair, T. (2006) 'We need ID cards to secure our borders and ease modern life', *The Daily Telegraph,* 6 November.

Clarke, R. (1988) 'Just another piece of plastic for your wallet: The Australia Card Scheme', *Computers & Society* 18(1). Online. Available: http://www.anu.edu.au/people/Roger.Clarke/DV/OzCard.html

Gandy, O. (2006) 'Data mining, surveillance and discrimination in the post-9/11 environment', in K. Haggerty and R. Ericson (eds) *The New Politics of Surveillance and Visibility*, Toronto: University of Toronto Press.

Grande, E. and Pauly, L. (2005) *Complex Sovereignty: Reconstituting Political Authority in the Twenty First Century,* Toronto: University of Toronto Press.

Haas, P.M. (1992) 'Introduction: epistemic communities and international policy coordination', *International Organization* 46: 1–35.

Higgs, E. (2004) 'Identity crisis', *History Today* 54(12): 15–16.

Hood, C. (1983) *The Tools of Government: Public Policy and Politics,* New Jersey: Chatham House.

Hood, C. and Margetts, H. (2007) *The Tools of Government in the Digital Age,* New York: Palgrave MacMillan.

Hosein, I. (2004) 'The sources of laws: policy dynamics in a digital and terrorized world', *The Information Society* 20(3): 187–99.

Introna, L. (2007) 'Making sense of ICT, new media and ethics', in R. Mansell, C. Avgerou, D. Quah and R. Silverstone (eds) *The Oxford Handbook of Information and Communication Technologies*, Oxford: Oxford University Press.

Jones, R. (2000) 'Digital rule', *Punishment and Society* 2(1): 5–22.

Jones, R. (2007) 'The architecture of surveillance', *Criminal Justice Matters* 68: 33–4.

Lessig, L. (1999) *Code and Other Laws of Cyberspace*, New York: Basic Books.

London School of Economics (LSE) (2005) *The Identity Project: An Assessment of the UK Identity Cards Bill and Its Implications,* LSE: Department of Information Systems. Online. Available: http://identityproject.lse.ac.uk/identityreport.pdf

Lyon, D. (ed.) (2006) *Theorizing Surveillance: The Panopticon and Beyond*, Cullompton: Willan.

Lyon, D. (2007) 'The Card Cartel: an oligopoly on the means of identification', unpublished paper. The Surveillance Project, Queen's University, Kingston.

Lyon, D. (forthcoming) *Identifying Citizens*, Cambridge: Polity Press.

Migdal, J.S. (1988) *Strong Societies and Weak States: State-Society Relations and State Capabilities in the Third World,* Princeton: Princeton University Press.

Moore, B. Jr. (1984) *Privacy: Studies in Social and Cultural History*, Armonk: M.E. Sharpe.

Noiriel, G. (2001) 'The identification of the citizen: the birth of republican civil status in France', in J. Caplan and J. Torpey (eds) *Documenting Individual Identity: The Development of State Practices in the Modern World*, Princeton: Princeton University Press.

Prevent Genocide International (2001) *Global Survey of Group Classification on Identity Cards*. Online. Available: http://www.preventgenocide.org/prevent/removing-facilitating-factors/IDcards/survey/index.htm

Privacy Commissioner of Canada (2007) *Identity, Privacy and the Need of Others to Know Who You Are: A Discussion Paper on Identity Issues*, Ottawa: Office of the Privacy Commissioner of Canada.

Privacy International (1996) *Identity Cards: Frequently Asked Questions*. Online. Available: http://www.privacy.org/pi/activities/idcard/idcard_faq.html

Rose, N. (1999) *Powers of Freedom*, Cambridge: Cambridge University Press.

Scott, J.C. (1998) *Seeing Like a State*, New Haven: Yale University Press.

Skocpol, T. (1985) 'Bringing the state back in: strategies of analysis in current research', in P. Evans, D. Rueschemeyer and T. Skocpol (eds) *Bringing the State Back In,* Cambridge: Cambridge University Press.

The Times (1995) 'Questions of identity', editorial, 25 May.

Torpey, J. (2000) *The Invention of the Passport: Surveillance, Citizenship and the State*, Cambridge and New York: Cambridge University Press.

2 Governing by identity[1]

Louise Amoore

> Identity requires difference in order to be, and it converts difference into otherness in order to secure its own self-certainty.
>
> (William Connolly 1991: 64)

> The secret identification directive acts as a legal obligation that directly affects millions of people while providing no public notice or allowing for checks on arbitrary or prejudicial enforcement.
>
> (Gilmore v. Gonzales 2006: 2)

On 4 July 2002, a US citizen, John Gilmore, arrived at Oakland International Airport for a South-west Airlines flight to Baltimore. Faced with the by now familiar demand 'passengers must show identification', Gilmore declined to show identification documentation and was denied passage. Making a second attempt to travel within the USA without presenting identification, this time from San Francisco, Gilmore was informed that he could proceed, but on condition that he submitted to a secondary and more intrusive set of searches. Again he declined and was denied boarding. In 2006, Gilmore filed a 'Writ of Certiorari', challenging, at the Supreme Court, the 'secret law' – concealed on the grounds of 'sensitive security information' – that requires citizens to 'identify themselves' for security screening (Gilmore v. Gonzales 2006: 2).

The Gilmore petition to the US Supreme Court is illustrative of a broader political move in the deployment of identity as a means of governing in the era defined as a 'War on Terror'. Moreover, it is suggestive of life in a world where formal identification systems are 'voluntarily adopted' (UK Home Office 2004), but where the failure to self-identify itself becomes a basis for suspicion and risk-based targeted searching. Gilmore encountered in the space of the airport – as one also experiences on the London Underground, at the railway station, at toll booths on the roads and on the city streets – a multitude of nebulous demands for identification. As the Electronic Privacy Information Center (EPIC) testified to the Supreme Court on the Gilmore case, the citizen was confronted with: 'a rule which may be either a government rule or an airline policy; which was required either at the check-in counter, at the gate, at a security checkpoint, or at some combination of these locations' (EPIC Amicus 2006: 8). It is this perennial obligation to identify oneself and others, and to do so in the absence of a visible, clear or challengeable rule of law, that both underlies and exceeds the debates on systems of identification – from ID cards and biometric identifiers, to automatic recognition systems and the use of commercial data mining for security (cf. Lyon 2003, 2004; Gates 2005; Amoore 2006; Amoore and de Goede 2005). The foundation of Gilmore's petition was precisely the blurring of categories of law, policy, rule and obligation in the Transportation Security Administration's Identification Directive. As in Giorgio Agamben's claim that, within the state of exception, acts proliferate 'that do not have the value of law but acquire its force' (2005: 38), the constant demand for identification operates as though it already had juridical status. Not only the state, but the security guard, the biometrics software engineer, the ticket sales clerk, even the citizen, acquires the power of policing the security policy (Bigo 2002).

This chapter explores how identification has become represented at the forefront of the techniques and technologies of so-called homeland security. In so doing, I am suggesting that the ID card itself, and the partially integrated databases to which it is a gateway, is already exceeded by the authorization of identity as a means to security more broadly. Not only are we witnessing the emergence of multiple and overlapping private players in the market for identification – best captured in Lyon and Bennett's 'card cartels' (see Chapter 1) – but there is an amorphous declaration of emergency and special measures, seemingly capable of limitless demands for identification. In a very real sense, the ID card itself is already deployed by other means. For the plaintiff John Gilmore, for example, what mattered was not strictly the requirement to produce identification *per se*, but rather the profound uncertainty as to the authority of the demand. Who is authorized to ask 'identify yourself'? What is the basis of that authority? Can there be effective redress for prejudicial or otherwise abusive demands for identification, when the site of the demand is never clearly locatable?

While in some ways the ID card debate in the UK, for example, is already surpassed – by an e-borders system, multiple trusted traveller schemes, monitoring of credit card and urban transit card transactions, biometric visas and work permits – the specific assemblage of diffuse authorities that demand identification is only scantily understood.[2] To propose a 'voluntary' national ID card system, or indeed to compel take-up via passport or visa application as in the UK case, is to expose how this specific mode of identification functions as but one element of a broader assemblage of practices of identification. Thus, for example, where privacy cultures mitigate against a national ID card system in a particular place, we tend to find the most advanced and proliferating forms of identification by other means. There is a case, then, I will argue, for focusing not strictly on identity as though it could be a fixed, settled and accessible domain, but instead on the practices and modes of identification that make an identity claim possible. As Stuart Hall (1990) reminds us, there can be no singular 'identity', but only multiple 'unstable points of identification' that temporarily and arbitrarily 'position' us (see also Hall 1990; Butler 1990). It is precisely these processes of identification that I will argue exceed the ID card itself, and whose novel contemporary forms demand our attention. Not least, because some of the most targeted and vulnerable groups are experiencing a perpetual exposure to governmental practices of identification: 'where is your return ticket?'; 'is your travel card expired?'; 'show me your student card'; 'why is your Oyster card unregistered?'[3]

In the discussion that follows, I will begin by situating the contemporary mode of identification in the War on Terror, focusing specifically on the historical example of global consultants *Price Waterhouse*. As accountants in the Second World War, *Price Waterhouse* were seconded to Whitehall to lend expertise to the devising of rationing systems for wartime Britain. This was (as Scott Thompson argues in Chapter 9), an important moment in the authorization of systems of identification. In the context of a declared emergency, statistical and survey methods were deployed to devise secure identity regimes for the population (see Hacking 1990). Some 60 years later, *IBM* having bought *PricewaterhouseCoopers Consulting*, we are seeing renewed emphasis on identification, but of rather a different kind. Where wartime modes of identification relied on evidential statistical data, contemporary modes of identification seek to incorporate the uncertain and the unknown into the calculation itself. They do not simply wish to verify the identity of an individual, but instead to identify and pre-empt a future potentially risky body.

Second, I propose that governing by identity has become the principal means of reconciling mobility – or more specifically the feigned picture of a world in which people, objects and money move smoothly – with the idea of securability. For, as William Connolly (1991) suggests in the opening citation of this chapter, identity 'converts difference into otherness in order to secure its own self-certainty'. Hence the reliance of contemporary border control practices on mobile forms of bordering that use identification to shore-up the 'homeland' from the 'strangeland', or as the Department of Homeland Security displays at all ports of entry 'keeping America's doors open and our nation secure'. Illustrating my point with one specific form of mobile identifier – radio frequency identification devices in immigration documents – I show how the *address* that has always been integral to identification, once mobile, is capable of novel conversions of difference into otherness.

Finally, this chapter concludes by reflecting on the implications of novel forms of identification for political contestation and, specifically, the capacity of privacy and rights to privacy to respond effectively. Different regimes and systems of identity are deployed in the security domain, primarily to reveal a picture of a person, or to 'pay attention' to those who are designated risky or suspicious (Crary 2004). Contemporary modes of identification, I argue, operate primarily via the screen and not via the card. The distinction matters profoundly to our sense of the political implications of new modes of identification. While the card is one interface with a picture of a person, the screen offers a different visuality – a projection of a person built from fragments, bits and bytes of data, suspicions and prejudices (Amoore 2007). These projected and pixilated people confront privacy laws and human rights agendas in new and problematic ways. When human rights and civil liberties NGOs, such as the ACLU, EPIC or Privacy International seek to challenge 'false identification' today – whether names on a 'no fly' list; money transfers frozen; or stop and search abuses – they confront precisely this screened and projected person. As they testify, it is almost impossible to challenge, to refute one's own (mis)identification.

ity: A war by other means

...at has been described as a 'risk society' reaching its limits – facing the unknowable risks and incalculable catastrophes of an uncertain world (cf. Ericson and Doyle 2004; Baker 2002; Ericson 2007) – the category of identity has become a particularly appealing means of governing. Ulrick Beck's (1999: 4) established claim that the uncertainties of, for example, climate change and terrorism, signal the limits of risk society, limits reached when science can no longer respond to the problems it produces, is at the very least premature. For, in the burgeoning scientific domains of identification, from DNA databases to finite anatomic metrics of the iris or face, there appears to be a pushing of the limits of the risk calculations that can be made. In the technologies of the war on terror in particular, systems of identification have become the tool of choice for new forms of risk calculation. Algorithmic models of identification that had long been used to identify unknown and uncertain characteristics in the worlds of consumerism and commercial management appeared as though they were novel technologies after 9/11. Giving evidence at a US Congressional hearing only five months after 9/11, *IBM*'s federal business manager testified that 'in this war, our enemies are hiding in open and available information across a spectrum of databases' (Kestelyn 2002: 8). Thus, in the immediate aftermath of the 9/11 attacks, the systems of identification traded by companies such as *IBM* and *Oracle* became the focus of US inquires that concluded: 'on September 11, enough relevant data was resident in existing databases', such that 'had the dots been connected, the events could have been exposed and stopped' (US Joint Inquiry 2003: 14). It is precisely this *joining of dots in advance*, this *identification before the event*, that captures the specific contemporary way of governing by identity. The proliferation of new juridical and quasi-legal measures such as the 'Real ID' Act, the 'Advance Targeting System', and the 'identification directive', deploy identity primarily as a means of assigning a risk value to an individual and, thus, making a security intervention possible even in face of profound uncertainty (Amoore and de Goede 2008).

To be clear at this point, it is not that systems of identification, nor indeed ID cards or identity registers, are at all a novel means of governing within a declared emergency or war. Indeed, the chapters of this book offer profound insights into the genealogy and historical specificity of the ID card itself. Rather, it is the specific mode of *pre-emptive identification* that is novel to contemporary security decisions, and it is this mode of identification that I am interested in here. It is worth reflecting for a moment, though, on one other historical moment, when the problem of uncertainty in war was addressed via identity. In 1940s wartime Britain, the Board of Trade turned to the expertise of accountants to devise and administer a system of clothing rationing. The *Price Waterhouse* accountants, seconded to Whitehall from European offices, were to become 'the body of men who played an invaluable part in all the Board of Trade's essays in control' (Hargreaves and Gowing 1952: 110). In the absence of reliable census data, the accountants produced a system of number that could both reveal information about the habits and behaviours of the population, and reliably identify and verify the claims of individuals (Jones 1995). In one sense, the decisions taken by *Price Waterhouse* accountants, on matters such as how to secure the rationing system from fraudulent claims, are simply one example of the use of statistical calculation and numeric identification in the 'taming of chance' (Hacking 1990). Yet, in 1940s Britain, the state's deferral to 'expert' systems of identification and classification (of people, families, professions) involved the routinized collection of data on the population (Rose 1991). It was strictly a 'preventative' and not a 'pre-emptive' means of governing, where prevention 'prescribes and produces order' and pre-emptive security 'intervenes and guides disorder' (Agamben 2002: 1; Massumi 2005). Capturing a situated and specific survey of the population, the accountants' measures were devised strictly to prevent clothing shortages and inflated prices. By contrast, the contemporary expert models of identification are not confined to a specific temporal survey or spatial location, but instead 'allow for opening and globalisation' and act on the future (Agamben 2002: 1).

To a degree, there is a common thread linking the wartime accounting techniques of *Price Waterhouse* to the contemporary 'homeland security solutions' of commercial players, such as *IBM*. *IBM* acquired the consulting arm of *PricewaterhouseCoopers* in 2002, making it possible for integrated databases and software models to be wrapped in consulting practices of risk management and future-proofing. It is not the commercial histories that are of primary significance here, though, but the exemplars of different logics of identification. Where wartime models of identification relied on evidential statistical data – reported numbers, recorded addresses and so on – contemporary modes of identification seek to incorporate what is uncertain and unknown into the identity calculation itself. Where the Board of Trade's key identity problem was how to verify the identity of an individual making a rations claim, now we see the emergence of the problem of identifying future risks. The logic of the ID card as we conventionally think of it dwells within the former mode of identification, yet the contemporary practices of identification embody the logic of the latter. Put simply, identification in the 'prevent' mode may mean that one's documentation denies access or the crossing of a border, while identification in the 'pre-empt' mode takes a risk decision long in advance of a border or boundary being reached.[4]

In short, then, the modes of identification deployed within contemporary ID card schemes and proposals – as well as in biometric identifiers, data mining and social network analysis, for example – have less in common with historical identity schemes than they do with mathematical models used to identify in other spheres. In the commercial world of the 1990s, an important shift took place in the use of data on consumers. No longer content with survey-style data on existing customers, the Holy Grail became the mathematical models that could identify the unknown individual – the as-yet-unencountered consumer to be targeted.

One particular resonance between the mathematical sciences and commercial worlds is especially worthy of discussion for its subsequent role in securitization. In the summer of 1992, *IBM* research fellow Rakesh Agrawal met for lunch with a senior executive of UK retailers *Marks & Spencer* (*M&S*). Working on mathematical models for locating associations between items in 'accumulated data' at the IBM-Almaden research centre, Agrawal proposed that *M&S*'s vast data on daily

tions could be used to take strategic corporate decisions. The research paper ;ulted from the *IBM–M&S* meeting, and from subsequent work with US *Wal-Mart*, has become the world's most cited paper on commercial algorithmic techniques (Agrawal *et al.* 1993). In simple terms, the model claimed to provide a method for building a profile of an unknown identity based on the knowledge of 'normal' transactions and their associated patterns of behaviour. Thus, for example, data on the patterns and associations between film choices at a cinema and food purchased in the foyer, could be used to target vouchers at particular customers, even if they were 'unknown consumers' and had never left their own data trail. The significance here is in the move that is enabled by algorithmic modes of identification – a shift from the effort to predict future trends on the basis of fixed statistical data, to a means of pre-empting the future, drawing probable futures into imminent and immediate commercial decision.

The *IBM* work on association rules in the mathematical and computer sciences, though it achieved ubiquity long before 9/11 by 'connecting the dots' in prosaic settings and everyday transactions, has subsequently established a way of thinking about taking security decisions in the face of an uncertain future. By 2004, Agrawal and his *IBM* team were leading the export of commercial algorithmic techniques to the security sphere, presenting the possibilities of association rules for the 'mathematical sciences' role in homeland security' (BMSA 2004). The promise that algorithmic calculations held out to the commercial authorities of the 1990s – to enable surveillance from a distance, to make market judgements in advance, to generate patterns of normal and atypical consumer behaviour – is now being re-made in the context of state security desires. At the time of writing, *IBM* have the software contracts for the Heathrow airport 'MiSense' biometrics system, the UK e-borders 'Iris' and 'Semaphore' trials, and the software for the US biometric borders programme. As the logics of commercial data mining cross into security spheres, association rules become a form of 'guilt by association', within which 'risky' identities are designated.

In the proliferation of modes of identification that identify in advance, then, we find practices that both underlie and exceed the 'card' in ID card. As in Michel Foucault's inversion of Clausewitz, where 'politics is the continuation of war by other means', practices of identification work to continually wage war on an other whose very identification serves to shore-up the 'we' in the homeland. 'The role of political power', writes Foucault, 'is perpetually to use a sort of silent war to reinscribe the relationship of force, and to reinscribe it in institutions, economic inequalities, language, and even the bodies of individuals' (2003: 16–17). Understood in this way, the political practices of homeland security – what Gregory and Pred call 'expert solutions' (Gregory and Pred 2007: 1) – are actually sanctioning and reproducing the war-like relations of power seen in the overtly militarized spaces of Afghanistan and Iraq. They target individual bodies, designate communities as dangerous or risky, delineate safe zones from targeted locations, invoke the pre-emptive strike on the city streets. The spiralling violences of systems that identify/target matter greatly to the political space to intervene in debates such as those surrounding national ID cards. In the imagination of a 'nation', the other who is not us is integral to the imagined community (Shapiro 1997; Gregory 2004).

Understood in this way, it may scarcely matter whether or not a particular ID scheme becomes law, what matters instead is whether it is able to act with the force of law. In more concrete terms, for example, the *Oracle Corporation*'s offer after 9/11 to provide free software for a US federal identity card and database, though it was rejected, has come into practice by other means. Already ubiquitous in our daily lives – in software platforms for payroll, pensions, healthcare, the bibliographic searches used in academic research, and so on – *Oracle*'s algorithmic 'identity management' systems lead the way in homeland security markets. Their Non-Obvious Relationship Awareness (NORA) software – developed for the entertainment industry and used in the Las Vegas casinos – are now deployed by the US Justice and federal intelligence agencies for counter-terror. According to *Oracle* consultants, NORA enables clients to identify 'obscure relationships between customers, employees, vendors, and other internal and external data sources'. NORA searches for behaviour patterns or personal associations that hint at terrorist activity, turning data into actionable intelligence' (IDC 2004: 11). It is this conversion of data into 'actionable intelligence' that makes pre-emptive identification possible in practice. Currently, the suspicious associations include past travel to Pakistan and transactions made from particular travel agents and money transfer agencies. The conversion of difference into otherness – William Connolly's *raison d'être* of identity – is everywhere being concealed inside the glossy technoscience of algorithmic identification.

Mobility: 'Keep the data flowing and the planes flying'

Moving quickly through the crowds of the ticket hall at a London Underground station, a young woman stops to top up her *Oyster* payment card at a nearby machine. The transaction cannot be authorized, the machine tells her, she must report to the officials in the booth. From behind the glass, the *Transport for London* worker taps at the computer keyboard:

'Yes, I can see the problem, you did not complete your journey on September 29th'.
'But I must have … I am here now'.
'No, we have no exit record of your smart card, your journey is incomplete. If you can just tell me where you completed your journey that day, I can reactivate your card'.
'But, I don't remember, it is two weeks ago'.
'I can tell you that you began your journey at Russell Square at 15.20 pm … we just need the exit data to complete the transaction'.[5]

In the travel transactions data of the payment card, the mobile people of the city leave their mapped traces. The completion of a journey and the registration of the travel card to a verifiable address – like the timely repayment of a loan, or a pattern of no-claims on motor insurance – identifies and marks out risk rating of the traveller, allowing her to be targeted, for coupons and discounted travel, or for intervention and interception. In effect, when established patterns are breached, the is asked to repair her risk rating, to complete her transaction, identify and leave verifiable data.

The nebulous and perennial demands to 'identify yourself' in public space has become an enduring feature of contemporary securitization. In the post-9/11 context, multiple sources of data are used to enable an uneasy reconciliation between security and mobility. If one is amenable to 'confessing' at the many borders of the subway, the rail network, the air transport system (Salter 2007) – 'where was your last destination?'; 'why did you pay cash?'; 'why is your card registered to an address outside London?' – then, the many trusted traveller and security pre-screening programmes will enhance the experience of a mobile world. This is the deal that is struck in contemporary modes of identification: verify a credible and secure identity and trade this for mobility (cf. Sparke 2006). Hence, the secondary security checks demanded of John Gilmore in the absence of his confessional identification. Indeed, the demand for identification has become *the* sovereign demand, even the condition of citizenship. When the European Union sought to annul the 2004 Passenger Name Record (PNR) agreement with the USA, for example, the US Secretary for Homeland Security made the condition that to 'keep the planes flying', people must be identified (by 34 items of data) and European states must 'keep the data flowing' (DHS 2006). When the transatlantic airliner plot was uncovered in 2006, the US authorities threatened to remove the visa waiver from 'Britons of Pakistani origin' unless the UK government agreed to 'enhanced verification procedures' on these people (Chertoff 2007).

At stake in contemporary programmes of identification, then, is the very mobility of identity itself. Because by now we are all familiar with the idea of identity as something that is never finally fixed and is always in process of identification, perhaps we should not be surprised that governmental techniques now seek out these mobile forms of identification. One example of this, particularly important to the demand for identification in contemporary border control, is the use of mobile 'tagged' forms of address. Systems of address, while always integral to identification, once rendered more mobile become capable of novel forms of tracking and targeting.

In August 2004, the US Department for Homeland Security (DHS) announced the testing of a new tracking technology at five US land border ports of entry. The trial – conducted by consultants *Accenture* and *Deloitte* in collaboration with *Philips Semiconductors* – embedded radio frequency identification (RFID) tags into paper I-94 customs and border protection forms. The RFID tags contain a 'passive' chip and antenna, capable of transmitting a unique numeric identifier to a remote reader. By October 2006, the same RFID technology became a US entry requirement for visa waiver programme passports. Later the same year, the UK's Transport for London announced that its RFID-enabled Oyster travel payment card was to integrate with a Visa credit card, allowing the tracking and tracing of all small transactions, actions and movements on the London Underground system.

How might we understand what is at work here? A virtually invisible technology, concealed within a paper document or 'smart' card, is deployed with the precise purpose of rendering a person visible, identifiable and locatable. As architect

Dana Cuff has noted, 'there is an irony here', it is 'invisible, miniaturized sensors that are making formerly inaccessible realms visible' (2003: 45). In part, of course, the apparent invisibility of the techniques for making visible is assured because of their already existing ubiquity in everyday commercial transactions. As the Vice President of *Philips Semiconductors* had testified to the US Congress Committee on Energy and Commerce in 2004, 'consumers are already likely to encounter RF-enabled personal identification devices in their daily lives, such as secure access cards for building entry, speedy gasoline purchasing, such as the *Exxon Speedpass*, vehicle anti-theft systems, and in transportation systems all over the world' (US House of Representatives 2004: 3). What is taking place, then, is the redeployment of sensor technologies used in the commercial identification of mobile things, objects, animals and vehicles into the domain of the identification of mobile people.

The emergence of knowledges of location, what Nigel Thrift has called 'our conventions of address', follows a tacit and often unacknowledged sense that we somehow know 'what will show up where and what will show up next' (2004: 176). In other words, a system of address has been central to our ability to spatially and temporally identify events, objects, people and so on. The history of addressability displays a significant playing back and forth of military logistical knowledges and commercial supply and transportation knowledges. Thus, for example, the origins of the 1940s bar code technologies lie in the communication techniques of Morse code. As computing technologies began to enable the electronic reading and recognition of patterns, new relationships between the identifier (postal code, barcode, personal identifiers, such as date of birth) and the identified (people, places, parcels, vehicles) become possible. Consider, for example, *IBM*'s 'punch cards' of the 1950s – patterns of punched holes in a card to be fed into the pattern recognition programmes of *IBM* machines.[6] The 'patterns of data on the IBM cards', writes Reinhold Martin, 'made visible what was invisible' (2003: 158). The machine's ability to 'read' the cards extended beyond the mere processing of data and into the almost magical realm of animating a life unseen. In a 1955 publicity brochure, *IBM* reminded the American public of how their lives were locatable in the traces of actions and transactions left in the card and 'read' by the machine:

> IBM first came into your life when your birth was recorded on a punched card. From then on many such cards have been compiled, giving a lifetime of history of your important decisions and actions. If you went to school, entered a hospital, bought a home, paid income tax, got married or purchased an automobile, the chances are that permanent records were made of these and other personal stories.
>
> (Cited in Martin 2003: 159)

What we begin to see with the intersection of systems of address with systems of pattern recognition, or the marrying of addressability and readability, if you like, is a computer-enabled system of *locatability*. While even rudimentary systems of address involve recognizing identifying markings, whether these are numbers, features of the natural landscape, or codes, the computer reading of markings and the recognition of patterns makes possible novel forms of location. Here, the emphasis is on a more mobile and agile mode of address that does not 'stop at the door' of delivery, but instead dwells inside, making visible, readable and locatable the traces of daily life. With the rise of what Kang and Cuff (2005) call 'computer addressability', the fixed location of the address is loosened via 'unique identification codes' (2005: 94). Because the codes dwell inside a body or object in the physical environment, they do, at least in theory, make it locatable in movement.

In this shift from addressability to locatability, the ability to track and trace mobility is achieved by animating the physical environment so that it is able to 'respond directly to what it sees' (Kang and Cuff 2005: 94). Thus, the 'reader' of traces, markings or transactions, established via the early technologies of punch cards and barcodes, becomes ever more important to the system of identification as 'addresses move with human and non-human actants' (Thrift 2004: 183). Rather as *IBM*'s early computers inferred people's life histories from the patterns punched into the cards, and from the intervals between them, contemporary readers of location, as a group of researchers at Intel have put it: 'infer people's actions from their effect on the environment, especially on the objects with which they interact' (Smith *et al.* 2005: 39). The embedding of RFID tags into objects, as Smith and his colleagues have shown at Intel, can be understood as one means to achieve a novel and mobile form of identification. The proximity chips inside ID cards form one element of systems of mobile identification, but they are one access point in a multi-layered series of gateways to plural databases. For a supermarket shopper's 'loyalty card', the gateway opens up onto patterns of past purchases, coupons or vouchers for savings and such like. For a US–Mexico border crossing card holder, the passive RFID tag signals an identifier that can be mapped across past patterns of travel, criminal convictions or terrorist watch lists. In this way, the RFID identifies the target for algorithmic calculation, at the border, at the supermarket check-out, at the entrance to the sports stadium, in the underground ticket hall. 'Through RFID tags', as Jerry Kang and Dana Cuff have it, address is specified 'to a fine level of granularity, much finer than a zip code', so that we 'will likely authenticate our identity to multiple queries of 'who are you' made by the enacted environment' (Kang and Cuff 2005: 106).

It is worth saying clearly that it is not the chips within 'smart cards' themselves that are the primary means of mobile identification, but rather the techniques of tracking and targeting that classify and categorize people. The practice of tracking, according to media theorist Jordan Crandall, seeks to 'detect, process and strategically codify a moving phenomenon in a competitive theatre', whether this space is a 'battlefield, the social arena, or the marketplace' (Crandall 2005: 4). In this sense, tracking technologies enable the identification and location of moving targets. RFID's military origins, and its playing back and forth between supply chain and logistics techniques and state security practices, bear out what Samuel Weber (2005) calls a 'target of opportunity', a competitive 'seizing' of 'targets':

> However different the war on terror was going to be from traditional wars, with
> their relatively well-defined enemies, it would still involve one of the basic

mechanisms of traditional hunting and combat, in however modified and modernized a form: namely 'targeting'. The enemy would have to be *identified* and *localized*, *named* and *depicted*, in order to be made into an accessible target .... None of this was, per se, entirely new. What *was*, however, was the mobility, indeterminate structure, and unpredictability of the spatio-temporal *medium* in which such targets had to be sited .... In theatres of conflict that had become highly mobile and changeable, 'targets' and 'opportunity' were linked as never before.

(Weber 2005: 3–4; emphasis in original)

Samuel Weber's key point of discussion is the theatre of war, though his argument sheds significant light on the modes of identification that I depict here. The *identification*, *localization*, *naming* and *depiction* of mobile targets is, in this war by other means, conducted in and through daily life, in advance of any possible future strike or intervention. The targeting of mobile bodies, things, objects or monies is becoming a matter of locating – positioning in the sights, if you like – so that the opportunities of a mobile global economy might be seized, while the capability to identify and secure the target remains. As consultants, *Accenture*, *Deloitte* and *IBM* lead the drive for multiple networked public and private applications of identification software, the commercial 'targets of opportunity' that allowed the production of goods to become dispersed and diffuse are clearing space for more diffuse modes of sovereign power. The technologies that have made possible a global supply chain of export processing zones and offshore sites, are simultaneously being embedded into border crossing cards, visas, passports and immigrant ID cards that include mobile people within governable space by means of their targeted exclusion.

Conclusions

Reflections on privacy

There can be little doubt that some of the most significant political challenges to the governing of security *via identity* have come from critical lawyers, many of whom represent those people most subjected to racism, prejudice and violence in the identification regime (cf. Rotenberg 2003, 2007). For these juridical challengers of identity systems – from REAL ID and USVISIT in the USA, to the National Identity Register and the Borders Bill in the UK – it is the right to privacy that provides the way into the problem. Moreover, for some it is privacy measures that can restore civil liberties within the securitization of identity, for example in Privacy Impact Assessments, data transparency, designation and restriction of purpose, and so on. And yet, the idea of privacy, at least in many of its contemporary manifestations, is an inadequate means of politicizing the drive for identification. Indeed, we might even say that it depoliticizes the positioning of our identities, replacing the struggles of politics and difference with more technologies, this time of law and regulatory control. The appeal to a human right to privacy and bodily integrity, as Irma van der Ploeg (2003) has argued, 'does not entirely match wit' the informatization and digitization processes evolving' (2003: 66). Thus, the use of identity to govern pre-emptively, or to secure mobility, as I have suggested in this chapter, raises new questions for how we think about the idea of privacy itself.

First, the appeal to privacy itself restates the unity of the subject that is intrinsic to the mode of identification I have described. Put simply, where the mode of identification assumes a nation-state, a citizenry, an identity that is securable, can be secured, the idea of privacy itself imagines an individual whose private data can be secured and unequivocally protected. The reduction of a person to their rights recognizes, as legal philosopher Costas Douzinas puts it, only 'a non-substantial, a thin personality, a public image that seriously mis-matches people's self-image' (2002: 397). This leaves people, as is increasingly the case, contesting the identification that is made of them, both by the law and in security practice. Not only is this bare and pared down rights-oriented privacy mirroring the sovereign practices of securing and protecting, but it is also all too readily incorporated into the mode of identification itself. So, for example, the bodily incursions of the *Backscatter* X-ray at US and UK borders are apparently ameliorated by the use of privacy enhancing digital 'fig leaves'; the algorithms developed by Rakesh Agrawal are now accompanied by his programme of 'humane data mining' that anonymizes personal data; the European objections to PNR transfer are eroded by the reduction of identity data fields. The imagination of a world that can be secured through the authentication of identity is scarcely interrupted or unsettled by a counter-appeal to make private the traces of our identity in the residue of daily life.

Second, a key implication of my argument here is that the person whose identity is to be protected is not limited to the situated and surveilled individual of wartime ID cards. Superficially, all modes of identification appear to demand a 'picture of a person' – whether this is photograph ID or biometric scans – but the form of image specific to contemporary modes does not stop at the surface of a document or card. Where a snapshot or photograph embodies a time and location-specific image of a person, the screen and screened visualities delve into layers of data images (Friedberg 2007). The image on an ID card or passport, even the databased images of Backscatter or electronic fingerprinting, is projected forward into what appears as a visualization of a person with a risk value attached. As Friedrich Kittler has argued in his works on filmic images, projections are produced from fragments of visual data, from individually isolated characteristics that are then selected, differentiated and reintegrated into a visual whole (1997). Of course, gaps persist between the lines that join the pixilated dots. These gaps, though, are filled with mobile and projected images that produce a seamless whole. In a sense, then, the missing elements are crucial to the projected and pre-emptive identifications of people. If the homeland security vision is to identify and intercept in advance, then pre-emptive identification positively relies upon missing elements and gaps. someone is misidentified, or that the full picture is not known, or that visible to the subject, is to mistake the logic of identity that is ation, simply put, is that the increasingly visual identification me gaps and invisibilities, these are simply 'filled in' by the it penetrates and projects forward in time, and because it seeks a picture of a person from data fragments, it is the multiple screened identifications that should concern us more than the image on the surface of a card or other document.

Finally, given the problem of political action in relation to privacy, what would constitute responsible and ethical decision in the context of the forms of identification I have discussed? 'To act ethically', writes William Connolly, 'is often to call some comforts of identity into question' (1991: xix). In contrast to a diminished privacy that is located in an individual, then, ethical action would put the very idea of identity at risk, recognizing and confronting the difference that makes all identity claims possible. The project, as Connolly proposes, is not to reject the rights claim itself, but to consider the ambivalence of all identity at the heart of all 'responsibilities', 'judgements' and 'rights' (1991: xx). In concrete terms, one implication for my argument here would be that we must confront the way that modes of identification, operating through difference, have become normalized. In the prosaic obligation to identify and to confess identity, the suspicious and the malicious can proliferate (Amoore 2007). At the time of writing, for example, London's Underground stations display a poster calling for passengers to 'use all their senses' in the detection of that which is abnormal and potentially dangerous. The Metropolitan Police posters, illustrated with images of eyes, noses, ears and lips, extend the pre-emptive mode of identification into the realm of the senses and affective experience.

In the face of this kind of governing by identity, to call the comforts of identity into question would mean constructing a more fully fleshed out form of privacy. One that does not deploy the private as a means of distancing the other and shoring-up our identity position, but instead asks that privacy be possible in the very public spaces that demand 'who are you?' It is not so much a lack of privacy that is the political problematic, but rather a lack of social space in which we can see and be seen, engage with the differences and difficulties of our world. As the American novelist Jonathan Franzen writes: 'the networked world as a threat to privacy? It's the ugly spectacle of a privacy triumphant', 'we are flat out drowning in *privacy*' (2002: 50). What is absent, as Franzen sees it, is not strictly the possibility for privacy – this he sees as the guiding principle of a data-driven world where the encounters, differences and difficulties of public space are effaced by 'the right to be left alone' – but rather the ability *to be visible* in public space without judgement or suspicion. At the same time as the demand for identification is made in the spaces of shopping precincts, underground or city plaza, a demand to render ourselves visible to security authorities of many kinds, our ability to simply walk around, to see and be seen in public space diminishes.

Notes

1 The research is supported by UK Economic and Social Research Council (ESRC) award RES 155 25 0087: 'Contested Borders: Non-Governmental Public Action and the Technologies of the War on Terror'.
2 Leading NGOs contesting the UK ID card and ID register, frame the problem as 'the visible face of deeper systems already in place', with ID cards the 'low-hanging fruit' that

is more readily publicly challengeable; interviews conducted with Privacy International and Liberty (Brussels 26 March 2007; London 10 August 2007).
3 These are some of the demands for identification reported by a group of North African young people studying in London, interviewed 12 April 2007. Under Section 44 of the UK's Terrorism Act 2000, powers to stop and search without grounds for suspicion were granted to all places with a known intelligence-led security threat. The special measure has become a permanent rule for the whole of the London Metropolitan area.
4 It is for this reason, for example, that Gareth Crossman, Director of Policy for Liberty, has greater privacy concerns for the National Identity Register than for the National ID Card Scheme itself and, indeed, considers the UK Borders Bill to 'go far further than either' in its use of 'profiling techniques'. Testimony to Westminster Forum, 12 July 2007.
5 This example is drawn from the documented experiences of a participant in 'London in a Time of Terror', Birkbeck College, London, 8 December 2006.
6 IBM's generation of punch-card computers used technology derived from Herman Hollerith's patterned cards developed for the US census of 1890, itself having roots in pattern cards used in weaving. Hollerith's company was one of three parent companies of *IBM* (Hacking 1990: 53).

Bibliography

Agamben, G. (2002) 'Security and Terror', *Theory & Event* 5: 4.

Agamben, G. (2005) *State of Exception*, translated by Kevin Attell, Chicago: University of Chicago Press.

Agrawal, R., Imielinski, T. and Swami, A. (1993) 'Mining association rules between sets of items in large databases', *SIGMOD Proceedings,* pp. 914–25.

Amoore, L. (2006) 'Biometric borders: governing mobilities in the war on terror', *Political Geography* 25: 336–51.

Amoore, L. (2007) 'Vigilant visualities: the watchful politics of the war on terror', *Security Dialogue* 38(2): 139–56.

Amoore, L. and de Goede, M. (2005) 'Governance, risk and dataveillance in the war on terror', *Crime, Law and Social Change* 43(2): 149–73.

Amoore, L. and de Goede, M. (2008) 'Governing by risk in the war on terror', in L. Amoore and M. de Goede (eds) *Risk and the War on Terror*, London: Routledge.

Baker, T. (2002) 'Liability and Insurance after 9/11: embracing risk meets the precautionary principle', *Geneva Papers on Risk and Insurance* 27: 3.

Beck, U. (1999) *World Risk Society*, Cambridge: Polity.

Bigo, D. (2002) 'The Möbius ribbon of internal and external security(ies)', in M. Albert, D. Jacobson, and Y. Lapid (eds) *Identities, Borders, Orders: Rethinking International Relations Theory*, Minneapolis: University of Minnesota Press.

BMSA (2004) *The Mathematical Sciences' Role in the War on Terror*, Washington: National Academies Press.

Butler, J. (1990) *Gender Trouble: Feminism and the Subversion of Identity*, New York: Routledge.

Chertoff, M. (2007) 'Remarks by Secretary Michael Chertoff to the Johns Hopkins University Paul H. Nitze School of Advanced International Studies', 3 May. Online. Available: www.dhs.gov/xnews/speeches/sp_1178288606838.shtm (accessed May 2007).

Connolly, W. (1991) *Identity/Difference: Democratic Negotiations of Political Paradox*, Minneapolis: University of Minnesota Press.

Connolly, W. (2005) *Pluralism*, Durham and London: Duke University Press.

Crandall, J. (2005) 'Envisioning the Homefront: militarization, tracking and security culture,' *Journal of Visual Culture* 4(1): 17–38.

Crary, J. (2004) 'Conjurations of security', *Interventions: International Journal of Postcolonial Studies* 6(3): 423–30.

Cuff, D. (2003) 'Immanent domain: pervasive computing and the public realm', *Journal of Architectural Education* 57(1): 43–9.

DHS (2006) 'Survey of DHS Data Mining Activities', Washington DC: Office of the Inspector General.

Douzinas, C. (2002) 'Identity, recognition, rights, or what Hegel can teach us about rights?' *Journal of Law and Society* 29(3): 379–405.

EPIC Amicus (2006) 'On petition for writ of certiorari to the United States Court of Appeals', Washington DC: Electronic Privacy Information Center.

Ericson, R. (2007) *Crime in an Insecure World,* Cambridge: Polity.

Ericson, R. and Doyle, A. (2004) 'Catastrophe risk, insurance and terrorism', *Economy & Society* 33(2): 135–73.

Foucault, M. (2003) *Society Must be Defended: Lectures at the College de France*, New York: Picador.

Franzen, J. (2002) *How to Be Alone*, London: Fourth Estate.

Friedberg, A. (2007) *The Virtual Window: From Alberti to Microsoft*, Cambridge: MIT Press.

Gates, K. (2005) 'Biometrics and Post 9/11 Technostalgia', *Social Text* 23(2): 35–53.

Gilmore v. Gonzales (2006) 435 F.3d 1125. Washington DC: Ninth Circ.

Gregory, D. (2004) *The Colonial Present*, Oxford: Blackwell.

Gregory, D. and Pred, A. (eds) (2007) *Violent Geographies: Fear, Terror and Political Violence*, New York: Routledge.

Hacking, I. (1990) *The Taming of Chance*, Cambridge: Cambridge University Press.

Hall, S. (1990) 'Cultural identity and diaspora', in J. Rutherford (ed.) *Identity: Community, Culture, Difference,* London: Lawrence Wishart.

Hargreaves, E.L. and Gowing, M. (1952) *Civil Industry and Trade*, London: HMSO.

IDC (2004) 'Identity Management's Role in an Application Centric Security Model', White Paper, Framingham: IDC.

Jones, E. (1995) *True and Fair: A History of Price Waterhouse*, London: Hamish Hamilton.

Kang, J. and Cuff, D. (2005) 'Pervasive computing: embedding the public sphere', *Public Law Research Paper Series,* No.04–23, Los Angeles: University of California.

Kestelyn, J. (2002) 'For want of a nail', *Intelligent Enterprise* 5(7): 8.

Kittler, F. (1997) *Literature, Media, Information Systems: Essays*, Amsterdam: Arts Limited.

Lyon, D. (2003) *Surveillance after September 11*, Cambridge: Polity Press.

Lyon, D. (2004) 'Identity cards: social sorting by database', *Oxford Internet Institute Brief* No. 3, November. Online. Available: http://www.oii.ox.ac.uk/research/publications.cfm

Martin, R. (2003) *The Organizational Complex: Architecture, Media and Corporate Space*, Cambridge: MIT Press.

Massumi, B. (2005) 'The future birth of the affective fact', *Conference proceedings: Genealogies of Biopolitics*.

Rose, N. (1991) 'Governing by numbers: figuring out democracy', *Accounting, Organizations and Society* 16(7): 673–92.

Rotenberg, M. (2003) 'Testimony to the national commission on terrorist attacks on the United States', 4 December, Washington DC: 9/11 Commission.

Rotenberg, M. (2007) 'Privacy developments in the United States with respect to travellers using air transport', Evidence given before the European Parliament's Committee on Civil Liberties, Justice and Home Affairs, 26 March, Brussels: Europarl.

Salter, M. (2007) 'Governmentalities of an airport: heterotopia and confession', *International Political Sociology* 1(1): 49–56.

Shapiro, M. (1997) *Violent Cartographies: Mapping Cultures of War*, Minneapolis: University of Minnesota Press.

Smith, J., Fishkin, K., Bing, J., Mamishev, A., Hilipose, M., Rea, A., Roy, S. and Sundara-Rajan, K. (2005) 'RFID-based techniques for human-activity detection', *Communications of the ACM* 48(9): 39–44.

Sparke, M. (2006) 'A neoliberal nexus: economy, security and the biopolitics of citizenship on the border,' *Political Geography* 25(2): 151–80.

Thrift, N. (2004) 'Remembering the technological unconscious by foregrounding knowledges of position', *Environment and Planning D: Society and Space* 22: 175–90.

UK Home Office (2004) *Identity Cards Bill: Regulatory Impact Assessment*, London: HMSO.

US House of Representatives (2004) 'Radio Frequency Identification (RFID) Technology: What the Future Holds for Commerce, Security and the Consumer', July 14, Washington DC: House of Representatives.

US Joint Enquiry (2003) 'Report of the Joint Inquiry into the Terrorist Attacks of September 11, 2001', Washington DC: House Permanent Select Committee on Intelligence (HPSCI) and the Senate Select Committee on Intelligence (SSCI).

Van der Ploeg, I. (2003) 'Biometrics and the Body as Information', in D. Lyon (ed.) *Surveillance as Social Sorting: Privacy, Risk and Digital Discrimination*, London: Routledge.

Weber, S. (2005) *Targets of Opportunity: On the Militarization of Thinking*. New York: Fordham University Press.

Section Two

Plus ça change:
Colonial legacies

3   The elusive panopticon

The HANIS project and the politics of standards in South Africa

Keith Breckenridge

Imagine it.

A secure, single means of identification for 43 million citizens.

Done.

South Africa's Department of Home Affairs partnered with several contractors, including Unisys, to develop the Home Affairs National Identification System (HANIS) one of the world's largest civilian fingerprint databases.

(Online. Available: http://www.unisys.com)

More than a decade ago the South African Department of Home Affairs issued a tender for the building of an Automated Fingerprint Identification System (AFIS), a database system for the biometric data that would integrate with the existing Population Register, and the issuing of identity cards to the entire population. Some of the elements of the Home Affairs National Identification System (HANIS) have been implemented, but South Africans are still waiting for their new identity cards. In the meantime, the Home Affairs Department – the division of the state that provides citizens and foreigners in South Africa with all of the essential documents of identification – has spun slowly into administrative collapse. This chapter is an attempt to explore the reasons for the HANIS debacle; I also want to consider another question, which may be of interest to those who live far from South Africa: Can a centralized and interoperable system of biometric identification actually be implemented? Or, to use the words of our contemporary theory, is the biometric panopticon possible?

The significance of HANIS

The South African biometric project is often used as a precedent for the biometric identification systems that are now currently underway in many liberal and social democracies. When the CIA's John Woodward, the leading policy advocate of administrative biometrics, began to map out their possible uses in government in 1997, he used South Africa and the Philippines as examples of societies that had resolved to introduce a biometric national identification card. Similarly, when the

(Conservative) British government began to re-consider the introduction of a national identity card in 1996, journalists pointed to the South African grants system as the single case that combined both the new smart card applications and identification technologies. The stories in the British financial press, which described the extension of the cutting-edge of banking technology to some of the most underdeveloped regions of Africa, gave the South African story particular power. Here was an excellent example of the use of biometrics for purely civilian and humanitarian ends. After 9/11, as the western democracies scrambled for a bureaucratic remedy to the danger within, the South African HANIS project was widely cited as an example of nationwide civilian biometric smart card identification. Recently, the global IT conglomerate, NEC, has used its involvement in the South African project as evidence of its suitability for selection as the provider of biometric border control systems in Britain (NEC Corporation 2006). In the effort to build support for a biometric smart card to control access to government health and welfare benefits, the Australian government used the example of smart card usage in Finland, France, Germany, Italy, Taiwan and South Africa. As *Electronic Frontiers Australia* has noted, of the countries cited as precedents, only the South African HANIS project includes the three elements of photographic identification, biometric registration and smart card applications (*Electronic Frontiers Australia* 2006). As the United States' Department of Homeland Security has become preoccupied with building an integrated global biometric surveillance system, the complexity of the HANIS experiment needs, I think, to be more widely understood than is currently the case (Chertoff 2007).

South Africa is, of course, a special society. For decades, scholars have studied it as the capstone of the system of racial capitalism that developed in the Atlantic world after slavery. In the years since the democracy began in 1995, and following the demise of formal segregation in the Americas, some of this significance has dissipated. As I have suggested elsewhere, in an era of increasingly centralized and coercive surveillance, the South African state is important because it is the first example of a truly biometric order (Breckenridge 2005a). Much of what the advocates of biometric registration systems around the world have been calling for since the start of the War on Terror has already been implemented in South Africa.

Some features of this society deserve special mention. The bureaucracy in South Africa is very radically centralized, especially in relation to the processes of vital registration. All births, marriages and deaths are recorded by the Department of Home Affairs in Pretoria: the state delegates no registration functions to local or provincial government. The same pattern is true of driver's licences, passports and the primary tool of identification, the ID book, which are also issued and registered centrally. (There is also only one centrally controlled police force.) Interlaced with this intensely centralized bureaucracy, is a pervasive reliance on fingerprints for official identification. For much of the twentieth century, the South African state sought to use large scale fingerprint registers to control the movements and identity of African, Indian and Chinese people. This enthusiasm for administrative biometrics reached its apogee in the 1950s when Hendrik Verwoerd built a single, centralized fingerprint repository called the Bewysburo – or the Bureau of Proof – into the foundations of the Apartheid state (Breckenridge 2005b). In the decades that followed, some of the key functions of the central government were dismantled under the policy of Bantustan self-government, but since the early 1990s, the energy of centralization has been revitalized. Today all South Africans have a bio-metrically authenticated official record of identity, and millions of people make daily use of their fingerprints in their dealings with the government. This means that the South African biometric identification project, quite unlike the cards currently being considered in other countries, had a multifunctional character from the outset: the designers of the HANIS system intended it to function as a biometric panopticon.

On the face of it, then, the history of biometrics in South Africa is a special instance of Foucault's now very widely used theory of biopolitical government (Burchell *et al.* 1991). In fact, I think, the theoretical importance of HANIS may lie elsewhere. In the first instance, I would like to reaffirm the scholarly significance of specific regional and temporal details in the face of what is very often a circular and derivative interest in the power of Foucault's analysis of the discourse of the subject. In asserting the significance of this South African history, I want to resist the tendency to relate it to a handful of metropolitan theorists and scholars, a very common analytical move which tends to ignore the specific, and difficult, histories and historiographies of this region, and many others. Similarly, I want to show that the fractures and contradictions that obstruct the development of biometric surveillance are at least as important, politically, as the imperatives of convergence.

The origins of the HANIS system lie over a century ago when the founding figure of administrative fingerprinting, Sir Edward Henry, spent six short months on the Witwatersrand between his appointments as Inspector-General of the Bengal Police and Deputy-Commissioner at Scotland Yard (Sengoopta 2003). Following the suggestion that Francis Galton had made in his book *Fingerprints* in 1891, Henry's repositories were very rapidly put to use as tools of labour recruitment and control. This dependence on coercive systems of labour mobilization culminated in Verwoerd's grand project for a centralized biometric identification register, and the infamous Dompas pass system. In the decades that followed this system of control was applied to all South Africans.

The immediate causes of the HANIS system lie in the national security concerns of the South African state in the early 1980s, in particular the decision by PW Botha's government in January 1981 to issue a single, fingerprint authenticated, identity document to all South Africans, white as well as black. In the preceding year the African National Congress's special operations unit, under the command of the white communist, Joe Slovo, had staged flamboyant attacks on the fuel refineries in Secunda and Durban. These attacks coincided with Botha's energetic militarization of the South African state (Cock and Nathan 1989). Key members of the government, like Chris Heunis, the new minister of the Department of the Interior, had begun to set in place a constitutional order called the National Security Management System that re-drew the lines of political authority around a set of regional committees dominated by the South African military (O'Meara 1996: 255–269). The military and its Cabinet supporters argued that South Africa faced a Soviet-sponsored 'Total Onslaught'. Establishing a national fingerprint register of all white, Indian and coloured South Africans was one of the key elements of the 'Total Strategy' they had designed to preserve white power. On the day of the Minister's announcement, a spokesman for the South African Defence Force explained that the military believed that it was necessary to 'upgrade the sophistication of identity documents'. In 1981, as the *New York Times* observed at the time, the fledgling biometric access control technology was 'a solution to a problem that no one's aware of yet'. With the decision to set up universal fingerprint identification as an anti-terrorist strategy the South African government was creating the *raison d'être* of the newly christened biometric access control industry.

Many white people, especially those who had the original *Book of Life* issued in the 1970s, did not apply for the new, fingerprinted, identity document until the deadline approached in 1990, the same year that the African National Congress was unbanned. There is some irony in the fact that thousands of white South Africans queued to be fingerprinted for ID books designed as an anti-terrorist measure, and instrument of white racial supremacy, in the year after Nelson Mandela was released from prison. By this time, officials had begun to stress different reasons for holding the books, like the usefulness of fingerprints for 'orderly public administration', for business or for identifying dead bodies, but the desire for closure, for completing the national register, had now become both the end and the means of the state's policy (Brits 1990; Stirling 1988).

The HANIS project also has roots in the intensely-contested debate about the character of the post-Apartheid welfare system. The first meaningful discussions for a biometric identity card took place in 1994 during the inter-departmental planning for the implementation of the ANC's first economic and social policy, the 'Reconstruction and Development Program' (RDP). The RDP expressed the economic policy goals of academics and activists associated with the internal political organizations, unions and civics, and at its core it was an argument about the provision of basic services and welfare benefits to millions of very poor South Africans (Marais 2001: 122–159; The Reconstruction and Development Programme 1994; Bond 1996). The Home Affairs representatives on this committee, Piet Fourie and Peter Payne-Findlay, were saddled with the responsibility of ensuring that the benefits were fairly distributed amongst the potential beneficiaries, and that only South Africans would qualify. The grants, land, housing and basic service reforms envisioned for the RDP would involve a much larger group of recipients than the 20 million people then being recorded in the Population Register (although they probably did not have in mind a doubling of the size of the database). With the huge amount of work involved in the processing of fingerprints in mind, they proposed that Home Affairs should implement an Automated Fingerprint Identification System and an identity card. Payne-Findlay persuaded the Director-General to support this idea and he was given the task of drafting the proposals for the AFIS. Over time, this task expanded into requests for proposals from the largest international computer companies for the three different parts of the HANIS system: the AFIS, the cards and the building of the Home Affairs computer systems. Payne-Findlay drafted the R800 million tender that was announced by the Minister in December 1996 (Informant 8 2007).

The announcement of the HANIS project catapulted Home Affairs back into the limelight of the international government computing industry. After decades of being international pariahs, the Home Affairs officials and their new ANC political leaders, were being feted by the largest multinationals. The list of IT companies tendering on the South African project was a Who's Who of international government computer contractors: TRW, Sagem Morpho, Unisys, ICL, Olivetti, Printrak, Labat-Anderson, Lockheed-Martin, Marubeni. Each of these firms set up complex joint ventures that brought in local companies closely associated with the old state – Denel, Plessey, Persetel-Qdata and a string of Empowerment partners, the South African term for companies controlled by black shareholders – Don Ncube's Real Africa Holdings, Bhekisizwe Computer Systems, Robert Gumede's Gijima Holdings. Here was a potent political cocktail indeed (Lunsche 1997, 1998; Stones 1997; Delaney 1998a,b).

Each of the companies bidding for the HANIS contract approached the task of convincing the tender board in a different way, but the overall effect was to suggest that in adopting biometric identification, South Africa was joining the cutting edge of international bureaucratic practice; the tender process nicely demonstrates the ways in which states and private contractors work in an intrinsically international field of practice. A special representative from the British Home Office where, in Buthelezi's words, 'much progress with the implementation of an automated fingerprint system has been made', assisted in the evaluation of the proposals (Buthelezi 1997). Lockheed-Martin traded heavily on its experience as the AFIS contractor for the FBI's similarly sized repository of 40 million fingerprints. Sagem Morpho, the massive French defence corporation that dominates the global market in digital fingerprint readers, emphasized its role in the large scale biometric ID projects then under development in Honduras, Philippines and, most importantly, Malaysia. When Unisys wanted to demonstrate the usefulness of their systems they had a clear advantage in that they could present systems actually in place in South Africa. The evaluation committee was invited to tour the California prisons system to view the Unisys tools at work and, drawing on the longer history of Datakor, its sanctions-era subsidiary inside the country, they visited the Lindela Repatriation Centre and another local juvenile detention facility to observe biometric identification at first hand.

The first real shock came a year later with the elimination of the major international biometrics companies in the second round of the evaluation process. The two consortiums left in the race were both dominated by older South African firms: QData/Persetel were opposed by the Marpless Consortium (consisting of Unisys, Plessey, Marubeni and Gijima). The consortiums dominated by Lockheed-Martin and Sagem complained vociferously to the press, the State Tender Board, the Auditor-General and the Parliamentary Portfolio Committee that their exclusion imperiled the entire project. ICL's local representative hinted at underhand dealings when he protested that Sagem's AFIS had never 'been disqualified prior to benchmarking in the context of international open tenders'. Even the French Ambassador lobbied the Minister to review his decision not to grant the tender to Sagem (Delaney 1998a; Buthelezi 1998).

Under this pressure, the Parliamentary Portfolio Committee duly subjected Payne-Findlay to a grilling. He was publicly accused of tampering with the HANIS tender, and stripped of any decision-making authority over the project. Sagem commended the Parliamentary Committee, thanking them for 'doing a good job in investigating our complaints'. These complaints precipitated the first significant delay in the evolution of the HANIS project. At the Committee's suggestion, both the Auditor-General and the Public-Protector initiated investigations into the tendering process. Six months later, in December 1998, the Protector's report found no significant problems. A contract was signed with the Marpless Consortium in February 1999 (Delaney 1998; Buthelezi 2002).

Behind the scenes the actual content of the contract began to change almost immediately; most importantly the physical and technological features of the card were dramatically altered. One key change was the decision to use NEC fingerprint verification equipment in the final version of the Marpless proposal. Another was the later decision, subsequent to the awarding of the tender but before a contract was signed, to abandon the bar-code equipped cards provided by Polaroid. This decision to move to smart cards was critical, for it opened up a wide field of theoretical possibilities for HANIS, turning it from a dual-purpose identification and electronic purse project into a multi-purpose vehicle for the state's many information processing requirements. In practice it also meant that the HANIS project was awarded without a card issuing contract.

The decision to abandon the bar-coded cards came before the granting of the tender in March 1999. It was later justified in the computer press as an obvious choice of new technologies over old, but the reasons for the shift to the smart card were more convoluted. Security is the most common reason for adopting smart cards in identification systems. It is the security of cards equipped with integrated circuits (because they can store and process the very large numbers necessary for public key encryption) that is conventionally offered as the explanation for the claim that biometric smart cards mark a qualitative change in the history of state identification systems. But in the late 1990s smart cards, because of their very limited memory and processing power, were not dramatically more secure than magnetic stripe cards.

The move to a smart card based identity card followed intense lobbying at the highest level of the state, leading to a meeting of the Directors-General to discuss the issue in April 1998. At this meeting, Andile Ngcaba, the Director-General of the Department of Communications and the ANC's key IT expert in the first decade of their rule, seems to have played the key role (Van den Heever 2001). The example of two contemporary Asian biometric identification schemes loomed large. 'South Africa has looked overseas for implementation models', *SA Computer Magazine* reported, 'to countries such as Malaysia, which recently rolled out one million smart cards to its population, and to Hong Kong, which announced its interest in swapping the two-dimensional bar code for the smart card' (Wright 2002).

A single view of the customer

Very soon after the decision to adopt the smart card, the Department of Home Affairs began to chart out the possibility of using the identity cards to host all of the key functions of government information processing. No longer a single-purpose tool of identification, the card had now become the lynch-pin of a host of bureaucratic and commercial functions. 'The smart card that we are introducing is not confined to the limited identification/verification realms of the Home Affairs strategic engagement only', Minister Buthelezi announced to the media in February 2000. 'Rather, it is a magnanimous, multi-applications, government smart identity card with extensive capabilities contained in a chip that boasts enough intelligence to allow other departments and perhaps even other forms of industry permissions to utilize the card technology' (Buthelezi 2000). With a prospective budget for the smart cards now being proposed at the nice round number of R1 billion – some 25% more than the entire project was originally estimated to cost – the Department began to gather the different commercial and bureaucratic interests that might want to use them. An inter-departmental committee, involving over a dozen different departments and staffed by the most powerful officials in the national bureaucracy, began to consider the possibilities for the new smart card. In the early stages of the process there was widespread enthusiasm from these different departments for the HANIS smart card. Gareth Warner, who had taken over from Payne-Findlay as the outside consultant of the HANIS project, remembered that, at this time, 'everyone had the same issues' (Warner 2007a).

With encouragement from an enthusiastic and very powerful inter-departmental committee, Home Affairs began to look around at the most common transactions in the other departments; very early on it became clear that the success of the card would lie in two areas: banking and welfare. Early in 2000 three separate teams were appointed: the first looked at existing smart card systems inside the country like the millions of GSM cards in the exploding cellular phone market and the proprietary system used by Aplitec to deliver pensions and other grants; the second was charged with the investigation of a set of technical specifications for the cards; and the third considered the possibilities and mechanisms for making the cards interact with the existing card infrastructure (Whitby 2000). Right at the outset the success of the cards was tied to tight integration with the requirements of the social grant system and the emerging Europay–Mastercard–Visa standard that promised access to the robust and extensive banking network. Buthelezi stressed both goals in his parliamentary briefing, just weeks after the Marpless contract was signed, when he explained that the interdepartmental committee had 'decided to honour our senior citizens with the privilege of being the first beneficiaries of this world class project', which would give them the 'ability to draw, should they elect to do so, their grants from bank ATMs using their smart cards' (Buthelezi 2000a).

By the middle of 2000, under the general influence of the fast waning dotcom frenzy and the particular encouragement of Andile Ngcaba, the smart card had grown into an instrument of digital social transformation. During the month of August, Home Affairs called for proposals from businesses for applications on the smart card. The response, in the Minister's words, 'was overwhelming with more

' companies and interested parties submitting responses'. In the wake of ﹍ proposals the department began to argue that 'e-governance and e-commerce will be closely coupled to the envisaged identity card'. In these months, the role envisaged for the cards expanded from 'key enabler' to a dozen government departments into a general purpose instrument of electronic commerce. Adopting and extending the role of the current population register, which is accessed by the banks and insurance companies for official confirmation of death, the biometric HANIS cards would provide businesses with a foolproof mechanism of identity. 'The card', Buthelezi promised, 'will eventually be used by a number of private organisations such as banks, insurance companies, medical aid schemes and many more, to combat fraud' (Buthelezi 2000c). Some 18 months later, at the commissioning of the Marpless system, the Minister's sense of the pool of commercial users had expanded to include 'any branch of government and any private entity which adopts the system required to read it electronically'. The biometric smart cards, in this scheme, would deliver automated access control across the borders of the country and 'building access control or by vending machines which intend to restrict their products, such as cigarettes, to adults only' (Buthelezi 2002).

As the range of possible users for the smart card expanded so did the Department's sense of the cards' function as the lynch-pin of all state activities. Holding out the triple promise of automated record keeping, public key encryption and biometric authentication, the smart cards seemed to realize the project of the original Book of Life, providing a secure, single record of the citizen's entire engagement with the bureaucracy. With proposals from over a dozen departments, the Interdepartmental Technical Committee began to plan for the smart card itself to coordinate and record the dozens of different transactions between the departments and citizens (and non-citizens). After more than a year of discussions about the possible uses of the card the Committee sent the first of many proposals to the Cabinet. 'The vision', Patrick Monyeki explained, 'is that the smart card should provide the single interface between citizen and government'. Indulging the fantasies of corporate customer relations systems developers for a single summary record of the huge pool of electronic transactions swamping businesses, he implied that the cards would provide the state with a focused lens into the life of any individual. 'Envious corporates will note that this will, in theory at least', *Computer Week* told its readers, 'give government the elusive "single view of the customer"' (Van den Heever 2001).

The elusive panopticon

Monyeki's claim that the proposal for the card tender had been sent to Cabinet was the first of half-a-dozen similar claims that would be made over the next five years. In fact there was no technical mechanism to actually implement the grand project that the Interdepartmental Committee then had in mind. In November 2001, six months later, Home Affairs gathered together the most important actors in the emerging field of biometric smart card authentication to consider the difficult problem of the competing and incompatible technical standards offered by the different biometrics companies. The problem was the same one that has bedevilled finger-print classification and storage in general, and the construction of centralised reg-istries in particular, since the turn of the twentieth century: no uncontested standard existed for smart card fingerprint identification, either in South Africa or interna-tionally. 'Each respective manufacturer is offering his own preferred system as the ultimate solution', Gareth Warner warned, 'while the respective international com-mittees push forward on the development of biometric standards which are still a long way off in terms of the development of comprehensive specifications' (Peachey-Warner 2003).

The situation presented a special problem in South Africa precisely because fin-gerprinting was so common. Drawing on the half-century of fingerprinting in the Central Reference Bureau, many other Departments had adopted fingerprinting as their preferred means of identification, and they had begun to purchase electronic solutions to automate the work of authentication and storage. At least five separate nationwide systems had been adopted by different government Departments in 2000: police, social welfare, drivers' licensing, and the courts and prisons had all already purchased massive biometric systems, each with millions of records, inde-pendently of Home Affairs. Some departments, like Social Welfare, had contracted different companies to undertake the work in each province. 'Currently five provinces use smart card technology coupled with fingerprint biometric technol-ogy to pay out state grants', Warner wrote at the time 'and there is no development of common standards across these provinces both in terms of smart cards and fingerprint biometrics' (Warner 2001: 13).

In some cases, this absence of standards created exactly the same problem as the early 20th century conflicts over modifications of the Henry system, but the new format also created new, even more intractable, difficulties. In the large scale AFIS systems, designers would create subsets of records that were obviously similar in order to avoid the necessity of undertaking matches across millions of records, using the arches, loops and whorls of Francis Galton's original classification (Warner 2001). Differences over the rules for the implementation of these clusters of records could build exactly the same classification incompatibilities into electronic systems as existed in locally customized manual registries.

A more serious problem has its roots in the huge difference between the elec-tronic storage required to retain the original fingerprint and its mathematical tem-plate. The advocates of smart cards often play up their computational powers in deeply exaggerated terms; in fact the cards have very limited capacity. These phys-ical limits on the storage available on the cards are aggravated by the budget con-straints of large scale identification projects: the cards used in national identity cards tend to be the cheapest and smallest. When the HANIS project adopted the smart card format they were planning on 8 kilobytes (Kb), or at the most 16 Kb of memory. The significance of these physical memory limits becomes obvious in the context of the storage requirements of a normal fingerprint image. The compressed image of an individual fingerprint requires some 20 Kb of electronic memory, which means that even the largest and most expensive smart cards can accommo-date only one or two complete fingerprint images. Even the oldest cards have enough space to store copies of the mathematical representation of a fingerprint, called a minutiae template like Galton's original fingerprint classifications, these templates express the geometrical relationships between a limited number of details (or minutiae) from the dense patterns of individual fingerprint lines – the location and the direction of ridge endings, splits, loops (Information Technology Laboratory, NIST 2000). These are recorded numerically and combined in a carefully ordered sequence in to a single large number, which despite its complexity, takes up less than 250 bytes of memory – the mathematical template uses just 1 per cent of the memory used to store the image.

The immediate result is that all of the dominant manufacturers of biometric identification systems store only the templates on their cards. Each of these companies uses its own proprietary system of minutiae for encoding and interpreting the template on the card (Peachey-Warner 2003). This is potentially very problematic because, until recently, the different commercial systems could not interpret each other's templates, nor can the original print be reconstructed from the mathematical template. But it is catastrophic where, as is definitely the case with some of the social welfare grants systems developed by Aplitec, the original image is not retained at the database end. These problems of classification are not specific to South Africa; the same problems have also affected the US military in Iraq, another site of ubiquitous fingerprint registration (Gerth 2004).

Digital technology also introduces another problem that had not much troubled manual fingerprinting. 'Manufacturers of fingerprint scanners currently cannot deliver convincing evidence that they can make a distinction between a real, living finger and a dummy constructed of silicone rubber or any other material', Warner reported. For those companies planning to use and sell unattended biometric readers, a reliable mechanism to test for what he called 'liveness', was evidently a matter of some urgency.

The Biometric Standards workshop that Billy Masetlha hosted in November 2001 was called to address this 'grave challenge to government'. Home Affairs brought the main state contractors in South Africa – NEC, Sagem, Siemens and Oberthur card systems – together to plan the development of a local standard for the exchange of fingerprint templates between smart cards. Aside from the now glaring problems of incompatible proprietary systems, the Department returned to the idea that a properly designed smart card system could revolutionize both state and commercial transactions. The development of the local standard would make possible 'electronic interchange of biometric identifiers between government jurisdictions and commercial service providers requiring positive and secure methods of person identification of individuals'. The workshop came to rapid agreement on the specification of the image size and quality, but then quickly became mired in the conflicting systems of minutiae that each company used to generate the key produced from that image. The last resolution of the workshop set up a special committee under the control of the South African Bureau of Standards and the Council for Scientific and Industrial Research to work on a 'national biometric standard' compatible with the emerging international standard. 'Gone are the days when you can run to a province and sell each one a different product that does not conform to a national standard', Patrick Monyeki warned the contractors (Dudley and Otter 2001).

Over the course of the next 18 months, two major agreements seemed to put in place the standards that were required to make HANIS work as the lynch-pin of a revolutionized networked society. Under Warner's influence, the different manufacturers, and their government clients, agreed to a standard fingerprint image format and they drafted a local standard for the sequencing of biometric data on the cards, called ARP 054, closely modeled on the standard then being developed in the USA by the National Institute of Standards and Technology. Home Affairs announced that this new local standard would be 'modified in the near future' to 'include an ameliorated definition of minutiae points and location' (South African Department of Home Affairs 2003).

Five years later a practical standard for biometric devices was still not available. Each of the major companies involved in the field of fingerprinting in South Africa retained its own system of minutiae for producing the numerical template. 'We could never come down to a biometric standard', Gareth Warner noted in 2007, 'each of the companies still uses a proprietary system' (Warner 2007b). Under pressure from the new US Homeland Security laws, international standards making bodies worked energetically in the years after 2003 to create templates that would allow the different commercial systems to exchange information reliably, but these new methods are still not 'defined well enough to allow for practical interoperability' (Warner 2007b). The HANIS project's dilemma derived from the fact that it could not, given the pervasiveness of biometrics in South Africa, adopt a single-supplier, fully proprietary system, like those being developed by Sagem around the world, and it preceded, probably by decades, the emergence of a practical interoperable standard for biometric devices.

The companies involved in the provision of biometric identity cards, particularly Sagem Morpho who claims to have captured '1.5 billion fingerprints worldwide', have very good reasons to resist the development of an effective open standard (Hi-Tech Security Solutions 2004). The most obvious of these is that they earn a licence fee for the proprietary template for every card issued over the lifetime of the identification system; revenue that will very likely last for a generation. In addition to those fees, the nationwide adoption of a single, proprietary minutiae template would mean, as Monyeki and Warner warned in 2001, that the state is forced to pay for hardware from the supplier who owns the license for the lifetime of the cards. In South Africa, and internationally, Sagem occupies a formidable position in the economy of identification, and it is vigorously supported by the diplomatic resources of the French government. The company's contract for the AFIS system used by Interpol gave them an inside track on the tender for the South African Police Services Criminal Records Centre. Sagem also sell the mobile Morphotouch machines that are widely used by the police and the private social welfare grant delivery companies to search for fingerprint matches. When the HANIS contractors built a smart card production facility, they duly chose Sagem equipment and templates. But this system was never used to produce cards, because of Home Affairs' desire to coordinate the HANIS system with the other existing biometric systems using an open standard.

Under pressure from the US government, the most powerful international standards-making bodies worked busily after 2001 to compose an interoperable standard, but the results of these efforts were complex, and they came, in any case, much too late for HANIS (International Committee for Information Technology Standards 2003). The political and financial energy behind this movement towards an open standard for fingerprint minutiae was unmistakable: all of the documents cite US Department of Defense, Patriot Act or Presidential Homeland Security directives citing the same concerns for interoperability that had troubled the South Africans in 2001. Two issues loomed large in these workshops: the first was avoiding vendor lock-in, or technological dependence on a proprietary standard, and the second was the digital panopticon or interoperability, the goal to make all biometric devices interact with each other. Under this pressure the major biometrics contractors had agreed by March 2004 on a basic open standard for biometric minutiae, INCITS 378.

The tests that the US government commissioned of the open standard in 2005 have some startling implications for the project of an interoperable biometric identification system (National Institute of Standards and Technology 2006). These investigations were undertaken on millions of fingerprints taken from the largest digitized collections in the USA, which means that they do not address the first difficulty of fingerprints that resist templating altogether. The massive tests showed that the use of the INCITS standard in place of the three most accurate, proprietary systems (produced by the dominant companies NEC, Cogent and Sagem) doubled the rate of incorrect rejection (False Non-Matching), and produced a ten-fold increase in the much less likely errors of mistaken identification (False Matching). If, in other words, the open standard was used on the most accurate matching systems to test the identity of 1,000 people it would falsely reject twice as many people as the proprietary system (20 instead of 10). It would, also, incorrectly identify one or two people out of every 1,000 where the proprietary systems would be unlikely to do that in a population of 10,000.

The obvious remedy for the increased rate of error produced by the open standard was to move away from a single biometric measurement to multiple indicators. This, in turn, raises a host of new incompatibilities for already existing biometric systems. Some of these have only recorded a single biometric, while others, like the Aplitec biometric smart cards, have selected the best fingerprint impressions on a case by case basis. The use of an open template on multiple fingerprints would first require agreement on the fingers being captured, with very onerous administrative implications for the already existing systems that do not meet this requirement.

The obvious question is this: did the HANIS project fail solely because it preceded the development of a viable system of biometric surveillance? Will subsequent schemes work more effectively? Certainly, the current drive to biometric convergence is intensive, with the political and economic pressure of powerful divisions of the US government leading the most important technology corporations towards an open standard, and it is extensive, with institutions in Europe and the USA working in an independent but coordinated project. But the movement to an interoperable standard, and with it the project of the biometric panopticon, is also strongly contradicted by the technological and administrative consequences of an open system. For the largest companies (especially Sagem Morpho) the goal of locking national identification systems into a proprietary system remains a very attractive and viable project. The most likely outcome, in the context of very vigorous lobbying, is that the proprietary systems will prosper, interacting with the open standard in a fashion that remains subject to significant rates of error.

Banking on standards

The difficulties that the HANIS developers faced in securing an interoperable standard for fingerprints were mirrored in another key aspect of the biometric panopticon: the development of a smart card standard for the banking system. From early in 2000, Home Affairs worked with representatives from the banking industry to map out the electronic payment systems that would be required for the HANIS smart card to meet the requirements of the Europay–Mastercard–Visa standard for the banking infrastructure. In June of that year, all of the major South African banks agreed to implement the EMV standard for payment systems, which was, at that stage, nearly a decade old. In these discussions the banks appeared to be working to a deadline of January 2005 for the introduction of a nationwide system of ATMs and point of sale machines capable of reading the smart cards (South African Department of Home Affairs 2003).

The commercial banks proved much slower than anyone had predicted in adopting the EMV smart card standard. By the middle of 2007, more than two years after the agreed deadline, most of the banks were still using the magnetic stripe technology, and they had scarcely begun the massively expensive project of replacing existing teller and point of sale machines. While the banks proposal, in 2003, for their own smart card based 'Account for Life' (Duminy 2003) seemed to run across the bows of the HANIS project, the real difficulty was that the functionality proposed for the HANIS card presumed a much higher degree of synchronization between the banks, and a much more urgent timetable, than was actually the case (Engelbrecht 2006). 'The banks were brought into the picture', one of the project managers observed, 'but there was never a time that we actually reached a compromise as to what the card should actually contain' (Informant 8 2007).

Added to the difficulty of herding the banking cats was the even more sensitive problem of adopting fingerprinting in private banking. South African banks have been flirting with the use of fingerprint authentication for as long as the HANIS project has been under development (Engelbrecht 2006; *The Guardian* 1999; *Electronic Payments International* 1996). The same problems of proprietary technical standards threaten the banks but the real issue is that the banks are very nervous about public outrage over the adoption of fingerprint authentication. Without a statutory requirement that customers provide biometric authentication the banks were not likely to impose fingerprint checking on their customers, which meant that there was no immediate benefit for commercial fraud detection. By the beginning of 2007 the EMV standards-based electronic purse had been effectively abandoned as part of the HANIS project. When the Minister was asked if the Banks or the

Department had 'washed their hands of the smart card project', she pointedly responded that the 'Department had not' (Justice, Crime Prevention and Security (JCPS) Cluster briefing 2007).

Where the four major banks in South Africa have been very slow to adopt smart cards for individual financial transactions, the opposite has been true in the privatized field of social welfare payments. In these transactions, biometric authentication was ubiquitous as early as 1996, and by 2003 the field was dominated by a single company bearing its own patented smart card interchange standard and providing a massive network of point of sale devices across the continent. Aplitec, or Net1 UEPS to use its new Nasdaq trading name, is the brainchild of Serge Belamont, a Frenchman who developed the South African interbank ATM network in the late 1970s. His project is to build an anti-bank, a smart card-based financial system that makes almost no use of the existing banking network infrastructure, in order to deliver financial resources and products to the global poor. At the heart of this campaign, a deadly serious attempt to build a non-EMV financial empire, is the UEPS anti-standard for intercard data exchange. Aplitec shares this facility with no one, not even their bureaucratic paymasters, as the cards themselves are the bearers of all the financial data required to track funds to individuals, merchants and the company (Net 1 UEPS Technologies, Inc 2006).

Since 1999, the company has grown spectacularly rapidly, attracting investments from the major banks and, more recently, a listing on the NASDAQ stock exchange. In the single year, 2004–2005, the stock price of Net1 rose 15-fold, reaching nearly US$1.5 billion (Sergeant 2005). In 2000, Belamont was asked about the threat to his business from the HANIS smart card. 'Government will separate the payment application from the ID card', he replied, 'and leave the payment card to the financial industry' (Lloyd 2000). He has proven surprisingly prescient. Aplitec has a history of sailing very close to the wind of government, but those who have been involved in the HANIS project see nothing underhand in the company's dominance. 'Welfare eventually gave up on us as they said we would never issue a card and that they had to pay out pensions', one of the managers explained, 'how right they were' (Informant 8 2007). By 2007, Aplitec Net1 had some 4 million bearers of its biometrically authenticated smart cards for the delivery of welfare grants, and more than 4,000 point of sale machines capable of transacting only with those cards. The company has effectively constructed its own proprietary banking infrastructure and welfare payment system, fulfilling the two trophy projects of the HANIS smart card without any of its interoperability.

Conclusion

This study of the HANIS project suggests that a biometric panopticon that will allow states to monitor the movements and behavior of their citizens across the different fields of social life – migration, social welfare, banking, policing – is not currently possible. Indeed it suggests that biometric systems that are strictly targeted at a single set of transactions – healthcare or migration – are much more likely to work in the short term than the interoperable systems that national security policy advocates have in mind (see Etzioni 2000: 103–37). It also seems likely that national identification systems that are wholly owned by one of the largest firms, like Sagem, Cogent or NEC, are likely to be much easier to implement and more efficient than an open system. Yet there are also unmistakable signs that the implications of this kind of monopoly for control of the means of identification are unacceptable to policy makers in all of the wealthiest states (see Torpey, the introduction to this volume).

It is also clear that the individual national debates about the costs and benefits of biometric identification cards form part of an integrated transnational field. On this political terrain, the most powerful actors are the multinational firms and multilateral standards making bodies. This South African example demonstrates the difficulties of an isolated national effort to shape this debate. The politics of biometrics is driven by arguments about globally acceptable practice and precedent. In this debate the move to a set of open standards is ongoing, but the global firms have lobbying, diplomatic and financial resources that are not available to the advocates of open systems. If, as seems possible, the OECD countries now withdraw from the project of introducing biometric identity cards, that will leave the global identification economy in the hands of its current incumbents, in particular Sagem Morpho.

This study of HANIS shows that the errors of classification that have plagued large scale fingerprinting systems since the end of the nineteenth century do not disappear in the digital world. The advocates of biometric technologies stress the efficiencies and high levels of accuracy of computerized systems. But it is important, especially in the context of large scale and interoperable systems, to emphasize that biometric systems are in fact prone to error. These errors may be failures to enroll, or they may be matching errors. The errors will certainly increase if multiple systems and larger populations are subjected to a single biometric test. What is critical is that the citizens affected by these errors must be provided with a means for challenging these mistakes without the indignity of losing well established rights of due process.

In the attempt to answer the question: Is a biometric panopticon possible? – I have been drawn to Bowker and Starr's characterization of the development of 'technical standards as a site of political decisions and struggle' (Bowker and Starr 1999: 49). In this conflict, the interests of modern capitalist firms and state bureaucracies pull in both directions, but so does history. Actually existing biometric systems have inherited the interests and associations of at least six politically very different axes in the twentieth century: imperial labour controls, prisons and policing, national security, social welfare, banking and computing. These systems are not naturally compatible, and in some respects they conflict directly. In the HANIS case the conflict between a tool designed for national security and the demands of the banking and social welfare systems have proven, to date, irreconcilable. It is these conflicts that have played themselves out in intractable difficulties over technical standards. Over time, the conflicts may diminish, producing the kinds of open standards that will allow for interoperable digital surveillance, but that day is still a long way off.

Bibliography

Bond, P. (1996) 'Neoliberalism comes to South Africa', *The Multinational Monitor*, May.

Bowker, G. and Starr, S. (1999) *Sorting Things Out: Classification and its consequences*, Cambridge: MIT Press.

Breckenridge, K. (2005a) 'The biometric state: the promise and peril of digital government in the New South Africa', *Journal of Southern African Studies* 31(2): 267–82.

Breckenridge, K. (2005b) 'Verwoerd's bureau of proof: total information in the making of apartheid', *History Workshop Journal* 59(1): 83.

Brits, E. (1990) 'Kwessie van ras en vingerafdrukke pla nog', *Die Burger* 15 June.

Burchell, G., Gordon, C. and Foucault, M. (1991) *The Foucault Effect: Studies in Governmentality*, Chicago: University of Chicago Press.

Buthelezi, M. (1997) *Min Buthelezi: Parliamentary Briefing – Sept '97*, 10 September. Online. Available: http://www.info.gov.za/speeches/1997/0916HOME97.htm (accessed 11 April 2007).

Buthelezi, M. (1998) *Budget Debate*, 14 May. Online. Available: http://www.info.gov.za/speeches/1998/98908_2459810879.htm (accessed 31 May 2007).

Buthelezi, M. (2000a) *Home Affairs National Identification System: Project Launch*, 31 January. Online. Available: http://www.info.gov.za/speeches/2000/000301503p1001.htm (accessed 31 May 2007).

Buthelezi, M. (2000b) *Parliamentary Media Briefing*, 10 February. Online. Available: http://www.info.gov.za/speeches/2000/0002111208p1001.htm (accessed 31 May 2007).

Buthelezi, M. (2000c) *Parliamentary Media Briefing*, 21 September. Online. Available: http://www.info.gov.za/speeches/2000/0009221010a1003.htm (accessed 31 May 2007).

Buthelezi, M. (2002) *HANIS Basic System Commissioning*, 18 February. Online. Available: http://www.info.gov.za/speeches/2002/0202191046a1001.htm (accessed 11 April 2007).

Chertoff, M. (2007) 'Remarks by Secretary Michael Chertoff to the Johns Hopkins University Paul H. Nitze School of Advanced International Studies', *Department of Homeland Security*, 3 May. Online. Available: http://www.dhs.gov/xnews/speeches/sp_1178288606838.shtm (accessed 8 May 2007).

Cock, J. and Nathan, L. (1989) *War and Society: The Militarisation of South Africa*, Cape Town: David Philip.

Delaney, Jeff (1998a) 'Failed HANIS bidders in the dark', *Computing SA*. Online. Available: www.computingsa.co.za (accessed 11 April 2007).

Delaney, Jeff (1998b) 'Hanis decision expected "shortly"'. Online. Available: http://www.ictworld.co.za/EditorialEdit.asp?Archive=1&EditorialID=2844 (accessed 21 April 2007).

Dudley, G. and Otter, A. (2001) 'Standards critical to State biometric projects', *ITWeb*, 21 November. Online. Available: http://www.itweb.co.za (accessed 11 April 2007).

Duminy, B. (2003). *Account for life – a feasibility assessment prepared for Finmark Trust*, May. Online. Available: http://www.finmarktrust.org.za/documents/2003/MAY/AFL_Report.pdf (accessed 11 April 2007).

Electronic Frontiers Australia (2006) *Australian Govt. Access Card – Comparison with Other Countries*, 26 May. Online. Available: http://www.efa.org.au/ Issues/Privacy/ac-intcomparison.html (accessed 24 April 2007).

Electronic Payments International (1996) *South Africa: Biometrics set to revolutionise banking*, 25 September.

Engelbrecht, L. (2006) 'Banking on biometrics', *ITWeb*, 17 November. Online. Available:

http://www.itweb.co.za/sections/quickprint/print.asp?StoryID=168621 (accessed 11 April 2007).

Etzioni, A. (2000) *The Limits of Privacy,* New York: Basic Books.

Gerth, J. (2004) 'Fingerprinting glitches are said to hurt antiterror effort', *New York Times,* 27 October.

The Guardian (1999) 'The eyes have it', 20 May.

Hi-Tech Security Solutions (2004) *Ideco Technologies – perfection in biometric technology,* October. Online. Available: http://securitysa.com/regular.aspx? pklRegularId=1860 (accessed 15 August 2007).

Informant 8 (2007) HANIS Project Employee.

Information Technology Laboratory, NIST (2000) *Fingerprint Comparison Flash File,* February. Online. Available: http://www.itl.nist.gov/iad/894.03/fing/ fngcmps.html (accessed 13 August 2007).

International Committee for Information Technology Standards (2003) *Smart Card Biometric Interoperability Study Report*. INCITS Secretariat, Information Technology Industry Council, Washington DC: International Committee for Information Technology Standards. Online. Available: http://www.ncits.org/tc_home/m1htm/docs/m1030398.pdf (accessed 14 August 2007).

Justice, Crime Prevention and Security (JCPS) Cluster briefing. (2007) 16 February. Online. Available: http://www.pmg.org.za/briefings/briefings.php? id=319 (accessed 30 May 2007).

Lloyd, T. (2000) 'Strange bedfellows, but they make a smart pair', *Financial Mail* 14 July.

National Institute of Standards and Technology (2006) Minutiae Interoperability Exchange Test 2004. Online. Available: http://fingerprint.nist.gov/minex04/ (accessed 7 August 2007).

NEC Corporation (2006) 'NEC UK shows how global biometric solutions could enhance UK Border Control', 18 October. Online. Available: http://www.prnewswire.co.uk/cgi/ news/release?id=181837 (accessed 27 May 2007).

Lunsche, S. (1997) 'Arm wrestling to take the nation's fingerprints', *Sunday Times* 1 June.

Lunsche, S. (1998) 'IT companies scramble for lucrative ID tender', *Sunday Times* 15 February.

Marais, H. (2001) *South Africa – Limits to Change: the Political Economy of Transition,* London: Zed Books.

Net 1 UEPS Technologies, Inc (2006) Net1 UEPS Technologies, Inc Annual Report, 30 June.

O'Meara, D. (1996) *Forty lost years: the apartheid state and the politics of the National Party, 1948–1994.* Johannesburg: Ravan Press.

Peachey-Warner, G. (2003) 'Biometric standardisation: HANIS smart ID card project and ARP 054 standard', *Elekron Journal – South African Institute of Electrical Engineers* 20(4): 55–6.

The Reconstruction and Development Programme (1994) Online. Available: http://www.anc.org.za/rdp/rdpall.html (accessed 25 May 2007).

Sengoopta, C. (2003) *Imprint of the Raj: How Fingerprinting was Born in Colonial India,* London: Macmillan.

Sergeant, B. (2005) 'Moneyweb – Historical news: Daily news – South Africa's $1.5-bn champion', *Moneyweb,* 5 August. Online. Available: http://www.moneyweb.co.za/mw/ view/mw/en/page62053?oid=39903&sn=Daily%20news%20Detail (accessed 12 April 2007).

South African Department of Home Affairs (2003) 10 March. Online. Available: http://www.home-affairs.gov.za/projects.asp (accessed 3 June 2007).

Stirling, Tony (1988) 'Black sash claims on black IDs repudiated', *The Citizen* 8 January.

Stones, Lesley (1997) 'Race on to supply state ID system', *Business Day* 9 October.

Unisys & South Africa's Department of Home Affairs (2004) Combating fraud with instant identification verification. Online. Available: http://www.unisys.com/services/clients/ featured_case_studies/sa_department_home_affairs.htm (accessed 4 January 2004).

van den Heever, J. (2001) 'IT in Government: slow and steady wins the race', *Computer Week*, 30 July. Online. Available: http://homeaffairs.pwv.gov.za/ news.asp?id=2 (accessed 11 April 2007).

Warner, G. (2001) *Establishment of a national fingerprint biometric standard for government*. Online. Available: http://home-affairs.pwv.gov.za/documents/presentations/ position%20paper.zip (accessed 11 April 2007).

Warner, G. (2007a) *Interview*.

Warner, G. (2007b). *Interview 2*.

Whitby, P. (2000) 'Research on new citizen card begins', *Business Day* 7 April.

Wright, B. (2002) 'eGovernment', *SA Computer Magazine* 18 February. Online. Available: http://www.sacm.co.za/Feature.asp?NewsID=4203&Item=4835&Title =e%2DGovernment (accessed 11 April 2007).

4 China's second-generation national identity card

Merging culture, industry and technology

Cheryl L. Brown

Nearly two decades after the official introduction of its first-generation identity card in 1985, China launched its second-generation ID card (二代身份证 *er dai shenfenzheng*), a computerized ID citizen card to facilitate population management, reduce identity fraud, and digitize the information databank related to its citizens for authentication and storage. Following four rounds of deliberation, the National People's Congress Standing Committee voted to approve the ID card draft legislation on 28 June 2003, with implementation to begin on 1 January 2004 (Standing Committee 2003). The ID card law applies to mainland China. Hong Kong and Macau, special administrative regions of China, have their own ID cards with different technological regulations and policies (see Chapter 5). Taiwan, as a separate entity, has its own identification card with its own policies. The new law stipulates compatriots of Hong Kong, Macao and Taiwan settling in the People's Republic of China (PRC) and foreigners seeking citizenship or restoring nationality in the PRC are to apply for an ID card. The 2004 law has not only designed a new ID scheme for domestic management and authentication on the mainland but catapulted China to the forefront of the international smart card industry.

This chapter examines the introduction of China's computerized, second-generation ID schema as a national and international development of the smart card industry. The chapter addresses the description and function of the ID card, the integration of technology into the ID scheme, rollout plan for implementation, the domestic and international motivations for the ID scheme, and lessons learned that are applicable for ID schemes and policies merging technology and culture.

The second-generation card

China's second-generation card presents a significant change from the black and white, paper-laminated first-generation card that the government introduced in 1985, utilizing the standard language of the country. The new ID card, made of durable, recyclable polyester plastic, has a grey design of the Great Wall, a red national emblem, decorative pattern ranging in colour, full name of China and the card issuing department, and validity dates on the front. The back of the card contains the card holder's name, gender, ethnic nationality, birth date, address and ID number, with the person's colour digitized photograph to the right side. The

Figure 4.1 China's identity card.
Source: Wikimedia Commons 2006.

law allows autonomous regions to use minority nationality language characters or universal language characters of the region to complete the registration information of the ID card. Wikimedia Commons (2006) provides an illustrative image of the second-generation ID card in Figure 4.1. The new card, measuring 85.6 mm long and 54 mm wide, is slightly smaller than the 96 mm by 66 mm of the first ID card.

The ID card costs 20 yuan for a new card, 10 yuan for a temporary card and 40 yuan for a new card to replace a lost one.[1] Persons living on minimum social security allowances in the urban areas and disadvantaged rural residents are not charged a fee when replacing the old, first-generation ID card with the second-generation card for the first time. Citizens living in poverty due to accidents, disease, or natural disasters will pay half the fee for the ID card. Issuing agencies collect all card fees for the state treasury.

The second-generation card purports to safeguard citizens' legal rights, a benefit not comparable in the regulations for the 1985 first-generation ID card. Under the new law, individuals and organizations cannot arbitrarily check or hold citizens' ID cards except for the police with acceptable reasons. Article 6 stipulates that any information police gain in checking citizens' ID cards must remain confidential. The new law also gives the rights of card ownership to citizens below the age of 16. The government issued first-generation cards to persons age 16 and older.

The first-generation card contains a 15-digit ID number. Digits 1–6 indicated the administrative unit; 7–12 for birth data – birth year (2 digits), birth month (2 digits), birth day (2 digits), and 13–15 for a sequence and gender code to differentiate people sharing the same birth date and living in the same county or district, with the last number as odd for males and even for females. Prior to the Y2K in August 1999, the Twelfth National People's Congress Standing Committee passed a decision to give each citizen an ID number at birth and upgrade to 18 digits to record four instead of two numbers for the birth year. Digits 1–6 of the first-generation ID card with 18 digits represents the cardholder's administrative unit, 7–14 for the birth information – birth year (4 digits), birth month (2 digits), birth day (2 digits); 15–18 code assigned to persons that share the same birth date and live in the same district or county, with the second to last digit as an even number for female and odd number for male. While the issuing agencies manually assigned digits 15–18 to accommodate the Y2K card, the Ministry of Public Security Bureau (MPS) uses an algorithm calculating the first 17 numbers to arrive at the last number, with X for 10, for the second-generation card.

Application for the first- and second-generation cards is related to the household registration (*hukou*) system, which indicates the citizen's birth location in the rural or urban area of China. Citizens applied for the first-generation card at the location of their permanent residence, and the local public security organ issued, printed, and controlled the cards. The second-generation card also requires local application at the public security organ of the permanent residence. Applicants complete the Identity Card Application Registration Form, submit the *hukou* booklet for local public security officials to review, and receive the second-generation ID card within 60 days of submission and acceptance of the form. Regions with communication problems may require up to 30 extra days. Temporary ID cards are available in approved cases of urgent need.

Technology advancements of the second-generation card

The first-generation ID card sometimes used handwriting to record information on the card, especially for uncommon characters not accessible for typing. The second-generation card utilizes computerized characters on the card. The announcement of the card included plans to create a database of '20,000 rarely used Chinese square characters' to facilitate recording characters from the first-generation card (*People's Daily* Online 2003b). The either handwritten or typed first-generation card presents information only visible to the eye. The second-generation card, however, integrates a thumbnail-sized chip-module allowing sight reading and machine processing of the information it holds.

The second-generation ID card employs radio frequency identification (RFID), which uses wireless, radio waves to relay and transmit data through transponders or RFID tags to automatically identify a person or object, or any other information. It requires a special card reader for the ID cards. This automatic-identification method is similar to a bar code except bar code identification requires human contact or line-of-sight scan to receive information. RFID allows collecting data and entering data directly into computer systems without human participation and reaching greater distances than bar coding. It reduces the time and labor required to manually input data. The RFID tags consist of a microchip or integrated circuit (IC) attached to an antenna. Retrieving the stored data on the RFID tags requires a stationary or mobile reader with one or more antennae. The Internet allows two entities to share information about the location of identified items at any time. Fifteen Chinese government ministries and commissions, including the Ministry of Science and Technology (2006), released China's White Paper on RFID Technology Policy at a Beijing conference on 9 June 2006. The five-chapter document acknowledged China's use of RFID for ID card management and projected plans and strategies for increased research on this application.

The government initially planned the new ID card to hold fingerprints. A Ministry of Public Security press conference on 13 March 2001 announced the demonstration phase of a second-generation, multi-application card that would include identification and integration of passport, driving licence, and other applications in the future. The conference addressed the possible inclusion of fingerprints or other biometrics. The released second-generation card, however, has one application – identification – and no biometrics. Wang Lijian, deputy director of the National Registration Center for Integrated Circuit Cards, through an interpreter, shared the government's concerns with a *Card Technology Today* (2003) reporter: 'Such an effort to introduce biometrics, the huge quantity (of cardholders), is not feasible to start (with).' The government has considered biometrics as a later possibility based on trial testing for bar code ID cards with genetic codes (*People's Daily* Online 2002a) and R&D activities in biometrics.

The digitized photo on the new ID card does not integrate face-recognition biometrics, but the Ministry of Public Security issued photo stipulations to authenticate the person's true identity. Card applicants must have proper hair – not messy, not too tall, and not dyed – and must eliminate all accessories such as necklaces and earrings.

Plans and pilots for the second-generation ID card

Qiu Xuexin, director of the First Research Institute of the Ministry of Public Security (MPS), announced China's forthcoming ID card at the Fourth International Fair of Smart Cards in Beijing in June 2001. He reported the Ministry had submitted plans to the State Council for the new ID card and received its approval. The ID card scheme moved beyond the Ministry, as the next step involved proceeding with plans following 'positive feedback from other government departments' (*China Daily* 2001). The State Council approved China's use of IC technology in June 2001. At another conference in Beijing, Zhang Qi, director of the electronics products administration department of the Ministry of Information Industry, announced the government would emphasize policies on IC cards and the industry during the tenth Five-Year Plan for 2001–2005 (Foreign Ministry 2001).

Two years after Qiu's announcement to the international forum, the MPS held a meeting to outline the pilot implementation and highlight the safety measures of the second-generation ID card. The Ministry identified trial cities and referenced the start as 'the first half of the next year' and the completion of replacing paper cards as the 'end of 2008'. Wu Dongli, director of the Ministry's security administration bureau, accented the safety measures of the new card in guarding against the forgery common with the paper-laminated, first-generation card. The Ministry also emphasized the need to strengthen computer networks at all levels of the public security bureau to facilitate service to citizens and assist police with crime control. National People Congress leaders reiterated the significance and convenience of a computerized ID and suggested the forthcoming ID link between identification cards and centralized databases in using digital identification machines to scan the data on the participants and match it with the information stored in the system (*People's Daily* Online 2003b).

The Ministry announced the nationwide rollout of the second-generation card and final release of the first-generation card in 2005. The anticipated rollout completion is 2008. Officials used different strategies to urge citizens to obtain the new card: websites featuring colorful ID card graphics and frequently asked questions about the ID card; news reports on fraud and counterfeit cases involving the first-generation card; press coverage on services, e.g. hotel registration, bank loans, marriage application, Internet café login, and online gaming login, requiring the second-generation card; extended card distribution time to include workday evenings and weekends; and televised press conferences with the Ministry of Public Security officials promoting the benefits of the card.

As China prepared for the Spring Festival celebration of the Year of the Pig in 2007, the MPS held a videophone conference to communicate with other officials about processing ID cards. The conference directed public security organs to use television, circulars, newspaper, broadcasts to widely publicize the ID card, timing and process during the Chinese New Year (Ministry of Public Security 2007). The MPS designed this announcement to target those rural migrant workers lacking ID cards and who were returning home for the festival.

Domestic and international motivations for the ID scheme

The government's development of the first-generation identity card stemmed from China's increasing movement of citizens to meet the needs of the growing market economy and efforts to modernize population management. The country required a mobile, efficient system of identification to shift from the household registration (*hukou*) system, which China introduced in 1958 as a major tool for social control and population management, to a system of individual identification via the ID card. Even before the development of the *hukou* system, traditional Chinese government maintained population records for statistics and taxation. Neither the paper-laminated first-generation card nor the chip-integrated second-generation cards has replaced the *hukou*, however.

For years, the *hukou* system has separated urban and rural residents as a system of classification and restricted residents according to their birth. Children inherited their mother's *hukou* classification, with a law in 1998 allowing inheritance of the mother or father's *hukou* status, thus entrenching the generational effect of the system. The *hukou* system provides each household with a *hukou* booklet, requires registration with local authorities at birth, and designates the person's residential location – typically where born – and socioeconomic benefit status as agricultural or non-agricultural.

The *hukou* booklet, as a form of citizen identification and sorting for family members, lists the household name and type, issuing agency and date, handling person's signature, seal, registration date, and data on each family member: name, name of householder or relationship with householder, former name, gender, birth location, ethnic group, origin location, birth date, other address in the city, identity card number, height, blood type, educational level, marital status, employment location, position, when and from where moved into the city, and when and from where moved to the address (China: Reform 2005). *Hukou* registration is required for all citizens of China. To register, citizens must use their birth certificates and apply in person. To replace a lost *hukou* booklet, however, one can use the identity card. Members of the household must present the *hukou* for events requiring identification verification, e.g. registration for passport, marriage, employment, school, and ID card (original or replacement). The holder must report to the *hukou* registration issuing authority any changes in the number of household members.

As economic reforms in 1979 and the 1980s led to a surplus of labor in the rural areas and the demand for more urban workers continued, the government began to issue *hukou* reforms allowing rural residents to seek work in urban areas. The reforms varied per region, but notable ones include the temporary residence certificate for rural workers staying in urban areas for longer than six months, the permit to live away from home for people staying in another area for a lengthy period of time, and the blue chop or blue stamp *hukou* allowing urban migration for rural workers with a stipulated level of income and education.[2]

In a study of the *hukou* and crime control, Chen (2002: 6–7) maintains that China's 'basic identification instrument of every urban citizen throughout his or her life' is now inadequate for managing the population. Recent reports support this premise. Millions of rural residents of China have moved to cities in search of jobs to enhance their rural incomes. This migration has yielded a large floating population, often with no registration in the urban areas, but an inexpensive labour source to businesses. Urban locations often lack schools for migrant children and housing, healthcare, and employment for migrants, who maintain the label of rural residents with a temporary residential certificate or without a permit for urban migration. The government fears migrants may resort to crime without employment to support themselves. Li Zhang (2001), however, studied a major transient community of Beijing, to find not only unwelcomed social conditions among the floating populations but network organizations and urban entrepreneurs. Zhang's work and other studies (Wong and Huen 1998; Solinger 1995) highlight the variation among the floating population category from temporary workers to vagrants or drifters with plans for employment and survival.

Chen views the first-generation ID card as 'a modification of the hukou rather than a substitute for it (8)'. Zhu (2003) also contends that the framework for the rural and urban barrier of the *hukou* remains in China. Alexander and Chan

(2004) explore the existence of an apartheid pass system in this control of migrant workers. In more recent years, many provinces and municipalities have relaxed *hukou* restrictions or explored *hukou* reforms, addressing criticisms of human rights abuse of migrant workers and the continued need for inexpensive human capital in the cities. In Wang Fei-Ling's prepared statement before the United States Congressional-Executive Commission on China (2005) and earlier analysis of *hukou* reforms (Wang 2005), he contends the Chinese government computerized the *hukou* system in the 1980s to allow an instant police check of a person's information via the computer transmission of data, but floating populations have increased in the cities. Wang maintains that the campaign to eliminate the identification of *hukou* location and the use of ID cards without *hukou* data are misleading as an indicator of improved human rights. He asserts one can still discern the cardholder's residential location through the address. The government's efforts to link the second-generation ID card to a data network and RFID may offer higher level controlling and policing of mobile populations, but monitoring will remain difficult without ID registration of large floating populations.

A second motivation for China's ID scheme is the management of movement and behaviour the government identifies as a public security risk, especially via Internet use. Within a decade after the Tiananmen Square incident shared student protests and violent reaction with the international world via CNN, television and radio broadcasts, cable networks, cell phones, and fax machines in 1989, China began to witness increasing use of the Internet in work and social settings. The country faced the quagmire of needing the Internet and other information and communication technologies (ICTs) to boost its development in e-commerce and wanting to maintain control of information flow among the public. The government relied on official regulations, laws and organizations to ban information it deemed as violating state secrets or threatening state security.

In 1998, China's Ministry of Public Security proposed a five-year, two-phase plan of 1998–1999 and 1999–2002 to build the Golden Shield Project 金盾工程 (*jindun gongcheng*), a three-tiered, networked computer system, to facilitate management of economic and social developments; unify a rapid, coordinate effort against crime; standardize information technology applications; enhance surveillance detection; and increase public security information sharing at all levels of the Public Security Bureau. China recognizes the Golden Shield Project, 80 million yuan investment, as one of 12 major national projects using networked computer-based systems to manage government and develop e-government services (*People's Daily* Online 2003a).

The Beijing Public Security Bureau signed a contract with Qinghua University on 2 September 2001 for the digital wide-bank network of Golden Shield (*People's Daily* Online 2001) and researchers reported its development (Walton 2001), but the project did not begin operations two years later in September 2003. China's Vice Premier, Huang Ju, announced the need for additional, coordinated efforts from all levels of public security officials to construct the networks (*People's Daily* Online 2003a). The project underwent formal government inspection in Beijing on 16 November 2006 (Ministry of Public Security 2006).

Within one year after the initial proposal for the Golden Shield Project, the Chinese government realized another threat to its authority. On 25 April 1999, more than 10,000 practitioners of Falun Gong lined the streets near Zongnanhai, the Chinese Communist Party (CCP) leadership compound, seeking official recognition and protection against reports of beatings and arrests in Tianjin. Although a peaceful assembly, the organization demonstrated the ability to gather in a major public setting unbeknownst to the Party. More importantly, Falun Gong boasted a total population of 10 million, then rivaling the population of the CCP. Falun Gong members not only used cell phones and the Internet to communicate in China but participated in a triangular communicative network of cell phones, websites, fax machines, and e-mail linking three nodes of home country members in China, international supporters worldwide, and a long-distance leader living in New York (Brown, 2001). Meanwhile, a proliferation of chat rooms critiquing politics of China began to penetrate cyberspace as Internet use increased in China.

The Golden Shield Project to enhance surveillance and curb security risk is often dubbed the 'Great Firewall of China' for its efforts to control penetration and activity of the Internet in the country and in reference to the firewall of networks and China's Great Wall. The Ministry blocked or restricted access to obscene or politically subversive content by using firewalls and proxy servers to restricting routing of Internet Protocol (IP) addresses, filtering Uniform Resource Locators (URLs), censoring search engine pages and slow uploads of international pages. The Ministry called for registration of Internet users in cybercafés and other outlets for Internet use to maintain records of activity. International companies such as Yahoo! appeared to lend support to the Great Firewall as it acknowledged China's public security regulations and laws instead of users' privacy rights by revealing the names of users to the Chinese government. In July 2007, the Chinese government launched a campaign to restrict teenagers' online gaming to three hours. The programme mandates gaming companies to use software requiring gamers to enter their identification numbers to screen the users. The Ministry announced the requirement of gamers under 18 to restrict gaming to three hours and stop for physical exercise. Although gamers use their ID numbers to log on, new reports have highlighted the use of using fake IDs (China Daily 2007a).

Within four years of completion of the Golden Shield in 2003 and research on China's Internet filtering (Zittrain and Edelman 2003) and challenges (Mulvenon and Chase 2006), Crandall *et al.* (2007) have created a Doppler test to measure China's Internet filtering and censorship by testing penetration of the firewall. The researchers' Doppler measurements of firewall penetration yield results questioning if the Golden Shield or Great Firewall is a weak chain-link fence. Another challenge to the use of database linked to the ID is technology savvy citizens' ability to figure out the algorithm for configuration of ID numbers. Bloggers have revealed their strategies online for cyber audiences. A crucial part of resolving the ID card and database technology for China is innovative research, which President Hu Jintao vowed to increase in his address to the 17th National Party Congress on 15 October 2007.

A third motivating factor for China's ID scheme is the boost the ID card brings to domestic R&D development and national pride in the look of the card. Citizens displaying their new ID card in Beijing in 2007 had a sense of pride about the new card as opposed to the old, tattered, paper-laminated card. The second-generation card celebrates national research and design, as the chip-module represents the combined work of two units – the Institute of Microelectronics of prestigious Qinghua University (Tsinghua in Wade-Giles Romanization) and the Qinghua Tongfang Microelectronics Co., Ltd, a subsidiary of Qinghua University. The units jointly founded the Beijing Qinghua Tongfang Microelectronic Co., Ltd in December 2001 for collaborative research and development of second-generation ID card chips (Institute of Microelectronics of Tsinghua University, n.d.; *People's Daily* Online 2004a). Tan *et al.*'s (1998) article on contactless IC ID cards reveals the early work of the Qinghua University researchers on the chip-module.

China's Eastcompeace Smart Card Co., Ltd, established in 1988, is the main supplier for China's national ID card project. The company supplied more than 12 million cards to the Chinese government in 2005, and received a contract to supply 20 million more national ID cards (*Card Technology Today* 2006). Huaxin Plastic Industry Development Co., Ltd, created the organic-friendly polyester plastic material for the ID card. The government acknowledged it is easier to sell the data management factor if the card and technology are home grown and managed. Press reports sought to quell suggestions that Japanese companies were involved in production of the card.

An international factor supporting the country's ID scheme is the market attraction to expand the integrated circuit (IC) card production in China. The national ID card, as one of many IC cards in China, demonstrates the talent of R&D in China. The ID card market not only attracted computing companies and vendors, especially with RFID technology, in the smart card market, it also threatened the European third-party markets. France's Gemplus, a major world IC card producer, established Gemplus Tianjin as its Asia IC card production headquarters in China's municipality of Tianjin (Gemplus 2004). Subsequently, Gemplus received an order to produce 10 million SIM cards for China Unicom (Smart Card Alliance 2003).

A major international benefit of the ID card scheme is the use of RFID in a large order of cards, which catapulted China to the forefront of international development in this technology (*Card Technology Today* 2007). China has emerged as a major leader in the radio RFID technology for contactless cards (Xiao *et al.* 2007) and is already using tags on pet dogs to monitor their care. RFID tags can help monitor production of goods for exporting and improve the image of China's many health-endangering recalls of food, pet products, toys, and medicines. China can emerge as international leaders in reaching out to collaborate with other countries and retailers via RFID. China's ID scheme also brings attention to the country's advancements in technology and compliance with international laws (addressing accusations of apartheid for migrants) and image building for the 2008 Olympics in Beijing (Zissis 2007). China will incorporate RFID technology for contactless tickets for the Olympics.

The ID card offers a system of population management and surveillance for China and protects the government against security threats. At the same time, the new, computerized ID also represents China's national pride in domestic R&D that has catapulted China to the forefront as international leader in the RFID market.

Lessons learned: Identity management and Chinese culture

China's ID scheme offers insight into the complexity of shifting to the digital management of such a huge population and the usefulness of having a preexisting census or population management programme. Countries such as India without a central population database experience a level of organizational complexity in starting from scratch as India is now doing (see Mehmood, Chapter 7). China, however, is switching from the paper card to an IC card. At the same time, the change in ID schemes had another set of problems. The MPS has reported cases of overlapping ID numbers and duplicate identities (Lu 2006) with no systematic strategy for individuals with the same number to resolve the duplication.

Another lesson for ID card schemes in other countries is the security issue of the database and surveillance. The integrated circuit in the card makes it more difficult to forge. Also, computers can read the cards and store information. Computer reading allows police to check an abundance of cards in a shorter period of time than the first-generation card. Through the database network, the Internet allows two officials to share information about the location of identified individuals at any time. Even if the government were using it to legitimately avert public security, a digital eavesdropper can obtain the transmitted information. Hackers could obstruct networks and alter data.

Digital interference raises another concern about the right of privacy and the use of obtained information. Although privacy has not been an expressed value as in other societies, scholars in China are beginning to explore its meaning. Lu (2005) contends that a changing view of privacy is emerging in China that does not support the government violations reported by the Global Internet Liberty Campaign (2004) and Rotenberg and Laurant (2005). A particular example of privacy issue concerning ID cards in China occurred when ID card photos of entertainment stars appeared on the Internet (*China Daily* 2005).

China's ID scheme reveals a lesson about technology management. Maintaining an R&D program to further the advancement of the ID card for maximum use is costly in human and intellectual capital. Beyond maintenance, the Ministry's initial focus on a multi-purpose card integrating biometrics is costly. China has released social security cards and health cards to citizens but not integrated with the ID card. The Renmin University of China Campus Information Card Project, dubbed the 'Campus Card', is the first attempt to produce a multi-purpose ID card that includes identification information and financial applications. Planned in conjunction with the Ministry of Public Security, the 'Campus Card' can be used to certify ID and other purposes such as the library, shops, cafeteria, stores and gyms.

The Chinese government's policy on names for the second-generation ID card offers a lesson for future leaders in planning ID cards, which must address major technical and cultural issues. Chinese names typically have two to three characters. One character, the surname, is written first. Second and third characters represent the given name. Sometimes, parents choose only one character for the given name. In an example of three names, Wang Meili, Wang is the surname and Meili is the given name. In the case of only two names, the child is Wang Mei. Computerization required for the second-generation ID card makes it difficult to code rarely-used Chinese characters for given names that do not exist in current databases for ID card use. Rare characters stem from parents' desire to select a meaningful and unusual name for their child, a practice common in Chinese history. Names also portrayed the social setting or times such as 'Yonghong' ('forever red') during the Cultural Revolution of 1966–1976.

Using names not included in the databanks poses problems when registering for a second-generation ID card, opening a bank account, or seeking a hotel room. The Beijing Municipal Security Bureau reported the temporary problem of not being able to produce second-generation ID cards for 41,000 citizens and renew 900,000 cards because of the names. In the case of names not available in the computer databank of names for producing cards, citizens would need to apply for a temporary provisional ID card. Using the temporary card remained a problem, however, because hotels and banks requiring ID cards lacked the names in their systems (China Network 2005).

Surnames and common names pose additional challenges for ID card processing, as China is experiencing a dearth of available family names. The MPS 2006 national survey revealed approximately 85 per cent of China's population of 1.3 billion shares 100 surnames. Wang is the family name of 93 million, Li for 92 million, Zhang for 88 million, and Chen, Zhou, Lin, and four other surnames for about 20 million. Parental selection of rare or unusual names to accompany a popular surname prevents children from having a commonly used full name such as Wang Wei or Wang Fang. The Marriage Law of 1980 allowed the child to take the father or mother's surname. To address the dearth of surnames and avoid repetitive names, the MPS introduced draft legislation in 2007 to allow parents to combine their surnames for their child. A father with the last name Wei and mother with the surname Zhang could select either surname for their child or combine the names to give the child the surname of Weizhang or Zhangwei (*China Daily* 2007b; *People's Daily* Online 2007c).

One couple exceeded the selection of a rare Chinese name in choosing the symbol @ as a distinctive name for their son. Li Yuming, vice director of the State Language Commission acknowledged the boy's father remarked that @ was not only used worldwide for e-mail but the Chinese enunciation of 'at' resembles 'ai ta' or 'love him' in Chinese (Attewill 2007). Although the State Language Commission initially addressed the issue of unconventional and rare names, the police would make the final decision on the name. The conflict between database characters and naming traditions in China lends itself to addressing other issues of conflict between technology and culture when adopting new identification technologies.

Another issue other jurisdictions can glean from China's ID scheme experience is the differences among local police forces, tension between the public and police in the country, and fraudulent practices among law enforcement. Higher-level public security bureaus found inconsistencies in police enforcement of central laws in local areas. Police failed to uniformly implement the ID card laws. In some locations, for example, police charged additional fees in renewing ID cards. The Ministry of Public Security issued the Provisions on Administration of the Usage of People's Police Certificate, effective 1 June 2006, a regulation mandating unified ID certificates for almost 1.6 million Chinese police. The new certificates seek to facilitate ordinary people's identification of the police, curb fraudulent use of police credentials against citizens, standardize management of local police forces throughout the nation, and integrate international technology standards for global cooperation. The unified certificates replaced the former certificates, which the local public security administrations issued to police. The former certificates varied according to the region or province, hindering investigations across locations and citizens' identification of the police. In a press conference on 30 May 2006, Fan Jingyu, a senior official handling MPS personnel training, announced the banned use of the former local certificates as of 1 January 2007 (*China Daily* 2006a; *People's Daily* Online 2006, 2007a).

Conclusion

China introduced its computerized second-generation ID card in 2004 to facilitate population management, reduce identity fraud, and digitize storage and authentication of citizens' data and ID. The new card law states the protection of citizens' legal rights. The government's motivation for its first-generation ID scheme in 1985, emanated from the country's need to modernize population management in a developing market economy and shifting population from rural to urban areas. The country required a mobile, efficient system of identification to shift from its 1958 household registration (*hukou*) system of population identification and management to individual authentication via the ID card.

As China moves in the direction of *hukou* reform and digital identification, the country faces challenges in the implementation of the second-generation ID card. The social sorting of urban and rural birth place may cease to exist in the form of population monitoring, but government surveillance and digital databases of ID information – along with police, health and childbirth records – may challenge citizens' legal rights and threaten digital intrusion. Stored information, easily accessible to public security officers and used at the discretion of the local police, has the potential to infringe citizens' rights in a vast country that currently lacks the democratic traditions that may limit abuses in other countries. Apart from information misuse by government sectors, hackers pose the risk of network obstruction and data modification. Along with technological development for ID schemes, comes the cost of maintenance.

A related issue is violation or compromise of citizens' privacy. Although China may not have experienced privacy debate in the past, the advancement of technology in ID authentication, data storage, and citizen surveillance may evolve the discussion in the future, especially if China witnesses an increasing public emphasis on privacy rights. This privacy threat for Chinese citizens has the potential for converging to the privacy risk of ID schemes in other political cultures.

Another challenge of the second-generation ID card stems from using technology in shifting from traditional practices. Computerized identification has challenged naming practices. The gradual move from a *hukou*, family-based identity to an individualized, digital identity presents another societal change. The country's exploration of merging culture and technology exposes the potential of future developments in technology that must reconcile traditions in China and other countries.

As China resolves the political, cultural, social, and technological issues of its ID card, the card's rollout has catapulted the country's position in the international smart card and RFID markets. The commercial potential for ID cards enhances the role for domestic and international technology companies in the specification and development of ID schemes in China and worldwide.

Notes

1 The exchange rate is about 14 cents (in US dollars) for every China Yuan Renminbi. The exchange amount for 20 yuan, 10 yuan, and 40 yuan is US$2.70, US$1.35 and US$5.40.
2 See Zhu Lijiang (2003), Wang Fei-Ling (2005) and Wong, Linda and Huen Wai-Po (1998) for an overview of these reforms.

Bibliography

Alexander, P. and Chan, A. (2004) 'Does China have an apartheid pass system?', *Journal of Ethnic and Migration Studies* 30(4): 609–29.
Attewill, F. (2007) 'What's in @ name? Chinese watchdog queries parents' choice', *Guardian Unlimited* 16 August. Online. Available: http://www.guardian.co.uk/china/story/0,,2150301,00.html (accessed 18 August 2007).
Brown, C.L. (2001) 'Triangular networks and e-government: communicative power in cyberspace', paper presented at the Annual Meeting of the American Political Science Association, San Francisco, 1 September 2001.
Card Technology Today (2003) 'Fingerprints are missing from Chinese National ID card', 1 October 2003. Online. Available: http://www.cardtechnology.com/article.html?id=200505091INLFLGE (accessed 2 September 2007).
Card Technology Today (2006) 'New Chinese ID card contract awarded', *Card Technology Today* 18(2): 6–7.
Card Technology Today (2007) 'National ID project moves China to head of the pack in radio frequency technology', 2 February. Online. Available: http://www.cardtechnology.com/article.html?id=20070221PGYABPF5 (accessed 2 September 2007).
Chan, K.W. and Zhang L. (1999) 'The Hukou system and rural–urban migration in China: processes and changes', *The China Quarterly* 160: 818–55.
Chen, X. (2002) 'Community and policing strategies: a Chinese approach to crime control', *Policing and Society* 12: 1–13.

Chen, Y. and Kluver, R. (2006) 'Information society and privacy in the People's Republic of China', *Journal of E-Government* 2(4): 83–103.

China Daily (2001) 'New microchip ID card expected', 12 June. Online. Available: http://www.china.org.cn/english/GS-e/14478.htm (accessed 30 July 2007).

China Daily (2005) 'Mainland celebrities' ID card photos exposed online', *Shenzhen Daily* 14 July. Online. Available: http://www.chinadaily.com.cn/english/doc/2005-07/14/content_460113.htm (accessed 19 December 2006).

China Daily (2006a) 'China police granted unified certificate', 30 May. Online. Available: http://www.chinadaily.com.cn/china/2006-05/30/content_603991.htm (accessed 3 June 2007).

China Daily (2006b) 'Surveillance increase sparks privacy concerns', 7 December. Online. Available: http://www.china.org.cn/english/MATERIAL/191484.htm (accessed 19 December 2006).

China Daily (2007a) 'China clamps down on Internet gaming', 17 July. Online. Available: http://www.chinadaily.com.cn/china/2007-07/17/content_5438062.htm (accessed 20 July 2007).

China Daily (2007b) 'China gripped by name shortage', 26 July. Online. Available: http://www.chinadaily.com.cn/china/2007-07/25/content_5443465.htm (accessed 30 July 2007).

China Network (2003) 金盾工程 [Golden Shield], 27 February. Online. Available: http://www.china.org.cn/chinese/zhuanti/283732.htm (accessed 30 July 2007).

China Network (2005) 北京4.1万人因冷僻字问题无法制作二代身份证 [In Beijing 41,000 people cannot get second-generation ID cards produced because of rare words], 4 November. Online. Available: http://www.china.com.cn/chinese/zhuanti/chwlsh/1019698.htm (accessed 30 July 2007).

China: Reforms of the Household Registration System (Hukou) 1998–2004 (2005). Research Directorate of the Immigration and Refugee Board. Online. Available: www.unhcr.org/home/RSDCOI/4305fbc04.pdf (accessed 12 September 2007).

Chinabyte.com (2004) 二代身份证的换装起 [The second-generation ID card replacement start], 13 February (in Chinese). Online. Available: http://news.chinabyte.com/117/1768117.shtml (accessed 28 July 2007).

Chinabyte.com (2007) 2007 中国国际 RFID 技术高峰论坛会 [China International RFID Technology Summit Forum], 6–8 September (in Chinese). Online. Available: http://data.chinabyte.com/rfidgflt/ (accessed 16 September 2007).

Chinese Government Official Web Portal (2005) 'ID numbers go online in Guangdong', 22 August. Online. Available: http://english.gov.cn/2005-08/22/content_25419.htm (accessed 24 March 2007).

Chinese Government Official Web Portal (2006) 'New ID card ensures privacy', Shenzhen Daily. 10 February. Online. Available: http://english.gov.cn/2006-02/10/content_184763.htm (accessed 19 December 2006).

Crandall, J.R., Zinn, D., Byrd, M., Barr, E. and East, R. (2007) 'Concept Doppler: A weather tracker for Internet censorship', paper presentation at the 14th ACM Conference on Computer and Communications Security, 29 October – 2 November.

Eastcompeace Smart Card Co., Ltd. (2007) 'About us'. Online. Available: http://eastcompeace.en.alibaba.com/aboutus.html (accessed 11 February 2007).

Foreign Ministry (2001) 'China on way to becoming IC card king (12/19/01)', Consulate General of the People's Republic of China in New York. Online. Available: http://www.nyconsulate.prchina.org/eng/xw/t31294.htm (accessed 15 September 2007).

Gemplus (2004) 'Gemplus expands China operations with the new plant in Tianjin'. Online.

Available: http://www.gemalto.com/press/gemplus/2004/corporate/17-11-2004-new_plant_in_tianjin.htm (accessed 3 September 2007).

Global Internet Liberty Campaign (2004) Privacy and human rights: an international survey of privacy laws and practice. *Global Internet Liberty Campaign.* Online. Available: http://www.gilc.org/privacy/survey/intro.html#invasion (accessed 10 March 2004 and 9 January 2007) (Website has not been updated since 2003).

Huang Shan (2007) 'World's biggest ID database complete', China.org.cn, 11 April. Online. Available: http://www.china.org.cn/english/China/206827.htm (accessed 28 July 2007).

Institute of Microelectronics of Tsinghua University (no date) 'Major achievements in recent years'. Online. Available: http://dns.ime.tsinghua.edu.cn/english/research/2.htm

Liu, H. (2004) 'The child's right to birth registration-international and Chinese perspectives', National Institute of Law. Chinese Academy of Social Sciences. Online. Available: http://www.iolaw.org.cn (accessed 9 August 2007). Also published by the Norwegian Centre for Human Rights, University of Oslo.

Lu, H. (2006) 'China strives to solve "identity duplication cases"', 23 October. Online. Available: http://english.gov.cn/2006-10/23/content_421147.htm (accessed 17 December 2006).

Lu, Y. (2005) 'Privacy and data privacy issues in contemporary China', *Ethics and Information Technology* 7(1): 7–15.

Ministry of Public Security (2006) 国家发改委主持召开大会 通过 '金盾工程' 建设项目国家验收 [National Development and Reform Commission issues national approval for the 'Golden Shield' construction project at management conference], 17 November. Online. Available: http://www.mps.gov.cn/cenweb/brjlCenweb/jsp/common/article.jsp?infoid=ABC00000000000035645 (accessed 19 July 2007).

Ministry of Public Security (2007) 公安机关春节前后为外出返乡群众办理二代身份证 [The Ministry of Public Security Spring Festival on returning to one's native village for the populace to handle the second-generation ID card]. The Central Government of the People's Republic of China. Online. Available: http://www.gov.cn/fwxx/sh/2007-02/06/content_518877.htm (accessed 19 July 2007).

Ministry of Science and Technology, People's Republic of China – Fifteen Ministries and Commissions (2006) 中国射频识别 (RFID) 技术政策白皮书 [White Paper on RFID Technology Policy in China], 9 June.

Mulvenon, James C. and Chase, Michael S. (2006) 'Breaching the great firewall: external challenges to China's Internet controls', *Journal of E-Government* 2(4): 71–82.

National Citizen Identity Information Center (2007) '50 most frequently used Chinese Names', 25 July. Online. Available: http://www.xmnext.com (accessed 27 July 2007).

Open Beijing's Residence Laws. (2007) *China Daily*, 25 April. Online. Available: http://www.china.org.cn/english/GS-e/208898.htm (accessed 26 April 2007).

People's Daily Online (2001) 'Beijing to expand public security information network', 3 September. Online. Available: http://english.people.com.cn/200109/03/eng20010903_79170.html (accessed 27 November 2006).

People's Daily Online (2002a) 'China to develop genetic identification card', 25 September. Online. Available: http://english.peopledaily.com.cn/200209/25/eng20020925_103874.shtml (accessed 27 November 2006).

People's Daily Online (2002b) 'China starts working out law on citizen ID card,' 31 October. Online. Available: http://english.people.com.cn/200210/31/eng20021031_106032.shtml (accessed 27 2006).

People's Daily Online (2003a) 'More efforts needed in public security computer system: Huang Ju', 3 September 2003. Online. Available: http://english.people.com.cn/ 200309/ 03/eng20030903_123628.shtml (accessed 19 December 2006).

People's Daily Online (2003b) 'Chinese citizens to use new ID cards next year', 18 December. Online. Available: http://english.people.com.cn/200312/18/eng20031218_ 130715.shtml (accessed 19 December 2006).

People's Daily Online (2004a) 'China to issue new intelligent ID cards', 28 January. Online. Available: http://english.peopledaily.com.cn/200401/28/eng20040128_133413.shtml (accessed 19 December 2006).

People's Daily Online (2004b) 'China starts to launch second-generation ID cards,' 30 March. Online. Available: http://english.peopledaily.com.cn/200403/30/eng20040330_ 138863.shtml. (accessed 19 December 2006).

People's Daily Online (2004c) 'China to build world's largest database', 24 July. Online. Available: http://english.people.com.cn/200407/24/eng20040724_150673.html (accessed 19 December 2006).

People's Daily Online (2004d) 'Beijing begins to use second-generation ID cards', 7 April. Online. Available: http://english.peopledaily.com.cn/200404/07/eng20040407_139729. shtml (accessed 19 December 2006).

People's Daily Online (2006) 'China starts to issue nationwide-unified police certificate', 1 June. Online. Available: http://english.peopledaily.com.cn/200606/01/eng20060601_ 270328.html (accessed 3 June 2007).

People's Daily Online (2007a) 'China to unify police identity card from Jan 1,' 1 January 2007. Online. Available: http://english.people.com.cn/200701/01/eng20070101_ 337432.html (accessed 10 June 2007).

People's Daily Online (2007b) 'Virtual Beijing police to patrol in cyber world,' 29 August. Online. Available: http://english.people.com.cn/90001/90781/6250833.html (accessed 30 August 2007).

People's Daily Online (2007c) 'What's in a surname? A combination of mother's and father's, 20 June. Online. Available: http://english.people.com.cn/200706/19/ eng20070619_385662.html (accessed 27 June 2007).

Remin (People's) University of China (2004) 'Campus Information Card'. Online. Available: http://english.ruc.edu.cn/en/100375/18906.html (accessed 10 June 2007).

Rotenberg, M. and Laurant, C. (2005) *Privacy and Human Rights 2005.* Online. Available: http://www.privacyinternational.org/survey/phr2005/PHR2005.pdf (accessed 1 May 2007).

Smart Card Alliance (2003) 'China Unicom Orders Over Ten Million SIM Cards From Gemplus'. Online. Available: http://www.smartcardalliance.org/articles/2003/06/27/ china-unicom-orders-over-ten-million-sim-cards-from-gemplus (accessed 3 September 2007).

Solinger, Dorothy (1995) 'The floating population in the cities: chances for assimilation?', in D. Davis, R. Kraus, B. Naughton and E.J. Perry (eds) *Urban Spaces: Autonomy and Community in Contemporary China,* Washington, DC: Woodrow Wilson Center Press and Cambridge: Cambridge University Press.

Stalder, F. and Lyon, D. (2001) 'Electronic identity cards and social classification', in D. Lyon (ed.) *Surveillance as Social Sorting: Privacy, Risk and Digital Discrimination,* New York: Routledge, p. 77–93.

Standing Committee of the National People's Congress of the People's Republic of China (1980) 中华人民共和国婚姻法 [Marriage Law of the People's Republic of China] Adopted at the Third Session of the Fifth National People's Congress and promulgated by

Order No. 9 of the Chairman of the Standing Committee of the National People's Congress on 10 September 1980 and effective as of 1 January 1981.

Standing Committee of the National People's Congress of the People's Republic of China (1985) 中华人民共和国居民身份证条例 [失效] [Regulations of the People's Republic of China Concerning Resident Identity Cards] Adopted at the 12th Meeting of the Standing Committee of the Sixth National People's Congress and promulgated for implementation by Order No. 29 of the President of the People's Republic of China on 6 September 1985, and effective as of 6 September 1985.

Standing Committee of the National People's Congress of the People's Republic of China (2003) 中华人民共和国居民身份证法 [Law of the People's Republic of China on the Resident Identity Cards], Adopted at the Third Meeting of the Standing Committee of the Tenth National People's Congress on 28 June 2003 and promulgated and implemented by Order No. 4 of the President of the People's Republic of China on 28 June 2003, and effective as of 1 January 2004.

Tan Xuebin, Yang Xingzi, Ge Yuanqing, Zeng Ying (谭学斌,羊性滋,葛元庆,曾莹) (1998) 一 用于身份识别的非接触式 IC 卡的设计与研制 [The Development of a Contactless IC Card Used as ID Card] *Microelectronics* (微电子学) 28(3): 12–15.

United States Congressional-Executive Commission on China (2005) China's Household Registration (hukou) System: Discrimination and Reforms: Roundtable before the Congressional-Executive Commission on China, One Hundred Ninth Congress, first session, 2 September 2005.

Walton, G. (2001) 'China's Golden Shield: corporations and the development of surveillance technology in the People's Republic of China', Rights & Democracy, Online. Available: http://www.ichrdd.ca/english/commdoc/publications/globalization/goldnShieldEng.html (accessed 3 March 2007).

Wang Fei-Ling (2005) *Organizing through Division and Exclusion: China's Hukou System*, Stanford: Stanford University Press.

Wikimedia Commons (2006) 'Image: Jumin shenfenzheng.jpg,' Creative Commons Attribution 2.5. Online. Available: http://commons.wikimedia.org/wiki/Image:Jumin_shenfenzheng.jpg (accessed 10 September 2007).

Wong, L. and Huen Wai-Po (1998) 'Reforming the household registration system: a preliminary glimpse of the blue chop household registration system in Shanghai and Shenzhen', *International Migration Review* 32(4): 974–94.

Xiao, N., Crotch-Harvey, T., Harrop, P. and Das, R. (2007) *RFID in China 2007–2017*, Cambridge: IDTechEx Ltd.

Xinhua News Agency (2005) 'New ID card for all citizens by 2008', 29 April. Online. Available: http://www.china.org.cn/english/Life/127471.htm (accessed 19 December 2006).

Xinhua News Agency (2006a) '100,000 Chinese share one name "Wang Tao"', 27 January. Online. Available: http://www.china.org.cn/english/Life/156552.htm# (accessed 23 January 2007).

Xinhua Online (2005) 'Overlapped ID numbers affect one million people', *Shenzhen Daily*, 25 May. Online. Available: http://news3.xinhuanet.com/english/2005-05/25/content_2999289.htm (accessed 19 December 2006).

Xinhua Online (2006c) 'What's in a name? Destiny, Chinese say,' *China Daily*, 18 March. Online. Available: http://news3.xinhuanet.com/english/2006-03/18/content_4330416.htm (accessed 5 May 2007).

Xinhuanet.com (2007) 'China trying to unify urban, rural household registration', 29 March. Online. Available: http://english.people.com.cn/200701/24/eng20070124_344244.html (accessed 12 August 2007).

Yu Zhu (2007) 'China's floating population and their settlement intention in the cities: beyond the *Hukou* reform', *Habitat International* 31(1) (March): 65–76.

Zhang Li (2001) *Strangers in the City: Reconfigurations of Space, Power, and Social Networks within China's Floating Population*, Stanford: Stanford University Press.

Zhu Lijiang (2003) 'The Hukou System of the People's Republic of China: A Critical Appraisal under International Standards on Internal Movement and Residence', *Chinese Journal of International Law* 2(2): 519–65.

Zissis, Carin (2007). 'Olympic Pressure on China', Council on Foreign Relations. Online. Available: http://www.cfr.org/publication/13270 (accessed 29 July 2007).

Zittrain, J. and Edelman, B.G. (2003) 'Internet filtering in China', Harvard Law School Public Law Research Paper No. 62, *IEEE Internet Computing* March-April: 70–8.

5 Hong Kong's 'smart' ID card

Designed to be out of control

Graham Greenleaf[1]

Hong Kong has had an ID card system for nearly 60 years, used primarily for purposes of immigration control, and for identification by government, but at the turn of this century, it decided to convert it to a chip-based 'smart' ID card. This was only a few years after Hong Kong became part of the People's Republic of China. The Hong Kong Administration took the opportunity to make the smart card multifunctional from the start, but claimed that use of all the additional functions would be voluntary. This chapter questions to what extent these uses of additional functions will be voluntary, and whether this is significant. It examines the potential for further expansion of the functions of Hong Kong's ID system, commonly known as 'function creep' and the extent to which any such expansion will or will not be under democratic control.

Sixty years of ID cards in Hong Kong

ID cards have become a pervasive fact of life in Hong Kong since their introduction following the Second World War and the enactment of the *Registration of Persons Ordinance* (ROPO) in 1949. The UK colonial government gave a commitment that the scheme would be withdrawn once the turbulent post-war conditions, particularly the influx of refugees from China, had subsided (Waters and Clarke 2000: 15). By 1960, when the ROPO was overhauled, the laminated ID card included the holder's fingerprint and photograph, but new cards from 1973 no longer included fingerprints (*Wikipedia* 2007). Neither the 1949 nor 1960 ROPO made it compulsory for the card to be carried, only for the ID number to be provided in dealings with government. However, by the late 1970s, the levels of illegal immigration had become overwhelming, rising to over 100,000 in 1979 (2% of the population), and the ID card became a principal means of controlling this influx, and consequently obtained a high level of local acceptance (Bacon-Shone, pers comm 2007). In 1979, ROPO was amended to allow regulations to be made requiring persons to carry their ID cards in designated areas and produce them, on request, to police, and by 1980 regulations had designated all of Hong Kong's territory (Waters and Clarke 2000: 15; *Wikipedia* 2007), influenced by the influx of illegal immigrants into Hong Kong following the wars in Indochina. Further legislative amendments in 1980 (*Immigration Ordinance* s17C), supporting prohibitions on employment of illegal immigrants, made it mandatory for *all* Hong Kong residents over 15 years to carry a recognized 'proof of identity' in public places and produce it to police on demand (Waters and Clarke 2000: 16; *Wikipedia* 2007). Children aged 11 were required to obtain an ID card, but not to carry it until they turned 15.

The content on the ID card was a person's name (in English and/or Chinese), sex, date of birth (DOB), photograph, various registration dates, ID card number (including a prefix such as W for domestic helpers), and symbols indicating where the holder was born, conditions of their residence in Hong Kong, and whether their reported name or DOB had changed since first registration (Waters and Clarke 2000: 29; *Wikipedia* 2007).

The political and constitutional context into which one of the world's more technically sophisticated ID systems is being introduced strongly influences the prospects for protection of privacy. Hong Kong was a British colony until 1997, when sovereign control was resumed by the People's Republic of China (PRC), and since then has been a Special Administrative Region (SAR) of the PRC. Its relatively short history of privacy protection is shaped by the conditions of that 'handover' of sovereignty.

The colonial administration's desire to legislate on pre-handover 'unfinished business', particularly in relation to protection of civil rights, gave Hong Kong a data protection law, the *Privacy (Personal Data) Ordinance* of 1995. Hong Kong is still the only Asian jurisdiction that has a Privacy Commissioner. The continuation of UK-influenced common law means that, as in the UK, there is no common law right of privacy. Hong Kong's 'high degree of autonomy' (*Sino-British Declaration* 1985) from the PRC involves only limited democracy. The Chief Executive is appointed by the Central People's Government. The members of his 'cabinet', the Executive Council, are all appointed by him. Legislation is made by a 60-member Legislative Council (LegCo), of which half are elected by direct elections from geographical constituencies and the other half from functional constituencies such as specified occupational groups and industries. Despite a decade of stability since the 1997 handover, there is little 'democratic dividend' for Hong Kong beyond a slight increase in the number of elected representatives. Although it is restrained in its interference, the mainland government shows no immediate sign of allowing Hong Kong to become more democratically governed, let alone fully democratic.

Uses of the ID card and number

In practice, the main official uses of the ID card (as distinct from the ID number) have been the requirement to produce it on demand to Police or Immigration Officers, as a travel document in some circumstances (particularly in travelling to and from the People's Republic of China), and to present to prospective employers (Waters and Clarke 2000: 29).

Where required, 'in all dealings with government', individuals must provide their ID card numbers and the numbers of any other persons for whom they are required to produce details, such as family members notwithstanding any other law to the contrary (ROPO s5(1)(b)). This has been one of the main factors leading to the largely unconstrained range of uses of the ID number in the public sector. It has accustomed people to producing their ID cards as well, since that is a convenient way to provide and 'verify' your number. Common situations of use of the ID number by government include: its inclusion on the driver's licence (and hence its availability to anyone to whom that license is produced); its use by the Inland Revenue as the primary identifier for individuals; its compulsory collection by employers; its use in police systems (Waters and Clarke 2000: 30); and its use as the file number of hospital patients.

In the absence of any law that prevented this, use of the card and number in the private sector has also been widespread. They were required to be disclosed or presented to a wide range of private sector organizations. The number was recorded in the visitors' books of businesses and apartments, and on contracts, demanded at the scenes of accidents and so on (Waters and Clarke 2000: 30). Production of the card is often required to verify a number already provided.

The use of number and card for many purposes created a great deal of convenience for individuals as well as business and government. Proving one's identity was, and is, a simple matter in Hong Kong, the one caveat being that only government authorities have the means to ascertain whether the ID card or number that is proffered is lost, stolen or a good counterfeit.

Post-1997 controls

Privacy Ordinance and ID number code

Hong Kong's 1995 *Personal Data (Privacy) Ordinance* (PDPO 1995) is a conventional 'European style' data protection law, based around Data Protection Principles (DPPs). Its enforcement mechanisms are weaker than most, with no effective means for victims of breaches to gain compensation, and a sporadically-used criminal enforcement process. The Privacy Commissioner's office has been energetic in securing government and business compliance with the Ordinance, in a culture that respects laws and authority.

In 1997, the Privacy Commissioner issued a Code of Practice on the ID number (HKPCO 1997), as required by the Ordinance (PDPO 1995: s12(8)). The Code's purpose is to specify, as a rebuttable matter of law, how the Ordinance applies to the ID number (PDPO 1995: s12), so the Commissioner was in effect required to work out whether existing uses of the number breached the DPPs. As a result of ROPO s5 the Code could not impose limits on the collection of ID numbers by government agencies, and it was questionable how it could affect other aspects of its public sector use. The Ordinance imposed separate controls on data matching. In relation to the private sector, the Commissioner was not so constrained. This was a historic opportunity to control the uses of the ID number and therefore the card, but the opportunity was lost when the Commissioner took the view that 'roll-back' was not a viable option, even in the private sector, in the absence of specific statutory direction or a strong body of public opinion calling for this.

In the public sector, the Code (HKPCO 1997) does not impose limits on the collection of ID numbers by government agencies. It also allows the ID numbers to be used as multi-purpose internal identifiers by any organization. The controls the Commissioner can impose on data matching because of other powers in the Ordinance take on greater significance in this context because the ability of Hong Kong agencies to collect and use ID numbers makes matching exercises so much easier. In the private sector, the Code allows routine collection of ID numbers by any organization that requires some reliability of identification in order to avoid non-trivial losses (HKPCO 1997: para 2.6.3). Although private bodies cannot legally compel disclosure, they can make it a condition of doing business with an individual. It allows such numbers to be used as multi-purpose internal identifiers by any organization. Copies of cards (e.g. by fax) may be required to verify identity remotely. ID numbers may be shared with other private sector organizations where collected for 'a purpose shared by both' but if the disclosure is for purposes of 'data matching', it would have to satisfy the separate rules that the Ordinance imposes on such activities. Prior to the introduction of the smart ID card, the main protection against more extensive use of ID numbers by the private sector has been the diffi-culty of collecting ID numbers by automated means.

The breadth of use of the ID card and number in Hong Kong is indicated by the diversity and number of complaints about them reported by the Commissioner (see HKPCO cases 2007; WorldLII cases 2007). The Commissioner's findings in these complaints also illustrate that, while the Code is very permissive, it is still possible to breach it and the DPPs underlying it (see Greenleaf 2007). Excessive collection (DPP 1) is not a source of complaints of importance, given the Code's liberal acceptance of collection of ID numbers. Wrongful disclosure (DPP 3) allegations make up more than half of the complaints received. Examples of where breaches have been found include a newspaper publishing a copy of a witness's statement including his ID number and name; a prosecuting authority providing a witness statement to a defendant including the witness's ID number; a finance company disclosing to its debt collector a copy of a debtor's ID card; a business disclosing an ex-employee's ID number to customers to stop him poaching business; inclusion of ID numbers in data provided to an affiliated company; a property company's dis-closure of tenants' ID numbers and other particulars to an affiliated 'club' that pro-vided services. The security principle (DPP 4) is also invoked where actions cause inadvertent disclosures, or make it easier for disclosures to others to occur. Breaches have occurred where a company used the first six digits of its customers' ID numbers as the default password; and where envelope printing errors or losses of a PC in a taxi have caused wholesale disclosure of customer ID numbers.

The 'smart' ID card system

A chip-based 'smart' ID card for Hong Kong was first proposed within the Hong Kong government in 1999 as part of a review of the Information Systems Strategy of the Immigration Department (ImmD), and a project team was established. In early 2000, it came to public attention through a discussion paper presented to

LegCo in the course of ImmD seeking funds for a position to oversee the project, and a succession of feasibility studies and reports followed (see Waters and Clarke 2000: Part III). The ImmD had requested consultants to advise on the feasibility of the smart ID system being used not only for its core business of immigration control, but also for other applications generally, including voter registration.

In March, the Privacy Commissioner expressed concerns in public about the risks of 'function creep' and recommended a Privacy Impact Assessment (PIA). Some legislators expressed concern about privacy issues, and attempted to link this issue to other proposed legislation concerning treason, sedition etc. (the 'Article 23' proposals). A PIA was completed for ImmD in November 2000 (Waters and Clarke 2000). Although an abridged version became available sometime late in 2002, its recommendations were largely ignored in the LegCo debates, and perhaps were unknown by most participants. The quality of public debate was diminished as a result.

The intended scope of the proposed system remained uncertain throughout the political debates of 2001–2002. It is clear that various agencies in the Hong Kong administration took the view that the new ID system had unlimited potential for expansion of uses. By 2000, the Information Technology and Broadcasting Bureau (ITBB) was coordinating a separate investigation into potential applications for a multi-application smart card, and this seems to be the genesis of the inclusion of the driver's licence, library card and digital signature functions in the smart ID card. Other functions were considered by ITBB including as a health card, for voting, and as a senior citizens concession card (Waters and Clarke 2000: 41). In December 2001, well into the debates, the ITBB (2001) said '[t]he potential use of the chip is large and new possible functions are emerging all the time'. The ITBB subsequently pointed out that the separate 'card face data' segment will give 'flexibility' and will allow 'case by case' approval of other applications for the purpose of 'authenticating citizens before services are provided' (ITBB 2002).

In mid-2002 a Bill to amend the ROPO to enable the introduction of the smart ID card was introduced to LegCo (*ROP Amendment Bill* 2001), together with an indicative draft by ImmD of likely amendments to the ROP Regulations (ROPR 2007). By this time, the administration had reduced the proposed initial functions of the smart ID card to four functions in addition to immigration control: a driver's licence; a library card; a token to carry a digital signature; and an authenticator to access e-government services. The administration insisted that all of these uses were voluntary, and that the only compulsory use of the card was for its normal immigration functions.

After hearings by LegCo committees, the legislation was passed in early 2003. Only a dozen organizations and individuals gave evidence or made submissions (LegCo 2001: Appendix II). Only two were critical (Greenleaf 2001; Lee 2002) and the Administration attempted a detailed rebuttal of one (HK Administration Response to Greenleaf 2002). The Committee's Report (LegCo 2001) endorsed the Administration's general approach, but stressed that 'the storage of [any non-ROP] data in a chip requires the consent of the card holder' and that this should be reflected in both the Ordinance and Regulations.

During this whole period of 2000–2003, there was no significant public disquiet at the proposed changes to the ID system. Hong Kong's newspapers took only intermittent interest, when prompted by some LegCo development, and no public protest, NGO opposition or even letters to the editor appeared. However, in June 2003, only a couple of months after the ID legislation passed, an estimated half a million people from a population of 6 million took to the streets to protest against attempts by the government to introduce a 'security' law.

The new Hong Kong ID card is a contact smart card which contains on its face the same information as the previous card. The chip on the card contains all of this information in a separate 'card face segment' and separately contains templates of two fingerprints. In some cases, it contains a digital signature and PIN, where the user has allowed a digital signature (a HK Post eCert) to be added.

The 'rollout' of smart cards to replace the existing ID cards started in 2003 and was only completed in March 2007. As of September 2007, all previous ID cards are invalid, and those who have failed to apply in time are potentially liable for a fine of HK$5,000 (HK Administration 2007). The effects of the smart ID card have therefore not yet been fully felt by Hong Kong's citizens. Both claims of its benign effect, and arguments about its potential abuses (as are found in this chapter) are still largely predictive.

The inadequacies of controls on function creep

The core problem of the Hong Kong ID system is the failure to define its purpose with precision. This was so with the previous 'dumb' paper-based system. Its conversion into a smart card-based system exacerbates that problem by being based around an intended but undefined expansion of functions, coupled with greater technological possibilities. To warn of this risk is not to posit a 'function creep conspiracy'. It is likely that the authors of future function creep will have had nothing to do with the introduction of the smart ID card, they will merely be opportunistic beneficiaries of the loopholes that have been created.

The longer-term risks of ID system expansion, while they did not capture the imagination of the Hong Kong public, were clear to some local commentators: 'The risk is that the smart ID card, once extensively used for all purposes, may enable the government and other personal data users to use the card as a means of abusive social control and massive invasion of privacy. This is the evil we must guard against' (Lee 2002: para 2).

The main question this chapter seeks to answer is to what extent did Hong Kong guard against the 'evil' about which Lee warns, when it enacted legislation to introduce the smart ID card in 2003? It could have been the appropriate time for LegCo to more precisely define the circumstances under which government agencies collect and use the ID number, and to re-assess the use of the ID number by the private sector. Even if it could not define all possible future acceptable uses of the ID card and number, LegCo could have ensured it had powers to examine proposed future expansions and approve them if they were in the public interest. In other words, it could have ensured legislative oversight of function creep. Like any identification system, Hong Kong's smart ID system cannot be understood by focusing on the ID card alone. We must also consider the ROP database that stands behind the card, and the ID number, the use of which is facilitated by the card and its chip.

New uses of the card and chip

The amended ROPO and ROPR give LegCo weak control over the expansion of uses of the smart ID card and chip. We need to consider both new functions that require changes to the card or chip, and those that do not.

Despite improvements made to the Bill during the legislative process, it still allows new content to be added to the card or chip, enabling new uses, merely by amendments to regulations. Such regulations do not require positive LegCo approval, but can be disallowed by LegCo. It is also possible that new uses of the card/chip may not require amendment of any other Ordinance. Such additional information can only be included in identity cards or their chips 'with the consent of applicants for or holders of identity cards' (ROPO s7(2A)), as required by the LegCo Bills Committee. The Regulations add that the person to whom the card relates can have such data removed on request, and that the purpose of adding new data, and the data to be added, must be listed in Schedule 5 (ROPR cl 4A(1). Parties entitled to add such data do not need to be listed in Schedule 5, but only need to have the permission of the Commissioner of Registration to add data. As yet, only the HK Post eCert is listed (see Greenleaf 2007). Function creep in the chip without a new amending Ordinance is therefore limited to data which can be described as added by consent, a valuable limitation achieved through the legislative process and the submissions that warned that the Bill was too broad.

Despite this useful limitation, we need to consider the types of expansion by regulations that this still leaves open. As described above, the structure is already in place to allow private sector additions to the content of the chip, because the Commissioner of Registration can give permission to 'any person' to add data. Such permission will also constitute 'lawful authority' to store, alter or add to data in a chip, so that doing so is not an offence (ROPR cl 12(1A)). The way is therefore open for medical data, stored value 'purses' or other data to be added to the ID card, making it much more seriously 'multi functional' than it is at present. The only check on this is that regulations adding to Schedule 5 can be disallowed by LegCo, assuming that the issue appears important enough. The Bills Committee noted, and was apparently satisfied with, an Administration undertaking 'to brief the relevant Panels before introducing subsidiary legislation to provide for the incorporation of new non-ROP related applications on the card face of a smart ID card or in the chip ...' (LegCo 2001: para 33).

Any additional government use of the card that does not require additional data on the card does not require a Schedule 5 change, so there is no LegCo opportunity for scrutiny. New uses of the card can arise if any government agency decides to use the ID card in replacement for some identification card of its own, relying on the power to require a person to furnish their card number when dealing with government (ROPO s5). Sometimes there will need to be some coincidental change to other legislation, as with the need to carry a driver's licence, and the library card application (see HK Administration Response to Greenleaf 2002: 4.3). However, there is no reason to expect that such coincidental changes will always be needed, and it was not needed with the fourth initial ID card application, the online change-of-address facility. LegCo has no power to disallow such uses, unless it passes new legislation, and may not even become aware of some new uses. The potential expansion of the uses of the ID system is therefore not tied to changes of the card or chip, and can occur without LegCo scrutiny.

The use of card readers to do ID checks (including fingerprint comparisons) was originally proposed to be open to any 'authorized persons' approved by the Chief Executive, without any LegCo scrutiny of the exercise of this power (Greenleaf 2007). The Bills Committee took up the argument in submissions that this could be used to allow private sector security guards, or even some mainland government officials, to fingerprint people (Greenleaf 2002). Reg 11A was amended to restrict this power to 'a police officer or a member of the Immigration Service' who would have to have reason to believe that the person concerned held an ID card that was not theirs (ROPR 2003, Reg 11A).

Expanded uses of the ROP database

An ID system can only be understood in the context of the databases behind it. Waters and Clarke (2000) set out in the first PIA the extent of the ROP database, and warned that it would be more attractive to external users, once it was augmented by the smart ID system, because of its expanded digital content (see also Greenleaf 2001; Lee 2002: para 5). The permitted uses of the ROP database by the Immigration Department itself are very broad, and were made broader by the 2003 amendments (ROPO as amended 2003: s9): (1) to enable public officers to verify the identity of persons; (2) to enable verification of identity 'for any other lawful purpose' and (3) for 'such purposes as may be authorized, permitted or required by or under any Ordinance.' Other than for its power of disallowance of (3), if it notices, LegCo has no role in controlling the expansion of uses of the ROP database.

Powers to allow new forms of disclosure from the ROP database by the Immigration Department to external organizations are equally broad. New classes of users only require approval in writing from the Chief Secretary for Administration (ROPO as amended 2003: s11), and may apply to a 'class or category of persons by name, office or description'. No regulations subject to LegCo scrutiny are required, and the Privacy Commissioner does not have adequate powers to control these disclosures (Greenleaf 2007).

Expanded uses of the ID number

As outlined above, prior to the smart ID system, the collection of the ID card number in Hong Kong was already largely uncontrolled because of the weaknesses of the privacy Ordinance (PDPO 1995) and the ID Number Code (HKPCO 1997). In this permissive context, the introduction of the smart ID card would be likely to dramatically increase the collection and retention of ID numbers and their use to link internal organizational data, *provided* it brought with it greater ease of electronic capture of ID numbers and other basic identity information such as the name.

This risk is heightened by the existence of the 'card face segment'. There is a separate segment on the ID card chip for 'card face data' (ID number, name, DOB and date of issue), which can be accessed electronically by libraries as part of the proposed library card function, 'and on a case by case basis for other functions that may be approved in future' (ITBB 2002). The chip therefore has differential levels of security for different segments.

The new s12 (ROPO 2003) creates an offence where anyone 'without lawful authority or reasonable excuse, gains access to, stores, uses or discloses, any record kept by the Commissioner on particulars furnished to a registration officer' but it is still an open question whether accessing card face data is ever illegal because of this (Greenleaf 2007). However, the new Reg 12(1A) (ROPR 2003) is more effective, providing simply that 'any person who, without lawful authority or reasonable excuse … (b) gains access to any data stored in a chip' is guilty of an offence. The only exceptions are where a person accesses their own data via a government-approved facility, and where a third party is authorized under Schedule 5 (e.g. a HK Post eCert) (ROPR 2003: Reg 12(1B)), so the remaining question is who can give a third party 'lawful authority' to access data on the chip? The Administration's answer (HK Administration Response to Greenleaf 2002: para 3) is that the Commissioner of Registration can do so, and can enforce this because the card face data is encrypted (Greenleaf 2007).

It seems therefore that the 2003 legislation provides for bureaucratic discretion, coupled with technical control and criminal sanctions, to determine who can access the card face data. LegCo oversight does not seem to be a necessary part of the picture. These controls, while valuable, still allow the possibility that the Administration could authorize any private sector or public sector party to use card readers (with the appropriate cryptographic keys) to read and capture card face data. The weak controls in the PDPO and the Commissioner's Code would have little effect on limiting where this could occur (Greenleaf 2007).

In summary, the 2003 amendments authorizing the smart ID card system ensured that LegCo control of its expansion could be largely bypassed once it was safely in place. Whether in practice it will be bypassed, or whether the Administration will seek LegCo approval for all forms of expansion, is of course a different matter. LegCo has the capacity to disallow any regulations providing for the addition of any new data to the card or chip and the addition of any other parties entitled to do fingerprint checks. On the other hand, it does not have any general formal control over new uses of the ID card or chip which do not require new data to be added, new uses of the ROP database, expansion of disclosures from the ROP database or decisions as to who will be given the technical capacity to access the data on the card face segment of the chip. Therefore, too many matters have been left to administrative discretion, and put outside the formal powers of LegCo to disallow expansions.

The limited 'voluntariness' in the four new functions

The Administration claimed that all four initial non-immigration uses are voluntary. This is correct in two limited senses: (1) it is not compulsory for anyone to have extra information on the ID card, and (2) it is possible to carry out the four applications by means other than the use of an ID card. However, in relation to each proposed use, the 'voluntariness' is significantly limited or qualified, either in that (a) citizens/consumers will not remain unaffected by new uses even if they ostensibly opt out of them, or (b) they are not being given a genuinely non-discriminatory choice. They are better described as 'quasi-voluntary'. It can also be argued that '[e]ven if the adoption of non-immigration applications by the users is optional, convenience and usefulness will eventually dictate adoption' (Lee 2002: para 6).

More important, the label of 'voluntariness' does not answer the question of whether an additional use of the ID card should be allowed, either for these proposed uses or any in future. One result of the 2003 legislation is that LegCo has to a large extent lost its ability to control extensions of the use of the ID system, provided those extensions can be labeled 'voluntary' in the weak sense described above.

The following discussion is not necessarily a criticism of the four applications now being carried out by use of the existing Hong Kong smart ID system. Rather it is a criticism of the lack of thorough investigation of what was being proposed that took place before its introduction. Furthermore, it is not a criticism of the extent to which these applications really are voluntary, the value of which was underlined in the first PIA, subject to the caveat that it was 'not implemented in such as way as to make the choice of the application a practical necessity' (Waters and Clarke 2000: 64). As the PIA authors recognized, voluntariness is not a slogan or an absolute: it needs examination.

Driver's licence on backend computer

It is proposed that the ID card will also serve in lieu of a driver's licence. At present, all drivers have a plastic licence which can be inspected by police. It is therefore not necessary in many cases for police who have pulled over a driver to do a 'backend' check, as they can readily establish that the person does hold a driver's licence and the driver's identity (if necessary by also requiring production of ID card with photo). They cannot check if it has been suspended unless they contact the backend system.

Under the new system, the default position will be that drivers will not have a separate licence (the plastic licence) unless they opt-in in order to obtain one. There will be no licence data on the ID card chip. Instead, the licence will be constituted by the data on the backend computer, which the police will access through a person providing their ID card. If (as seems likely) most drivers will not opt-in to obtain the plastic licence, then police who have pulled over a driver will always need to do a backend check, as they otherwise cannot even establish that the person has ever held a driver's licence. The Administration claims that 'circumstances for checking should be no different from (not more comprehensive than) the current practice' (HK Administration Response to Greenleaf 2002: para 1.1). This does not seem to be correct if most drivers will no longer hold a visible licence.

Furthermore, where a person does opt-in to obtain a plastic licence, police checking of the backend database could still become more likely than it was before. Holders of plastic driver's licences will not be exempt from producing their ID card 'for inspection' (ROPR 2003: Reg 11). Police will still be able to ask for production of an ID number so as to verify the person's identity (ROPO 2003: s5). The ID card may be able to be swiped, once police are equipped with card readers for online checks. If this becomes commonplace, then the plastic licence may indeed become meaningless in interactions with police, and only be used for hiring cars, overseas driving and other interactions where a visible licence is essential.

This change is only 'voluntary' if you consider that a requirement to opt-in in order to maintain the status quo is 'voluntary'. This is a compulsory change to a substantially different system from which you can only partly opt-out. It is not necessarily an objectionable change (particularly given that Hong Kong driver's licences are already based on ID number) but it is certainly not voluntary.

Library card use

The Leisure and Cultural Services Department (LCSD) will be able to read/copy electronically from the chip all data on the face of the card ('card face data') (ITBB 2002). No other proposed application requires reading only that data. The library application is the first of what may be other applications for 'authenticating citizens before services are provided' based on reading card face data, and it is very important for that reason. Without the library application, there would have been no current need to design a card with a separate card face segment. By adding what ITBB describes as the 'straight-forward and non-controversial' library application (ITBB 2002), the basis for many possible extended uses has been designed into the card from the outset.

The library card application 'has been designed to use the ID card number as a matching key to the library card number' (HK Administration Response to Greenleaf 2002: 1.4). This increases the risk that a person's library borrowings could become known to others because it is easier to find out a person's ID number than their library number. No doubt security measures have been taken to prevent this from happening, but the risk has been increased through correlation with another numbering system. A person's borrowing of books or films is sensitive information, which can indicate beliefs and interests, especially important in a jurisdiction which is part of the PRC.

It seems that this application will be 'voluntary' in the stronger 'opt-in' sense because at least existing library users will have to apply to use their smart ID card for library purposes (HK Smart ID 2007: 'Library Services' section). There was no need for the ID number to be used as the library number. The library card number could have been stored on a separate component on the ID card, providing the convenience of dispensing with a separate library card, without the dangers of expanding use of the ID number into another information system (Bacon-Shone, pers comm 2007). The Administration rejected this argument on the grounds of cost and arguable inconvenience if an ID card was lost or remote services were being used (HK Administration Response to Greenleaf 2002: para 1.4).

HK Post eCert on the chip

During the 'rollout' of the HK smart ID card from 2003–2007, all persons obtaining new cards have been offered the option of including a digital signature on the ID card chip, the e-Cert provided by Hong Kong Post. Use of the e-Cert was free for a period of time. The 'voluntariness' of this arrangement has to be considered in the context of what freedom of choice have Hong Kong citizens been given in obtaining and using digital signatures.

First, in 2007 no digital signature other than an e-Cert from HK Post can be included on a smart ID card, five years after the Administration's 2002 claim that it will 'consider allowing digital certificates by recognized certification authorities (CAs) ... other than HKPost' on the ID card 'when there is strong public support' (HK Administration Response to Greenleaf 2002: para 1.2). This statement conveniently ignored that: (1) there is no evidence of 'strong public support' for a government-provided digital signature on the chip; and (2) no other CA provider will ever be given the opportunity to ask all SAR residents whether they agree to have their company's digital signature on the chip.

The privacy dangers of digital signatures on ID cards are largely a matter of future occurrence, not of current policy or practice in Hong Kong. One danger of digital signatures on a government ID card arises from abuses of government power in breach of the law (e.g. governments obtaining access to the private key, or capturing data relating to digital signature use). Other dangers would require legislative changes, such as requirements that an ID number always be used in conjunction with a digital signature, or vice-versa, in electronic transactions. These potential dangers are less if there are multiple signature providers. The likelihood of collaboration in abuses is greatly reduced by the number of parties involved. The likelihood of effective opposition by signature providers to undesirable legislative changes is greater the more providers there are.

It is true that digital signature certificates are available on other media and from other providers in Hong Kong, but the only option put in front of every eligible person in Hong Kong was for a (free) HK Post e-Certs on an ID card. In theory, citizens were free to choose, but in practice, they may not have been making an informed choice. Despite its 'first mover advantage', HK Post has been unable to achieve a high take-up of e-Certs, with only 0.28% of those issued being renewed when payment was required, and only 10% of those issued ever being used (Ming Po 2007). The potential dangers of a government-endorsed *de facto* digital signature monopoly coupled with an ID card are unlikely to materialize for the present. The HK government is no longer requiring eCerts for online tax returns, and is allowing PINs instead (Bacon-Shone, pers comm 2007).

The Administration claimed that to allow for signatures from multiple CAs on one card would raise 'more issues on privacy protection' (HK Administration Response to Greenleaf 2002: 1.2). All this means is that it would have needed to get the protective measures right at the outset. The provision of only the e-Cert on the chip was and is unjustifiably discriminatory, denying citizens the full choice that should have been available to them. Also, if the use of a digital signature is ever made the only practical option in other contexts (as discussed below), this reduces the extent of voluntariness in holding an e-Cert on the smart card. Voluntariness is a matter of degree, here as elsewhere.

Online change of address use

'ESD Life' is the Hong Kong government's online service for provision of e-government services (ESD Life 2007). In 2002, use of a HK Post eCert was compulsory for online change of address with multiple government departments via ESD kiosks, but an additional Certification Authority (Digi-Sign) has now been approved. The HK Post e-Cert was also proposed as the only way by which drivers would be able to check the status of their licences online. It has also been the only way by which one could participate in voting by shareholders online (Webb 2002). The main issue here is whether the exclusive relationship between the e-Cert and the ID card is giving Hong Kong residents as full a choice of options for *electronic* change of address and other functions as is reasonably practicable. To the extent that it is necessary to use a HK Post e-Cert – as distinct from other authentication methods or other providers – in order to carry out online transactions, this application becomes less voluntary than it seems.

The smart ID card is not the only token on which the e-Cert may be carried. It is also possible to inform government departments by post or personal attendance of a change of address, but that is increasingly unattractive to many people – and to government. An alternative means of accessing government services, authentication by a PIN stored on the ID card, was explicitly rejected by the Information Technology and Broadcasting Bureau (ITBB), which proposed that the e-Cert use will be the only method implemented on the ID card without giving any convincing justification (see Greenleaf 2007). This unwillingness to consider inclusion of a PIN on the ID card seems to undermine its argument that the use of the e-Cert on the ID card is 'voluntary and non-discriminatory' (HK Administration Response to Greenleaf 2002: para 1.3). Users are denied the widest possible choice of options in electronic transactions.

In summary, the use of the ID card as a driver's licence is only 'voluntary' if a requirement to opt-in in order to maintain the status quo (i.e. keep a plastic licence) is 'voluntary'. The library card example illustrates how LegCo ought to consider the full context of even a 'straight-forward and non-controversial' application, and the cost-benefits of alternatives, before deciding whether it is justified. The provision of only the e-Cert on the chip was and is unjustifiably discriminatory. It unjustifiably denies citizens choice and is not 'voluntary'. Similarly, lack of other authentication mechanisms, such as a PIN on the ID card, undermines the argument that the use of the e-Cert on the ID card is 'voluntary and non-discriminatory'. Voluntariness is a matter of degree in arguments about identification, a relevant factor but not a conclusive one. These four examples show why close LegCo scrutiny of the whole context in which any proposed expansions of the ID system will operate is necessary. LegCo, not the Administration, should decide whether each change is in the public interest or involves unjustifiable dangers. 'Voluntariness' is a red herring, if used to deflect the need for proper legislative scrutiny.

Conclusions

Designed to be out of control

What could Hong Kong learn from its experience in re-building its ID system? The most obvious thing is that LegCo oversight has been diminished more than it should have been, partly because of exaggeration of the importance of 'voluntariness'.

Ongoing privacy impact assessments needed

If LegCo regained more oversight of the proposed expansions of the system, it should have some process for obtaining independent expert advice, because the issues are complex and the Administration should not be allowed to completely set the agenda. Despite various calls to do so (Waters and Clarke 2000; Lee 2002; Greenleaf 2002), the Immigration Department (ImmD) did not obtain a proper Privacy Impact Assessment (PIA) on the non-immigration uses of the ID card (see Greenleaf 2007).

There may be many more proposed applications of the ID system in years to come. LegCo should implement a better process by which it can approve or disapprove *any* proposed expansions on the basis of comprehensive, expert and independent PIAs. The ROPO would ideally be amended to require them, with the terms of reference for the PIA(s) requiring approval by LegCo, to ensure that all implications are canvassed, including whether or not the application should be an allowed use of the ID card. It should be necessary for PIAs to be published in sufficient time to allow public comment before LegCo assesses them.

The Privacy Commissioner should at least comment, to help ensure that the PIA consultant had appropriate privacy expertise. The Commissioner should have an ongoing pro-active oversight over the uses and expansions of the ID system, and could have more immediate and concrete input than a PIA, which might have to be justified in each instance. It is also possible that Hong Kong's bureaucrats might be more respectful of intervention by one of their own with established expertise and credentials.

A comprehensive code for the ID system is needed

The first PIA recommended a comprehensive code controlling all aspects of Hong Kong's ID system:

From a privacy perspective, it is desirable for the objectives of the HKSAR ID Card system to be expressly specified in law. The current situation, where there is a statutory framework for Registration, and for access to registration data; but where the uses of the Card and Card Number are not defined and only loosely controlled, is unsatisfactory. A comprehensive statutory framework for the ID card system as a whole, including registration and uses of the card and card number, would provide important privacy protection, and give re-assurance to the HK population in the face of concerns about 'function creep' and increased surveillance. It would also clarify and remove any uncertainty over the authority for specific uses and disclosures.

(Waters and Clarke 2000: 63)

The Administration claims that the current composite of the PDPO, the ID number Code, the ROPO and the ROPR, and the Immigration Ordinance, constitute such a comprehensive code (HK Administration Response to Greenleaf 2002: 5.3), but the numerous gaps and inconsistencies, let alone their nearly incomprehensible scatter over these documents, mean that this is not so.

Enactment of a comprehensive code could also provide an opportunity for a re-assessment by LegCo of all of the ways in which both the public and private sectors use the ID system, or may do so in future. The development of such a code would be an ideal assignment for Hong Kong's Law Reform Commission, which has extensive experience in privacy issues.

Caution in ID expansion appropriate in Hong Kong

The political context is the appropriate point on which to conclude this chapter. ID systems are an important element in the mechanisms by which States exercise control over populations. Fully democratic political systems have more checks and balances by which potential abuses of ID systems may be prevented. Expansions of ID systems carry a lower level of risk in such systems. An unavoidable factor which should be considered in this instance of the re-making of an ID system is that Hong Kong is part of the People's Republic of China (PRC). Although it does have a high degree of autonomy it does not have complete control over its political destiny. The PRC is not a democracy, nor is Hong Kong a full democracy. After ten years its democratic future is still uncertain (HK Administration 2007a).

When all these factors are considered, it seems appropriate for Hong Kong to take a very cautious approach to any proposals for expanded uses of its ID system. This is particularly so when the change to a smart card-based system is in itself a major technological and social change which may have consequences and difficulties not yet foreseen. The Administration claimed in 2002 that it was already taking a cautious approach (HK Administration Response to Greenleaf 2002: 5.6), and it is true that there has not been a headlong rush into more applications. Nevertheless, the current approach leaves too much control in the hands of the Administration and not in the hands of the more democratic body, LegCo. It is not yet a cautious enough approach, because the Administration trusts itself too much. There are insufficient checks against the temptation for expansion, which may become more powerful now that the rollout of the new smart ID system is complete.

In the re-making of the Hong Kong ID card from 2000–2003 the Administration got most of what it proposed: a technically sophisticated smart ID card system; no defined limitations on the eventual expansion of the system; a system that was (modestly) multi-functional from the start; and the ability to expand many aspects of the system with little likely interference from LegCo in the form of disallowances or need for LegCo approval. It is an ID system that is out of the control of the semi-elected representatives and largely under the control of Hong Kong's mandarins.

Note

1 Professor of Law, University of New South Wales and Director, Cyberspace Law and Policy Centre; formerly, Distinguished Visiting Professor, University of Hong Kong Faculty of Law 2001–2002. Work on this chapter was written in part as work on an Australian Research Council Discovery project, 'Interpreting Privacy Principles'; It was written while the author was a Visiting Fellow at the AHRB Research Centre in Intellectual Property and Technology Law, University of Edinburgh Faculty of Law. The assistance provided by Nigel Waters and Roger Clarke's 'Initial Privacy Impact Assessment Report' is acknowledged and will be obvious from the numerous references to it. Valuable comments were provided by Robin McLeish and Professor John Bacon-Shone. Joeson Wong, PhD student at UNSW provided information concerning e-Certs.

Bibliography

APEC (2004) 'Asia-Pacific Economic Cooperation (APEC) APEC Privacy Framework', APEC. Online. Available: http://www.asianlii.org/apec/other/agrmt/apf209/

Basic Law (1990) 'Basic Law of the Hong Kong Special Administrative Region', adopted 4 April, by the Seventh National People's Congress of the People's Republic of China, Third Session.

Berthold, M. and Wacks, R. (2002) 'Hong Kong Data Privacy Law: Territorial Regulation in a Borderless World Thomson', Hong Kong: Sweet & Maxwell Asia.

BORO (1991) 'Bill of Rights Ordinance', Ch. 383, *Laws of Hong Kong*, enacted 1991.

ESD Life (2007) (Hong Kong SAR government). Online. Available: http://www.esdlife.com/home/eng/default.asp

Ghai, Y. (1999) *Hong Kong's New Constitutional Order, The Resumption of Chinese Sovereignty and the Basic Law*, Hong Kong University Press, 1997.

Greenleaf, G. (2001) 'Submission to Bills Committee on Registration of Persons (Amendment) Bill', Hong Kong Legislative Council, October 2002. Online. Available: http://www2.austlii.edu.au/privacy/articles/hkidcard/

Greenleaf, G. (2002) 'Submission on the smart ID Card and the Registration of Persons (Amendment) Bill'; Hong Kong Legislative Council, October. Online. Available: http://www2.austlii.edu.au/privacy/articles/hkidcard/

Greenleaf, G. (2002a) 'Summary Submission Concerning the 'Smart' ID Card and the Registration of Persons (Amendment) Bill', LegCo Paper No. CB(2) 2620/01-02(01). Online. Available: http://www.legco.gov.hk/yr01-02/english/bc/bc56/papers/bc561011-2620-1e-scan.pdf

Greenleaf, G. (2007) 'Hong Kong's 'smart' ID card: The legal framework for function creep'. Online. Available: http://law.bepress.com/unswwps/

HK Administration Response to Greenleaf (2001) 'Information Paper on the Registration of Persons (Amendment) Bill 2001,' LEGCO PAPER NO. CB(2)21/02-03(01), 11 October 2002. Online. Available: http://www.legco.gov.hk/yr01-02/english/bc/bc-56/papers/bc561011cb2-21-1e.pdf (accessed 10 October 2007).

HK Administration (2002) 'Provision of Registration of Persons records', LC Paper No. CB(2) 150/02-03(01). Online. Available: http://www.legco.gov.hk/yr01-02/english/bc/bc56/papers/bc561028cb2-150-1e.pdf

HK Administration (2002a) 'HKSAR Identity Card Project – Latest Developments and the Second Privacy Impact Assessment Report', CB(2)2433/01-02(07), 10 July 2002. Online. Available: http://www.legco.gov.hk/yr01-2/english/panels/se/papers/se0710cb2-2433-7e.pdf

HK Administration (2007) 'Invalidation of old identity cards'. Online. Available: http://www.smartid.gov.hk/en/replace/invalidation.html

HK Administration (2007a) 'Green Paper on Constitutional Development'. Online. Available: http://www.cmab-gpcd.gov.hk/doc/GPCD-e.pdf

HKPCO (1997) 'Hong Kong Privacy Commissioner Code of Practice on the Identity Card Number and other Personal Identifiers'.

HKPCO (1997a) 'Transfer of Personal Data outside Hong Kong: Some Common Questions', Fact Sheet 1. Online. Available: http://www.pcpd.org.hk/english/publications/guid_note.html

HKPCO (2007) 'Complaint Case Notes and Enquiry Case Notes'. Online. Available: http://www.pcpd.org.hk/english/casenotes/case.html

HK Post e-Cert (2007) 'Hong Kong Post e-Cert Home page'. Online. Available: http://www.hongkongpost.gov.hk/index.html (accessed 8 October 2007).

HK Smart ID (2007) 'Government of Hong Kong Smart ID Home page'. Online. Available: http://www.smartid.gov.hk/en/ (accessed 8 October 2007).

ITBB (2001) 'Non-immigration applications for incorporation into the Smart ID Card', 20 December.

ITBB (2002) 'Update on non-immigration applications for incorporation into the Smart ID Card', 4 July.

Lee, M. (2002) 'Submission from Professor Matthew Lee to LegCo', CB(2)2785/01-02(02), 11 October.

LegCo (2001) 'Hong Kong Legislative Council Report of the Bills Committee on Registration of Persons (Amendment) Bill 2001', LC Paper No. CB(2)1473/02-03. Online. Available: http://www.legco.gov.hk/yr01-02/english/bc/bc56/reports/bc560319cb2-1473-e.pdf

Ming Po (2006, 2007) 'Chinese language newspaper', Hong Kong, 3 and 4 November 2006, 27 June 2007.

PDPO (1995) 'Personal Data (Privacy) Ordinance', Hong Kong. Online. Available: http://www.hklii.org

Privacy Law Project (2003) 'World Legal Information Institute (World LII) Privacy Law Project', commenced 2003 and ongoing. Online. Available: http://www.worldlii.org/int/special/privacy/ Includes Office of the Privacy Commissioner for Personal Data Hong Kong Case Notes and Office of the Privacy Commissioner for Personal Data, Hong Kong Administrative Appeal Board Case Notes.

ROPO (n.d.) 'Registration of Persons Ordinance'. Online. Available: http://www.hklii.hk/hk/legis/en/ord/177/

ROPR (2003/2007) 'Registration of Persons Regulations' (Hong Kong). Online. Available: http://www.hklii.hk/hk/legis/en/reg/177A/index.html

ROPR (n.d.) 'Registration of Persons Regulations'. Online. Available: http://www.hklii.hk/hk/legis/en/reg/177A/

ROP Amendment Bill (2001) 'Registration of Persons (Amendment) Ordinance 2003', September 2003.

Waters, N. and Clarke, R. (2000) 'Initial Privacy Impact Assessment Report', Pacific Privacy Pty Ltd. Abridged version of consultancy report to HKSAR Identity Card Project. Online. Available: http://www.legco.gov.hk/yr00-01/english/fc/esc/papers/esc27e1.pdf (accessed 8 October 2007).

Webb, D.M. (2002) 'DeVoted to failure – HK's share voting system'. Online. Available: http://webb-site.com/articles/devoted2failure.htm

Wikipedia (2007) 'Hong Kong Identity Card', 8 October.

WorldLII (2007) World Legal Information Institute, Privacy Law Library. Online. Available: http://www.worldlii.org/int/special/privacy/

6 A tale of the colonial age, or the banner of new tyranny?

National identification card systems in Japan

Midori Ogasawara

Introduction

In 2002, I visited South Korea to report on its national identification (ID) card system, which requires all nationals over 17 years old to carry a card. At the time, I subconsciously viewed this system as a vestige of a bygone age, lingering in a 'less-advanced' country. The Korean system, called the Resident Registration System, originated with the military dictatorship in the middle of the Cold War, and criticism of the system has been rising during Korea's democratization. As a reporter for a national newspaper, I covered the problems of the Korean system pertaining to privacy and democracy in order to warn the Japanese, whose government was about to implement a similar ID network. As I investigated the story, I came to realize the contradictions of adopting a 1960s anti-spy-system in the twenty-first century. And I wondered: If the Korean system is a remnant of the death squads of the Cold War, then where is Japan heading?[1]

Since the American 'war on terror' was declared, our reversion to the past has seemed to accelerate. A neo-liberal view of risk management, which thinks that scientific knowledge can calculate and eliminate risks in advance (Sakai 2001), has flourished in global policies, especially in national security of sorting out the population into 'terrorist' or 'innocent'. In this view, everyone has the potential to commit harmful acts against the state and capital – this is a matter of chance rather than individuality or social structure. So the new systems seek to control *everybody* beyond the borders of insider/outsider or citizen/non-citizen. As a means of targeting whole populations, national ID card systems are now being proposed in a number of 'advanced' countries, such as the United Kingdom and the United States, where ID systems were used in the past to check on the movements of foreigners, immigrants, and colonial natives (Cole 2001; Parenti 2003). The colonial surveillance that had targeted people outside of the national borders now covers insiders as well with new 'smart' technologies.

The national ID card system has colonial roots in Japan, too. One of the first examples was in North-east China in the 1920s, where the Japanese militarily occupied and declared 'the state of Manchuria'. Another early case was the Korean and Chinese workers in Japan, who were forced to contribute to the war economy until 1945. Fingerprinting underpinned these ID card systems to watch over the *enemy-within* in the empire. Although Japan lost all of its colonies with its surrender after the Second World War, the system survived and crystallized into the Alien Registration Card System in post-war Japan, involving intensive surveillance over the formerly colonial population, mainly the Koreans and Chinese. The ex-colonial natives were unilaterally categorized as aliens and deprived of Japanese nationality, although they stayed in Japan. This system still requires registered foreigners to carry the cards today. Fingerprinting had been part of the registration procedure until 2000 when ongoing resistance by Koreans and Chinese led to the abolition of fingerprinting. However, this biometric technique has returned to the immigration system in November 2007, no longer by ink and paper, but by biometric digital device.[2] Immigration takes fingerprints and photographs of almost all foreigners over the age of sixteen who enter Japan. It records this information digitally and compares it with the fingerprints and photographs on 'blacklists' (Ministry of Justice 2006; Immigration Bureau 2006).

Over nationals, modern Japan has established two kinds of identification system: Koseki and Juki-net. Koseki records personal information of each family and traces relationships of family members. Koseki emerged in the late nineteenth century, during Japan's drive to build up its modern state, catch up with the Western powers, and cultivate and shape its national population. The system embodied a patriarchal concept of family and played a role in educating individuals about the desirable forms of family and marriage for the modern state, and about the desirable relations between the emperor and his subjects. Koseki strictly excludes 'foreigners' and so represents membership in the state, but is not clearly citizenship as has been developed in Western history. Koseki rather fabricates an image of unity for the 'Japanese', the subjects of the nation-state, by repressing ethnic, linguistic and cultural diversities in Japan. It has a structure of the disciplinary power that Foucault suggests enhances patriarchy and nationalism. But the power operates not only in a panoptic way from the state to the individuals, Foucault reveals, but also in a lateral way among the family members and a synoptic from the society to the individual.

Juki-net, the most recent Japanese ID system, which I compare with the Korean ID system, is a computer network that lists every Japanese person by ID number and allows the government to share personal information on that number. It also supplies the optional ID cards containing an integrated circuit (IC) chip that can carry different types of memories for multi-use. Juki-net has expanded its data and purpose since its implementation in 2002. Similar to Koseki, Juki-net excludes non-nationals and includes nationals from the newborn to the elderly. But, unlike Koseki, it has innovative characteristics based on the new capacities of computer networks and data-mining. The state can transgress the classic boundaries of administration on the network, and so it can arbitrarily divide and aggregate personal information for various purposes. The boundaries that had once protected the individual by acting as a wall of defence for collective entity and action, can no longer protect the individual. Juki-net gives the state individualistic, fluid and direct intervention in personal life, that is superimposed on Japan's disciplinary society.

This chapter examines the colonial roots of the modern national ID system and the ways that they have resurfaced in contemporary Japanese identification initiatives. I argue that Koseki has been a powerful technique to maintain social categories and orders, controlling from interpersonal relation to the relation between the citizen and the state. Meanwhile, the colonial technique of the Alien Registration Card has made non-citizens visible and traceable with intensive surveillance, and has excluded their political power from the society. In addition, the state is using the new techniques to dissolve modern categories and directly intervene in individuals' lives. The individual can be exposed to multi-dimensions of surveillance by arbitrary data-mining in the latest complex of ID systems. Juki-net appears as part of a global strategy in this context: the individualistic and totalitarian security system.

Koseki: Constructing nationals

Documenting individual identity across most life-stages is one of the most basic infrastructures for the nation-state (Caplan and Torpey 2001). As Max Weber argues, bureaucracy works as a machine with the non-mechanical modes of production to serve the relation between the state and individuals (Weber 1946). By asking for birth date, address, gender, family size, and income-level, the government categorizes the population, taxes it, drafts it, and provides it welfare and healthcare. The modern political system demands registration, identification and categorization, and it rationalizes these demands as being necessary for the equal administration of state programmes. Such categorization, not only by the state, but also by corporations, has introduced social sorting which affects the individual's *life-chances* (Lyon 2001).

Michel Foucault suggests that state power intervenes in individual life to increase its power and exert its full strength (Foucault 1981). This power is repressive, but also productive; he calls it 'bio-power'. The general population became the new target of the modern era. It is not merely substantial residents, but 'men in their relation'. They include:

> their links, their imbrication with those other things which are wealth, resources, means of subsistence, the territory with its specific qualities, climate, irrigation, fertility, etc.; men in their relation to that other kind of things, customs, habits, ways of acting and thinking, etc.; lastly, men in their relation to that other kind of things, accidents and misfortunes such as famine, epidemics, death, etc.
>
> (Foucault 1991: 93)

These were the exact targets of modern Japan, when it drastically westernized its political and economic systems in the late nineteenth century. After a 300-year isolationist policy of the ruling warriors, which banned going abroad, restricted exports and imports, and punished Christians, it was urgent for the new regime of the Emperor to build political and economic institutions equivalent to the

Western empires, as Great Britain, Germany, France, the Netherlands and the United States expanded their territories in East Asia. In order to accomplish this task rapidly, the government first endeavoured to ascertain what kinds of people were in its land.

National registration started with the Koseki Act of 1871, in a series of modernization policies under the slogan: 'Enrich the Country, Strengthen the Soldiers'. Similar registration systems had existed before for taxation purposes, but these registrations belonged to local authorities such as feudal lords or Buddhist temples. The national registration focused on family-oriented records, whereas its European counterparts based theirs on the individual. This record is called Koseki, literally meaning register of a house. It was originally planned to investigate the national population, but it came to determine the Japanese 'family' system. All residents were required to register as the unit of family at municipalities. In other words, the individual had to belong to any family from the moment of birth. The records defined a master of the family and all members who belonged to him. One Koseki file sometimes covered several generations. It required one family member to report any changes in the family, and it created an official order among family members, such as oldest to youngest, lineal to collateral bloodline, and male over female (Ninomiya 2006). Thus, the original Koseki was designed for property lists of the humans and non-humans of the master. Civil Law also stated that the master of the family led his family members, that females did not have legal competence, and that the first son succeeded his father and inherited all the family property. Rather than recording actual living members, Koseki shaped the normative and desirable framework of the family. Even in the current Koseki system, women and children outside of the institution of marriage cannot get full legal status in Civil Law. Koseki culturally reified the frame of the family, wherein the whole family lived with the same honour and dishonour. False records and deviant behaviour threaten other members' social lives, so they laterally watch each other and help remove potential risks against family prosperity. If a member of an upper-class family wants to marry someone in a lower class or stigmatized social group, it is typical for other members to blame her for 'getting Koseki dirty', even today. Koseki envisioned on paper how the family should look in the modern state, and it facilitates the role of policing family members.[3]

The patriarchy of Koseki, at the same time, composed the most fundamental moral model for the emperor state. All individuals in Koseki were regarded as 'children of the emperor'. As sons and daughters obeyed their father, the nationals were trained to obey the emperor. This was often applied to other organizational relations as well, such as those in the military and in factories. Koseki incorporated individuals into the state system through family, and nationalized them as subjects of the emperor. In other words, having your name in Koseki signifies that you have the Japanese citizenship. But the Japanese modern laws have never literally defined citizenship. Instead, legal citizenship was concealed behind a vague concept of 'the Japanese', without any racial, ethnic, and cultural definitions (Sato 1996).[4] Simultaneously, an imaginary unity of the Japanese was constructed, which ignored ethnic and cultural diversities in the population, such as Ainu and

Okinawa, and normalized them. Loyalty for the emperor, rather than the rights of the citizen, was most highly valued and taught at school, in the workforce, and in the family. Koseki constructed a national identity as Japanese. In this system, citizenship can never appear as a matter of universal right. Rather, Japanese nationality is the reward for the subjects of the emperor, and loyalty is a duty more than anything else.

Consequently, foreigners have been strictly excluded from Koseki. Japan joined the colonial wars, taking Taiwan from China in 1895 and annexing Korea in 1910. The government deployed harsh assimilation policies there to produce more 'Japanese': coercing the natives to speak Japanese, to change their names to the Japanese style, and to participate in Shinto worship of the Emperor as the national god. The government also introduced the Koseki system of Japanese nationality to the colonies. However, the files were completely separate from the Koseki of mainland Japan, distinguishing the colonial natives from the records of 'the pure Japanese.' It was prohibited for the colonial natives to register their permanent address on the mainland or change their permanent address to the mainland, even if they moved to the mainland or married a Japanese national on the mainland (Sato 1996; Tanaka 1995). The modern state continued to categorize the new population during its expansion and dispose these new categories in ways which contributed to reinforcing the power of the ruling class. The Korean and Taiwanese Koseki became a powerful means of repressing colonial natives until 1945.

Koseki's centralized power has a characteristic of disciplinary power that Foucault analyses in his theoretical model of the 'Panopticon', originally introduced by Jeremy Bentham as an architectural design for low-cost supervision (Foucault 1977). The panoptic design lets a guard in a central tower watch over inmates; but the inmates are never able to see the guard in the shade of the tower, and so the presence of the guard is no longer important. This relation internalizes the gaze of supervision in the inmates, and automatic self-monitoring starts in the individual. The mechanism of self-discipline encourages human beings to conform to the dominant system. Koseki certainly exercises this kind of disciplinary power: the emperor represents the central tower overlooking his people through the Koseki system. It penetrates the frame of the family as a private entity, and turns individuals into subjects serving the imperial monarchy with their internalized gaze.

However, Koseki is more than panoptic. Family members laterally check each other with a critical gaze to see whether anyone damages their normative frame of family with deviance and disorder. The society, not the emperor, also condemns deviance of an individual synoptically. Ruth Benedict, an American anthropologist, observes that the Japanese family does not protect its members when the members exhibit deviant behaviours against the outside society (Benedict 1967); for example, the father disowns his son and apologizes for his lack of control to the society. Social sanctions break through the family protection because family is the end unit of social order, not an independent entity from the larger society, as is Koseki.[5] Three dimensions of gazes render Koseki more powerful than the panoptic model of disciplinary power. It exposes the individual to extreme isolation when he attempts to go against the status quo of Japanese society. Koseki is the basic chart of 'men in relation' in Foucault's words (1991: 93), covering all citizens. Each datum of Koseki can be used to measure their conformity to the social order: who belongs to whom, and who is inside and outside of the normative family. The pressure to be normal comes from the very heart of the privileged circle of citizenship, the nationalized family in Koseki.

Koseki survived after the Second World War, although the large part of the patriarchal Civil Law was reformed under democratization by the Allied General Headquarters (GHQ). In the current Koseki Act, one Koseki covers fewer than two generations, basically husband, wife, and children. Koseki over three generations was forbidden. Once the children marry, they register at a new Koseki. However, they are still required to define the family head, dominantly male, and its members on the same file. Only people with the same surname are allowed in the same Koseki.[6] In a sense, Koseki was re-born for the nuclear family that became the dominant structure in post-war industrial Japan, preserving the male-leading relationship in the family. It is not coincidental that the emperor system also survived the lost war with a new look at 'a symbol of the nation' and that only the Emperor Hirohito, the supreme commander of the war, was exempt from being charged as a war criminal among the political leaders in the Tokyo Tribunal. Today, Koseki is still a list of 'the pure Japanese', which is consistent with the fact that Japan forbids dual citizenship. If a woman marries a Japanese man, she is required to abandon her original nationality to obtain Japanese citizenship. For a hundred years from monarchy to democracy, Koseki has been an effective technique to ensure the people's loyalty to the state.

Colonial roots: Repress but produce

Since the Sino-Japan War in 1894, Japan had engaged in continuous military conflicts in China. In 1932, it claimed the nation of Manchuria in north-eastern China.[7] Japan installed the Last Emperor of the Qing dynasty, Puyi, in a puppet regime which ruled for the Japanese army. Japan did not enact the Koseki system in Manchuria, unlike in colonized Korea and Taiwan. The primary style of living in north-eastern China was very different from the southern colonies: the native residents were nomads, the Chinese seasonal migrants came in and out, and the Japanese immigrants were initially single male farmers (GSNF 1987; Sato 1996). The family-oriented Koseki system could not effectively track movements and relations of single families. In addition, the resistance against Japan's colonization was constantly on fire in this region. The fragility of this pseudo-state caused the ruling Japanese to impose intensive and individualistic surveillance over the general population.

The ID card in Manchuria started as an employee card in the 1920s. It is significant to note that the system appeared *before* the declaration of the state of Manchuria. The Group Saying 'No' to Fingerprinting, opposing the Alien Registration System, conducted field research on fingerprinting identification in this area in 1987. They interviewed men who worked for the South Manchuria

Railway Company and underwent forced fingerprinting for their employee ID cards. The South Manchuria Railway, like its Western counterpart the East India Company, was established under a joint agreement linking corporations and the government in 1906, following the Russo-Japan War. It owned the coalmine, the seaports, and the steelworks and was even in charge of administrative services in the area along constructing the railways. According to the interviews, the Chinese workers made ten fingerprints rolled on paper, and the company checked them to see whether the worker had escaped from other workplaces or had organized strikes before. If fingerprints matched those on the 'watch lists' that worker was sent back to the previous workplace or sentenced. In fact, the South Manchuria Railway did not hire 25 per cent of the applicants in 1937 because their fingerprints matched with the watch lists (Tanaka 1987). This early use of biometrics for labour management originated in the Fushun Mine in 1924, to select the workers who would not involve the anti-Japanese movement, and the same technique spread to other companies and regions. Japan intended to restrain the Chinese migrants and repress the resistance, but needed to accept the labour power to increase production for the war. Therefore, these identification techniques were crucial for the state to *repress* the rebels but *produce* more wealth.

The ID card came onto the scene after fingerprinting in 1938 when the Manchuria Labor Industry Association issued the 'labour card' to the workers. The Japanese army also started to distribute the resident ID card including fingerprint and photograph. The geographical area subjected to resident identification expanded every time the army deployed the intensive tactics against the guerrillas. The army surrounded the villages with mud walls and checked the residents with their cards at the entrances, in order to cut off the communication between the residents and the guerrillas. The army established the Bureau of Fingerprints to control all kinds of fingerprints in 1939. Between 1934 and 1940, more than 5.2 million people were fingerprinted for the national identification systems in Manchuria (GSNF 1987: 22). The fingerprint technicians not only worked in the office, but took part in the military operation to identify resisters. Fingerprinting identification developed in the military tactics of searching, isolating, and killing the enemy of the empire in Manchuria.

On mainland Japan, it was Koreans who were first required to carry the ID cards, following the experiment outside the territory. Because of land expropriation and high unemployment under Japanese rule, many Koreans had moved to Japan to make their living after the armed annexation of Korea in 1910. Those people were compelled to belong to a Korean association in their domicile called Kyowa-kai, whose heads were the police directors and the public investigation agents (Higuchi 1986). Kyowa-kai assimilated Koreans to the Japanese style of living and banned the Korean customs. The government began to issue a notebook type of ID, Kyowa-kai-techo, in 1940 during a 15-year undeclared war against China. In order to support the expanding war, the General National Mobilization Law was imposed on nationals, including Koreans and Taiwanese, who were forced to work for the government and for the military industries. Under this law, the number of Koreans in Japan reached 2.3 million by 1945 (Tanaka 1995: 60). Afraid of the growing population of colonial natives on the mainland, the Japanese accelerated both mass and individual-based surveillance with the ID card system.

Members were required to carry Kyowa-kai-techo, which had 30 pages, with their photographs (Higuchi 1991). The national anthem 'His Majesty's Reign' was printed on the first page, as was 'the Oath of Imperial National Subject' on the last page, which Koreans were directed to read together in every public meeting. The patriotic lyrics constrained Kyowa-kai members to have the collective identity of 'the Japanese'. Other pages recorded how much the card carrier donated for 'National Security', 'Building the Battleship', or 'Strengthening the Soldiers'. The Kyowa-kai-techo shows how the ID card attempted not only to verify names and contact information, but to impose desirable identities and to expose personal histories. Many companies kept Kyowa-kai-techo at the workplace, so if a Korean applied for a job without his ID, he was assumed to have escaped from the former workplace and was put under investigation (Higuchi 1986: 146).

Clearly, national ID cards were first imposed on populations seen as potentially dangerous to the imperial state, specific races and ethnic groups. ID cards played a role in creating a boundary between the outside and the inside of the expanding nation-state. Japan was not the first case; the Western mentality and techniques spread to contemporary Japan and other parts of the globe along with war and colonialism. As Torpey suggests, the passport system developed through the First World War has given states the best opportunity for monopolizing the legitimate means of movement (Torpey 2000, 2001). The state introduced ID card systems in the state of exception of the war, but never took away the emergency techniques in post-war periods, like the passport system that is taken for granted in today's world. Biometrics was inseparable from the colonial ID system. Cole finds that, while anthropometry, the measuring of body parts and indexing the data, emerged in the cities of Europe, fingerprinting was tried out on the colonial population because there were complaints among the officials. For example, in India, colonial natives had similar combinations of hair, eyes and skin colour to identify them (Cole 2001). Fingerprinting was used as a great way to recognize racial 'others'.

Alien registration: Manipulating citizenship

Like other emergency techniques during wartime, fingerprints remained in the post-Second World War ID system to categorize 'others' in Japan. The Alien Registration System was launched in 1947 with the Alien Registration Ordinance, which was the last ordinance by the Emperor Hirohito (Tanaka 1995: 64; Sato 1996: 88). After that, all laws had to be passed by the Diet. This ordinance explicitly reflected the fear of the ruling class of the ex-colonial population they had suppressed until the unconditional surrender. The ordinance assumed the Koreans and Taiwanese in Japan as aliens *temporarily* in legal status and compelled them to register. Koreans and Taiwanese were *permanently* deprived of Japanese nationality when the ordinance became the Alien Registration Law in 1952, and Japan signed the San Francisco Peace Treaty and regained its sovereignty (Tanaka 1995: 66; Sato 1996: 70, 89). At this point, 95 per cent of registered 'aliens' in Japan, approximately 600,000 people, were Korean and Taiwanese (Tanaka 1995: 46). The intent of this law was not to regulate general travellers coming and going along the Japanese border, but to watch over the activities and relations of the colonial natives whom the Potsdam Declaration emancipated and turned into the winners of the war. They began to claim their political and economical equality with the Japanese, and many including the Japanese were supportive or sympathetic of socialist movement because of their resistance to Japanese fascism during the wartime. The government and the Allied General Headquarters wanted to exclude this enemy-within from citizenship and treat them as outsiders in the post-war chaos and upheaval of the Cold War.

The original Alien Registration Law required all 'foreigners' over 14 years old and staying for more than 60 days in Japan to fingerprint at registration and renewals every two years (Tanaka 1995: 82, 90). The government issued the Alien Registration Card based on registration records, and it has been compulsory from the beginning to carry the card and show it to police if asked. One is fined up to 200,000 Japanese Yen (approximately US$1,800) for not carrying it, and is even sentenced to up to a year in jail for refusing to show it (Ministry of Justice 2004). Although the government insists that the Alien Registration is equivalent to Koseki for nationals, these severe punishments indicate that foreigners are not equal to nationals and are subject to additional surveillance.

The nation-state retains power over citizenship. The Koseki system, which registered the racial others separately from 'the pure Japanese' was used to remove Koreans and Chinese from the Japanese citizenship. The Kyowa-kai lists also provide the basic data for the Alien Registration System (Nakao 1997: 129). Koreans and Chinese who were forced to serve in Japan's war became non-citizens overnight. Although this is not typical of how colonial citizens are treated after independence,[8] it is clear that the state holds final determination of who deserves to be a citizen, and the citizen herself can never decide to which state she belongs (Jung 2003). Both the individuals who are included in and excluded from citizenship are inevitably incorporated into the state-citizen structure. As far as the state is entitled to define citizenship, citizens must be favourable for the state and be tested for their loyalty to the state. Moreover, the state must always keep some of the population outside of privilege, in order to maintain this political structure as a source of power. Yeong-hae Jung, a Korean sociologist in Japan, contends that the privilege of Japanese citizenship exists primarily to give Japanese citizens the illusion that they have rights, in comparison with foreigners who do not have any rights. She argues that Japanese citizenship is not substantial as a political right to the state, even though the new Japanese Constitution defines that sovereignty resides in people, no longer in the emperor. The state must maintain legal discrimination against foreigners to conceal that Japanese citizenship is 'a rice cake in the picture', which looks delicious but is useless (Jung 2003: 295). If citizenship was free from nationality, the characteristic of citizenship would depart from privilege for universal rights. The rice cake might come out of the picture and give the people in Japan the real taste and energy.

Fingerprinting was part of registration until 2000 when the foreigners' resistance achieved its abolition (Choi 2000: 4). Since the beginning of enforcement, there were a number of foreigners who refused to put their index fingers in ink. But these protests did not get much social attention until 1980, when Han Jong-suk, a Korean man who came to Japan at nine years of age, refused to be fingerprinted at city hall in Shinjuku ward, Tokyo. Han said, 'I have been fingerprinted many times before. But if I continue, my children and grandchildren are also going to be fingerprinted. I cannot leave anything for them, but, I want them not to be fingerprinted' (Tanaka 1995: 78). It was apparently the first time that the media covered the Alien Registration fingerprinting from a critical point of view. Following Han, many foreigners decided not to be fingerprinted for their own reasons. This movement was named 'the revolt of only one'. It also became a diplomatic issue between South Korea and Japan. In 1982, the Alien Registration Law was revised to apply its registry from 14–16 year olds and to extend card renewal from every three years to every five years. In spite of the partial compromise, according to the newspaper *Asahi Shimbun*, rejection of fingerprinting numbered more than 7,400 by September 1985 (cited in Sato 1996: 91). The government tried to push back the protesters by arresting, accusing, fining, sentencing and disapproving re-entry to Japan. Many fought back in the courts. Although the protesters never individually won in any court, the Korean–Japanese Memorandum of 1991 promised to abolish the fingerprinting of Korean residents in Japan within two years (Tanaka 1995: 98). The Japanese government finally announced the total abolition of fingerprinting of all foreigners on the day before South Korean President Kim Dae-chung visited Japan in 1998 (Choi 2000: 42).

Nevertheless, that was not the end of the story. Instead of fingerprinting, the government devised substitutes, which were added to registration forms: signatures and family records. The Ministry of Justice and the municipal governments store a handwritten signature. The family record includes the names, birth dates and nationalities of parents and spouses who live in Japan, and, if the person registering is the head of the family, he needs to add each family member's name, birth date, nationality and relationship to himself (Sato 1996: 94, 98–102). These items undeniably resemble Koseki. The government now attempts to merge outsiders into the relation-oriented surveillance of Koseki.

It reminds us that there are two essential techniques of identification; one is based on the individual and their unique biological information, the other is based on human relations involving the person's social activities. Stimulated by the developing biometric technologies, government administration in the twentieth century seemed to lean increasingly on individualistic identification more than relational identification. Cole suggests that fingerprint identification became preferable to anthropometry in the twentieth century because it saved on the cost of instruments and required less skill in law enforcement and administration. It matched the idea of modern industrialization, including rationalized bureaucracy, scientific management and mass production (Cole 2001: 166). Before biometric techniques were developed, a person was basically identified by the testimonies of people who had observed that person. Despite the development of biometric techniques, this old-fashioned surveillance using human eyes has never been abandoned. Moreover, this technique can be more efficient in recognizing 'men in relation', to use Foucault's words. So, the question here is: Is Koseki's technique the tale of a bygone age or the banner of new era? And, what if Koseki were combined with biometric ID cards? The biological data and relational data would go hand-in-hand to identify the individual in their body and with their history. It may be the concept of human identification that 'smart ID cards' linking many databases embody, which is currently proposed in the neo-liberal economy and 'war on terror'.

Juki-net: Numbered 'dividual'

In addition to Koseki, another registry for national Japanese was legislated in 1951, and revised as the Resident Basic Register System in 1967. While Koseki is permanent and family-oriented, this system focuses on updating the individual's movement. Japanese nationals came to be required to register their address at the municipality every time they move. This system is linked with Koseki, so that family relations can be tracked. The copy of the Resident Register is more commonly used as a means of social identification than Koseki, which contains a wider range of sensitive data. Individuals are often required to submit a copy of their Resident Register in order to apply for a job, a school, a passport and a driver's licence.

However, the Resident Basic Register System was essentially changed in 2002 when its part of the personal data was computerized, and networked with the central database owned by the government. This national computer network, the so-called 'Juki-net' is made up of all the resident registration databases belonging to 3,200 municipal governments, and it gives every Japanese citizen his/her specific ID number (Asahi Shimbun 2002b). Juki-net circulates up to 14 personal data items in the Resident Basic Register. The government can access six core items among them, without asking permission from the individual or local governments: name, address, date of birth, gender, the history of data changes, and the 11-figure ID number. This was the first time that all Japanese citizens, including newborns, became unitarily numbered by the state. If a family moves to a different city, the government can directly search the new address by the ID number. Moreover, the ID number enables the government to track personal changes, such as marriage and divorce.

The plan for this system had been discussed among law-makers since the late 1960s, when it was called the 'General National Back Number System'. The idea is that all nationals carry the single national ID card which can be used as a driver's licence and health insurance card. Taro Nakayama, the Diet member who wrote the book *100 Million All Back Numbers*, illustrated how a driver could be quickly saved from an accident, properly taken care of in the hospital, easily given compensation for the accident in court, and even found a suitable new job, all through his national ID card (Nakayama 1970). For this simulation, the unitary ID number is the key to unlock and connect all kinds of personal data, and so everybody must carry that card to access databases. But the plot was never realized because of a strong fear of a new technology at the time: the computer.

To mollify the long-term public opposition, the government declared that Juki-net would be restricted to only 92 administrative purposes before the Bill was passed in the Diets in 1999 (Ogasawara 2002). Yet after passage, these were expanded to 264 items through additional laws a few months after Juki-net was launched. Similarly, in 1999, the government insisted that Juki-net served to simplify administrative procedures for the public's convenience. But when implemented in 2002, Juki-net's main task was quietly changed to 'e-government', establishing Juki-net as the universal frame for on-line governance, and implying more proliferation of the network. Juki-net's development shows how data-sharing networks inevitably become multi-purpose, expand the scope of their data, and escape from legal restraints and democratic transparency, once they are established.

However, even a few weeks before Juki-net was implemented, more than 86 per cent in an opinion poll by *Asahi Shimbun* responded that they were afraid of leaking and the improper use of personal information (Asahi Shimbun 2002a). Correspondingly, 70 municipal assemblies and 29 mayors of the cities, towns and villages passed resolutions to demand the government to postpone implementing Juki-net. The Public Management Minister Katayama reacted to this public dissent in commenting; 'It is illegal if those cities do not participate in Juki-net. What happens to the money we already invested in Juki-net? The silent majority is waiting for the implementation' (Ogasawara 2002: 117). Despite his warning, the Mayor of Yamatsuri, Fukushima prefecture, expressed the boycott of his town to Juki-net a couple of weeks before the implementation. Following him, the mayors of Suginami and Kokubunji, Tokyo, expressed that they would not take part in Juki-net. The Mayor of Yokohama, Kanagawa prefecture, announced the system in which the citizens could choose whether they were contained in Juki-net or not. Eventually, Juki-net lacked 4.1 million citizens in its data for its first day, 5 August 2002 (Asahi Shimbun 2002b). In other cities, many refused to receive the mailings notifying the ID numbers, and returned them to their cities. A number of civil groups were organized and held demonstrations against Juki-net on the streets along with hosting 'the Big Brother Award' or screening the documentary of the Korean ID system. Some took further steps by suing the government for invading their privacy. Among 35 cases, in November 2006, the Osaka High Court judged that it was against the right to privacy that Juki-net contained the personal information of people who did not want to be listed, and ordered to eliminate the ID numbers of those that could be used as the 'master key' for data-matching by administrative departments beyond individual permission (Asahi Shimbun 2006). Although other courts did not decide Juki-net jeopardized privacy rights, it has been established through the cases that Article 13 of the Japanese Constitution guarantees the right to informational self-determination. However, in March 2008, the Supreme Court reversed this decision and decided that Juki-net did not infringe on the right to privacy guaranteed by Article 13 of the Japanese Constitution. The Supreme Court said Article 13 is limited to the right not to have personal information disclosed to a third party.

In 2003, the Japanese government began to issue an optional ID card linked to Juki-net. This 'Juki-card' is the first national card specialized for identification. It has the basic data of Juki-net printed on the surface with or without the photograph of the carrier. It also contains an integrated circuit (IC) chip, which can store and combine many types of data, such as biometric and banking information on a 'smart card' (Wood *et al.* 2007). In order to standardize technological schemes, the government has invested billions in pilot projects for local ID card systems over the past two decades. However, most of the cards were extremely unpopular and disappeared a few years after their implementation, not always because of concerns for privacy but due to administrative inefficiency, similar to the HANIS system in South Africa (Breckenridge, Chapter 3). For example, the City of Izumo launched a few different types of card systems that combined the data of the Resident Basic Register with other personal data in the IC chip: first, the 'welfare card' attached medical information for the elderly, second, the 'child card' attached development history for the youth and last, the 'citizen card' attached banking information. Some intentionally avoided keeping medical records in the card, because of privacy concerns. But most people did not carry the cards, and medical information was not standardized. The new mayor abolished the card, despite having spent 600 million yen (about US$5.5 million) on the policy. In six years, only one out of 7,700 welfare cards were used for a medical emergency (Ogasawara 2002: 123).

Ignoring the explicit failures of the local ID cards, the Japanese government has firmly encouraged cities and towns to attach Juki-card to other services and to increase the carriers. According to the Ministry of Public Management, there are 127 municipalities in 2007 that multi-use the Juki-card, for example, to access libraries, automatic machines issuing copies of Koseki or the Resident Basic Register, and other public facilities (Ministry of Public Management 2007). Yet four years after its advent, the distribution rate is still only 1 per cent of the national population. The unpopularity of the system clearly shows that few citizens need the national ID card. But the government is keen to attach it to the citizenry.

Theoretically, Juki-net has different characteristics from the disciplinary power of Koseki. It goes beyond the modern administrative categorizations, departs from legal control, and expands with state discretion. These aspects cause a fluid, individualistic and direct intervention in personal life, without any mediating entity, such as the role played by the family in Koseki. Juki-net cuts off family ties to the individual, which characterizes Koseki. It is the first ID system that purely targets the individual citizen. To be individualistic, a number is the key to align and sort out mass information on the population. Juki-net not only counts each person, it turns each one into a number.

Unitary numbering represents bio-power in Juki-net. It represents both the individual body and the population – Foucault suggests that bio-power links an anatomo-politics over the human body and bio-politics over the population as the biological species (Foucault, 1978). For the state, an ID number is the perfect tool to avoid double counting and no counting, and to create an inerrant chart of a population, while permitting no place to hide. It reduces a human being into a datum that can be identified, processed, and circulated without conflicting with other components of his being, such as physical and social relationships. The number has no historical or familial tie to the individual, while Koseki entails family history and relationship, such as the son or daughter of the master. One can see that personal data attached to the ID number on Juki-net are predominantly biological data, without social components of individuality and livelihood: like a sign on an animal in the zoo, the name, gender, age and home. Juki-net binds the ID number that represents the corporeal body to be registered and controlled by the state, with the biological history.

In turn, for the citizen, a number moors her to the totality of the state because her number is for the masses, not for herself. She starts her life as a particular number in the state's alignment, and her ID number does not have any meaning on its own, without the entire enumeration. Her number is a component of the total, not an independent entity of its own. Her number distinguishes her from the total, but embeds her in the total. It places every individual in an order. Contradictorily, but essentially, the ID number for one is for all.

In this duality the number links both poles of bio-power: the individual body and the mass population. It finds the individual in the mass and ties the individual to the mass. It always offers fresh biological data of the population to the state. In this mechanism, the individualistic technique paradoxically works for total efficiency of governance.

Foucault explains that there are two principles of political rationality that the modern state has pursued: the individualization and totalitarian principle (Foucault 1981: 254). Issuing unique numbers to nationals enables the state to exert both individualizing and totalizing powers of regulatory mechanism over a population, because the government can both accumulate and divide all kinds of data based on the ID numbers. Mehmood (Chapter 7) elaborates how excessively the state desires to enumerate the population by deconstructing many identities of the individual. Foucault asserts that, compared with individualizing power over the body as experienced in the Panopticon, totalitarian intervention is a relatively new practice by 'the police'. By this, he means 'a governmental technology peculiar to the state; domains, techniques, targets where the state intervenes' (Foucault 1981: 246).

> As a form of rational intervention wielding political power over men, the role of the police is to supply them with a little extra life; and by so doing, supply the state with a little extra strength. This is done by controlling 'communication,' i.e., the common activities of individuals (work, production, exchange, accommodation).
>
> (Foucault 1981: 248)

The intervention in individual lives can be qualified as totalitarian because the intervention provides the state its strength, its vigour. The government must ensure the "communication" among individuals, the common activities of individuals, for total efficiency of the state (Foucault 1981: 248). In other words, the individualistic technique is necessary for the state to accomplish a totalitarian agenda. Reducing the citizen to a number contributes to aligning the population and cataloguing it for the intervention, although it pinpoints the citizen simultaneously. The mobilization of the population during the wartime might have been easier if the state had had the unitary ID number system. The individualistic scheme of Juki-net functions as means of totalitarian intervention in the mechanism of bio-power. Koseki has already enacted the totalitarian power to intervene in personal relationships. However, Koseki's frame cannot capture mobile individuals, so the Resident Basic Resister System was constructed. Juki-net brought the individualistic technique one stage further with computerization that can process any type of individual data. Totalitarian power is now supported by individualistic techniques capable of fluidly changing the target and purpose of control.

Gilles Deleuze called this new phenomenon the 'society of control', which he believed Foucault viewed as part of the process replacing a disciplinary society. In a disciplinary society,

> [the] power both amasses and individuates, that is, it fashions those over whom it's exerted into a body of people and molds the individuality of each member of that body. [… In control societies, we are] no longer dealing with a duality of mass and individual. Individuals become 'dividuals,' and masses become samples, data, markets, or 'banks.'
>
> (Deleuze 1995: 179–80)

Juki-net distinctively has these characteristics of technology corresponding to control society. There, the individual floats in 'a modulation, like a self-transmuting molding continually changing from one moment to the next, or like a sieve whose mesh varies from one point to another' (Deleuze 1995: 178–9) in the data flow of Juki-net and the possibly linked databases. There is no end to the data flow that can be determined, and individuals become the fragmented data for the state, corporations, or software.

Conclusion

It is worth returning to the colonial roots of the national ID card systems to find how these techniques have excluded others and exploited them as a mechanism of bio-power: repress the resistant, but use it to produce more wealth for the national economy. More empirically, national ID cards were no more than the technology of subjugation and extermination for individuals who were categorized as political and economical minorities. As Cole asserted, identification, supported by the most scientific fashion of the time, fingerprinting, was developed to identify dark-skinned Indian natives for white officers, and to eliminate Manchurian rebellion for the Japanese Empire.[9]

Modern ID systems like Koseki categorize insiders and outsiders for citizenship, and maintain social order and discipline through nationalizing the population. This mechanism has never expired. Koseki still reproduces a patriarchal family structure and subjects of the state. However, in addition to disciplinary power of Koseki, the new individualistic ID system like Juki-net crosses the borders of citizenship that have been drawn by the modern state. Juki-net can process personal data for any purpose and combine data over different spheres nationwide. It disguises legal control, but tends to expand the scope of data and purposes. We do not know what kinds of new categorizations await us in the future, but state-run databanks will continue to produce divisive labels of risk and non-risk. Scrutiny never ends in this society of control, as Deleuze (1995) describes. Without the modern boundaries of categorization, the individual is more likely to be directly and arbitrarily searched and excluded. The ID card system exposes the individual to the pressures of normalization and conformism to the state power in order to be a desirable citizen.

Nikolas Rose analyses that the securitization of identity is imposed on the individual in order to access and enjoy social services and rights guaranteed to the citizen (Rose 1999). One is obliged to 'continuously and repeatedly evidence one's citizenship credentials as one recurrently links oneself into the circuits of civility' (Rose 1999: 246). As a citizen or consumer, we enjoy identifying our legitimate membership to the society, where the rationalization of ID card system is generated. The national ID card system is rationalized when it is said that the card benefits every citizen by blocking out 'terrorists', dangerous foreigners and the enemy-within. Therefore, *everybody* should be included. Biometrics is also said to be the reliable and ultimate means of scientific identification for *everybody* post-9/11.[10] Japan's new immigration system, which requires foreign travellers to be fingerprinted, was realized in this context, the first follower of the US system in the world, although few expected that it would reappear only a few years after its abolition in the Alien Registration System. The ethos of this colonial technique survived underneath the post-war democratic reforms and is now adapted to a larger population having been rationalized and facilitated by the global allies of security. The discourses supporting the more generalized fingerprinting system never refer to those who have been targeted in Japan's history and what this technology has brought to the targeted. Rather, they conceal those questions with the pervasive declaration of saying 'on behalf of everybody's safety'. However, this system does not benefit everybody because somebody has to be the 'terrorist' to continue the game. If we overlook the sophistry in this totalitarian logic of everybody, we may become blind to the excluded innocent. Or we may conform to power in order to protect ourselves within a fragile sense of safety as the innocent. At that point, we may not need many more steps to reach a new fascism defended by digitally networked identification techniques.

We may not be heading backwards to the death squads of the Cold War, as I thought in Korea, where the border between West and East was so clear. But we may be heading for a global tyranny of security. To break the totalitarian rationalization of security with the individualistic technology, we must unveil critical aspects of each national ID system: Who is targeted? Who receives the benefits? And who decides who is who?

Notes

1 The surveillance techniques in the Cold War are assigned to the new tasks in the context of the global 'war on terror', which seems also to reverse our time. It gives rise to political discourses defining those surveillance techniques as progress. The Japanese Minister of Justice, Seiken Sugiura, spoke admiringly about the Korean ID system. 'South Korea

has made more progress than Japan. When I went to Korea last January, I was surprised to find that individual photographs were attached to resident registration files, which were linked to the passport system and enable officials to identify the individual. Each country must make an effort, so Japan also needs to confront terrorism for international harmony' (The House of Representatives, 17 March 2006).

2 In May 2006, the Japanese Diet passed a revision of the Immigration Control and Refugee Recognition Act, in order to implement the new fingerprinting immigration system (Immigration Bureau 2006).

3 Ninomiya introduces a debate between family-law-makers over Koseki's role. While a lawyer who studied in France insisted on abolishing Koseki and replacing family records with individual records, a bureaucrat claimed that Koseki represented a master's responsibility for feeding his family members, enabling the poor to survive without going to a 'salvation house', and protecting the family morality (Ninomiya 2006: 38).

4 Japan admits the Japanese nationality to those who have a Japanese parent. Bloodline is only the source of the nationality, not the place of birth like other countries. The first Koseki registered all people in its territory, and they are assumed to be 'the basically Original Japanese'. Since then, only the children of the Original Japanese have been able to receive citizenship (Sato 1996: 14).

5 When three young Japanese were kidnapped by an armed group in Iraq in 2004, a public out-cry arose blaming the three for 'their selfish action of going to Iraq to get the government in trouble'. The condemnation increased when their families asked the government to withdraw Japanese troops from Iraq, which was the condition the armed group set to release the three. The families toned down their criticisms after putting up with harassment and social sanctions.

6 'Entering Koseki' is the common expression for marriage, not 'taking' it on your own. Most married couples choose the husband's surname.

7 Since 1894 Japan was involved in wars every ten years. It is important to note that Japan's nation-state building ran parallel to imperial wars over new territories. Many Japanese officials went abroad during this period and imported Western ideas of nation building, especially the German and French legal systems. The law-makers designed the nation to support constant wars. Colonial Wars were not exceptional situations from the beginning of the nation-state. Rather, they were necessary.

8 For example, the Federal Republic of Germany gave Austrians residing in Germany after the Second World War the right to choose German nationality (Tanaka 1995: 67–8; Jung 2003: 120). The United Kingdom also guarantees British Commonwealth citizenship to the citizens of newly independent countries by the law of 1948. The free entry of British Commonwealth citizens to Britain was restricted after the 1960s, but Irish nationals in Britain are still guaranteed equal citizenship to British nationals, even if they do *not* choose British nationality (Bunda 1993: 118, 126). Nationality and citizenship are often synonymous. However, as in the Irish case in Britain, nationality and citizenship can be separate, and citizenship does not necessarily belong to nationality.

9 Biological knowledge has contributed to rationalizing ID systems. Fingerprinting has been bound up with racist anthropology and biological determinism, as Cole describes: 'Fingerprinting has embedded firmly within our culture the notion that personhood is biological. [...Our] fingerprint patterns told the state who we were and even defined our individuality, our very personhood' (Cole 2001: 5).

10 It should not be overlooked that biometrics is sometimes used for privilege, and ITC businesses attempt to wipe out the negative image of biometric identification. The Japanese new immigration system imposing fingerprinting on foreigners will also offer privileges to some Japanese; it allows travellers who are willing to register their fingerprints in advance to go through immigration faster than other non-registered travellers.

Bibliography

Asahi Shimbun (2004a) '86% Anxious about Juki-net, 76% want to suspend implementation, Opinion poll', 22 July.

Asahi Shimbun (2004b) 'Juki-net starts, 4.11 million missing', 5 August.

Asahi Shimbun (2006) 'Juki-net is defective and unconstitutional, judged the Osaka High Court. Ordered eliminating information of four residents', 1 December.

Benedict, R. (1967) *The Chrysanthemum and the Sword (Kiku to Katana)*, Japan: Shakai Shiso Sha.

Bunda, J. (1993) 'Nationality and citizenship', *Bulletin of Fukuoka Education University*, 42(2): 115–29.

Caplan, J. and Torpey, J. (2001) 'Introduction', in J. Caplan and J. Torpey (eds) *Documenting Individual Identity*, Princeton: Princeton University Press.

Choi, S. (2000) *Inquiring 'My Country'*, Japan: Iwanami Shoten.

Cole, S. A. (2001) *Suspect Identities*, Cambridge: Harvard University Press.

Deleuze, G. (1995) 'Postscript on Control Societies', *Negotiations*, New York: Columbia University Press.

Foucault, M. (1977) *Discipline and Punish,* New York: Vintage Books.

Foucault, M. (1978) *The History of Sexuality Volume One,* New York: Vintage Books.

Foucault, M. (1981) 'Omnes et Singulatim', in S. M. McMurrin (ed.) *The Tanner Lectures on Human Values II*, Salt Lake City: University of Utah Press.

Foucault, M. (1991) 'Governmentality', in G. Burchell, C. Gordon and P. Miller (eds) *The Foucault Effect*, Chicago: Chicago University Press.

GSNF (Group Saying 'No' to Fingerprinting: Shimon nante minna de 'pu' no kai) (1987) 'Fingerprints in fake 'State of Manchuria',' *Institutes of Chinese Affairs* 41(6): 16–27. Online. Available: http://ci.nii.ac.jp/vol_issue/nels/AN00144813/ISS0000159093_jp.html (accessed 1 May 2007).

Higuchi, Y. (1986) *Kyowakai*, Japan: Shakai Hyoron Sha.

Higuchi, Y. (ed.) (1991) *Document Collection of Kyowakai,* vol. I *(Kyowakai Kanke Shiryo Shu I)*, Japan: Ryokuin Shobo.

House of Representatives (2006) 'Discussion of the Law Committee', 14 February – 29 March. Online. Available: http://kokkai.ndl.go.jp/ (accessed 1 July 2006).

Immigration Bureau (2006) 'The Public Announcement of the Immigration Control and Refugee Recognition Act, 2006 Amendment'. Online. Available: http://www.immi-moj.go.jp/keiziban/happyou/20060524_law43.pdf. English version available: http://www.immi-moj.go.jp/english/keiziban/happyou/law43_20060524.pdf (accessed 1 June 2006).

Jung, Y. (2003) *Sing People's Reign (Tamigayo Seisho)*, Japan: Iwanami Shoten.

Lyon, D. (2001) *Surveillance Society*, Buckingham: Open University Press.

Ministry of Justice (2004) 'The Alien Registration Law, 1947 original and 2004 Amendment'. Online. Available: http://law.e-gov.go.jp/cgi-bin/idxselect.cgi?IDX_OPT=1&H_NAME=%8a%4f%8d%91%90%6c%93%6f%98%5e%96%40&H_NAME_YOMI=%82%a0&H_NO_GENGO=H&H_NO_YEAR=&H_NO_TYPE=2&H_NO_NO=&H_FILE_NAME=S27HO125&H_RYAKU=1&H_CTG=1&H_YOMI_GUN=1&H_CTG_GUN=1 (accessed 1 June 2006).

Ministry of Justice (2006) 'The Immigration Control and Refugee Recognition Act, 2006 Amendment'. Online. Available: http://www.moj.go.jp/ (accessed 10 April 2006).

Ministry of Public Management, Home Affairs, Posts and Telecommunications (2007) 'Report on distribution and multi-usage of Juki-card'. Online. Available: http://www.soumu.go.jp/c-gyousei/daityo/ (accessed 1 July 2007).

Nakao, H. (1997) *Basic Knowledge on Issues of Koreans in Japan (Zainichi kankoku cho-senjin mondai no kisochishiki)*, Japan: Akashi Shoten.

Nakayama, T. (1970) *100 Million All Back Numbers (Ichioku Sosebango)*, Japan: Nihon seisanse Hombu.

Ninomiya, S. (2006) *Koseki and Human Rights (Koseki to Jinken)*, Japan: Kaiho Shuppansha.

Ogasawara, M. (2002) 'The forgotten origin: report on the Resident Basic Registration Network', in Y. Tajima (ed.) *Personal Information Protection Act and Human Rights (Kojin joho hogoho to Jinken)*, Japan: Akashi Shoten.

Parenti, C. (2003) *The Soft Cage*, New York: Basic Books.

Rose, N. (1999) *Powers of Freedom*, Cambridge: Cambridge University Press.

Sakai, T. (2001) *On Liberty (Jiyu-ron)*, Japan: Seido Sha.

Sato, B. (1996) *The Reader of Foreigners in Japan (Zainichi 'Gaikokujin' Dokuhon)*, Japan: Ryokufu Shuppan.

Tanaka, H. (1987) 'The origin of fingerprinting', *Asahi Journal* 9 October: 21–3.

Tanaka, H. (1995) *The Foreigners in Japan (Zainichi Gaikokujin)*, Japan: Iwanami Shoten.

Torpey, J. (2000) *The Invention of the Passport*, Cambridge: Cambridge University Press.

Torpey, J. (2001) 'The Great War and the birth of the modern passport system', in J. Caplan and J. Torpey (eds) *Documenting Individual Identity*, Princeton: Princeton University Press, p. 256–70.

Weber, M. (1946) 'Bureaucracy', in H. Gerth and C.W. Mills (eds) *From Max Weber*, New York: Oxford University Press.

Wood, M.D., Lyon, D. and Abe, K. (2007) 'Surveillance in Urban Japan', *Urban Studies*, 44(3): 551–68.

7   India's new ID card

Fuzzy logics, double meanings and ethnic ambiguities

Taha Mehmood

The present day 'terrorist' is a man who thinks. He is a planner. No one knows his name or his past. When and where does he come from? No one knows.

He could be anyone or no one. He could be the one sitting beside you in a theatre or a local train, or a bank's teller or a cigarette/tobacco vendor. He is intelligent and dangerous.

He has to be found.

(*Fanaa* 2006)

Introduction

The Indian Government is gearing up to prepare a national database of all citizens and distribute national identity cards to a billion people. This represents a historical milestone, and offers an opportunity to think about a whole spectrum of issues of technology, citizenship and governance. For instance, how does a modern nation-state grapple with issues of visibility and invisibility or identity and anonymity? What tropes of political and bureaucratic rhetoric does the state mobilize to assert its claim for initiating the processes of visibility? How do existing social conditions change in the face of such processes? What sort of transformations do these processes of visibility inaugurate, especially between the state and the individual? What strategies does an individual engage to respond to these transformations? Through this chapter, I explore some of the above-mentioned questions, specifically with regard to the introduction of the proposed 'Multipurpose National Identity Card' (MNIC) in India. The MNIC is the first citizenship document of its kind in the country, especially in its proposed comprehensive reach: a national register of citizens, a national register of non-citizens and a national register of residency.

Developments and shifts in the modes and meaning of state surveillance

The history of the consolidation of the idea of the nation-state, especially after the French Revolution, and the resultant anxieties of national bureaucracies to demarcate and delineate land, to map and measure territory, to create and sustain archives, and to know and register its populations, have been extensively researched. Ground-breaking work by various scholars, especially John Torpey (Torpey 1999; Caplan and Torpy 2001), Valentine Groebner (2001), Jon Agar (2001) and others, have opened exciting avenues towards in-depth investigation of linkages between information, documentation and governance. Their work has been crucial to our contemporary understanding of the historical role that identity documents, such as passports and ration cards, have played in the organization of a nation-state as a unitary body.

Historians of science and technology, particularly Simon Cole (2002) and Chandak Sengoopta (2004), have focused on unearthing the sociopolitical milieu that produced the technology of fingerprinting. The notion of individual identity, especially 'suspect identity', was seen in a new light in philosophical, legal and bureaucratic discourses after the introduction of fingerprinting. The human body (re)entered the discourse of identification as an inalienable bridge connecting societal signifiers like name, age and gender to the selfhood of a person.

The work of Gerd Gigerenzer and colleagues (1990), Ian Hacking (2001), Theodore Porter (1996), and others has been hugely instrumental in exploring the centrality of numbers in probabilistic statistical schemes that were increasingly adopted by many nation states during the twentieth century. Exploration of popular 'social engineering' ideas of determinism, deviation, and mean, for instance, has rekindled debates around the role of numbers in governmental thought and policy.

Reflections by Gary Marx (1989), David Lyon (1994, 2002, 2003), Erving Goffman (1999), and Manuel Castells (2000, 2003), among others, have sustained a debate over the ideas of individual identity and of identification regimes. In its wake, ongoing sociological scholarship has produced an invaluable amount of literature. Close reading of several texts and contexts has thrown up new frames of reference for understanding the human condition. Through my research, I have attempted to uncover the dominant *fabula* or story of individual identification, together with rather fragmented and discrete *sjuzhets* or smaller plots of surveillance assemblage, or what is called 'new surveillance'. This is where data-bodies, DNA profiling, fingerprints and iris scans act as portals to a nuanced scrutiny of technology and body. This has resulted in what David Lyon considers a 'shift', wherein the body has been reintroduced as 'a source as well as site of surveillance' (Lyon 2001: 291). The body can be used as a document.

Gearing up for the multipurpose national identity card

In this regard, it has become important to observe elusive changes happening in the Indian context. They are elusive precisely because of the conspicuous silence of the Indian Government on the topic of the MNIC, as contrasted with the enthusiasm of corporate media in announcing the arrival of a number of smart card manufacturing firms setting up production units in India. This dichotomy sets up a critical duality marked by official silence and unofficial excitement.

In April 2003, the Government of India decided to initiate a 'pilot project' for the introduction of the Multipurpose National Identity Card (MNIC) in select districts. This decision was based on the recommendation of a Group of Ministers (GoM) report on National Security. Some background on the GoM is useful here. The GoM was formed in April 2000 on the recommendation of the Kargil Review Committee (KRC), which had been struck in July 1999 to investigate the causes of the Kargil War. From May to July 1999, India and Pakistan engaged in a bloody conflict over the mostly barren but strategically important mountain peaks of the Kargil district. Kargil district lies on the Line of Actual Control facing the Pakistan border, which comprises the Pakistan Controlled Kashmir region of Baltistan. It is significant to note that the Kargil War was effectively what David Lyon (2003) calls – in relation to 9/11 in the USA – the 'big event' in that, far from being just a long-term process of bureaucratic accretion, stimulated certain specific measures to create a complete database of all 'Indian citizens'. The suggestions of the KRC mostly dealt with Indian defense and internal security policies. One such proposal was that 'steps be taken to issue ID Cards to border villagers in certain vulnerable areas on a priority basis, pending its extension to other or all parts of the State.' The KRC further urged that a policy like this 'would also be relevant in the North-East, Sikkim and part of West Bengal.' (For a detailed timeline regarding the origins of MNIC, see Appendix below.)

Timelines and structure of the MNIC initiative

By April 2007, the 'pilot project' for MNIC was complete. According to an official press release, the 'pilot project' was needed 'to understand and develop the processes for collection and management [of a] database of citizens'. The management of a citizen database will be done through 20 specially constructed centres, one at each Tehsil/Block (sub-district) headquarters. These centres are digitally equipped and connected to a national online database. The back-end management of these centres is done by Bharat Electronics Limited (BEL). The personalization of cards has been entrusted to the Consortium of Central Public Sector Undertakings (CCPSU) comprising BEL, Electronics Corporations of India Limited (ECIL) and Indian Telephone Industries (ITI). The design of the card has been prepared with the help of National Institute of Design (NID) at Ahmedabad.

On 26 May 2007, the Registrar General of India, D.K. Sikri, who is also the Registrar General of Citizens Registration, handed over the first MNIC to Mishro, a resident of the Pooth Khurd Village of the Narela District, of the National Capital Region of Delhi. This document, like many national identity card schemes elsewhere, has the following characteristics: fingerprint biometrics, photograph, digital memory, and standard identity signifiers like name, age, address, etc. The data were collected by asking 16 questions, each linked to a separate category. I will discuss the critical role played by the methodology of collecting data and its relationship to the larger idea of citizenship towards the end of this chapter. First, however, I will concentrate on the technology of smart cards generally, as well as how this technology has been rolled out in the MNIC.

The MNIC as a smart card

The MNIC is a 'smart card'. A smart card is a card with an embedded microchip that can be loaded with data. The card is equipped with a Radio Frequency Identification (RFID) chip, a data tag for storage and retrieval purposes. RFID is a system of Data Carriers and Base Stations. A Data Carrier can be any label, tag, or transponder consisting of an RFID Die, an antenna, and packaging. The Carrier can then be formatted into any plastic ticket. The Base Station acts as a reader that contains an antenna, a radio frequency receiver or transceiver, and a microcontroller or computer. The Base Station can be set up as a desktop, wall mount, or portal. RFID usually means a passive RFID. The transponder is powered by a radio frequency signal rather than a battery. The reader transmits the radio frequency power to the transponder. The transponder can do nothing unless it is near the reader. Depending upon the frequency band, the reader can communicate with the transponder within a range of 20–1,000 cm. The card's memory is a SCOSTA – Smart Card Operating Software for Transport Application – based chip with storage capacity of 16 Kb. With an active RFID, the transponder is powered by battery or fuel cell. The reader and transponders are basically radios that can detect each other within a distance of a kilometer.

The MNIC will be fitted with a passive RFID. In this regard, the card is a breakaway from earlier kinds of 'identity documents'. For instance, ration cards issued in India under the Public Distribution System (the Antyodaya card for the poorest, 'Above Poverty Line, APL' and 'Below Poverty Line, BPL' cards for others) are tactile in that the markers of an individual's identity (such as name, age, or gender) were handwritten, thus susceptible to tampering by the user. This gave way to Indian Photo Voter Identity Cards: laminated cards on which a photograph and identity markers (name, age, etc.) were machine printed.

Although this was an advanced form of technological use compared with the good old ration cards, users could still fudge the documents with false entries. The transformation from manual and mechanical inscriptions of identity signifiers to digital processes shifts the idea of a document to a plane that lies at the border between heterogeneity and homogeneity. For all the data at its root would be composed of Boolean binaries – homogeneous in a way, yet distinct from each other by the operation of a number – and individual personhood would be signified as an objective mark – a mark that could be stored, transmitted, linked, accessed, manipulated, shared and retrieved by what is regarded by their developers as the precise science of a software program.

Theodore M. Porter, in his influential work *Trust in Numbers*, wrote, 'when "philosophers" speak of objectivity of science, they generally mean its ability to know things as they really are' (Porter 1996: 3). Likewise, an 'objective' individual identity of a person – a person as he or she really is – may be a function of 'a body, a memory, and rights and responsibility' (Lyon 2001: 294), together with locatability, social categorization, symbols of eligibility/non-eligibility, etc. (Marx 2001: 312). In this respect, the number becomes useful, as it deconstructs individuals made up of many identities into a totally transparent being. The concern of the State first to know its citizens before governing them results in a desire for complete enumeration (see, e.g. Scott 1998).

The rise of suspicion: A popular culture and media backdrop to the MNIC project

Before returning to the topic of the MNIC specifically, I would like to explore some elements of popular culture, literature and recent events that may illuminate how the Indian population may perceive the MNIC. To that end, at this juncture, it is useful to consider the dialogue from *Fanaa,* a Hindi movie (2006), quoted at the beginning of the chapter. The lines are excerpted from a scene where Agent Tyagi, a surveillance expert, is called in to assist an Anti-'terrorist' Unit to track down an alleged 'terrorist'. She explains to a colleague from the Ministry of Defence methods of discovering more about the alleged 'terrorist', whom they refer to as the 'mastermind'. Throughout the sequence, the characters voice anxieties about not knowing the 'mastermind's' name, location or history. Agent Tyagi repeatedly states that '*no one knows*' who he is. Of course, by 'no one' Agent Tyagi means the State. Unable to deal with the anonymity of the alleged 'terrorist', Agent Tyagi conflates it with a generic assumption. She says, '*He could be anyone or no one*'. The film's narrative, especially after this particular sequence, revolves around determining the identity and personhood of the 'mastermind'. As Tyagi says, '*He has to be found*'. The pertinent question here is: how can this particular person, who could be 'anyone' or 'no one', be found?

In the epic poem *Ramayana*, the trope on which the scene from *Fanaa* seems to draw, there is an instance when Prince Rama's brother Laxmana is fatally wounded by Indrajeet, the son of rival King Ravanna. Laxmana could only be saved by one herb. Hanuman, the monkey god, is sent to fetch Sanjvani, the life-saving herb from the faraway Dronagiri mountain range. Now, Hanuman had no knowledge of herbs and unable to select the right herb, he uses his divine strength to lift the entire Dronagiri mountain range and bring it to the battlefield in Lanka at the southern tip of the Indian subcontinent.

Agent Tyagi's dilemma is similar to Hanuman's. A 'terrorist' who is imagined as a 'deviant personality' type as opposed to a 'normal or average' law-abiding citizen 'has to be found'. Categories, such as 'deviant' or 'normal' seem well-defined so long as they are articulated within a general administrative or policing context. But these categories call for a closer scrutiny, because central to the ideas of 'deviancy' and 'normalcy' lie a State's anxiety to render its population into a visible spectrum, where each hue suggests a particular category. Each category is then subjected to a slightly different legal framework. For instance in the Indian context, the idea of 'Scheduled Castes', 'Minorities', 'Scheduled Tribes', etc. is a very sensitive concern for millions, yet in the public domain, there is little reflection on the foundational logic of these categories. It is still not clear as to who can lay claim to be a 'Scheduled Tribe'. Even after 60 years of independence many 'Tribes' are still negotiating with the Government, often violently, to have their 'Tribe' to be included in the 'Schedule Tribe' Category. In this regard, the use of the word 'normal' as an imagined category becomes significant. It refers to the idea of 'norm' as advocated in a sociological context by Emile Durkheim. In *Empire of Chance*, Ian Hacking, reflecting on Durkheim, writes, 'A moral fact is normal for a determined social type when it is observed in the average of the species, it is pathological in antithetical' (Hacking 1990: 172) which in turn is marked by what is wrong.

In light of such explorations of what is 'normal', it should come as no surprise that media coverage of stories of 'national importance' in India are marked by narratives of 'disruption of normal life' and followed by the rhetoric of 'restoration of normalcy'. This is accompanied by the usual sorting out of 'anomalies'. In this regard, Foucault's burgeoning list of excavations concerning the mad, the recidivist, the insane and the sick could have some notable additions in the form of the 'terrorist' and the suspicious-looking person.

For instance, the Delhi Police, which underpins its public presence through the endearing punch-line *For You With You Always*, launched a media campaign in the wake of an alleged 'terrorist' attack on the Red Fort in December 2000. The campaign 'Let's Fight Terror Together' ran simultaneously with a massive tenant verification drive to register all tenants residing in the city. The seeming logic was that since the alleged 'terrorists' were outsiders to Delhi and had lived in the city for months prior to the attack, it was possible that some of them could still be present. The complementary media campaign ran as an advisory exhorting the citizen to be on alert and be on the lookout for potential 'terrorists'.

In a country such as India, where information superhighways co-exist with potholed lanes of misinformation and uncertainty, any advisory of the sort mentioned above tends to result in a situation where the human ear starts competing with the eye to arrest any seditious developments. Much as novelist Ismail Kadare writes in *The File on H*, '... the ear never rests, for people always want to talk and to whisper, what is said and especially what is muttered is always ... much more dangerous to the State than what can be seen' (Kadare 2006: 26–27).

One year later, in December 2001, in a classic case of tinnitus (a medical term connoting a buzzing sound that blocks all other sounds that is sometimes heard in one or both the ears), the Delhi police arrested a professor of Arabic in Delhi University on charges of waging war against the State. It was claimed that he had a hand in the conspiracy to attack the Indian Parliament on 13 December 2001. On this eventful day, five alleged 'militants' drove into the Parliament compound and started firing indiscriminately. What exactly happened is still not entirely clear, but the Parliament CCTV cameras and TV cameras show an exchange of fire between the police forces/security personnel and these men. All alleged 'militants' were killed in the shootout, and six arrests were made later.

It was alleged that these 'militants' attacked the Indian Parliament because of their dissatisfaction with the State for not granting 'freedom' to the state of Kashmir. The professor was sentenced by a High Court to death, but was later acquitted and absolved of all his charges by the Supreme Court of India in 2003. The sole 'evidence' for his arrest (which was later proved faulty) was transcripts of a 136-second telephone conversation between him and his 18-year-old half-brother in Kashmir. The 13 December attack was termed by the Government and media as 'an attack on the heart of Indian democracy'. So far, out of the six main accused, two have been acquitted for 'lack of evidence' and one is on death row, but there is a sustained campaign for a 'fair trial'. What we have are five dead bodies, and an 'event' that continues to raise questions among those who follow the news.

It is not my purpose to discuss the events of attack on the Indian Parliament *per se*. However, it followed close on the heels of the 11 September 2001 events in the USA, a 'big event' that led to a global overhaul as far as the passing of new 'anti-terror' legislation, such as the Patriot Act. In India, the 13 December event facilitated the passing of draconian anti-terror laws, such as the POTA (Prevention of Terrorism Act 2002).

Coming back to the 'Let's Fight Terror Together' campaign, a 'terrorist' could be any person acting 'suspiciously'. Specifically, this could be anyone wearing clothes unsuited for the season, or trying too conspicuously to blend in with surroundings by his dress and behaviour, or who is too fat or too thin. In other words, to use Agent Tyagi's proclamation, he could be 'anyone or no one'. This rhetoric tends to produce a situation where, on one level, the idea of normality becomes a performance of that which is imagined as 'normal' and on another, creates a perceptional filter of what Gary Marx calls, 'categorical suspicion'.

Perceptional filters have a long history of helping governments to 'see' things. But with regard to the specific idea of 'normality', this filter works both ways. That is, whenever members of a nation-state try to 'see' its population through lenses that are made to 'register' only 'normal' and/or 'abnormal/deviant' populations, more often than not, people respond by becoming more 'normal'. Hence the idea of 'normality' is constantly contested in this tug of war. As Hacking asserts, '… few of us fancy being pathological so "most of us" try to make ourselves normal, which in turn affects what is normal' (Hacking 1990: 2). What are 'normal clothes'? What does one mean when one is talking about 'blending in' with surroundings? What kind of contingent idea of 'normality' does this give rise to? Can one differentiate 'normal' from 'suspicious' behaviour?

The MNIC as proof of 'normality'

The case of a national identity card stretches the idea of 'suspicion' further. Affirming one's trust in the state is a two-fold process. First, one must be aware of one's personhood, or be in possession of a document that can vouch for one's claim. Second, one 'should' have a document that contains a fingerprint, or what Agamben calls 'the most private and incommunicable aspect of subjectivity … the body's biological life', to be not only enumerated but recalled and verified in an instant. Further, through the MNIC, a 15-digit National Identity Number (NIN) will be allotted to each citizen. The state will only recognize a person as him or herself if the memory of personhood as contained in his token matches exactly to a trace of his identity as indexed by the State archives. The link between the name, the person, and his memory is constituted by a number.

The NIN would become mandatory for a range of transactions. Here the 'multiple-purpose' of the national ID card would emerge. From a railway journey to bus travel, from gaining admission to a school to registering property, or from obtaining a driver's license to opening a bank account – for each of these transactions the card-carrying citizen would have to fill in a form and quote his or her NIN. According to an official estimate, the Government of India currently has more than 100,000 different forms pertaining to various departments. Because of increasing pressure by different private lobby groups, the Government has given the nod to mid- and large-sized software companies to actively participate in and share the burden of processing this 'national' information.

Incorporating these parameters and functions, the MNIC may precariously waver towards, as some scholars argue, the 'demeaning' of the identity of an individual. The argument is that personal identity stands to be 'demeaned' as it becomes an 'ersatz-identity', bereft of subjectivity and composed of numbers. As Richard Sobel (2002) explains in his exhaustive essay 'The Demeaning of Identity and Personhood in National Identification Systems', 'NIDS demeans political and personal identity by transforming personhood from an intrinsic quality inhering in individuals into a quantity designated by numbers, represented by physical cards, and recorded in computer databanks'.

However, any identity document gives a lot of 'meaning' when an individual's identity is documented. The urge to acquire identity cards underlines some fundamental assumptions, one being the legitimate claim to State benefits, irrespective of whether one is qualified or not. Beyond these 'benefits', to be unrecognized by the State, to be stateless is, not something that many would desire. Long queues outside Government offices for ration cards, voter ID cards, etc. show a need to be 'acknowledged'.

The coming together of public and private on the MNIC project entailing the sharing of information marks another first. It is the first time the Indian State will allow its memory to be accessed by non-state players. 'G to B' (Government to Business) has emerged as the newest mantra in the rhetoric of e-governance. The State, of course, stands to reap significant benefits if this works out. Instead of a multitudinous array of identity documents bearing different identification numbers, ranging form the Voter ID card to the Permanent Account Number (PAN) Card, driver's licences, and credit cards, it will have to manage only one document with just one identity number.

The MNIC in practice

In the absence of any contemporary or historical evidence of a workable implementation of a national identity card scheme, it is still unclear how successful this initiative will be in the long run. However, we do have strong evidence of a historical tendency by governments to rely on numbers. There seems to be an umbilical relationship between statecraft and the magic of numbers. At this stage, the idea of numbers can perhaps provide us with a suitable point of departure from thinking about numbers from the perspective of government and a governing mentality, of census and unique identity and of traceability and inventorying. To complicate the argument further, it would be worthwhile to think of events and conditions when numbers, in all their idiosyncrasy and abstraction, cannot perform their basic function. That is, when they cease to be unique.

Portuguese novelist Jose Saramgo's *All the Names* is a case in point. It is a riveting account of the Central Registry of Births, Marriages and Deaths. The novel deals with the disappointments, delusions and frustrations of a clerk, Señor Jose, who lives in a single room attached to the Registry. The story, set in a city which, to borrow *Fanaa* rhetoric, could be any or none, goes like this: Señor Jose works in the Registry during the day and 'by night, he ferrets for facts about the famous, compiling his own archive of births, deaths and marriages. One day he chances upon an index card of an ordinary woman whose details hold as much fascination for him as any celebrity's … Jose starts to track the woman down'. After much trial and tribulation he reaches the conclusion that the woman had committed suicide. But his conclusion turns inconclusive after he pays a visit to the cemetery. Señor Jose retells his experience: 'I walked through the general cemetery to the section for suicides, I went to sleep under an olive tree, and the following morning when I woke up, I was in a middle of a flock of sheep, and then I found that the Shepherd amuses himself by swapping around the numbers on the graves before the tombstones are put in place' (Saramago 1999: 243).

The historical desire of a nation state to identify an individual from cradle to grave through the agency of an identity document has taken a new turn. With the emergence of the digitally enabled national identity card we are moving towards the paradoxical specter of opaque transparency: as the citizen becomes more and more transparent in the eyes of the State, the State recedes behind a plethora of alphanumeric archives and databases. For instance, a Public Distribution System or PDS shop would have electronic kiosks instead of personnel from the Food and Civil Supplies Ministry who until now have been sourced locally. The operation and maintenance of the PDS shops would be subcontracted to various private vendors, while only those citizens who are eligible for the category of BPL (below poverty line) would have access to subsidized food. Their claim would, of course, have to be validated through the smart card.

The fabricated image of a person, together with other alphanumeric signifiers, contained in a digitally re-writable, retrievable memory embossed with a national emblem and laminated between transparent sheets, brings to mind the metaphor of a key. Like any key, the MNIC would enable its user to open locks and access various schemes and services. The MNIC will be just like this key, albeit a double-sided one, for it will allow both the State and the citizen to enter into each other's realms.

However, there is a caveat in this meta-narrative, and I am reminded of poet–philosopher Gaston Bachelard's assertion that 'the lock doesn't exist that could resist absolute violence, and all locks are an invitation to thieves' (Bachelard 1994: 81). How will this play itself out in the case of the MNIC? Will the MNIC be able to function as a 'key' as it is made out to be?

A notch gives an outline to a key. It lies on the periphery of a key and forms a firm boundary to a key. The NIN would similarly act as a crafted notch or groove to this key called MNIC. Its unique sequence of numbers will distinguish between the standardized memories of personhood, which acquire legal currency by being valid, and other memories which are too personal, too complex, and too multi-layered to be grouped into any category of time and space or sorted into any form of document, but nevertheless form the basis of who we are. The NIN, according to the proponents of the MNIC, will act as a virtual border between the State machinery and the citizens. Along this border, assuming the system works as planned, any act of transgression would be immediately noticed, no stealth or subterfuge could be practiced, and all acts of masquerade would reveal a hidden identity. This stands in stark contrast to the real frontier, characterized by razor wire fencing and check-posts, where the idea of territory is contested by security forces on a day-to-day basis, and where people may have lived and moved across an ever-changing line for years, where the terrain is marked by negotiated crossings, dealings with middle-men, farewells and promises of return.

At the borders of identity

The physical frontier becomes the space where the State confronts its biggest dilemma. How to sort individuals out? How to decide who is who? How to ascer-tain the truthful claim about an identity? How to gauge if the *lungi* clad person is from this side or that? Perhaps the answer is being looked for in the MNIC card.

In the case of Indian borders, like most others, the problem is compounded as the line between an alien and a citizen is very fuzzy. Border posts are places where identity documents assume hyper-significance, where a heightened state of alert-ness is the 'norm'. These are locations where 'anyone' can be asked to prove his or her identity, and where a lack of an identity document quickly transforms the pre-sumption of innocence into a presumption of guilt. India shares a 2,912 km border with Pakistan, a 4,053 km border with Bangladesh, 1,690 km border with Nepal, and a 3,380 km border with China. There have been border disputes with Pakistan, China, and Bangladesh. There have been three wars with Pakistan, and one with China. Borders lie on the edges of a nation-state. What kind of an imagination of lived experience would result if one were to think of a nation without a centre – where the distinction between the centre and the periphery collapses, where the centre becomes the border, where presumption of guilt is 'normalized' and where the 'citizen' needs to be distinguished from the 'alien' through a smart identifica-tion card?

'Border Management' is a chapter of a highly influential report on national secu-rity entitled 'Reforming the National Security System-Recommendations of the Group of Ministers'. It reads, 'In fact, barring Madhya Pradesh, Chhattisgarh, Jharkhand, Delhi and Haryana, all other States in the country have one or more international borders or a coastline and can be regarded as frontline States from the point of view of border management'. Quantitatively speaking, according to this report, out of a total of 28 states and 7 Union Territories in India, all but 5 states, for all administrative and political purposes, are to be regarded as a 'Border'. This may well transform to a situation where citizens may be seen as potential immigrants (read 'aliens') by the state. With an internal collapse of the periphery, the idea of the hinterland merges with notion of the border. In its wake, the self-sustaining myth of inside and outside is engulfed. Particular ethnic, religious and political identities are overtaken by an affective national identity underlined by a document.

Furthermore, the report puts the blame on illegal immigration. 'Illegal migration has assumed serious proportions. There should be compulsory registration of citizens and non-citizens living in India. This will facilitate preparation of a national register of citizens. All citizens should be given a Multi-Purpose National Identity Card (MPNIC) and non-citizens should be issued identity cards of a different color and design'. For the illegal immigrant to be marked and verified, the citizen has to be stabilized, and for the citizen to be marked and verified, the illegal immigrant has to be stabilized. For all purposes and unless stipulated otherwise, the not-so-apparent dichotomy between the legal citizen and the illegal immigrant is sorted out, and the state would find itself sinking deep in self-demarcated tautological quick-sands.

The national identity card appears as a desperate attempt to bolster what Arjun Apadurai argues is 'a fundamental and dangerous idea behind the very idea of the modern nation state, the idea of a 'national ethnos' (Appadurai 2006: 3). While in the act of taking off the ballast involving a whole set of other identities, the state seems to be prescribing a unitary identity, to keep its wobbly boat afloat. The rhetoric of one nation, one land, one border, one citizen seems to assert itself through a dreamlike gaze of the state underwritten by – highly technologized – ideas of modernity.

Given the internal haemorrhage that the MNIC may potentially have initiated between the fringe and the core, albeit at a very minute scale, it is interesting to note how subtle changes in the syntactic structure of this minutely calibrated grandiloquence has helped push the dreams of mobility beyond national boundaries. This was evident in the misreading of the Hindi language title of the MNIC by the people of Pooth Khurd, the village north-west of Delhi. Pooth Khurd was earmarked for the pilot project of the MNIC scheme. The erstwhile farmlands of this village have been transformed into urban clusters following the rapid expansion of Delhi and the absorption of the frontline rural/semi-urban areas into the metropolis. Malls, multiplexes and high-rise apartment blocks have appeared. Compensation money for the displaced farmers was supposedly 'adequate' but when I visited this village in 2006, the dominant narrative was one of lack of livelihood. Former agriculturalists were finding it difficult to move into newer occupations and work cultures. I conducted a series of interviews with a group of men from this village. One of them complained: 'We don't have work, but this does not mean we are poor'. This was evident in the range of new cars parked along the yet-to-be-constructed *pucca* roads of the village.

When I asked them about the MNIC, their faces lit up. They all remembered the day when the Sub-Divisional Magistrate (SDM) came to their village and told them about a '*Hara Card*' or a 'Green Card'. Many people told me how they would take foreign tours; some also said that their dream of settling abroad would finally come true in the near future. This narrative, though somewhat odd, was a recurrent theme in all my subsequent visits to Pooth Khurd. Still, the connection between the MNIC and going abroad was unclear. Many visits later, while I was listening to an illiterate farmer talking about places he would visit in England, I chanced upon the possible link. I was admiring the jute presented to him by the SDM, on account of his role as responsible community elder. The farmer had mobilized over 50 people to share their biometric and other personal information with the officials of the State. The letters 'MNIC' were inscribed on either side of the jute bag in English and Hindi. MNIC, in Hindi, reads as *Bahu-uddeshye Rashtriya Pechan Patra* or Multipurpose National Identity Card. But what the people of Pooth Khurd read was *Bahu deshye Rashtriya Pechan Patra* or Multi 'Nation' National Identity Card. Phonetically, there is little difference between *Bahu Deshye* and *Bahu Uddeshye*. But semantically, it inverts the very idea of a national identity card with its notions of fixed citizenship and singular national identities.

Much has happened since that particular visit to Pooth Khurd. A whole range of smart cards have surfaced, from biometric passports to smart health cards and smart cards for access to subsidized food grains under the Public Distribution System. There is talk of an Integrated Smart Card, which will collapse these other cards into the MNIC. And according to a Planning Commission Report of January 2007, recommendations are being put forth to include children within the smart card project.

Creating membership: Taking everyone into account

'How to take children into account?' This is the predicament the Government of India seems to be grappling with. A report entitled 'Entitlement Reform for Empowering the Poor: The Integrated Smart Card' deals with problems pertaining to the distribution of benefits under various governmental schemes. This peculiar quandary has arisen as the MNIC would only be given to persons who are 15 years of age and above, thus depriving a lot of children of benefits. The report recommends, 'the biometric information of all family members needs to be in-built into the smart card'. On the question of citizenship status, the report suggests, 'The creation of a data base of residents and assignment of a unique ID to each resident is much easier than the creation of a database of citizens, because of the difficulty of authentication of citizenship and the legal implications that it may have'.

The idea of the MNIC began as an attempt to mark all citizens permanently and accord them with formal national membership – a membership which would surpass other memberships denoted by filial relations, region, religion, language, gender, caste, community, locality, etc. and result in a creation of a unitary club. Significantly, the project failed to take into account the complex praxis that exists between the idea of an individual identity as imagined by the State and an identity as lived by people. To complicate matters further, the Planning Commission Report (January 2007) makes it abundantly clear that the Government is tinkering with the idea of collapsing individual identities into group identities. This move would create new membership pools within a larger sea of already existing sets of memberships.

In a country with a documented history of mass internal migration, a national register of residency would facilitate the creation of hitherto unimagined membership pools – unimagined because these pools will tend to push valid citizens without a formal residency status towards the brink of illegality, while genuinely 'illegal' immigrants would try to mask their existence by acquiring all available tokens of legitimate identification.

Blurred borders among 'citizens'

The creation of newer sets of membership would create fresh categories for identification. Together with existent categories, the emergent categories will tend towards an amorphous idea of national group membership where at least some of the members will be neither totally included in nor excluded from the group. In the absence of distinct forms of identification, the ongoing experimentation is producing a somewhat 'Fuzzy Logic' of national identity. According to Lotfi Zadeh, mathematician and co-author of *Fuzzy Logic*, Fuzzy Truth is something which represents membership in vaguely defined 'sets' and not a result of an event or condition. Fuzzy Logic allows for 'set membership' to range from 'Slightly' to 'Quite' to 'Very'.

In a frontier-like situation, a national identity card would create a 'universal set' of Indians, but as the Planning Commission Report (January 2007) suggests, this 'set' may have many 'subsets'. For instance, the state of Kerala has its smart cards for Commercial Sex Workers, the Indian army is considering a proposal to issue health smart cards for HIV-positive soldiers, and car drivers have smart driver's licences. Subsets around occupations, health conditions, and mode of transport are just a few of the many that may arise. The Fuzzy Logic of the MNIC will make 'Indian-ness' an attribute dependent not just on the document, but also on one's projected image of being a 'normal' Indian. The contestations for claims to national membership through the MNIC card will arise in the domain of truth claims. They will be marked by attempts to look like or furnish proof of evidence of 'Indian-ness', which would make one 'Slightly Indian' or 'Quite Indian' or 'Very Indian'. Depending on the success of an individual's claims, a person would get a Multi-purpose National Identity Card (MNIC) or a Multi-purpose Residency Card (MRR).

In the not-much-talked-about case of 400 Iranian immigrants to the small town of Murshidabad, in the state of West Bengal, the logic of Fuzzy Logic becomes apparent. These people settled in Murshidabad 80 years ago – well before the independent Indian nation-state was formed. The MNIC survey party failed to accord a single one of them Indian citizenship status. So what are they: Persian-speaking Indians or Bengali-speaking Iranians? Are they 'Slightly', 'Quite' or 'Very' Indian?

The 16 categorical questions in the Government Performa for MNIC, mentioned earlier in the essay, must be answered not through a straight tick or a cross but by giving information supported by evidence. This evidence is then turned over to a verification team headed by a supervisor. The verification team will ascertain the citizenship status of each individual. If evidence is unavailable, the decision of the verification team and the sub-divisional magistrate would be crucial in granting citizenship to a hitherto undocumented individual. Thus, by its very nature the MNIC questionnaire generates slippages within categories. For an individual to arrest these slippages and be verified correctly he must either produce evidence or show by some other means that he is 'very Indian'.

Hence, cases like those of the Iranian migrant community discussed above, with their 'slightly Indian' features, clearly escape the bureaucratic exercise of rendering an individual into a citizen. In order to belong to a nation, an individual must conform to categories anchored by questionnaires, certificates, oaths, and affirmations. Non-conformance results in new categories, which in turn produce narratives of illegality and suspicion.

Likely consequences

In the scenario discussed above, 'under-represented' sections of the Indian society, like the 'undocumented', the 'poor' or the 'minorities', could be subjected to discrimination. Although at this stage this proposition might be regarded as a conjecture, it underlines the importance of *a priori* evidence made necessary to be granted a MNIC card. Unfortunately, millions of un-credentialed Indians do not have any evidence of their existence. MNIC card project proposes to create a centralized database linked to individual card holders, which would then be connected to social benefit schemes. Hence a non-possession of the card on account of lack of evidence needed for its procurement might result in denial of services to the very people it was meant to be for in the first place.

Another important aspect of the MNIC debate is a moral one. It is still not clear as to how the data garnered by the MNIC will be used. Who will access this database? A report by Human Rights Features cautions the idea of storing personal information of an entire country in 'one database'. The report suggests that the MNIC card may infringe on the privacy of individuals as there is a 'possibility of corruption and exploitation of data'.

The proposed data gathered through the MNIC project would concretize existing categories. However, the right or the privilege to belong to these categories is still being disputed by people. 'Categorical suspicion' by the State is deeply contested by 'categorical affirmation' by a large chunk of society, which regard legible identity documents as the only vehicle for legible citizenship. Far from a scenario of total surveillance by a 'Big Brother', the Indian experiment with identity documents is a case of the fuzzy logic of membership.

Bibliography

Agar, J. (2001) 'Modern horrors: British identity and identity cards', in J. Caplan and J. Torpey (eds) *Documenting Individual Identity*, Princeton: Princeton University Press.
Appadurai, A. (2006) *Fear of Small Numbers: An Essay on the Geography of Anger*, Durham: Duke University Press.

Bachelard, G. (1994) *The Poetics of Space,* reprint ed. Uckfield: Beacon Press.

Caplan, J. and Torpey, J. (2001) *Documenting individual Identity,* Princeton: Princeton University Press.

Castells, M. (2000) *The Rise of Network Society*, 2nd ed. Oxford: Wiley-Blackwell.

Castells, M. (2003) *The Power of Identity,* 2nd ed. Malden: Blackwell Publishing.

Cole, S.A (2002) *Suspect Identities: A History of Fingerprinting and Criminal Identification*, Harvard: Harvard University Press.

Fanaa (2006) A Hindi movie.

Gigerenzer, G., Swijtink, Z., Porter, T. and Daston, L. (1990) *The Empire of Chance: How Probability Changed Science and Everyday Life*, Cambridge: Cambridge University Press.

Goffman, E. (1999) *The Presentation of Self in Everyday Life,* Gloucester, MA: Peter Smith.

Groebner, V. (2001) 'Describing the Person, reading the signs in late medieval and renaissance Europe: identity papers, vested figures, and limits of identification, 1400–1600', in J. Caplan and J. Torpey J. (eds) *Documenting Individual Identity,* Princeton: Princeton University Press.

Hacking, I. (1990) *The Taming of Chance (Ideas in Context),* Cambridge: Cambridge University Press.

Hacking, I. (2001) *An Introduction to Probability and Inductive Logic.* Cambridge: Cambridge University Press.

Kadare, I. (2002) *The File on H*, reprint ed. New York: Arcade Publishing.

Kadare, I. (2006) *The File on H*, reprint ed. New York: Arcade Publishing.

Lyon, D. (1994) *The Electronic Eye: The Rise of Surveillance Society*, Minneapolis: University of Minnesota Press.

Lyon, D. (2001) 'Under my skin: from identification papers to body surveillance', in J. Caplan and J. Torpey (eds) *Documenting Individual Identity.* Princeton: Princeton University Press.

Lyon, D. (2002) *Surveillance as Social Sorting: Privacy, Risk and Automated Discrimination,* London: Routledge.

Lyon, D. (2003) *Surveillance after September 11,* Cambridge: Polity Press.

Marx, G. (1989) *Protecting Privacy in Surveillance Societies*, Chapel Hill: University of North Carolina Press.

Marx, G. (2001) 'Identifying anonymity: some conceptual distinctions and issues for research', in J. Caplan and J. Torpey (eds) *Documenting Individual Identity.* Princeton: Princeton University Press.

Porter, T.M. (1996) *Trust in Numbers,* reprint ed. Princeton: Princeton University Press.

Prevention of Terrorism Act (2002) 'Interception of communication in certain cases', Chapter V, Government of India Act No. 15.

Scott, J. (1998) *Seeing Like a State*, New Haven: Yale University Press.

Saramago, J. (1999) *All the Names*, London: Harvill Panther.

Sengoopta, C. (2004) *Imprint of the Raj: How Fingerprinting was Born in Colonial India*, London: Pan Books.

Sobel, R. (2002) 'The demeaning of identity and personhood in national identification systems, Spring', *Harvard Journal of Law & Technology* 15: 2.

Torpey, J. (1999) *The Invention of the Passport: Surveillance, Citizenship and the State,* Cambridge: Cambridge University Press.

Appendix

Timeline of MNIC

a   26 May 1999: Kargil War with Pakistan begins.

b   26 July 1999: Kargil War ends.

c   29 July 1999: Government of India appoints the Kargil Review Committee (KRC) through Order No. 361/6/4/99-TS.

d   7 January 2000: The KRC submits a 228-page report to the Prime Minister. One of the key recommendations of the report is to take steps 'to issue ID Cards to border villagers in certain vulnerable areas on a priority basis, pending its extension to other or all parts of the State'.

e   17 April 2000: On the advice of the KRC, the Indian Government forms the Group of Ministers (GoM) through an order No.141/2/1/2000-TS.

f   22 December 2000: Red Fort in Delhi attacked by alleged 'terrorists'.

g   January 2001: Delhi police launches 'Tenant Verification' drive – the first ever compilation of data on 'Tenants' in Delhi.

h   26 February 2001: The GoM submits its report to the Prime Minister. A paragraph in Chapter V of the report, entitled 'Border Management', reads, 'There should be compulsory registration of citizens and non-citizens living in India. This will facilitate preparation of a national register of citizens. All citizens should be given a Multi-Purpose National Identity Card (MPNIC) and non-citizens should be issued identity cards of a different color and design'.

i   23 April 2003: Pilot Project on Multipurpose National Identity Card is initiated.

j   26 May 2007: RGI DK Sikri hands over the first tranche of National ID cards to the villagers of Pooth Khurd.

8 Population ID card systems in the Middle East

The case of the UAE

*Zeinab Karake-Shalhoub**

Introduction

Over the past few years, there has been a rapidly growing awareness among governments worldwide of the necessity to secure the protection of digital identities, assets and transactions, and, as such, to develop nationwide IT infrastructures in order to deliver more secure, efficient and convenient ID services to their citizens. Each year carries more declarations from governments of initiatives and projects to bring into play smart cards as national identity documents. Although many of those plans are modified or cancelled due to political pressures or budgetary constraints, some are indeed initiated. A number of Middle Eastern countries, especially members of the Gulf Cooperation Council (GCC),[1] are rolling out biometric chip-based National ID cards that all citizens must carry.

The many transformations brought about by the 'digital revolution' are countless, and the diffusion of wired and wireless technologies is growing at an unprecedented rate; the figures speak for themselves; by the end of 2006, there were 1 billion Internet users, about 3 billion mobile phone subscribers, and more than 3 billion bank card holders. Forecast data shows that, worldwide, revenues from what is known as Identity and Access Management (IAM) Technology is expected to grow from US$3.4 billion in 2006 to more than US$5 billion in 2010, exclusive of services.[2] Despite the many benefits brought by the new technology, fears and other issues were brought with them, such as identity theft, security, privacy of information, intrusion into data systems, and phishing; these are holding people back from taking full advantage of the new systems.

This chapter will examine ID Card System Projects in countries of the Gulf Cooperation Council (GCC), in general, and the United Arab Emirates, in particular. In addition to a descriptive review of the features of the proposed ID cards and associated tools, the chapter will also examine the institutional mechanisms enacted by governments of those countries to ensure the success of the projects, as well as those management issues and challenges faced by citizens and governments.

Biometric National ID cards and programmes

Biometrics is an automated method of identifying or verifying the identity of a living human being based on a physiological or behavioural characteristic unique to that individual. The most common biometrics in use today include: fingerprint verification; iris recognition; hand geometry; voice verification; signature verification; and facial recognition (Ryan 2006). The application of biometric technologies is not a new phenomenon; for a long time, they have commonly been utilized in the private sector, such as in the banks and other financial institutions, secure nuclear or chemical sites, or for the security of particular products, such as narcotics. Furthermore, biometric technologies have been consistently used as surveillance tools to track the comings and goings of employees in large institutions.

National ID programmes have proliferated in the past few years, especially after the 9/11 terrorist attack. These programmes are motivated by a myriad of factors, however, and based on the author's review of the various programmes worldwide, concerns related to security, border control and financial criminality are the main incentives behind such programmes. Programmes involving smart cards vary from one country to another. For instance, with the largest smart card ID programme in the world, China is in the process of issuing in excess of 800 million contactless ID cards (called the Second Generation National ID Card) with no biometrics and no other applications. On the other side of the spectrum, Malaysia's 18 million MyKad smart cards carry fingerprint biometrics and digital signatures, and are designed to function as a payment card with e-purse, to have health data embedded into them and even to pay transit fares and tolls.

ID cards are also being introduced in some democratic countries. The UK government is drawing up plans for a compulsory ID card combining biometrics with a smart card in an effort to tackle identity fraud, which costs the country UK£1.3 billion each year. Trials involving 10,000 volunteers have been launched from the passport office in London and three other centres around Britain. Recently, legislation for the British national identity card was passed under the Identity Cards Act 2006 (ICA).[3] The cards are linked to a database known as the National Identity Register (NIR). Despite the controversy and heated debate concerning the UK card, early in August of 2007, the UK government has formally launched the selection process to choose a contractor to run the controversial National Identity Card scheme which is due for rollout from 2009, and would become compulsory in time (see Wills, Chapter 10).

In addition to national ID card initiatives around the world, there has been an international move towards the introduction of biometrics into identity and travel documents. The International Civil Aviation Organization (ICAO), an agency of the United Nations, has recommended that all countries adopt biometric passports, and the USA has made it a future requirement for entering the USA under the visa waiver programme (Luce 2007). The standards of contactless passports set by the ICAO will add momentum to push for chip-based national ID.

With many governments now considering, or upgrading, their identity cards, biometrics and smart cards are coming of age in a variety of countries. Malaysia,

Brunei, Bahrain, Saudi Arabia, Oman and the United Arab Emirates are just a handful of developing countries that have recently adopted national ID smart cards using fingerprint technology. It is believed that these cards will provide advantages to government and citizens alike. The government is able to enhance its identification processes, improve its infrastructure, modernize its national registry system, increase homeland security and provide better quality services to citizens. Cardholders, meanwhile, can identify themselves electronically. Many countries, including those of the Middle East in general, and the GCC in particular, are applying biometric technology primarily for the purpose of securing their borders and, especially in the case of the GCC, controlling the influx of foreign workers. Biometric smart ID card technology is becoming considerably more common in the Middle East and around the world because of the advancement of standards governing biometric ID cards, and because governments and corporations are becoming more cautious about security, especially when it comes to border control.

The GCC countries

The Gulf Cooperation Council (GCC) was established in 1981 between Bahrain, Kuwait, Oman, Qatar, Saudi Arabia and the UAE. The main objectives behind the creation of the GCC are their geographic proximity and their general adoption of free trade economic policies. The ultimate purpose of forming the GCC was to effect coordination, integration and inter-connection between member states in all fields in order to achieve unity between them, to deepen and strengthen relations, links and areas of cooperation between their peoples, to promote the development of industry, agriculture, science and technology, to establish scientific research centres, set up joint ventures and encourage economic and trade cooperation by the private sector. These goals have been very far from being attained, mainly for political reasons.

The involvement of the GCC countries as active participants in the information/knowledge society and their move to electronic governments has motivated a number of them to undertake biometric ID card initiatives. Member countries' involvement as active participants in the 'digital revolution' is apparent when one looks at a number of international indicators and standards developed by multinational organizations, such as the Economic Freedom Index, the Information Society Index and the Digital Access Index (Karake-Shalhoub 2006).

The Countries of the Gulf also have distinctive cultural, social, economic and political structures. With a total population of approximately 34 million people, on the economic front, the revenues gained from the exportation of crude oil over the last 35 years have made rapid modernization of the GCC economies and infrastructures possible. The GCC holds 45 per cent of the world's oil reserves and supplies 20 per cent of global crude production.

Over the past three decades, GCC countries have witnessed unparalleled social and economic changes. Oil revenues, to varying degrees, have been put into modernizing infrastructures, creating jobs and enhancing social structures. Average *per capita* income in the GCC countries was estimated at about US$26,000 in 2006 ranging from US$13,300 for Saudi Arabia to US$49,700 for the UAE, with their combined nominal GDP reaching close to US$571 billion, ranging from US$12 billion for Bahrain to US$277 billion for Saudi Arabia (more than half the GDP of all Middle Eastern countries). With very low inflation, overall real economic growth has averaged 4.2 per cent per year during the past three decades, while the importance of non-oil economic activities has grown steadily, reflecting GCC countries' efforts at economic diversification. Moreover, central bank international reserves alone in some GCC countries are equivalent to about 10 months of imports. This progress has been achieved with an open exchange and trade system and liberal capital flows, as well as open borders for foreign labour. The GCC area has become an important centre for regional economic growth.

Security is a major issue for the GCC, but finding an agreeable prescription that satisfies all GCC member countries is a challenge. While member countries of the GCC state that they desire to reduce their dependence on the USA for security, there is no consensus over alternative ways of achieving their security goals. Differences have surfaced over the depth, scope and pace of political reform. The escalation of militant Islam and its consequences throughout the whole region is a big challenge for these countries. Differences also surfaced over the US-led invasion of Iraq. While some GCC states opposed the action, others served as bases for military and political campaigns.

On the social front, the most important issue to discuss is the population imbalance. The infusion of petrodollars since the beginning of the 1970s allowed the GCC countries to initiate large-scale infrastructure and development projects. Short of labour, these countries turned their eyes to Asia for this resource, initially importing labourers from South Asia, mainly India and Pakistan, and currently tapping the markets of East Asia and South-east Asia. Initially, the GCC countries intended to keep migration temporary, and this was the main reason why they turned to Asian, as opposed to Arab, workers. In line with this objective, workers are hired on a contractual basis and are required to return home at the end of their contracts. More than 30 years later, the GCC countries continue to employ Asian workers in very high numbers. Not only do migrant workers account for a large percentage of the population, the foreign population is larger than the local population in most of the Gulf countries. If we take the UAE as an example, 17 per cent of the total population are locals (emiratis) and the remaining 83 per cent are foreign expatriates. This heavy dependence on foreign workers and the demographic imbalance has been a source of unease for the GCC governments, prompting them to promote the nationalization of their labour force. However, most of these programmes are facing challenges mainly caused by demographics and social structures. Given this reality, the biggest threat for the GCC governments comes from the inside and not the outside. Somehow this threat has to be managed.

To summarize, the healthy economic conditions and the goal of modernizing their economies, coupled by the political structure in the region and the population imbalance, have led the GCC governments to embark on National ID cards projects. Furthermore, many of these countries do not have Population Register Databases.

Thus, one of the objectives of these initiatives is the creation of such centralized databases.

National ID card projects in the GCC

Experts agree that oil and heightening security concerns are stimulating the planned and existing introduction of complex National ID cards in the Middle East in general, and the Gulf countries in particular. Among other initiatives, these projects are making the region stand out relative to the rest of the world. Table 8.1 represents the main features of the smart card-based national ID projects in the GCC countries.

The proposed chip-based National ID cards in the countries of the Arabian Gulf are quietly moving ahead with plans for the introduction of millions of cards. Currently, five out of the six member GCC countries – Oman, United Arab Emirates, Saudi Arabia, Qatar and Bahrain – are in the process of issuing ID smart cards to their citizens and legal residents. Other states in and around the Arabian Gulf and the Middle East plan some type of chip-based ID cards of their own, either for government employees or for citizens and residents.

Worldwide concerns related to security, border control and financial criminality have prompted governments in the Gulf Cooperation Council (GCC) to fight identity theft; the growing need of governments to authenticate remote users, combined with the increasing concerns of traditional ID theft and fraud, has influenced technologically proactive governments in the GCC, such as the UAE, to convert to smart card-based ID solutions. The UAE, as an early adopter of smart National ID cards, is standing at the forefront of global e-government trends. The five abovementioned countries are combining their smart card chips with some kind of biometric identifier, such as fingerprint and facial images. To facilitate coordination, the GCC countries have formed a special committee, The Specialized Committee on Implementation of ID Cards, with the main purpose of synchronizing and managing the process of issuing National ID cards. In April 2006, the Committee recommended the launch of a pilot phase of the 'ID Card Recognition' initiative between the UAE, Oman and Bahrain borders.[4]

Notwithstanding the similarities among the GCC member states, each country has unique challenges balancing political and administrative demands with citizens' privacy. Early evaluation of the systems implemented so far shows that, from a technical perspective, the system operates smoothly when assessed on the usability, accuracy and scalability dimensions. In other words, the issuing and scanning procedures appear to be sound.[5] There are, however, concerns that citizens' rights and data protection might have been addressed only marginally. Furthermore, there might be significant concerns over the lack of legal and technological provisions to ensure data protection in a number of these countries, a fact which is particularly worrying considering the wide range of personal information stored. Many of the projects have not been fully executed, and as they unfold, we will be following their implementation and evaluating the issues pertaining to citizens' privacy/security, and the legal and technological dimensions.[6] With respect to Internet privacy laws

Table 8.1 Smart card-based national ID projects in the GCC countries

Country	Launch date	Cards issued	Cards projected	Biometrics	Mandatory	Extra features (existing/planned)	Department in charge
Bahrain	2005	30,000	700,000	Fingerprint	Yes	Health, Driver's Licence, e-purse	Bahrain Central Informatics Organization (CIO)
Oman	2002	1.2 million	2.5 million	Fingerprint	Yes	Government services, travel	General Department for Civil Affairs of the Omani Police/ Police and Customs Department
Qatar	2007		700,000	Fingerprint	Yes	e-Government, travel/contact and contactless technology	Qatar Ministry of Interior
Saudi Arabia	2006		15 million		Yes	Data stored on optical stripe as well as chip	Ministry of Interior
UAE	2005	150,000	5.0 million	Fingerprint	Yes	Driver's licence	Emirates Identity Authority (EIDA)

and legislation, no specific law for data protection exists in the GCC countries, although the recent Electronic Transactions and Commerce Act of the UAE (June 2006) may contain data protection clauses in Part 2. The UAE constitution grants the right to privacy and the UAE Penal Code protects individuals from the interception and disclosure of their data.[7]

One of the biggest challenges in the UAE ID Card projects is to build a National Registry System (NRS) or a Central Population Registry. It is believed that a central population database that allows a country to build a record with data collected from different databases where data is stored per category, e.g. pictures, fingerprints, demographics, etc. is a major objective of these initiatives. Currently, the UAE does not have such population registry service in place. Through the central population databases, authorities can now register details for each UAE citizen and foreign resident (i.e. births, marriages, divorces and deaths), in a single centralized system. Data is collected in real-time in regional offices, where each citizen can receive his/her ID card within just half an hour. The creation of central population databases is an integral part of the ID programmes in the various GCC countries, and will act as the pillar of a country's future e-government initiatives.

In addition to the ID programme, many of the GCC countries have implemented electronic gates (e-gates) for border control. Instead of standing in long lines waiting to get a passport stamped, e-gate card holders can show up at a terminal, swipe the card, give a fingerprint and head off to baggage claim. The e-gate is a smart card which includes a person's name, address, nationality, picture and fingerprints as a biometric identification. Citizens and foreign nationals with work visas can get cards. Initially, the system was established in Dubai, and has been used at Dubai International Airport since 2004; but was expanded to other airports in the UAE. This system has proven to be a success with hundreds of thousands of people in the UAE holding e-gate passes. Recently (beginning of 2006), the Dubai Naturalisation and Residency Department (DNRD) announced that it was working towards establishing IT connectivity between Dubai International Airport (DIA) and Heathrow Airport in London to facilitate use of e-gate card by passengers at the two airports. According to a UAE official, the objective of providing IT connectivity between UAE ports of entry and Heathrow is the first step towards establishing better coordination between various airports of the world, which in turn will help simplify passenger travel (*Khaleej Times* 2005).

The use of biometrics technology is not new to the UAE government; in fact, the UAE had implemented iris recognition as a means of border control in 2003. The country has found iris recognition to be an effective overt security means for preventing expelled foreigners from re-entering the country. Foreign workers expelled from the country were trying to re-enter with different passports including different names and date of birth, and were admitted back into the UAE (Rosenzweig and Kochems 2004). Indeed, back in 2002, the UAE started the development of a biometric-based system that scans all individuals arriving in the country to verify whether or not the individual is banned from entering the country. The UAE has generally found that a biometric that did not change over time, that could be quickly acquired, was easy to use in real time, is safe and non-invasive and could be scaled in the millions.

As of early March 2007, the UAE had enrolled close to 1 million irises. It enrols approximately 600 new irises per day. At the time of writing, some 7 billion iris comparisons are performed every day in a national security deployment covering all 27 air, land, and sea ports of entry into the UAE, comparing arriving passengers against a central database of iris patterns (about 9,000 daily arrivals are each compared by real time exhaustive search against an enrolled database of close to 1 million iris codes, making 9 billion iris comparisons per day). According to the UAE Ministry of Interior, over the past 4.5 years, this system has caught some 50,000 persons trying to enter or re-enter the UAE under false travel documents (House of Commons Science and Technology Committee 2006).

In general, the UAE has found iris recognition technology easy to use, and the system is regularly used by people unfamiliar with or unskilled in the technology, and in transit areas. The UAE is now considering creating a unified Arab list. The country is also considering a similar system to identify all individuals. Currently, the UAE identity cards are smart cards that contain fingerprints, and the UAE is considering including a person's iris code in the near future. Iris codes may also be placed on passports. The UAE's experience with iris recognition technology is that biometrics enhance the nation's security (*Al Ittihad Newspaper* 2004).

The United Arab Emirates is the second country (after Oman) in the Gulf to implement a smart National ID initiative; on 9 June 2006, a new law giving the Emirates Identity Authority (EIDA) responsibility for the introduction of a modern Population Register and ID Card system for all citizens and residents was proclaimed and signed by the President of the United Arab Emirates (Federal Law No. 9 for 2006 for the Population Register and ID Card System). This law consists of 32 articles addressing definitions, establishing the system and registration process, the ID card itself, and data retrieval and penalties. The purpose of this project is motivated by the promise that issuing an advanced personal ID card will replace many other identification methods, such as Labor cards, driving licences, health ID cards, to name just a few. The Emirates Identity Authority is an independent federal authority established by virtue of the federal decree No. 2 of 2004 (issued in September 2004). The decree has empowered the Authority with ultimate powers required for the execution of Population Register Project and the new identity card. Through this project, the Authority shall achieve two fundamental tasks, which are:

1   The establishment of a modern population register in order to facilitate the obtainment of government services for the public as well as to provide the required information for supporting decision-making, strategic planning and the allocation of sources in the fields of education, healthcare, housing, energy and other domains.
2   Issuance of identity cards for the whole population in the country, in order to verify and confirm the identity of each individual through the personal number and the smart card thus it shall be related to the biological features of the individual.

Early discussion of the UAE National ID card project started in early 2000, and it was not until July 2003 that the Ministry of Interior (then the organization in charge of the project) outsourced the development and design of the system. June 2005 witnessed the first pilot project where a limited number of citizens in the UAE armed forces were to register and issued ID cards. The mass rollout for the project started in mid-2007; already 14 service points were established around the country. It is expected that the registration process for all citizens and residents in the country (close to 5 million people) will take three years. The cost of the project is expected to be close to US$55 (AED 200 million).

The strategic goals of the UAE National ID card project are motivated by security and economical reasons.[8] From the security angle, three benefits were identified: (1) to enhance homeland security; (2) to minimize identity theft; and (3) to improve access/delivery of public service. It is believed that an integrated population database will enhance homeland security by being able to accurately identify a person within the UAE population; in addition, it will provide a foundation for a government trusted and robust identity verification infrastructure based on advanced technologies that will protect individuals against identity theft. Further, it will provide identification and authentication services to other ministries, banks and hospitals, such as driving licences, ATM cards, health cards, Labor cards, border control, iris scans, e-gate, and so on.

The economic goals of the project are identified as: (a) one card, multi-use; (b) strategic decision-making support; and (c) e-government and e-commerce support. Decision-makers at EIDA believe that unification of existing cards (labour, health, driving licence, etc.) into one ID smart card will reduce management and production costs; in addition to facilitating cross border and travel within the GCC countries. The smart ID card will also help in better planning and resource allocation and utilization; a centralized population registry will provide timely, accurate statistical information for strategic decision-making and long-term planning for education, healthcare, energy, etc. The smart ID card is also believed to support the country in its journey toward becoming a digitized economy, by building a national e-authentication infrastructure which will form the foundation for e-government services and e-commerce initiatives.

The card will be required for all citizens and residents (close to 5 million people), with biometrics captured for all those 15 years old or above (optional for those under 15). As of 31 December 31 2006, and as part of the second phase of its implementation, the UAE Population Register and Identity Card (PIRDC) system has been linked with the ministries of Interior, Labor, Health, Justice and Education. The first phase of the project started on March 2005 and included members of the UAE Armed Forces and Interior Ministry. The second phase of the project, completed in December 2006, included the registration of employees at federal ministries, government departments and non-government establishments. The number of ID cards issued in the UAE is currently around 150,000, and is expected to be finalized by the end of 2009. It is expected that the third phase will begin in mid-2007, and it will cover the whole of the UAE population (citizens and expatriates); a total of about 5 million people.

The UAE government had earlier in 2007 finalized a fee structure for the National ID card, under which the UAE nationals would pay AED 100 (US$27) to register and obtain the new card with a validity of five years. The registration fee for expatriates is linked to the validity period of their visas. An expatriate holding a one-year visa will be charged AED 100, with the fee going up in multiples of AED 100 for each year up to AED 300 for an individual holding a three-year visa.

In January 2007, EIDA reported that new registration centres will open in the first quarter of 2007. These are located in Sharjah, Delma Island and Dubai. The Delma Island registration centre will function in cooperation with the Tam Center for Integrated Services. The Dubai centre will be dedicated to register municipal employees. The objective of these new registration centres is to make it easier for people to register under the Population Register and ID Card (PRIDC) system. EIDA has adopted a multi-phase registration strategy designed to facilitate orderly registration of all people in the UAE. In the first phase, only citizens[9] are being registered selectively, beginning with government employees. This process will continue until the end of 2009. The registration of residents will start later on.

The UAE ID registration cycle is comprised of four phases: the first is verification where government issued credentials, such as passport and visas, are checked and verified. The second phase is enrolment where the documents are scanned, a photo is captured and biometrics are taken. The third phase is a background check where the person's biometrics is cross-checked against the government watch list. The fourth and last phase of the registration process is card issuance, which results in the production and issuance of the National ID card. Figure 8.1 is an example of the UAE ID card.

The card is digitally signed and the data is encrypted. Public data include the name, nationality and two fingerprints. Restricted data include digital image,

Figure 8.1 The UAE ID card. Taken from The Emirates Identity Authority, www.EIDA.ae

fingerprints and other personal information. Both cards held by UAE nationals and residents are going to be identical, as demonstrated in Figure 8.1. The front side of the card demonstrates the holder's name, nationality, personal photograph and the ID number which will be composed of 15 digits, in addition to the electronic chip which will bear the personal data of the holder including a face photograph, the digital certification and fingerprints. However, the back of the card shows the date of birth, sex, signature specimen of the holder, number and date of card validity. The ID number is to be allocated for the user for his or her lifetime. This 'personal number' is the only recognized number in the country for the purpose of obtaining government services and certain non-government and commercial services, which require identity confirmation. Moreover, the ID card will substitute for many currently used personal cards including labor card, health card, driving licence. In later stages, the card will be used as passports for residents to travel between the GCC countries.

The card is being produced in accordance with the most modern smart card technologies, including micro letters, ultraviolet ink and calligraphy. It will enjoy nine security features, which make a forgery very difficult, for such features have superiority over the currently used standards for many cards such as banking credit cards. The approved number of the new ID card will be composed as in Figure 8.2. The validity of the card will be for five years, after which it will be replaced. The data which does not appear on both sides of the card (saved in the electronic chip) may be updated without the need to replace the card.

In order to raise awareness about this project, EIDA has started launching ID registration programmes in public schools; back in late December 2006, students in a high school in Abu Dhabi took some time off their daily routine to register under the population register and ID card (PRIDC) programme. Students were taken by bus to a Registration Centre of the Emirates Identity Authority (EIDA), where they were briefed about the programme and the registration procedures. The PRIDC programme is considered to be one of the most advanced IT projects in the UAE.

The UAE is not the only country in the GCC that is implementing National ID cards. For example, the first phase of the ID programme in Oman began in January 2004 and has already enabled 1.2 million Omani citizens and residents to benefit

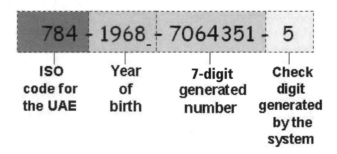

Figure 8.2 The approved number of the new ID card. Taken from The Emirates Identity Authority, www.EIDA.ae

from a secure and convenient identification that stores personal credentials, such as name, address, digital photograph, fingerprints, driving licence, etc. On September 2006, the Sultanate signed a contract with Gemalco, a leader in digital security, to implement the second phase of the Country's national ID programme providing 2.5 million National ID cards. The contract appoints Gemalco to be a provider of an update of the current National Registration System, of integration services, and to supply smart ID cards that will enable the Sultanate to provide faster and more secure public services to its population. According to an Omani source, the Oman National ID card programme is the first smart card-based e-government solution ever deployed in the Middle East. This official states that the implementation of the ID card project is part of the country's policy to improve the quality of public service and homeland security infrastructure. The core objective, as it is stated 'is to modernize the country's identification system and processes, making it more efficient and secure, both for citizens and government authorities'. This National Registry System will form the basis for all future Omani 2-government initiatives, including proposals to improve technical skills for the police force and other authorities managing the ID programme.

Conclusion

While National ID card initiatives have been debated and discussed by the various stakeholders in other countries around the world with both support and opposition, these initiatives are being rolled out very quietly in countries in the GCC. Based on the survey conducted by the author,[10] a large number of residents in the UAE, both citizens and expatriates, are not even aware that such a project is being implemented (47 per cent have heard of it but know nothing about it, while 22 per cent have not even heard of the programme); 43 per cent of those surveyed are indifferent towards this initiative (neither for nor against it). It is also interesting to note here that this initiative has not been covered extensively by the local media.

It seems that people are concerned about their privacy and security, and are nervous that the government might use the card to discriminate against non-citizens and religious minorities in the country. When asked about the reasons they are opposed to a national identity card programme, 41 per cent responded that they were concerned about their personal data being used without their permission; 32 per cent expressed concern that the scheme would discriminate unfairly against non-citizens. These results are not surprising given the fact that more than 80 per cent of the residents of the UAE are expatriates, and 57 per cent of those surveyed were non-GCC nationals (including Indians, Pakistanis and other Arab countries).

In addition to nationals, all expatriates living in countries of the GCC will be required to have these biometric ID cards. In the UAE, for instance, all will be issued multipurpose identity cards from next year (2008). In other words, registration with the Emirates Identification Authority (EIDA) and the obtaining of ID cards will become mandatory for nationals and expatriates older than 15 years starting January 2008. By mid-2008, electronic scans will be taken of both eyes, as part of the enhanced security measures. The UAE ID card will replace the driver's licence, labor, residency and health cards. It will also act as an e-gate, ATM card and e-passport when crossing into other GCC countries.

The countries of the GCC are in a situation where 'national security' is a major issue; but finding the collective formula that satisfies all member states is a challenge. The GCC seeks to reduce its dependence on the USA for security, but there is no consensus over alternative mechanisms. Members are divided over the roles of Iraq, Iran and Yemen in possible future security arrangements. Differences have arisen over the extent and pace of political reform. The rise of militant Islam and its uneven effects throughout the region may require greater flexibility and coordination among members.

The GCC countries are in a situation where they have to do something. With these new technologies, they are able to modernize their infrastructures and provide better services to their citizens. However, some GCC officials and political experts believe that the drive behind these initiatives is primarily to control large expatriate labour and worker populations, as well as deal with sensitive security concerns. Government officials expect that the advanced ID cards with biometrics will help them manage the growing flood of workers from Pakistan, Iran, India and other Arab and Western countries. The cards could also be used to track members of Islamic extremist groups and control budding dissent.

While five of the six GCC countries have officially embarked on National ID card schemes, there are clear signs that many questions regarding the privacy of information collected, who will have access to it, and how it will be utilized by local governments are still unanswered. Even though economic reasons were stressed by the GCC governments, as the main drive behind these National ID card initiatives, this author believes that there are strong political motives associated with these initiatives as well. The GCC countries, to varying degrees, have sensibly moderate relations with the West, especially the USA and the UK; and to this author based on her knowledge of the sociopolitical make up of the region, the GCC countries might have been, if not pressured, at least encouraged by the West to develop those systems. The USA publicly raised concerns with governments of the GCC (especially the UAE and Saudi Arabia) seven years ago about possible ties between some groups in these countries and Osama bin Laden; the majority of the 9/11 terrorists were Saudis and Emiratis. These countries have a high interest in being reliable and trustworthy (economic and political) partners to the USA. Having some of the best biometric-based ID card systems in the world might be regarded a sign of good will to the Western world that they have an interest in security and in deterring and fighting terrorism. It is also the case that these governments want to better manage their populations and introduce modern technology and e-government.

Notes

* The views in this paper represent those of the author.
1 Countries of the GCC are comprised of: Oman, Qatar, Saudi Arabia, Bahrain, Kuwait and the UAE.
2 *Worldwide Identity and Access Management 2006–2010 Forecast*, IDC No. 202728, August 2006.

3 The Identity Card Act, 2006. Online. Available: http://www.opsi.gov.uk/ACTS/acts2006/20060015.htm
4 Based on the author's discussion with Mr Khouri.
5 Presentation made by Mr Ali Khouri at the First GT Summit in Dubai, 3–5 September 2006.
6 The author administered a sample survey to 320 people in the UAE; the results are in Appendix A.
7 Law No. 1 of 2006 on Cybercrime; Law No. 2 of 2006 dealing with E-Commerce and Law No. 9 of 2006 dealing with the Population Register and Identity Card (PIRDC).
8 Based on a discussion with Mr Ali Khouri, Assistant Director General for Central Operations – Emirates Identity Authority, 4 September 2006.
9 Out of the close to 5 million people living in the UAE, less than 10 per cent are UAE Citizens.
10 To the author's knowledge, this is the first survey of its kind in the Middle East. The questions are adapted from various surveys published on the Internet.

Bibliography

Al Ittihad Newspaper (2004) 'Iris recognition system on the watch for expellees and convicts', 23 January, A1.

House of Commons Science and Technology Committee (2006) 'Identity Card Technologies: Scientific Advice, Risk and Evidence'. Online. Available: http://www.identityblog.com/wp-content/resources/id-cards-report.pdf (accessed 12 February 2007).

Karake-Shalhoub, Z. and Al Qasimi, L. (2006) *The Diffusion of E-Commerce in Developing Economies*. London: Edward Elgar.

Khaleej Times (2005) 'IT links between Dubai and Heathrow soon'. Online. Available: http://www.spt.aero/press/2771.html (accessed 25 July 2007).

Luce, E. (2007) 'US visa policy to come under attack', *Financial Times*, 30 January.

Prince Saud al-Faisal (2005) 'Saudi Arabia and the International Oil Market: An Executive Summary of the Special Presentation', *The James A. Baker III Institute for Public Policy*, 21 September, p. 2.

Rosenzweig, P. and Kochems, A (2004) 'Biometric technologies: security, legal, and policy implications'. Legal Memorandum No. 12. Online. Available: http://www.heritage.org/Research/HomelandSecurity/lm12.cfm

Ryan, R. (2006) 'Identity assurance and the protection of the civil infrastructure', *Sensor Review* 26(1): 18–21.

Stinson, J. (2007) 'Britons tolerate security cameras' prying eyes; some concerned about further intrusions', *USA Today* McLean, VA: 5 July: A.8.

Section Three

Encountering democratic opposition

9 Separating the sheep from the goats

The United Kingdom's National Registration programme and social sorting in the pre-electronic era

Scott Thompson

> They had in mind a short term solution to an immediate problem; viz. the sorting out of the eligible population into those required for industry and those available for the Army, and sought that solution in a census which would at once distinguish the sheep from the goats.
>
> (Sir Sylanus Vivian 1951,
> National Registration Programme Director 1921–1945)

The reinstatement of National ID cards has been the subject of heated debate in the UK in recent years and has led many to speculate on the social impact that these technologies *may* instil (*BBC Action* 2006; Webb 2007: 95–101). Although the heightened devotion to security experienced within western countries in recent years seems to be subsiding from mainstream discourse, many nations nonetheless remain interested in investigating the 'benefits' provided by nation-wide identification technologies (Blair 2006; *BBC News* 2006; Lyon 2003a: 13; Webb 2007: 91–102). As Lyon (2003b: 1) correctly notes, mainstream debates in the UK, USA and Canada have surrounded the weighing of ideas of 'security' against concepts of 'privacy', while little public media attention has been directed towards any of the other sociological implications of these technologies that do not happen to fit within this limited scope. One element that is central to the utility of these technologies, although remains nearly absent from public debate, is that of social sorting – the 'identification, classification and assessment' of individuals in order to 'determine who should be targeted for special treatment, suspicion, eligibility, inclusion, access, and so on' (Gandy 1993: 15; Lyon 2003a: 20). Unlike 'security' or 'privacy,' social sorting remains the unstated necessary means for these technologies to achieve greater population management.

The UK, in modern history, has been the subject of two implemented nationwide National Registration (NR) programmes centred around identity cards and infor-mation databases, as well as one non-initiated programme in the early 1950s (Vivian 1951; Ministry of Food 1955). In all cases, including the current models being presented to Parliament, these technologies are specifically designed to sort individuals by specified criteria as a means of better managing risk and non-risk associated populations (Lyon 2003a: 13). The initial goal of the First World War and Second World War NR programmes in the UK was simply that of sorting and extraction; 'to supply material enabling military authorities to discriminate between eligible personnel which could be called up for military service, either as volunteers or under a liability to compulsive service' (Vivian 1951: 8). However, after the NR's success in the late 1930s, the utility of identification technology displayed by NR officials quickly asserted itself as a competent method of population control by means of individual identification and a sorting of the population according to their perceived relative risk to the state.

This system reached its high point during the Second World War with the issuance of colour-coded identity cards in 1943 that quickly enabled one to distinguish to which strata of the population the holder was attributed to. Not only did this carding system sort and stratify the UK population during the war period, it furthermore became integrated as a measuring stick into discourses surrounding 'Britishness' identity, national unity and citizenship. This chapter seeks to explicate the social sorting function of the UK's second National Registration Programme, and review how it impacted individuals living during the Second World War period, in order to develop a better theoretical understanding of the phenomena of social sorting and its consequences.

Data for this analysis were drawn largely from archival material presented to the Canadian government by the government of the UK in the 1950s, laying out the UK's National Registration programmes and the benefits of these programmes on population management during the war years (Library and Archives Canada RG-2-B-2, Vol. 173, File N27, Vol.1). The series comprises three files of textual records consisting of a variety of UK government documents as well as a detailed report by the Historical Branch regarding the development, enforcement and maintenance of the National Registration programme in the UK written by the programme's central architect and director Sir Sylvanus Vivian in 1951. Supplementary data were also obtained from the UK's National Archives in London consisting of the complete records of files from the RG 28 series entitled *General Register Office: National Registration: Correspondence and Papers*, specifically: RG 28/48 *NR enumeration; employment permits; registration of aliens*; RG 28/144 *National Registration letter codes and identity numbers*; RG 28/111 *Green identity cards: permit office; persons in 'protected areas'*; RG 28/170 *Vagrants* (General Register Office 1915–1969). In all, the series consists of over 310 files and volumes with a date range from 1915 to 1969. These two main sources, the UK's RG 28 series and the Canadian RG-2, Vol. 176 series, detailed both programme development and implementation of the First World War and Second World War National Registration programmes within the UK and informed the argument presented in this paper. Further information was also drawn to a lesser degree from individual accounts submitted to the BBC's *Second World War People's War* series (2006).

The motivation for the Second World War
National Registration programme

The UK's Second World War National Registration programme was placed under development soon after the conclusion of the First World War. The programme's specific goal was to place at the government's disposal the ability 'to tell whether a man was necessary to his district or not' in order to 'avoid taking men who ought not be taken and ought remain' – essentially, in the words of the programme's director: 'to separate the sheep from the goats' (Hansard (commons) O.R.LXXIII, Vol.73, 1915: cols. 53–4, cited in Vivian 1951(5): 35–6). Not only was the programme to supply the government with vital occupational information, but NR data was also to allow for the effective coordination of the country's human resources by sorting individuals into categories of 'necessary' and 'available', in order to bring the highest level of efficiency to both industry and the armed forces (Standing Inter-Departmental Committee 1928; Vivian 1951: 26, 35, 56). Although the programme was deemed of the utmost importance by the Standing Committee of Imperial Defense, the Second World War NR programme was handicapped by the utter failure of its First World War predecessor to create a functioning register (Vivian 1951: 13–15; Elliot 2006: 175). In light of the past failures and the resulting pressure from government officials, the UK's second NR programme was meticulously designed to solve the problems of non-compliance and clerical errors that plagued the First World War register (General Register Office 1919: 14; Vivian 1951: 13–15). Specifically, the new NR system would seek compliance by being deeply incorporated into the ration programme and the new register would decrease clerical errors by being centralized in London so that programme officials would be better able to control the filing, updating and accessing of NR documents (Vivian 1951: 18, 31, 58, 79). Also due to the NR's history of failure the Second World War programme's initial mandate was restricted to simply that of extraction – the identification of men who were not 'necessary in his district' and thus 'available' for the armed forces, as well as the ability to 'round up' those men (Hansard (commons) 1915: cols. 53–4, cited in Vivian 1951: 5).

Data collected for the NR was commenced on National Registration Day, 29 September 1939 (*The Times* 1939a). To accomplish the massive feat of recording the personal information of 'all' individuals living within the UK, the government employed over 65,000 clerks called 'enumerators' to travel from house to house (Ministry of Labour and National Service 1938; Mills 2006: 2; *The Times* 1938; *The Times* 1939b). Enumerator officials were instructed to document each individual's name, address, sex, age, occupation, profession, trade or employment, condition of marriage, membership in the Naval Military or Air Force Reserve or Auxiliary Forces or Civil Defense Service or Reserve, into volumes called Enumeration Books which would then be transcribed onto cards and form the NR's Central Index (Vivian 1951: 21; General Register Office 1945–1949). This provided 'a central record of the whole registered population indexed in accordance to th[eir] number' (Vivian 1951: 21, 58, 72). Secondary copies were also sent to local NR officials forming a local index of individuals that lived within the local district.

Figure 9.1 National Registration Identity Card (1939–1943).

Note: The first edition of the ID card was issued when the initial information was gathered by registration officials. Although the numbering system remained identical, technological improvements to the card were needed, leading to formal re-issuing of NR ID cards in 1943.

Second World War National Registration Identity Cards

The Second World War National Registration Identity Cards issued by the NR programme were approximately the size of a modern-day passport. The card opened like a book and had only one section inside for the name and address of the owner – although there was other space delegated to further addresses should the bearer relocate (Figure 9.1). Within the NR's sorting programme, the identity cards played four vital roles. First, the cards acted to effectively identify individuals, specify their classification and allow bureaucratic machinery to manage populations via the initial sort; second, the cards ensured the visibility and ability to locate individuals on a national scale; third, the cards ensured a means of maintaining the validity of central index records; and finally the cards were used to ensure compliance to general governmental policies.

The innovative key to success of the UK's WII ID card in performing the necessary tasks allocated to it was the individual number printed on it. The ID card's number allowed NR personnel the ability to distinguish 'that person from all others, in the form of a distinct letter code, the number of the household and the number in the household of its particular member' (Vivian 1951: 72). The initial letter in the sequence depicted the general area, mostly separated by city or district. The initial letter 'S', for example, depicted Scottish areas, while 'U' depicted Northern Ireland and the rest of the letters of the alphabet were distributed across England and Wales. The next three digits distinguished a more precise area within the first general area, while the subsequent numbers, separated by a colon, depicted the number of the home, as it corresponded to NR maps. Finally, the position of the individual in the household, was indicated by the last digit with '1' indicating head of the household on down. Additional letters, designed to locate and identify the individual with greater ease, were also added to the ID card number in special cases. If the number was preceded by the letter 'V' then the bearer had been found to be either a vagrant or homeless by police or registration officials. The prefix 'Q' was allocated to those relocated to a new general area, 'FO' was used for distinguishing diplomats, and finally a prefix of 'P' or suffix of 'X' indicated a re-issued card

(General Register Office 1948–1949). Legally, cards had to be carried at all times and officers of the law could stop and demand that the documents be produced (*National Registration Act*, 1939 c.91, s.6(4); *The Times* 1939c; *The Times* 1940).

From the simple appearance of these documents one may think, as many individuals did, that the cards were as Berry (2005) claimed 'surely one of the easiest of documents to copy'. However, all NR ID cards were carefully protected from fraud by the use of several technological and procedural innovations (Vivian 1951: 95). The innovation of basing the distribution of food and other rationed goods on the ID card and NR structure was an element hard fought for by NR administrators as it was (correctly) seen as vital in ensuring the compliance of citizens to the NR programmes' regulations as well as the central means of detecting fraudulent cards.

When applying for ration cards, the Food Department required the applicant to show their NR Identity card. The ID card number was then recorded within the Food Department's documents, linking the individual through their number to the particular ration book provided to them. Subsequently the ration book itself was inscribed with the number of the individual to whom it was to be given along with the NR number. Finally, the ID card was stamped with the octagonal Food Department authority stamp.

To ensure that the NR files were up-to-date and to avoid possible deception, ration books were sent by post using the address of the individual on file in the NR's Central Index. This ensured that not only did each person receive one ration book but it also saw to the maintenance of up-to-date addresses of all registered individuals as well as the inability to produce fraudulent cards. If fraudulent cards were produced they would quickly be detected by the ration system in that the number would be already allocated to another individual. Also any police officer or National Service (NS) agent would easily be able to detect ID card forgeries presented to them since 'the absence of a stamp w[ould] afford strong prima facie grounds for further inquiry if not immediate suspicion' (General Register Office 1940a). In these ways, not only were forged ID cards effectively detected and collected, but registered citizens' locations were tracked through their ID card, making them readily accessible through governmental machinery (Vivian 1951: 95).

How the system worked

Once military and industrial conscription arrived in April 1939, proclamations called individuals specified by age to report for assessment (Vivian 1951: 229). Once the individuals had reported and were assigned to either armed forces or industrial work, calls to service were posted and individuals were directed to report for duty. The names of individuals who had reported were recorded, and lists were made and matched against the central index to identify those who were found to be non-compliant with governmental regulations (Vivian 1951: 56). Specifically, requests for National Service workers were issued by either the Ministry of War or the Ministry of Labour, depending on the services required, and sent to the NR office. The Central index was then used to generate lists of 'available' individuals, and these lists were then forwarded to the requesting Ministry. There officials

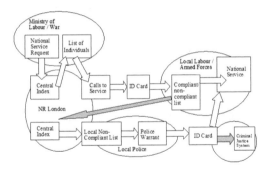

Figure 9.2 National Service Conscription Procedure.

issued calls to service that were delivered by post to the address listed upon the individuals' NR record. Compliant individuals' ID cards were checked when they reported for duty and lists of those who had not reported were sent, via the NR office to local police who were to apprehend the listed individuals based on ID card identification/verification procedures. Discovered non-compliant individuals were then either directed to their required National Service (conscripted labour) or fed into the UK's criminal justice system. Ultimately, the non-compliant individual discovered by this system was to be faced with a choice of either compliance with National Service requirements, imprisonment at the hands of the Criminal Justice System or engage in some form of resistance (Figure 9.2).

The Second World War NR system was heralded within government as an incredible success. As the programme's director Vivian asserted, identity cards and their system of numbering people had increased database searching efficiency by over 50 per cent and had successfully functioned as 'a mechanism sufficiently constructed and fuelled ... capable of developing latent power as an instrument of population control' (General Register Office 1942a; Vivian 1951: 79, 85, 181). For these reasons, NR technology was quickly integrated into several governmental services and ministries including health, insurance, immigration, voting, policing initiatives, refugee control, mercantile marine identification and control, internment programmes, pensions, population statistics and assessments, births, deaths, marriages, as well as others.

Colour-coded identity cards and social stratification

Although the basic underlying technology described above was present throughout the UK's NR system, after the outbreak of war, government officials at the Home Office expressed the need for a stratified system of identification based on the perception of a notable variance in the risk associated with various populations. Although policing agencies had already begun checking individuals' ID cards, they argued for a system that could easily separate those who were 'above suspicion' from those who were not (Vivian 1951: 166). The result was an assortment of colour-coded identity cards that allowed for the quick assessment of an individual's validity and risk, successfully sorting the population and differentially applying the scrutinizing gaze of the state's surveillance apparatus (General Register Office 1942–1949). Even though the NR programme was initially designed solely for identification and extraction, the adopting of colour-coded cards further sorted the public, empowering some while disempowering others.

The Blue Card

When NR cards were issued across the UK in 1939, individuals were issued brownish coloured 'buff' ID cards (Figure 9.1). These cards were then replaced with colour-coded cards in the early 1940s for those occupying particular occupational positions or holding a particular social status (*The Times* 1943). Citizens not selected for either the Green or Pink Cards (discussed later) came to be known as 'Blue Card' holders, as the re-issuance of cards in 1943 bore this colour (Figure 9.3).

Blue Cards delineated the vast bulk of the UK's civilian population and bore all of the technologies indicated above. Compared with the Green and Pink Cards, Blue Card holders were allocated to the 'small people' who were restricted in their movements within particular zones, as their cards did not allow them to pass any of the many road blocks and restricted areas dividing the country (General Register Office 1940b). The Blue Cards' main innovation over their earlier incarnation was that they held several different portions to fill in one's address, keeping a record of individual movement as well as avoiding the costly re-issuance of cards in the case of homes being destroyed or an individual's relocation due to government National Service. Furthermore, these new blank Blue Cards were issued individual numbers allowing the cards to be traced back to the issuing NR officer, as well as the printing factory and distribution networks. Anytime an individual moved to a new address, NR officials had to be notified and identity cards and ration books updated (Edds 2004). Blue Cards had originally been issued to children as well, however a barrage of thefts by unscrupulous adults led to the creation of a specialized under age 16 ID card.

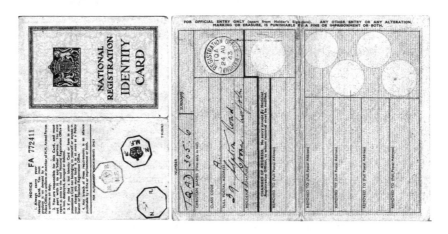

Figure 9.3 National Registration Blue Identity Card (1943–1952).

Since the other colour-coded cards signified individuals who were protected from being conscripted into the National Service, the Blue ID Card informally denoted those who were the usable 'human resources' at the disposal of the state. Although conscription was initially limited to men, by 1941 the *National Service Act* was amended as to apply to 'all persons of either sex' – drawing both men and women from the Blue Card classification into the armed forces and industry (*National Service (Amendment) Act*, 1941 c.4, s.1). As the war progressed and National Service conscripted more and more individuals into various positions, those carrying the Blue Card were looked at with greater suspicion. Particularly, not being registered with either the armed forces or the home guard was seen as not contributing enough to the war effort and negatively stigmatized (Rose 2003: 170, 174; Elliot 2006: 150).

Within a short period of time, those with Blue Cards working in protected occupations (and thus ineligible for National Service), were issued specific 'Certificates of Employment in Essential Services in War', denoting to policing officials and others their commitment to the war effort. The added separation of Blue Card holders had a reinforcing effect of pressuring those who wanted to avoid the negative stigma of not 'pulling their weight' to in some way serve and be issued a means of distinguishing their service – like an ID card of an alternate colour (General Register Office 1940b; Rose 2003: 33). As Grayzel (1997: 145) explains, visible items that depicted service played a strong social role during the war years, pressuring individuals to seek out 'demonstrable emblems of patriotism and full commitment to the national cause'. This shift only acted to deepen the validity of the Blue Card stigma and further distinguish these individuals as immoral and self-interested, the exact opposite of the self-sacrificing, egalitarian and patriotic 'Britishness' that permeated the war culture (Rose 2003).

The Green Card

When national registration was conceptualized in post-First World War UK, programme designers pushed by Home Office and Security Service personnel understood the need for a specialized ID card that would allow access to 'prohibited or protected areas into which entry was forbidden' for the general public (General Register Office 1940c: 1; Vivian 1951: 167). To ensure security, NR authorities felt 'that a document of bodily identity was essential to prove that the person producing the permit was the person to whom it related' (Vivian 1951: 167). The 'Green Card', as it was called, denoted who could access public utilities, large industrial concerns and other spaces in which 'security was essential' (Vivian 1951: 167). The main innovation of these Green Cards was a photograph that bore the image of the permit holder as well as the requirement of the signature and photograph to be endorsed by a signatory (Figure 9.4). In addition to this, the records held on these individuals were more detailed and included the addition of parental and spousal nationality information, and required the signature of 'a public figure, such as a minister of religion, JP [Justice of the Peace] or civil servant' who vouched as to the individual's 'character' (General Register Office 1939). Due to the card's added

Figure 9.4 The Green Card (1939–1952).

security features, the NR office went so far as to boast that their Green Cards were 'a stricter document of personal identity than the British Passport' (General Register Office 1940b).

Green Cards were often referred to as cards with 'positive endorsements' (General Register Office 1942b: 8). This meant that in addition to being granted access to restricted areas, the individual was 'recommended for favorable treatment' by government and policing officials. For the most part, the endorsements enabling the acquisition of a Green Card denoted an individual's official capacity within specified homefront military or civilian organizations, allowing them 'to perform their duties without being hampered by police suspicions' (Vivian 1951: 166). As the war progressed, the differential treatment enjoyed by Green Card holders led to widespread public demand for universal picture bearing ID cards, as an association had been made within media that the preferential treatment originating from the Green Cards was attributed to those individuals' increased ability to prove bodily identity (Vivian 1951: 163). Some Blue Card carrying individuals even began to affix photographs to their Blue Cards in hopes of increasing their card's validity, however since treatment was based on the colour of the bearer's ID card this technique was unsuccessful (General Register Office 1942b: 8; *The Times* 1941a,b).

Although the permit application for a Green Card required a significantly increased amount of personal data to be disclosed, demand for cards driven by 'personal self-interest' and political pressure pushed the registrars to offer photograph-bearing cards to all 'independent and responsible persons' with 'satisfactory credentials' (Vivian 1951: 163; General Register Office 1940d: 1, 1940b: 1). Photograph-bearing Green Cards started to be issued to those outside the previously defined 'classes' of people in 1943 to appease the public, although the processing of applications requiring photographing and authentication bottlenecked production and greatly limited the distribution of Green Cards to non-endorsed individuals, ultimately maintaining the validity of the colour classification (Vivian 1951: 163; General Register Office 1942b: 8, 1940c).

The need for increased numbers of 'secure' individuals reached a point by the mid-1940s that the lengthy application process required to obtain a Green Card was no longer a viable solution for policing needs. The solution was to produce ID cards for those who had access to mid-level security positions such as staff and labourers employed by the Air Ministry and Civil Defence personnel. These new NR 107 ID cards still bore photographs but were brown in colour, required a less lengthy application process and offered the bearer less access to secure areas. Further photograph-bearing cards were issued to police, mercantile marine, local NR Officials, Civil Defence personnel and other specialized personnel, accounting for over one million cards by 1942 (General Register Office 1940c, 1942b; Mills 2006: 25).

The Pink Card (DR 1)

The 'Pink' DR 1 card was developed as an extension of the Green Card and was distributed to only senior government officials, civil servants and service officers. The application process was identical to that of the Green Card with the addition of governmental department information (General Register Office 1939). Pink Cards were considered to be the ultimate of positive endorsements as they allowed for access to all prohibited places and protected areas specified under the *Emergency Powers (Defense Act) of 1939*, and the *Official Secrets Act of 1911* (Mills 2006: 48).

The security of these cards was similar to that of the Green Cards, although Pink Cards were supplemented with the inclusion of a department number, in order to indicate the individual's associations, as well as being embossed with an official seal.

The Alien Card

Although specified regulations in regards to citizenship and non-citizen rights have an extensive history within the UK, Alien Identity Cards can be traced to legislation put forward in 1919 (*Aliens Restriction (Amendment) Act*, 1919 ch. 92). The 1919–1920 changes to the treatment of aliens in the UK were designed within the political culture of post-First World War. Aliens, particularly those associated with 'enemy' nations, were seen as suspect and alien prisoners of war were in the process of being deported.

During this period, there existed a strong anti-alien discourse, as aliens not only were seen as a restricting force to British unity but were also viewed as the 'other', limiting integration and participation within British culture (Cesarani 1993: 25; Rose 2003: 104). Although these sentiments were most strongly directed towards aliens defined as Jews, Chinese and 'blacks', all nonetheless felt the stigma and alienation that was associated with the classification (Cesarani 1993: 25).

The Alien Registration Card itself was slightly smaller than the NR cards and contained information regarding the individual's nationality, date of birth, marital status, occupation, employment, residence and date of arrival. A secondary section, consisting of 23 blank pages, was used for police to record notes such as changes of residence, travel, or the issuance of permits. Alien Registration Cards were issued unique six-digit numbers that linked the card with held databases that were later integrated into the NR programme (General Register Office 1942b: 10). The cards also bore a photograph, endorsed by the issuing officer and local police organization, as well as a place for the individual to sign their name or place their thumbprint if they were unable to do so in 'English Characters' (Figure 9.5).

Figure 9.5 Alien Registration Card (1920).

Aliens were also associated with a sense of elevated risk and as such were regulated in their actions and movements. As Green and Pink Cards carried positive endorsements, alien cards were understood to carry 'adverse endorsements' (General Register Office 1942b: 9). Specifically, the alien classification required individuals to report any travel or changes in residence to local police officers in both the district that they departed and arrived in.

Furthermore, any changes to the collected information, including changes in profession, marriage status or the death of a spouse, were required to be reported to police within 48 hours. After the outbreak of the Second World War, aliens were further restricted to within a five mile radius of their residence unless they had obtained a special permit from police officers.

In addition to the Alien Registration Card, registered aliens were required to apply for and carry Blue Cards once National Registration had commenced in 1939. Initially, identical ID cards were issued to aliens, however public criticism over the lack of definition between citizens and non-citizens led to the addition of a stamp indicating one's alien status, in July 1940 (Vivian 1951: 187).

These stamps, it was argued would then allow for aliens to be traceable through the general NR programme and 'would strengthen the control over the alien population' since they could no longer 'avoid the disclosure of their status on challenge' or 'conceal his[/her] alien status' (Vivian 1951: 187; General Register Office 1942b: 9). Individuals labeled as aliens by the NR programme did in fact seek to remove their differentiated and lowered status through the alteration of permit books. Although, in preparation for such an event, the NR programme had developed an integrated triplicate system of files, matching alien registration to NR numbers and thus ensuring that any classification of non-citizens could not be removed (General Register Office 1940e). By 1941, the records of just under 220,000 aliens were incorporated into the NR machinery (Vivian 1951: 192).

In the early 1940s, distinctions regarding the risk attributed to particular aliens led to a splitting of the alien category into that of 'enemy' and 'friendly' (*The Times* 1941c). 'Enemy Aliens' specifically denoted individuals of Austrian, German and Italian nationality, although this list was expanded in 1942 to include Bulgarian,

Finnish, Hungarian, Japanese and Romanian aliens as well as ex-nationals (General Register Office 1942c). In the latter part of 1940, 'fears about 'fifth column' traders led the government to intern all Italian, German and Austrian men', accounting for over 30,000 individuals, many of which were Jewish refugees (Rose 2003: 94; Wasserstein 1999: 81). After the eventual detainment of all 'enemy aliens' in internment camps, tribunals were set up 'to consider the background of interned [individuals]' (Wood 2005). These tribunals investigated individual associations with various prescribed pro-NAZI and Fascist organizations, reviewed personal information and ruled on the individual's level of risk and resulting fitness to return to their homes in the UK. Released individuals, however, faced greater restrictions than they had before the war, as they were then denied access to specified areas, the possession of a car or bicycle, being out of doors between certain hours as well as other specific stipulations (*Defense Regulations* 1940, s.18a, b). 'Undesirable Aliens' remained within UK internment facilities until the end of the war (Jaconelli 2005).

The Yellow Card

The Yellow Card was initially distributed in 1943 as a response to calls for greater security on imported Irish labourers (Vivian 1951: 193). During the war, shortages in labour had prompted the government to sanction greater numbers of Irish immigrant labourers' travel to work in the UK. Prior to 1943 these workers were tracked through the use of travel permits. However, these documents were criticized by government and law enforcement officials as being inefficient in ensuring the removal of these workers once their permits had expired. For this reason the government turned to the NR programme in order to 'induce measures to render the system of control more effective' (Vivian 1951).

When the NR programme took over the control of immigrant worker populations it began to target specific occupation types when granting travel and labour permits. Specifically the programme sought the labour of those educated or being educated in the fields of Nursing, Midwifery and Probationers (Vivian 1951). When these individuals arrived in the UK, yellow identity cards were issued to them by police, stipulating their name, class code, postal address and temporary residence.

Specific to the Yellow Card was a stipulated expiry date, usually within 3–6 months of the card's issuance (Mills 2006: 27). These expiry dates were key to the Yellow Card system as 'the necessity for its renewal on its expiry date afforded NR officials an opportunity for checking by reference to the holder's travel document whether the permitted period of stay had been exceeded, and if so, of withholding the renewal and notifying the police' (Vivian 1951: 194).

Like Aliens, Irish immigrant workers were considered to be high risk and were required to adhere to the conditions, specifically those regarding employment, of their granted stay. However, if a Yellow Card holder could prove to the police their character, the police could endorse the individual's permit, allowing them to exchange their yellow ID card, along with its regulations, for a blue one (Vivian 1951: 195).

The end of the NR?

The use of NR cards in the UK after the end of the Second World War continued due to their necessity within the food rationing system, and it was not until 1952 that the programme was cancelled. Although the disbandment of the ID card system is often attributed to the actions of Clarence Willcock, a dry-cleaning manager who refused to produce his identity card upon being stopped for a speeding violation in 1950 (Mills 2006: 2; Agar 2001: 110–111), internal NR documents describe a more generalized public action against the continued use of the cards. Vivian, the NR programme director, noted that the compliance of both the general public and NR employees to the NR regulations was lost with the end of the war (Vivian 1951: 242). Until that time government propaganda and media sources had linked the NR with the maintenance of efficiency and equality within National Service and the discovery of German interlopers. With the end of the war these justifications were lost and government officials were unable to impose on the public mind any 'peace time necessities' for the NR and it was reported within governmental internal documents that individuals in the general public and in governmental positions across the UK had simply stopped following NR rules and regulations. In this way, Vivian (1951) argued that the ID card system had been 'crippled by the withdrawal of wartime support' and by the 1950s was already 'rapidly sinking into impotence and chaos'. Media reports and op-ed pieces from this time period also expressed a degree of hostility vented towards the NR and identity cards. As Agar notes: 'anti-card argument[s] echoed from heavyweight papers such as the *Manchester Guardian*, or the *Scotsman*, to the mass-circulation *News of the World*, to smaller papers, such as the *Hendon and Finchley Times and Guardian*' (Agar 2001: 110–111).

Although the Second World War register had officially been disbanded in 1952, its legacy remains within various governmental services and programmes with which it had been integrated. As Agar (2001: 102) points out the NR had to it a 'parasitic vitality'. Due to the unpopular nature of conscription it had to attach itself to other services, most notably the ration system, in order to convince individuals to both register and carry their cards (Vivian 1951: 43). However, the NR also supplied evidence to governmental officials that state wide databases could function efficiently and could effectively centralize the oversight and management of populations on a large scale (Vivian 1951: 227). Specifically, the NR number remained as a Universal Personal Identifier (UPI), in some cases to this day, within Public Heath Services records, UK voting registration and National Insurance programmes, while information gathered by the NR flowed into other governmental agencies including the offices of the Security Service, the Ministry of Labour, the Ministry of Pensions, the General Post Office, the Civil Defence, Inland Revenue, the Board of Trade and Trade Enforcement Inspectors (General Register Office 1939–1953).

Within a year of the end of the Second World War, NR governmental officials began formulating plans for the generation of a third NR programme. The UK's third NR was ultimately never implemented, but detailed plans were made as to how to quickly regenerate updated files and cards by using medical cards (which still bore the individual's Second World War NR number) and census data (Ministry of Food

1955: 3). It was argued that through these means, the NR officials could, within a minute timeframe, produce useable records for over 97 per cent of the population (General Register Office no date). New ID cards and supporting NR documents were scheduled to be printed on 25 March 1954 (HM Treasury, no date). In 1955, lists were generated containing all individuals who had entered the country from 1952–1955; all persons released from the armed forces since 1952–1955; all children born from 1939–1955; all individuals born after 1952 that were exempt from the Health Act (and thus would have no Medical Card number); and individuals who had died after 1952, in order to increase the efficiency of the re-registration process. The UK's third NR programme was to again play a centralizing role in the delivery of services, social sorting and population management in the event of war. However, the war that governmental officials had envisioned requiring a new NR never materialized and the third NR programme was never initiated (HM Treasury).

Conclusions

This historical case study of the UK's National Registration programmes offers four main relevant theoretical insights into social sorting and classification. First, classification and social sorting were an effective means of population management even before the electronic era. Not only is this of historical significance but it also lends credence to the argument that the specific techniques employed in the pre-electronic and in present-day technologies can be understood as causal mechanisms of social sorting systems. In particular, this study reaffirms the use of individualizing Universal Personal Identifiers (UPI) and database linking Universal Identifiers (UID) as key features of effective social sorting systems (Clark 1988: 501–502; Shattuck 1996), as well as the reliance upon database information checking as a central means of maintaining ID card/individual validity (Stalder and Lyon 2003: 86; also see Amoore, Chapter 2).

Second, social sorting technologies carry with them the possibility of incredibly formative unintended social consequences that can manifest as they are inserted into public discourses and made visible within populations. In this particular case, one can see how a social sorting mechanism, designed solely for the extraction of 'unnecessary' individuals became a key technology within debates over identity, citizenship and identification. Interestingly, in this case it was public discourses that had co-opted the social implications of the ID cards, pushing the development of the NR technology away from its original design to that of establishing visible technological distinctions of 'Britishness'. Also in this regard, the visibility of technological distinctions on the cards and between types of cards, the generally held perception of a measured degree of 'Britishness' generated by coded ID cards, and the relatively secretive functions of these technologies embedded within the cards, each present themselves as attributing factors to the resulting tight relationship between ID cards, identity and discipline in the UK during the Second World War period. As the information which the cards physically showed (colour, number, stamps etc.) was absorbed into discursive arguments about 'Britishness', the social validity of the cards themselves, the social validity of speculative discursive arguments around what the cards' attributes were thought to be (citizenship, war contribution and social status) and the social desirability of certain ID card attributes, became mutually reinforcing, resulting in the direction of social action towards compliance to state initiatives and policies.

Third, social sorting technologies foster stratification along socially visible lines. One can see this in the stratification matching the colour-coding of the ID. In this case, ID cards provided clear boundaries upon which the discourses of 'Britishness' could readily be laid. As the war progressed, the divisions of the public along governmentally defined lines of utility and security, embodied within the colour of one's ID card and illuminated by the NR programme's technologies, not only pushed those seeking to be proper Brits from certain classifications but also led to the application of non-British stigmas upon aliens, resident labourers and those not participating 'enough' in the war effort.

Fourth, governance plays an important and necessary role in the maintenance of social sorting systems. Within this chapter, one can see the dual forces of technological classification and self-definition at work in constructing social interactions. However, what is perhaps most interesting is the degree to which such a large, technologically advanced and legally empowered system was ultimately dependant on the support of self-governance within the population. In both the UK's First World War and Second World War NR programmes, determinative social properties were disrupted and ultimately rendered useless by means of non-participation and indifference by subjects and programme officials (Elliot 2006: 145; Vivian 1951: 242). In the pre-electronic era, these technologies relied heavily upon a vast number of individuals strictly adhering to policy of a centralized body. With the end of the war and National Service came the end of the justifying linkages that so firmly tied individuals to their self-disciplining link to 'Britishness' and good citizenship. For this reason, one should perhaps not be surprised that the effectiveness of an ID card programme is dependent, to some extent, upon the degree to which it is adopted, or ties into, the individual's constructed identity. Not only is this of interest for those seeking to oppose such systems of classification, but for those seeking to develop social theory in regard to surveillance systems, it also illuminates the importance that self-governance, as described by Foucault (1977), plays in even the most complex, top down and bureaucratic state programmes.

Although the relationship between social sorting, classification and its social consequences requires further analysis, this chapter nonetheless displays important trends linking ID technology – particularly when connected to socially visible personal identifiers – with the stratification and compliance of targeted populations. Although this may be exactly what those currently seeking to bolster 'national security' may be looking for (see Wills, Chapter 10), citizens facing registration would be advised to consider the history of coercion, deception and compliance that was targeted not only at external threats but more importantly used for the management of individual activity and life chances that can be found in historical accounts. As the UK's First World War and Second World War NR programme director explained: 'National Registration', constructed in this way, must be understood as 'a mechanism sufficiently constructed and fuelled to be capable of developing latent power as an instrument of population control which could be adapted and applied to specific purposes' (Vivian 1951: 227).

Bibliography

Agar, J. (2001) 'Modern horrors: British identity and identity cards', in J. Caplan and J. Torpey (eds) *Documenting Individual Identity: The development of state practices in the modern world,* Princeton: Princeton University Press, pp. 101–20.

Amenta, E. (2003) 'What we know about the development of social policy', in J. Mahoney and D. Rueschemeyer (eds) *Comparative Historical Analysis in the Social Sciences,* New York: Cambridge University Press, pp. 91–130.

Berry, R. (2005) 'Article ID A4895058', in *BBC The People's War,* London: BBC. Online. Available: http://www.bbc.co.uk/ww2peopleswar/ (accessed 5 December 2006).

BBC (2006) *Second World War People's War: An Archive of World War Two Memories.* Written by the Public, gathered by the BBC. Online. Available: http://www.bbc.co.uk/ww2peopleswar/ (accessed 11 April 2006).

BBC Action Network Team (2006) *ID Cards: An action network briefing.* London: BBC. Online. Available: http://www.bbc.co.uk/dna/actionnetwork/A2319176 (accessed 5 December 2006).

BBC News (2006) *ID Cards 'Should be Compulsory',* London: BBC. Online. Available: http://news.bbc.co.uk/2/hi/uk_news/4633822.stm (accessed 5 December 2006).

Blair, T. (2006) 'Downing Street briefing, 6 November 2006', as presented by the BBC, London. Online. Available: http://news.bbc.co.uk/1/hi/help/3681938.stm (accessed 1 December 2006).

Bonnell, V.E. (1980) 'The uses of theory, concepts and comparison in historical sociology', *Comparative Studies in Society and History* 22(2): 156–73.

Cesarani, D. (1993) 'An alien concept? The continuity of anti-alienism in British society before 1940', D. Ceasarani and T. Kushner (eds) *The Internment of Aliens in Twentieth Century Britain,* London: Frank Cass.

Clark, R. (1988) 'Information technology and dataveillance', *Communications of the ACM* 31(5): 498–512.

Edds, A. (2004) 'Working at the Food Office'. Online. Available: http://www.bbc.co.uk/ww2peopleswar/stories/67/a3236267.shtml (accessed 11 April 2006).

Elliot, R. (2006) 'An early experiment in national identity cards: the battle over registration in the First World War', *Twentieth Century British History* 17(2): 145–76.

Foucault, M. (1977) *Discipline and Punish: The Birth of the Prison,* Alan Sheridan, trans, New York: Vintage.

Gandy, O.H. (1993) *The Panoptic Sort: A Political Economy of Personal Information,* Boulder: Westview Press.

General Register Office (n.d.) *List of Records with N.H.S. (former N.R.) Numbers at Southport and in Local Executive Council Offices* (Report). General Register Office: National Registration: Correspondence and Papers, RG 28/98, London: The National Archives.

General Register Office (1915–1969) *General Register Office: National Registration: Correspondence and Papers,* RG 28, London: The National Archives.

General Register Office (1919) *Memorandum on the National Register* (Circular). General Register Office: Circulars, RG 41/13, London: The National Archives.

General Register Office (1939) *D.R. Form 5* (National Registration Form). Green identity cards: permit office; persons in 'protected areas', RG 28/111, London: The National Archives.

General Register Office (1939–1951) *Vagrants*, RG 28/170, London: The National Archives.

General Register Office (1939–1953) *NR 131, 134, 151, 167, 186, 202* (Circulars). National Registration: Circulars, F5/530/4, Chippenham: Wiltshire and Swindon History Centre.

General Register Office (1940a) *NR 143* (Circular). National Registration: Circulars, F5/530/4, Chippenham: Wiltshire and Swindon History Centre.

General Register Office (1940b) *30/05/1940* [Letter]. Green identity cards: permit office; persons in 'protected areas', RG 28/111, London: The National Archives.

General Register Office (1940c) *Minute Sheet 02/04/1940* [Letter]. Green identity cards: permit office; persons in 'protected areas', RG 28/111, London: The National Archives.

General Register Office (1940d) *Draft Press Notice*. Green identity cards: permit office; persons in 'protected areas', RG 28/111. London: The National Archives.

General Register Office (1940e) *NR 110* (Circular). National Registration: Circulars, F5/530/4, Chippenham: Wiltshire and Swindon History Centre.

General Register Office (1940–1942) *Green identity cards: permit office; persons in 'protected areas'*, RG 28/111, London: The National Archives.

General Register Office (1942a) *HQ/NRF/10* [Circular]. National Registration: Circulars, F5/530/4. Chippenham: Wiltshire and Swindon History Centre.

General Register Office (1942b) *Memorandum Prepared by the Registrar-General for the Information of Research United States Manpower Commission 1942* (Report). Identity cards replacement registers, RG 28/256, London: The National Archives.

General Register Office (1942c) *NR 136* (Circular). National Registration: Circulars, F5/530/4, Chippenham: Wiltshire and Swindon History Centre.

General Register Office (1942–1949) *National registration papers including comments on the History of National Registration by Sir S P Vivian*, RG 28/265, London: The National Archives.

General Register Office (1945–1949) *Channel Islands: NR enumeration; employment permits; registration of aliens*, RG 28/48, London: The National Archives.

General Register Office (1948–1949) *National registration letter codes and identity numbers*, RG 28/144, London: The National Archives.

Grayzel, S.R. (1997) 'The outward and visible sign of her patriotism: women, uniforms, and national service during the First World War', *Twentieth Century British History* 8(2): 145–64.

HANSARD (Commons) O.R.LXXIII, Vol.73 1915, cols 53–54.

HM Treasury (n.d.) *National Registration* (Letter). General Register Office: National Registration: Correspondence and Papers, RG 28/98, London: The National Archives.

Hasselbladh, H. and Kallinikos, J. (2000) 'The project of rationalization: a critique and reappraisal of neo-institutionalism in organization studies', *Organization Studies* 21(4): 697–720.

Jaconelli, T. (2005) *Undesirable Alien?* Online. Available: http://www.bbc.co.uk/ww2peopleswar/stories/06/a4147706.shtml (accessed 11 April 2006).

Lyon, D. (ed.) (2003a) 'Surveillance as social sorting: computer codes and mobile bodies', *Surveillance as Social Sorting: Privacy, Risk and Digital Discrimination*, New York: Routledge, pp. 11–12.

Lyon, D. (2003b) 'Introduction', in D. Lyon (ed.) *Surveillance as Social Sorting: Privacy, Risk and Digital Discrimination*, New York: Routledge. pp. 1–10.

Mills, J. (2006) *Identity Cards, Permits and Passes – Within the Island Fortress – The Uniforms, Insignia and Ephemera of the Home Front in Britain 1939–1945*, London: Wardens.

Ministry of Food (1955) 59A (Circular). General Register Office: National Registration: Correspondence and Papers, RG 28/98, London: The National Archives.

Ministry of Labour and National Service (1938) Instructions to N.R.O and R.B.D.'s 1938, Private Office Papers: War Emergency Measures, UK National Archives, LAB 25/84:1, London: The National Archives.

Rose, S.O. (2003) *Which People's War?: National Identity and Citizenship in Wartime Britain 1939–1945*, New York: Oxford University Press.

Rule, J. (1974) *Private Lives and Public Surveillance; Social Control in the Computer Age*, London: Allen-Lane.

Shattuck, J. (1996) 'Computer matching is a serious threat to individuals' rights', in R. King (ed.) *Computerization and Controversy: Value Conflicts and Social Choices*, 2nd ed. San Diego: Academic Press.

Skocpol, T. (1984) 'Emerging agendas and recurrent strategies in historical sociology', in T. Skocpol (eds) *Vision and Method in Historical Sociology*, New York: Cambridge University Press.

Stalder, F. and Lyon, D. (2003) 'Electronic identity cards and social classification', in D. Lyon (ed.) *Surveillance as Social Sorting: Privacy, Risk and Digital Discrimination*, London: Routledge.

Standing Inter-Departmental Committee (1928) NS 14 (Circular). Committee of Imperial Defence: Standing Inter-Departmental Committee on National Service in a Future War and Sub-committee on Man-Power: Minutes and Memoranda (NS and MED Series), CAB 57, London: The National Archives.

Star, S.L., Bowker, G.C. and Neumann, L.J. (1997) 'Transparency at different levels of scale: convergence between information artifacts and social worlds', in A.P. Bishop, N.A. Van House and B. Buttenfield (eds) *Digital Library Use: Social Practice in Design and Evaluation*, Cambridge: MIT Press. Online. Available: http://epl.scu.edu:16080/~gbowker/converge.html (accessed 7 January 2006).

The Times (1938) A national register, 24 March.

The Times (1939a) Registration day, 18 September.

The Times (1939b) The national census, 29 September.

The Times (1939c) What to do with identity cards, 6 October.

The Times (1940) Identity cards must be carried, 6 August.

The Times (1941a) Identity card rules, 28 July.

The Times (1941b) Unofficial entries on identity cards, 2 September.

The Times (1941c) Allied nationals to register, 6 June.

The Times (1943) New identity cards, 31 March.

Thelen, K. (2003) 'Insights from comparative historical analysis', in J. Mahoney and D. Rueschemeyer (eds) *Comparative Historical Analysis in the Social Sciences*, New York: Cambridge University Press, pp. 208–40.

Vivian, S. (1951) *History of National Registration* (Cabinet Office Paper). History of National Registration – Filed Separately, RG-2-B-2, Vol. 173, File N-27 (Vol. 1). Ottawa: Archives of Canada.

Wasserstein, B. (1999) *Britain and the Jews in Europe, 1939–1945*, 2nd ed. London: Leicester University Press.

Webb, M. (2007) *Illusions of Security: Global Surveillance and Democracy in the Post-9/11 World*, San Francisco: City Lights Books.

Wood, R. (2005) *A British born Alien*, Part One. Online. Available: http://www.bbc.co.uk/ww2peopleswar/stories/67/a4847367.shtml (accessed 11 April 2006).

10 The United Kingdom identity card scheme

Shifting motivations, static technologies

David Wills

Since the passing of the Identity Cards Act 2006 on 30 March 2006, the UK has an Act of Parliament legislating for identity cards, but as yet has not started to issue such cards. The government is currently in a technological procurement phase and is starting to bring online the administrative components of the system. From the legislation and the government's supporting announcements, the Labour government seems to be aiming for a highly complex ID card system. There have been a number of recent changes in the intended design of the system over the last year. While there are still questions about what the impacts of ID cards on the UK will be, this chapter aims to analyse a process in motion.

This chapter first provides an overview of the history of the ID scheme in the UK, including opposition to the proposals. This is followed by examination of the administration and operation of the scheme in both administrative and technical senses. Finally, the chapter provides an analysis of the motivations and drivers behind the ID card scheme. The technological element of the chapter draws upon insights from information security to highlight a number of issues with the projected operation of the ID card scheme. The analysis of the motivations for the cards reveals a shifting discursive landscape where differing justifications for the scheme are put forward over time whilst the core design of the system remains static. The most recent justifications for the scheme centre on the vulnerability of identity and construction of a need for governmental action to secure identity.

History and opposition

The UK is somewhat unusual in Europe in not having a national identity card. The UK had identity cards during the First and Second World Wars (Agar 2001; Thompson, Chapter 9), but these were withdrawn shortly after the end of the wars. There have been a number of proposals to re-introduce identity cards since that time but these have generally met with opposition or limited enthusiasm. The Conservative government introduced a scheme in 1996 in order to deal with the threat posed by Irish Republican (IRA) terrorism. This scheme would have been based upon the driving licence with the addition of more detailed information and a more stringent issuing process, supported by a newly created database. However, this proposal was curtailed by the 1997 general election defeat of Major's Conservative government by Tony Blair's New Labour.

After the events of 11 September 2001, the issue of identity cards re-emerged onto the political stage. Initial moves were made in the forms of the biometric 'Asylum Registration Cards' issued to applicants for political asylum (Lyon 2005: 85). These were intended to prevent multiple applications by the same individual. However, because they were generated from information presented by the applicant, often without established chains of documentary evidence, they did not in any sense 'prove' identity (Ward 2005). The proposal to extend this system to a model of 'entitlement cards' for the general population was first floated in 2002. For a thorough analysis of the Entitlement card proposals, see 6 (2003). Public and media responses re-articulated 'entitlement cards' as identity cards by another name and the government responded by re-phrasing the proposal in terms of identity cards. A draft Bill was introduced to Parliament in 2004 along with a public consultation exercise, before suspension in March 2005 due to a general election.

After the Labour government's return to power, and following a manifesto commitment (Labour Party 2005: 52–53), a Bill was introduced to parliament in May that was substantially the same as that which had run out of parliamentary time. It is this 2005 Bill that became the Identity Cards Act 2006. A number of political resignations, re-appointments and changes in portfolio seem to have had a limited effect on the parliamentary progression of the ID card scheme. First introduced by Home Secretary David Blunkett, ID cards were supported by his successors, Charles Clarke, John Reid and the current Home Secretary, Jacqui Smith. Under John Reid, a number of scandals at the Home Office forced Reid to declare the ministry 'not fit for purpose' and initiated a split between the Ministry of Justice (with responsibility for criminal justice, prisons and probation) and the Home Office (which would retain responsibility for terrorism, security, immigration and, importantly, identity cards). The new Labour leadership under Gordon Brown is continuing with the implementation of the ID cards scheme. The Home Office intends to introduce biometric identification for foreign nationals in 2008 and the first ID cards for British citizens will be issued in 2009 (BBC News 19 June 2007). Currently occurring are ID trials in conjunction with the Criminal Records Bureau and the Borders and Immigration agency, involving employment, age and criminal record checks (Identity and Passport Service 2007).

There has been notable opposition to the proposals from the established political parties, smaller campaigning and lobbying groups and from academic researchers. Nine labour party members rebelled against the party whip to vote against the 2006 Bill, an unsurprising occurrence given the tendency of a small group of labour MPs to regularly rebel against the government on issues ranging from Afghanistan and Iraq to university tuition fees (Cowley 2005). While they previously supported the entitlement cards and the 2004 ID card Bill, the Conservative party under the leadership of David Cameron are now officially against the ID cards Act, with 86 per cent of Conservative MPs voting against the Bill. The Conservatives argue that the scheme is a '£20 billion white elephant' (BBC News 19 December 2006) and are opposed to the 'infringement of ancient liberty' and the experience of 'papers please sir', seeing this as characteristic of totalitarian societies. They argue that ID cards are an expensive distraction from real solutions and a 'plastic alternative' to real policing and stronger borders.[1] The Conservative opposition therefore reflects both Burkean and libertarian strands of conservative philosophy as well as euro-scepticism and a belief in narrative of British uniqueness in comparison with Europe. The Liberal Democrats and the Scottish National Party are also opposed to ID cards; the Liberal Democrats arguing that the scheme is expensive, intrusive and ineffective.[2]

The arguments of campaigning groups opposed to ID cards can be roughly divided between two forms. Groups, such as NO2ID[3] and civil rights group Liberty,[4] focus upon pragmatic and technical arguments such as the cost of the scheme and arguments demonstrating why they believe ID cards will not work. This position is explicitly critiqued by groups such as Defy-ID,[5] and by Privacy International (Wickins 2005). Privacy International argues that arguments against ID should be principled rather than simply pragmatic. That the majority of opposition is predicated upon pragmatic grounds fits the critique raised by Muller that in the post 9/11 environment, with biometric technology appearing 'timely' and appropriate, questions of reliability are likely to remain the sole site of contestation and political debate (Muller 2005: 85). Yet some groups are clearly aware of the tactical problems of remaining within this 'pragmatic' frame. Dismissing the 'write to your MP' tactics of NO2ID, they claim that the stated aims and motivations of the scheme are distractions from the real aims of social control. Defy-ID in particular stresses the need for grass-roots action, especially with the passing of the 2006 Act, although this has so far been limited. Despite their ideological differences, there is overlap between the two types of groups in terms of specific goals, and smaller groups such as Defy-ID are willing to 'piggyback' on the resources and infrastructures of better funded groups (e.g. linking to documents hosted on the NO2ID website).

A final strand of opposition to the ID cards scheme has come from The Identity Project hosted at the London School of Economics Department of Information Systems. In 2005, after the reintroduction of the Bill to Parliament, the LSE published a report on the proposals. The report concluded that the proposals were 'too complex, technically unsafe, overly prescriptive and lack a foundation of public trust and confidence' (The Identity Project 2005: 5) and that the estimated cost of the ten year rollout will be between £10.6 billion and £19.2 billion. The government reacted strongly to the report, especially with regard to projected costs (The Identity Project August 2005). While focusing solely on the technical means of the ID scheme, rather than its underlying stated motivations (which the report accepted) the LSE report was significant in its depth of analysis. It also contained a technical proposal for an alternate card system that would meet the government's stated aims for the ID cards but without what the LSE saw as the major security issues of the government's proposal. This alternate model involved ID holders retaining control over their personal data and using a distributed 'token' mechanism to authenticate identity to particular sectors.

The administration of the identity card scheme

This section sets out the provisions of the Identity Cards Act 2006, the organizations and actors involved in the identity card scheme and the intended operation of the system. It is worth stating that the proposed system, provided for in the Act, is more than an identity card. Its core is the *National Identity Register* (NIR), of which identity cards are a physical manifestation. Surrounding the register sit a cluster of policies and legal statutes that ensconce the identity scheme within the wider framework of UK governance. Whitely and Hosein argue that the lead department on an ID card project strongly affects the nature of the scheme.

> The choice of government department that designs the policy on this issue directly influences the kinds of approaches and other policy agendas enrolled in the solution. The response and emphasis of a department of consumer affairs is likely to be very different from that of a department with policing responsibilities and will differ again from departments responsible for trade and industry.
>
> (Whitely and Hosein 2007)

The UK Identity scheme will be administered by a newly formed executive agency of the Home Office and as such can be expected to be oriented towards policing and security. The Identity and Passport Service (IPS) was formed in April 2006 from the UK passport service and the Home Office's internal identity card programme. Despite the planned availability of a separate ID card, the ID card is tightly integrated with the passport, drawing heavily upon the infrastructure of the previously existing passport service. In a change from previously stated plans (Lyon 2005: 74), issuing of the UK ID card is no longer integrated with the driving license, although the driving licence number is one of the 'identification numbers' that can be stored on the register, creating a functional link between the two databases.

The stated statutory purpose of the Act is to establish a 'secure and reliable record of registrable facts about individuals in the UK'. This is perceived as performing two functions. First, a 'convenient method for such individuals to prove registrable facts about themselves to others who reasonably require proof' and 'a secure and reliable method for registrable facts about such individuals to be ascertained or verified wherever that is necessary in the public interest' (Act 2006: 1). Public interest is further defined as national security, prevention or detection of crime, enforcement of immigration controls and prohibitions on unauthorized working and 'securing the efficient and effective provision of public services'. 'Registrable facts' include identity, address of principal place of residence and other places of residence, previous residences, current and previous residential statuses (nationality, entitlement to remain in the UK), identification numbers, when information on the individual has been provided from the register and information recorded in the register at the individual's request. The Act explicitly exempts this information from the definition of sensitive personal data in the Data Protection Act 1998. It is worth including the Act's definition of 'identity'. 'Identity' refers to full name, other names by which an individual might previously have been known, gender, date and place of birth and 'external characteristics of his that are capable of being used for identifying him' (Act 2006: 2).

The Act creates new criminal offences: the possession of false identity documents, identity documents obtained improperly, or identity documents that pertain to somebody else, with the intent to use this documentation to establish 'registrable facts' about themselves or another. These offences carry a potential sentence of up to ten years imprisonment and the relevant 'identity documents' include ID cards, immigration documents, UK passports, passports issued by external authorities, and UK driving licences. The Act also introduces offences relating to the national identity register: unauthorized disclosure of information from the register (up to two years imprisonment), providing false information to the register (up to two years) and tampering with the register (up to ten years). Additionally, given that any tampering with the register will involve computers, the provisions of the Computer Misuse Act 1990 are likely to apply.

The act also creates a new official regulator, the National Identity Scheme Commissioner, independent of the IPS. The Commissioner will have oversight powers regarding the uses to which ID cards are put. He cannot, however, exert any influence over the imposition of fines, criminal offences related to the scheme or information provided to the security services. The Commissioner will provide an annual report to the Home Secretary to be placed before Parliament for scrutiny. The Home Secretary may edit from this report information prejudicial to national security or prevention or detection of crime (Ward 2005). In addition to the role of the National Identity Scheme Commissioner, oversight roles are to be played by a number of bodies. During the passage of the legislation both the House of Commons Science and Technology committee and the Home Affairs Committee produced reports on the legislation. The Office of the Information Commissioner will have powers of oversight under the Data Protection Act 1998, where these have not been explicitly overridden. The Information commissioner has previously published a number of 'concerns' and guidance notes regarding the ID scheme. The Information Commissioner believes the scheme to be excessive and disproportionate, that identity should be a tool in control of the individual, and that ID cards cannot be seen in isolation from other surveillance technologies (Thomas 2003; Information Commissioner's Office 2005a,b).

The rollout of the card system is intended to be staggered and 'evolutionary'. From 2008, all non-European individuals resident in the UK for more than three months will be expected to register for an ID card. ID cards will be issued alongside passports to UK citizens starting in 2009. Currently, approximately 80 per cent of the population holds a passport, which are typically renewed every five years and the first 'e-Passports' with biometric information were issued in 2006. ID cards are to be compulsory for anybody applying for a passport from 2010. Before 2010 it will be possible to opt out of being issued a card, although details will still be entered on the register, rendering the opt-out less significant. It is unlikely to become compulsory to carry the card even when registration becomes compulsory for all UK residents over 16. Compulsory registration, along with penalties for failure to register will require further primary legislation.[6]

While administered by the Home Office, the UK ID scheme is notable for the wide range of linked agencies and organizations. This breadth is associated with the wide range of functions the government perceives the card fulfilling. This assemblage of institutions includes the Department for Work and Pensions, The Immigration and Nationality Directorate, the police, the Criminal Records Bureau, the Department of Communities and Local Government and local governments themselves. It also spreads beyond what might be narrowly understood as government to include bodies in the private sector such as credit referencing agencies that will play a role in the checking of 'biographical footprints' during register enrolment.

While purposes of the scheme will be explored in detail below, it is worth demonstrating the breadth of potential uses envisaged by this multiplicity of agencies. This includes employability checks, background and criminal records bureau checks, proof of age, access to public services such as unemployment benefits or the NHS, and a range of private sector 'identity checking services'. While ID cards may have a range of uses set out in legislation, it is likely that others will emerge. For example, the chair of the Electoral Commission has suggested that as a 'universal identifier', ID cards would have to be shown at the polling booth (Sherman 2007). If ID cards become regularly checked during financial and commercial transactions (or going to a bar etc.), then carrying the card becomes a practical necessity even though there is no legal requirement to carry the card at all times.

A final controversial issue surrounding the administration of the ID cards scheme is the expected cost of the scheme. The Government's consistent position has been that most of the costs of the scheme come from updating the passport, and that much of the costs can be recouped from the holders of the cards themselves as the cards will cost between £90–100 for a combined biometric passport and ID card, or approximately £30 for an ID card. The anticipated compulsory registration raises an issue with regard to cost that is significant in the British context. If registration is compulsory, but cards cost between £90 and £100, then this cost is compulsory. The government attempts to minimize comparisons between such a flat rate fee and the 'poll tax' or Community Charge of the 1980s, opposition to which culminated in a number of riots and contributed to the fall of the Thatcher government in 1990.

The Identity Project report is sceptical about the government's cost projections due to the experimental, untested nature of the technology, high security demands and uncertain levels of public trust (The Identity Project 2005: 241). In many of the LSE's re-assessments, the assumption is that costs will be increased by the need to counter deficiencies of the scheme. For example, the need to provide private areas in enrolling stations for those who are sensitive about having biometrics taken in public, or the costs of sufficiently securing such a large database with multiple entry points. The report argues that these costs are not accounted for in the government's costing of the scheme. These needs *may* be realized at a later date, with a resulting increase in costs. It is also possible that these needs will not be sufficiently addressed, or be neglected because of costs, with socially negative implications ranging from embarrassment to information insecurity. The LSE also attacked the 'granularity' of the government's published costs, suggesting that they did not break down projected costs in sufficient detail to allow analysis of the claims (Identity Project 2005: 241).

The identity scheme: Technology

The main technological issues surrounding the ID card are information security, the NIR database and its accompanying audit trail. The overview in this section is situated in the context of the legal and governmental framework which serves to complicate an analysis of the technology. At of the core of this framework is The Identity Card Act as the *enabling* legislation. Many technological details of the scheme are left to secondary legislation at which point parliament is presented with a package it can either affirm or reject but not modify (The Identity Project 2005: 229). Because of this, many technical details of the operation of the scheme are not yet in the public domain, or are subject to change. For example, it has not yet been decided if the smart ID card will be a contact chip or RFID, and while the 2006 Act provides the legal grounding for inclusion of iris biometrics on the database, this may not be actively pursued in the initial rollout.

For any large information technology project, since 2000, the government must undergo a series of 'Gateway' reviews by the Office of Government Commerce. These include risk analysis and implementation options. The results of these reviews have not been made public. The government has argued that in order to get accurate responses from its private sector advisors and experts, it must ensure commercial confidence, which prevents publication of the results. Given that legislation was passed before technological systems were selected (and had to be, given that the act enabled the system to progress), it is possible for the Act to make claims that are not technologically feasible. This is important in the areas of computer security and the capabilities of biometric searches across large populations. For example biometric technology for regular, reliable identification has simply not been tested with population sizes of around 67 million.

Five concepts drawn from information security are useful with regard to analysing the technological component of the ID scheme. Security issues are at the heart of any large scale IT project, yet especially so for one that is so discursively associated with the goal of 'securing your identity'. Adequate security is a requirement of data protection legislation. In addition, information security raises the profile of a third element of the familiar state-commercial surveillance dyad, and asks 'to what extent can criminals be considered surveillance agents?'

First, there is a myth of a completely secure system. Information security is often a trade-off with usability. A perfectly secure system would be one with no connection to the outside world, with no users, no information on it, in a locked room with no key and preferably, turned off. This is obviously not particularly usable. This is not to say that a degree of security cannot be achieved, however it is problematic to assume that security can be simply 'bolted-on' to the exterior of a system rather than designed into it. The NIR will hold millions of records and be accessed millions of times per day, with data changing frequently. As a significant system, with a wide number of access points, multiple methods of use, an entry for each member of the population and positioned as a '21st century public good' (Byrne 2007), the system would not just be exposed to attacks that aim to gain access to the database, but also 'denial of service' attacks which attempt to shut the system down. The more services (access to healthcare, border control, benefits and welfare payments, access to financial services) that are linked to the database, the greater the dangers of system failure. The cause of system failure need not be malicious for the effects to be catastrophic (The Identity Project 2005: 218).

Second, in information security, attackers have a strong advantage over defenders. While a defender must locate and fix every potential vulnerability, a defender only has to find one exploitable entry into the system. The identity scheme has a complex and high risk threat profile. It will include at its core a massive database of 67 million individuals. It would become a high priority target for attack, especially if access to the database becomes necessary for the creation of identities. Any actor desiring a 'false' identity then requires database access. The Serious Organised Crime Agency highlights the use of multiple, altered or stolen identities by organized crime (SOCA 2006). There would be substantial incentives for criminals to access the database. If the ID card system was to become the trusted arbiter of identities, these false identities would be indistinguishable from 'real' identities. The more assertions that are made about the security and reliability of the system, the more this incentive structure applies. It should be assumed that the National Identity Register (NIR) will be compromised, and that it will be compromised to a significant extent.

The government's initial intention had been to create a new 'clean' database from scratch, to prevent the inclusion of multiple or false identities. However, the database will now be spread across a number of sites. Biometric information will be stored on the Immigration and Nationality Directorate's asylum system, biographical data by the Department for Work and Pensions, while the issue and audit trail will be stored on the IPS system. This should not be considered a federated identity system, as the NIR will be functionally integrated and simply hosted on these three systems. Existing data on the legacy systems will be migrated across during NIR enrolment but the government argues that it can still maintain a clean database by checking this information before it is allowed onto the NIR. This re-use of existing systems will arguably reduce the cost of the ID scheme, and lower some of the set-up risks. The concept of a centralized single database has been strongly criticized from an information security perspective in response to the government's consultation efforts, yet the government has not articulated the shift to three databases as a response to the problems of centralization.

Third, there is widespread acknowledgement that 'security through obscurity' is a bad idea. Derived from military logics, security through obscurity is the idea that systems are more secure if their security arrangements are not made public. By keeping a system's construction hidden, the users (and in this case the public) are reliant on the designers having built the system correctly. Obscurity can only slow attackers down, and while open systems may be exposed to serious attacks sooner, these attacks are inevitable for high value targets. Open systems allow flaws to be identified and can be associated politically with values of transparency and accountability.

Fourth, and arguing from an economics of information security perspective, Anderson (2001) contends that information security is a matter of incentive structures. He states that when those charged with protecting data are not those who will bear the costs of security failures, information security simply does not happen. From the perspectives of ID cards, the costs of failures will likely be born socially and economically by individuals with little control and influence over the operation of the system nor access to its design and structure.

Finally, information security is not simply an issue of barriers and protection. It also includes limiting the impacts of the failure of defences. What will happen when the database is compromised, when personal information leaks out, when false identities are placed upon the database? What recourse does an individual have if they believe their register entry has been maliciously altered? How much information needs be stored in one location? What information needs to be stored at all?

The most controversial aspect of the Identity Register is the access and audit trail, a record of every time the NIR is accessed regarding an individual. The Government has argued for this audit trail on the basis of security and protection of personal data, and has suggested that the audit trail is in response to concerns of the Information Commissioner and data protection legislation. Because of the audit trail, individuals would be reassured that their data were not being incorrectly accessed. However, there are no timescales for deletion of these data, for example after a specified time period in which such an audit might be made. It is important to realize the capacity of this audit trail to reveal a broad range of activities related to an individual (employment checks, criminal records checks, benefits, health, physical locations at specific times, etc.) which in *themselves* are important personal data. Additionally, certain state agencies (notably the security services) are allowed covert access to the database, which does not show up on the audit trail. Apart from immediate concerns of state misuse, this indicates that there is a class of system user except from the audit trail, a feature that could be exploited by attackers for their own covert access. According to The Identity Project report:

> The audit trail is the greatest challenge in the proposed UK system, complicating the architecture unnecessarily, placing the bill and the ID card system on legally problematic grounds, and ignoring the existing identification structures in British society.
>
> (The Identity Project 2005: 248)

Motivations for the identity card scheme

Unpacking motivations for policy decisions can be a problematic exercise. It is easy simply to attribute researcher created motivations with little justification, or to unreflectively apply simple accounts like 'Big Brother' in the manner of dominant UK media discourses. One can assess stated motivations through examination of official discourse. However, it is problematic to simply assume that publicly stated motivations for a particular policy are the sole drivers. Public discourse operates in a mutual relationship with its audience(s) and influential mediators such as the press and broadcasters, while the act of making a public statement should be considered a political act (Jackson 2005: 1). Governmental discourse can be reactive to its opposition, and strong opposing arguments can cause a re-framing of policy motivations and aims. With regard to ID cards, we can identify a number of discursive shifts in policy justifications. Some initially high profile motivations have diminished in importance over the six year development of the current scheme (e.g. prevention of terrorism), while others have increased in importance or have newly entered into the debate (e.g. the danger of identity theft and the associated need to secure identities).

What is significant about the UK ID scheme is that alongside these discursive re-articulations, there have been few, if any, major shifts in the design of the system itself – the ID card scheme is practically the same as that proposed as an 'entitlement card' in 2002 (The Identity Project 2005: 35). The responses to the various consultation exercises demonstrate that the government was made aware of a number of significant problems with the design of ID card but did not alter the design (Secretary of State for the Home Department 2004). This discontinuity between motivations and design allows an entry point into the field of potential motivations. Additionally, the government's rejection of the LSE's alternate model of ID cards suggests drivers beyond the publicly stated aims – requiring the full flow and centralization of information. However, it should be noted that this may simply be the inertia of a project to which the government has already committed itself overriding the inputs of policy outsiders.

International drivers

There are three key potential international drivers for identity cards in the UK: the International Civil Aviation Authority passport standards, the USA visa waiver programme and the European Union Schengen agreement. The first two of these have received high priority in the government's discourse, while the third is almost conspicuously absent. As stated earlier, the ID card is to be integrated into the passport, and the government has stated that most of the costs of the ID card scheme come from international obligations to produce biometric, machine readable travel documents, and that given the requirement to establish the necessary mechanisms, an ID card is a logical outgrowth of this. The ICAO requirement is simply for a machine readable passport and does not require that information be stored on a central register. This obligation has already been met, as all Passports issued by the UK from 2006 are 'e-passports'. The UK is currently a member of the visa waiver scheme, allowing UK citizens to travel to the USA without a visa. Given the importance of business and tourist travel to the USA, and the cost and hassle of applying for a visa, the government takes it as axiomatic that it should remain in this scheme. According to the US government, what is required is 'a machine readable chip with information from the data page of the passport and a digital photograph on passports issued after October 2006' that 'conforms to the ICAO standards for the e-passport'[7] (see Stanton, Chapter 15). Therefore, with the issuing of e-passports, with a biometric – the digital picture of the holder's face – the UK has met its visa waiver programme requirements. The UK is currently not a full member of the EU's Schengen agreement however, retaining control of its own borders and passports. It is therefore not obliged to pursue biometric identity documents. The government has however argued that it does not want 'second class' passports compared with other European countries. The discursive move here is to play down the agency of the government and ascribe policy motivators to the EU tapping into 'euro-sceptic' strands of UK politics. This is an example of 'policy laundering', in which policies are developed outside of national deliberative fora and then adopted locally in the interests of national governments (Hosein 2004). At the same time, other European countries are discursively used as examples of countries where ID cards are unproblematically accepted and used without complaint.

Domestic motivations

There are four key areas of domestic policy motivations for ID cards in the UK: Immigration and illegal working, personalized and joined up 'e-government', national security, terrorism and crime, and finally, securing identity. As with the distinction drawn between international and domestic motivations, these are analytical distinctions. It is particularly difficult to separate the final category from the other three in practical terms, but is quite revealing analytically. These four categories roughly map onto the Home Office's own policy objectives (The Identity Project 2005: 234).

The Identity Card in the UK is inextricable from the issue of immigration both in terms of the mobilized discourse and in terms of the project's history (Flynn 2005: 227). The Applicant Registration Card was the UK's first biometric ID, while the ID card scheme was first called an entitlement card, intended to allow the 'entitled' to prove their 'entitlement'. 'Entitlement' grew out of a discourse of drains on the Health Service and social services by those not so entitled, including concepts of 'health tourism', 'economic migrants' and 'bogus asylum seekers'. Immigrants have been portrayed for some years in the tabloid press as attempting to 'sponge off' the welfare state. This is despite demographics of migrants who are often young, in relatively good health and travelling to work, not to claim benefits. According to Liam Byrne:

> The identity challenge means that without identity systems we leave our borders vulnerable, we leave community safety nets vulnerable; and we leave individuals perhaps most vulnerable of all.
>
> (Byrne 2007)

The Government's strategic action plan on ID cards states 'much of what we will be delivering in 2007 and 2008 will be in support of the Government's commitments to transform the immigration system' (Home Office 2006).

On the other side of the immigration card is the argument that the card will encourage a sense of 'Britishness' in the face of 'the socially fragmenting tendencies of globalisation, countering the alienation of sections of society from civic affairs' (Flynn 2005: 215). This purpose, it is argued, would promote a shared sense of identity, belonging and citizenship and that people would be proud to carry a card because it would be a 'palpable badge confirming their membership of a community' (Flynn 2005: 227). Thus, the ID card functions as a token of group membership, and its necessary correlate – the absence of a card signifying exclusion. If one cannot present an ID card when applying for employment, financial, health or social services, then one is positioned discursively, both linguistically and materially by a political technology as external to that 'community'. The converse of ensuring that citizens get what they are entitled to is the denial of services to those who are not entitled. This is reflected in the heavy discursive emphasis given to benefit fraud, and like illegal immigration, the strain that this places upon overstretched social services. The Department for Work and Pensions states that benefit fraud costs the benefits system £800 million/year (Byrne 2007).

The Identity Project report argued that little benefit fraud (between 1 and 3 per cent) actually involved false identities; most benefit fraud involves misrepresentation of circumstances, an activity that would not be prevented by identity cards (2005: 256).

A strongly articulated motivation for the introduction of ID cards is the move towards 'e-government'. Lyon (2005: 72) identifies this as a long-term UK goal and it is strongly reflected in UK government discourse. The Strategic Action plan states that ID cards and the NIR are to be 'the 'glue' that allows personal and identity-related data to be joined up across government' (Home Office 2006, s. 85) and that 'a really effective identity management scheme is essential in order to shape public services around the citizen and realize the goal of truly joined-up and personalised government' (Home Office 2006, s. 92). The Cabinet Office's digital strategy states that 'ID cards are developed in such a way that they add value to the whole range of digital transactions' and positions ID cards as a crucial element of 'Government Connect', a local government programme 'wherein customers will be able to complete government transactions online without having to send by post their passport, driving licence or utility bill as proof of identity' (Cabinet Office 2005). The articulation of the subject-position of 'customers' is typical within debates about ID cards. The ID scheme is positioned to provide a unique and accurate identifier of the individual across government.

In a significant discursive move, Home Office minister Liam Byrne has argued that the card scheme will become a 'great British institution', drawing parallels between the identity system and the railways of the nineteenth century. This language of 'part of the fabric of British life' and 'just a normal part of British life' serves a normalizing function to suppress potential objections to what in essence is a novel system.

Stalder and Lyon (2003) argue that ID cards are not particularly effective for national security, while in security climates influenced by 11 September 2001, they are frequently presented as part of a (necessary) binary trade off between civil liberties and national security. While the first part is most likely as true of UK ID cards as others, what is notable is that national security has not been a predominant element of the ID card debates in the UK, and that this binary trade off is absent from the government's recent discourse. The Act does not attempt to utilise the national security exception from data protection legislation. The Home Office has openly admitted that ID cards are not powerful tools for combating terrorism, and that perhaps they had even been 'oversold' (BBC News 2005). Whilst the familiar binary has emerged in debates over extended detention of terror suspects without trial, ID cards have been articulated in a non-zero-sum manner. As we will see below, the issue is reframed as a benefit to the government *and* to the citizen. The argument is made that ID cards will actually protect liberties, and that the ID card is an enabling technology for individuals.

The government's discourse has however placed more weight upon the role of ID cards in preventing crime and aiding in the detection of crime. According to the Serious Organised Crime Agency, identity fraud underpins much serious organized crime by 'enabling serious organised criminals to conceal themselves, their activities and their assets, and minimise the risk of detection' (SOCA 2006, s. 4.24).

If the introduction of ID cards appears to be a way for governments to 'get tough' on crime and terrorism, this may make it harder to move away from such a policy even if presented with good evidence to suggest that it is ineffective. In an attempt to preserve face, and not be seen to back down 'in the face of terrorists', politicians must persevere with a programme and find ways to justify it. Harnessing a project to a rhetorically powerful issue (in the current climate) can therefore backfire.

Finally, the most recent discursive dimension of the ID card debates: concerns over 'identity theft', the construction of the vulnerability of identity and governmental needs to secure identity. This element of the discourse has grown in importance from a marginal element in 2002 to one of the core themes of government ID discourse. This follows the perceived need, post 9/11, for a long-term solution for 'managing identities' (Muller 2005).

Identity is constructed as a vulnerable characteristic; one that can be stolen, questioned and doubted. This is explicitly linked to globalization and hyper-mobility. It is also linked to crime. The boundary between the more emotive 'identity theft' and the more technically accurate 'identity fraud' is fuzzily articulated. Identity fraud is regularly stated as costing the country £1.7 billion a year, although these figures have frequently been disputed by opponents of the scheme (The Identity Project 2005: 104). In many ways, identity is constructed as property, something that needs protecting. This can be found in many of the 'responsiblization' efforts: exhortations to check bank statements and credit ratings, and to shred documents of any importance. Governmental discourses can be interpreted as constructing an understanding of identity that is objective and essential: an understanding that allows identities to be either 'true' or 'false', something that can be proven (or disproved).

Critically, the government ID card scheme is counterposed to 'uncontrolled response', 'laissez-faire' 'mish-mash of unregulated, potentially unsafe systems' for identity management and a 'proliferation of plastic, passwords and PINS'. It is argued that it is the socially vulnerable who will be worst affected by the vulnerability of identity. 'In the face of most of these risks, it is unlikely that the most well off will be hurt most. It will be those who cannot afford to buy their own defences' (Byrne 2007). In this sense, the government articulates the ID scheme as the only appropriate protector of identity. The government also positions itself as the sole source of 'identity assurance' to the private sector. The aim is therefore to provide a 'gold standard' of identity proof.

Conclusion

Pre-ID scheme identity is dependent on multiple social relationships. We have identities, which are placeholders for our relationships with a variety of institutions and organizations. These identities act as representations of ourselves to those organizations. To an important extent they are negotiated, with a distinct amount of flexibility, through relational processes. Identities are, in this sense, not pre-existing things with an essential ontological character, but something that is social constructed across a number of social domains and in a number of ways. The UK citizen has a birth certificate, a national insurance number, most likely a National Health Service number, possibly a driving license number, some credit cards, an address, a phone number (or two), a video rental card, a library card, maybe a university card or ID provided by their place of work. These are not officially and structurally linked together.

Discursive constructions of policy motivations serve to constitute particular problems, and this serves to shape the acceptable solutions that can be offered to those problems. The problem here is one of unstable, unfixed identities. The existing model of identity is not sufficient. It is constructed as open to abuse. Terrorists and criminals misuse multiple identities to leach off society, and even kill us. A single identifier is needed to prove who you are, or that you are who you say you are. The presumption is that when asked this question, some people will lie (Lyon 2005: 71) – and that enough people will lie, and the consequences of this lying are so bad (or so unallowable) that action must be taken to certify identity beyond a doubt. Currently existing identifiers are constructed as insecure and unstable. They therefore need to be replaced by more secure identities. The notion of identity at play in the government's ID discourse is an identity mediated, managed, protected and legitimated through the state (broadly conceived of course). This is how ID is presented as non-zero-sum. The government gains a number of benefits (crime prevention, less drain on resources, etc.) while the individual gets his identity protected from external threats.

However, the ability of the government to construct a secure system which can perform this function should be questioned. As we have seen from an information security perspective it should be assumed that the National Identity Register will be compromised. Information security concerns should be at the heart of identity systems, security incentives need to be properly balanced and attention paid to who has control over personal data. In a society with a high level of surveillance, and which places greater reliance upon machine-authenticated forms of identity, 'identity theft' becomes much more of a possibility (and from an attacker's perspective, necessary). Bureaucratically grounded, secured and governmental identities become valuable, producing incentives for criminal activity. The question that arises is what happens when a society assumes that its ID system is authoritative, secure, stable and accurate, and acts accordingly, when in fact the system may be unstable, insecure, inaccurate and prone to misuse? The government's attempt to secure identities causes problems, because identities are not something that can be secured. They are mutable, negotiable, relative and social. There are also lessons for opponents of ID cards. Government discourse is responsive to challenges, and incorporates arguments against ID cards. In the UK, this can be seen in the shifts in public articulated motivations. While the discursive constructions of the motivations for ID cards have only recently taken on their particular form, the design of the ID system has been remarkably consistent since 2002.

Notes

1 Online. Available: http://www.conservatives.com/tile.do?def=news.story.page&obj_id= 1-35823&speeches=1
2 Online. Available: http://www.libdems.org.uk/noidcards/
3 Online. Available: http://www.no2id.net
4 Online. Available: http://www.liberty.org.uk
5 Online. Available: http://www.defy-id.org.uk
6 Online. Available: http://www.identitycards.gov.uk/scheme-what-how.asp
7 Online. Available: http://travel.state.gov/visa/temp/without/without_1990.html

Bibliography

6, P. (2003) 'Entitlement Cards: Benefits, Privacy and Data Protection Risks, Costs and Wider Social Implications', The Information Commissioner.
Agar, J (2001) 'Modern horrors: British identity and identity cards', in Caplan, J. and Torpey, J. (eds) *Documenting Individual Identity: The development of State Practices in the Modern World*, Princeton: Princeton University Press.
Anderson, R. (2001) 'Why information security is hard: an economic perspective', Proceedings of the 17th Annual Computer Security Applications Conference.
BBC News (2005) 'Labour admits ID card oversell', 4 August. Online. Available: http://news.bbc.co.uk/1/hi/uk_politics/4744153.stm
BBC News (2006) 'Giant ID computer plan scrapped', 19 December. Online. Available: http://news.bbc.co.uk/1/hi/uk_politics/6192419.stm
BBC News (2007) 'ID cards to be a UK institution', 19 June. Online. Available: http://news.bbc.co.uk/go/pr/fr/-/1/hi/uk_politics/6767083.stm
Byrne, L. (2007) 'Securing our identity: a 21st century public good', Speech by Liam Byrne MP, the Minister of State for Immigration, Citizenship and Nationality, to Chatham House, 19 June. Online. Available: http://press.homeoffice.gov.uk/Speeches/sc-identity-21st-century
Cabinet Office (2005) *Connecting the UK: The Digital Strategy*, London: The Cabinet Office, March.
Cowley, P. (2005) *The Rebels: How Blair Mislaid his Majority*. London: Politico's.
Flynn, D. (2005) 'Immigration controls and citizenship in the political rhetoric of New

Labour', in E. Zureik and M.B. Salter (eds) *Global Surveillance and Policing: Borders, Security and Identity,* Devon: Willan Publishing.

Home Office (2006) *Strategic Action Plan for the National Identity Card Scheme: Safeguarding your Identity.* Online. Available: http://www.ips.gov.uk/identity/down-loads/Strategic_Action_Plan.pdf

Hosein, I. (2004) 'The sources of laws: policy dynamics in a digital and terrorized world', *The Information Society* 20(3): 187–99.

Identity Cards Act (2006) London: HMSO.

Identity and Passport Service (2007) *Identity and Passport Service: Identity Service Proposition – a 'joint venture' with the Criminal Records Bureau,* London: Identity and Passport Service. Online. Available: http://www.identitycards.gov.uk/downloads/IdentityServiceProposition_%20Joint%20VenturewiththeCRB.pdf

Information Commissioner's Office (2005a) *The Identity Cards Bill – The Information Commissioner's Concerns,* London: Information Commissioner's Office, May.

Information Commissioner's Office (2005b) *The Identity Cards Bill – The Information Commissioner's Concerns,* London: Information Commissioner's Office, October.

Jackson, R. (2005) *Writing the War on Terror: Language, Politics and Counter-Terrorism,* Manchester: Manchester University Press.

Labour Party (2005) *Britain, Forward not Back: The Labour Party Manifesto, 2005,* London: The Labour Party.

Lyon, D. (2005) 'The border is everywhere: ID cards, surveillance and the other', in E. Zureik and M.B. Salter (eds) *Global Surveillance and Policing: Borders, Security, Identity,* Devon: Willan.

Muller, B.J. (2005) 'Borders, bodies and biometrics: towards identity management', in E. Zureik and M.B. Salter (eds) *Global Surveillance and Policing: Borders, Security, Identity,* Devon: Willan.

Secretary of State for the Home Department (2004) *Identity Cards: A Summary of Findings from the Consultation on Legislation on Identity Cards,* October. Online. Available: http://www.archive2.official-documents.co.uk/document/cm63/6358/6358.pdf

Serious Organised Crime Agency (2006) *The United Kingdom Threat Assessment of Serious Organised Crime 2006/2007,* London: SOCA.

Sherman, J. (2007) 'Election fraud is "so great that photo ID is urgently needed"', *The Times* 28 April. Online. Available: http://www.timesonline.co.uk/tol/news/politics/article1717480.ece

Stalder, F. and Lyon, D. (2003) 'Electronic identity cards and social classification', in D. Lyon (ed.) *Surveillance as Social Sorting: Privacy, Risk and Digital Discrimination,* London: Routledge.

The Identity Projects (2005) *The Identity Project: An assessment of the UK Identity Cards Bill and its implications. Version 1.09,* June. London: LSE Department of Information Systems.

The Identity Projects (2005) *LSE Team Responds to Home Office's Criticisms of The Identity Project Report.* August. Online. Available: http://identityproject.lse.ac.uk/LSE_ResponseTo_HomeOffice.pdf

The Identity Projects (2007) *Submission to the House of Lords Inquiry into the 'Impact of Surveillance and Data Collection',* London: London School of Economics and Political Science Identity Project, Department of Information Systems, July.

Thomas, R. (2003) *Entitlement Cards and Identity Fraud: The Information Commissioner's Response to the Government's Consultation Paper,* 30 January. London: The Office of the Information Commissioner.

Ward, P. (2005) *House of Commons Library Research Paper 05/43, The Identity Cards Bill,* 13 June. London: House of Commons Library.

Whitely, E.A. and Hosein, I.R. (2007) *Departmental Influences on Policy Design: How the UK is confusing identity fraud with other policy agendas,* London: Department of Management, Information Systems Group.

Wickins, J. (2005) *UK Identity Cards and Social Exclusion,* Privacy International. Online. Available: http://www.privacyinternational.org/article.shtml?cmd%5b347%5d =x-347-228833

11 The politics of Australia's 'Access Card'[1]

Dean Wilson

In the mid-1980s, Australia witnessed a vigorous debate over the proposal to introduce a national identity document that came to be known as the 'Australia Card'.
The Government's proposal for a national identification system spawned a broad
coalition of opposition significant enough to defeat the concept. At the time, the
defeat of the 'Australia Card' proposal was heralded as a victory for the rights of
individuals to data privacy. It was also viewed as a victory against the totalitarian
potential of large-scale interconnected government databases. Although long considered politically unpalatable, the issue of a national identity card has re-surfaced
on the Australian political agenda. The re-emergence of the ID card concept has
been advanced by the notion that 'everything changed' post-9/11. While in April
2006 the Government ruled out a compulsory ID card, an 'Access Card' project is
proceeding apace. The Access Card will require Australians to possess a biometric
smart card to access government services. Moreover, the project will include a substantial biometric database of the population.

This chapter seeks to examine the Australian Government's 'Access Card'
project. While following global trends (Lyon 2006) in considering proposals for
a national identification scheme, the Australian debate is especially interesting
due to the fact that a proposal was so resoundingly defeated in the recent past.
The Australian case therefore provides an opportunity to assess the extent to which
global developments in securitization and surveillance are played out within the
confines of a particular nation-state. Moreover, it is argued, the Access Card
project is an important symbolic marker of new configurations of state power. This
chapter begins by tracing the historical lineage of state identification and surveillance in the Australian context through to the Australia Card proposal of the
1980s. It then proceeds to examine the recent proliferation of databases and mass
identification schemes post-9/11, concluding with an examination of the Access
Card proposal. The chapter then proceeds to examine critiques of the proposal. I
conclude by offering some tentative suggestions on the interplay between global
surveillance trends and Australian political culture in the trajectory of the Access
Card project.

History, surveillance and the Australia Card

Although it was not until the 1980s that a national identity scheme was proposed, the compilation of dossiers and identification of the Australian population has a considerable lineage. Creating 'legible people' was central to the advent of Australia as a nation-state, and was intrinsically intertwined with the colony's penal origins and the need for the exercise of state power. Sorting and classifying inhabitants to control movement and disorder was an imperative of early colonial government. From 1796, the Governor of the Colony of New South Wales introduced a pass system administered by the police. By the 1820s, the pass was an elaborate document issued by a magistrate stating the name of the person, the nature of the journey and its duration and purpose. The pass also contained a long list of personal characteristics and details and the signature of the holder (Davidson 1991: 36).

As an outpost of the British Empire, indigenous populations were also subject to intensive surveillance and control by the State. From the mid-nineteenth century, Australian police forces administered protection legislation that involved intense surveillance of Aboriginal populations. In the Northern Territory, the First Protector suggested that Aboriginal people have a means of permanent individual identification through a 'one or two square inch' lesion on the skin. While this suggestion was never enacted, in the 1930s, Aboriginal people in the Darwin district were fingerprinted, subjected to compulsory medical examination and issued with a gold disc to be worn around the neck or hat that was linked to a detailed government record (Cunneen 2001: 64). Indigenous populations had a particular relationship to the Colonial State, but other groups, such as prostitutes under contagious diseases legislation and 'rough' segments of the working class, were also criminalized and subjected to intensive surveillance practices (Finnane 1994: 118). Thus, the emerging dossiers and files of the colonial state remained partial and targeted.

Australians did have limited experience of more general identity schemes in the mid-twentieth century. Australians were issued with an identity card during the Second World War. The Australian scheme linked to wartime rationing was similar in many respects to the British wartime identity card (Davies 1992: 30; Agar 2001). A proposal for a national identity card in the form of the 'Australia Card' was raised in 1985 as a means of reducing tax evasion and social security fraud, and also potentially to control illegal immigration. The Australia Card was to be carried by all Australian citizens and permanent residents (with different cards for temporary residents and visitors). The Australia Card was to display a photograph, name, unique number, signature and period of validity. The card would be produced for a wide-range of transactions including opening bank accounts, investment, employment applications and property transactions (Davies 1992: 31; Greenleaf 1986; Clarke 1987). The Australia Card Bill was introduced to Parliament in October 1986. Later withdrawn due to a technical flaw, the Bill was never reintroduced. This was probably due to the strength of public opposition that mobilized against the proposal. A mass public campaign, a public rally of 30,000 in Western Australia and a national opinion that suggested 90 per cent opposed the Australia Card indicated that the identity card proposal had become politically untenable (Davies 1992: 30–43).

Databases and the emergence of the Australian security state

The Australia Card story has attained somewhat mythic status in Australian political history. Consequently, it was long considered that in Australia an identity card proposal was politically taboo. However, this does not mean that the informational capacity of the Australian State has not considerably deepened and extended since the 1980s. Attendant with the rise of what might be called the 'security state' has been a deepening and widening of surveillance capacities (Lyon 2003: 15). Since the 1980s in Australia (as in other nation-states of the global north), there has been a progressive 'hollowing out' of the state. The Australian State has increasingly extracted itself from the provision of services and turned instead towards the promise of security and safety as the core business of government (McCulloch 2004b). Consequently, social administration and problems are increasingly reconfigured through the prisms of risk and security, as there is a tendency to 'govern through security' (Valverde 2001).

The expansion of surveillance capacities is evident in the recent proliferation of databases and mass-identification projects within Australia. Unsurprisingly perhaps, the initial expansion of smart card technology and biometric databases has intensified historic categories of exclusion and criminalization. It is the poor, marginalized, immigrant and indigenous who have been the first to be coded and entered in the proliferating digital databases of the Australian State. These include the initiation in 2001 of the CrimTrac DNA and fingerprint database of convicted offenders (Heagney 2001) alongside biometric pilot projects involving welfare and healthcare recipients (Bajkowski 2005; Abbott 2004). In 2004, a Medicare Smart Card was piloted in the State of Tasmania in conjunction with HealthConnect, an IT-based health record system (Abbott 2004). In 2005, the use of fingerprint scans for clients of the Australian social security agency Centrelink was also mooted (Bajkowski 2005).

A particular focus of the expansion of surveillance capacity has been in efforts to control illegal immigration. This has particular political resonance in the Australian context, where border control was a pivotal issue in the 2001 Federal election and immigration control remains a highly charged political issue (Pickering 2005; Wilson 2006, 2007; Wilson and Weber 2008). The grounds for the surveillance and documenting of 'non-citizens' has therefore been considerably extended. In 2004, the Australian Parliament passed the Migration Legislation Amendment (Identification and Authentication) Act, which significantly expanded the grounds for collecting biometric identifiers such as photographs, signatures and fingerprints from 'unauthorized arrivals'. The Department of Immigration and Multicultural Affairs (DIMIA) is undertaking a generously funded (A$42.87 million) programme of expanded surveillance capacity to 'establish and authenticate the identity of non-citizens at various stages of immigration processing, and on entry to and departure from Australia' (DIMIA 2004). An integral component of an overall strategy of 'identity management' is a biometric database of asylum seeker details (Wilson 2007).

In 2004, the application of smart card technology as a component of 'mutual obligation' policies aimed at indigenous communities was also advocated by the

Federal Government. Proposals that members of indigenous communities be issued with smart cards to facilitate the monitoring of social security payment expenditure were condemned as racist and reminiscent of the policies of South Africa's apartheid regime. Indigenous leader Mick Dodson decried the proposal as tantamount to 'a new era of apartheid' and asked 'are non-Aboriginal people going to have apartheid-like pass cards, or apartheid-like smart cards that compel them to spend their money in a particular way?' (ABC Online, 11 November 2004).

Other initial projects have sought to assemble databases within particular state jurisdictions. In 2005, Australia's most populous state, New South Wales, passed the Photo Card Act 2005, legislation that permitted the NSW Roads and Traffic Authority (RTA) to issue a photo identity card to people older than 16 years of age. The legislation opened up the possibility of the NSW RTA developing a centralized database that would cover the entire adult population of the state. Privacy advocates complained that the legislation put few limits on the information that could be shared between departments (Riley 2005). Similar concerns have been raised about proposals in the neighbouring state of Queensland for a 'smart drivers licence' slated for introduction in 2008 (Beattie 2005). Critics have indicated that the uses of the card are likely to expand (ABC Stateline Queensland 2004). In 2006, the Federal Government planned to formalize guidelines for smart card projects, a move designed to ensure interoperability and the consolidation of disparate databases (Woodhead 2006).

The deployment of smart card technology linked to digital databases is expanding in the Australian context. In both New South Wales and Queensland, critics have raised the spectre of the Australia Card and expansive registration of the population. Moreover, the current Australian Federal Government has demonstrated considerable interest in large-scale data matching projects, often overriding existing privacy constraints in the process. For example, recent amendments to the secrecy provisions of the *Social Security Act,* passed as part of 'Welfare to Work' reforms, swept away regulations protecting thousands of individuals' personal details (AMA 2006: 4). Nevertheless, even the spectre of the Australia Card has not been powerful enough to deter the Federal Government from an ambitious national identification project, known as the 'Access Card'.

The 'Access Card' project

Since 9/11, there has been a marked increase in the domestic securitization of Australian society. A key element of securitization has been the progressive centralization of security provision and policy with the Federal Government rather than State and Territory Governments. With the prominence of 'national security' as an issue, the Australian Federal Government has increasingly encouraged and facilitated national measures for security, including national policies for CCTV, mass passenger transport, security industry standards and counter-terrorism (Council of Australian Governments, COAG 2005). These measures reflect a general trend towards centralism in the Australian political structure (Summers 2006). It is against this backdrop that the proposal for a national ID card first emerged.

Initial moves to reconsider a national identity card were framed primarily in terms of terrorism and crime. In 2004, senior Australian Federal Police (AFP) Officers were placing pressure on the Federal Government to institute an ID card scheme, arguing that it would be a valuable tool in preventing terrorism and identity theft (Riley 2004). Similarly in 2005, the Premier of the State of Queensland, Peter Beattie, referred to capacity of identity cards as a counter-terrorism measure proclaiming 'I'd rather have an ID card and have a system which actually protects us in a democracy than end up being dead' (ABC Insiders 2005). Following the London bombings of July 2005, Prime Minister John Howard announced that the question of an Australian national identity card should be revisited, despite his vehement opposition to such a proposal in the 1980s (Jordan 2006). However in mid-2005, the Federal Government remained divided over plans for an ID card, with one government backbencher labelling an ID card 'a dangerous idea' (*Sydney Morning Herald* 18 July 2005). In January 2006, Australia's Attorney-General Phillip Ruddock indicated the issue of a national identity card was under consideration as one element of the Government's counter-terrorism strategy (Ruddock 2006). The ID card proposal was one part of a whole of government Identity Fraud Project.

On the 26 April 2006, Prime Minister John Howard announced 'the Government is ruling out introducing a compulsory national ID card' (Howard 2006a). Rejection of a compulsory national ID card may well have been informed by Australia's particular political history. However, the Government has stated that Australians are to receive a biometric Access Card that critics argue will effectively function as a national ID card. From 2010 government health and social services will only be accessible to those possessing an Access Card (Burrell 2006). The Australian Access Card proposal is due to be implemented in 2008, and with $1.1 billion allocated represents Australia's most expensive Information Technology project to date. An estimated 16 million Australians will be registered with photographs taken and signatures digitally scanned and stored. Software will check photographs for duplication that may be a sign of fraud. The card has a microchip that will store details including name, address, names of children or other dependants, signature, card number, concession status, personal identification number (PIN) and digitized photograph (SCFPA 2007).

The Access Card involves the compilation of a biometric database on a hitherto unknown scale. Individuals will be required to register and the database will contain the person's name, date of birth, citizenship or residency status, indigenous status if requested, sex, contact details, benefit card details and registration status. The details of an Access Card issued will also be held on the database, including the Access Card number, the date the card was issued and its expiry date, a photograph and a numerical template derived from that photograph and a digitized signature. The database will also include information about the documents presented to establish identity (SCFPA 2007: 6).

The recent Australian Senate Committee commented that the Access Card database (or 'register' as it is termed) was 'the most contentious element of the Access Card system' (SCFPA 2007: 27). The significant advance in centralized database capacity this represents was noted by Professor Alan Fels, who remarked that 'no previous Australian government, even in wartime, has effectively required all its citizens to give a physical representation of themselves, nor contemplated having this stored in one national database' (SCFPA 2007: 27). The Government has stated that personal information stored on other government databases will not be amalgamated, emphasizing that a 'mega database' was not being assembled (SCFPA 2007: 26). Nevertheless the register represents a single national database on a scale hitherto unknown.

While earlier proposals for an ID card were justified in terms of terrorism and crime, the discursive rationale for the Access Card has increasingly focused on administrative efficiency and consumer convenience (SCFPA Hearings 2007: 3–4). The 'business case', prepared by consultants KPMG, indicates that the Australian Government will save between A$1.6 billion and A$3 billion in fraud over a ten year period. However, the section that purportedly provides the evidence for this estimate was deleted from the public document by the Federal Government as it 'represents a risk to government outlays' (*Canberra Times* 2007). Government discourse surrounding the Access Card project has subsequently centred on the domestic issue of welfare and social security fraud. The Budget papers suggest the card is to 'generate savings in health and social welfare outlays'. Accompanying the Access Card is a raft of measures related to 'fraud and compliance'. A package worth A$282.3 million over five years has been funded to ensure compliance and detect 'welfare cheats' (Australian Government 2006).

The Australian Federal Police have strongly argued for the benefits of the Access Card in reducing identity fraud. However, the figures used to date estimating identity theft to cost between A$1 billion and A$4 billion are questionable (SCFPA 2007: 19–20; APF 2007). While Cole and Pontell (2006) argue in their analysis that identity theft panics seek to get the public to accept responsibility, in the case of Australia's Access Card, the spectre of identity theft has functioned rather differently. Law enforcement have been key stakeholders in the development of the Access Card, with the AFP in particular being positioned as experts on identity theft. This has granted them a key role in the development of the Access Card project (SCFPA 2007: 14). Moreover, it provides a central platform in their arguments for access to the database.

Anticipating privacy concerns, the Federal Government established an Access Card Consumer and Privacy Taskforce to consult with the community and give independent advice to the Minister on how to minimize privacy problems. The Task Force is headed by Professor Alan Fels, former Chairman of the Australian Consumer and Competition Commission (ACCC) and a widely trusted and high profile public figure. Other members include a former NSW Privacy Commissioner and a former Director of the Federal Bureau of Consumer Affairs. However, critics have noted that the Taskforce has no statutory basis or detailed terms of reference and must report to the Minister rather than the public (Greenleaf 2006). In November 2006, the Task Force presented the Government with 26 issues that needed to be addressed before the Access Card project could proceed. Privacy advocates have been sharply critical of the task force, suggesting that it has been effectively manipulated by the Government to sideline privacy issues (Greenleaf 2006; Johnston 2007).

As was also the case with the 'Australia Card' proposal of the 1980s, a significant effort is being expended on rendering the Access Card electorally palatable. The Government is to provide funding of A$1.1 billion over four years, including capital funding of A$80.6 million. An even more interesting figure is the A$47.3 million over four years for a 'communications strategy' which is to 'ensure all Australians are aware of the processes for registering for the card' (Australian Government 2006: 14). The Australian Government Office of Access Card has established a 'myth busters' website that apparently refutes popular 'misconceptions' about the Access Card project (Office of Access Card 2007). Thus the Access Card is being accompanied by a significant public relations campaign.

The 'Access Card' and its critics

While the Access Card has not yet attracted the mass public mobilization that attended the Australia Card proposal of the 1980s, it has nevertheless not been free from controversy. There has been considerable concern that the project is rushed, poorly planned, and that the details of the project remain shrouded in secrecy (Johnston 2007). The Australian Senate Standing Committee on Finance and Public Administration, considering the first of three projected pieces of Access Card legislation, noted the haste with which legislation was being moved and the dangers of having tenders for the Access Card project in the public arena before legislation legitimating the project had been passed (Standing Committee on Finance and Public Administration, SCFPA, 2007: 13–14). In this section, I wish to outline the major critiques of the Access Card project that have emerged in public debate. These are that it is a national identity card, that it will be expensive and inefficient, that it will facilitate identity theft and fraud, that it will invade privacy, that it will inevitably be subject to 'function creep' and be utilised for a wide range of purposes and that it will have a discriminatory impact.

One of the most compelling criticisms in the Australian context, given the legacy of the Australia Card, is that the Access Card is an ID card. The political sensitivity of this distinction is revealed in the rather elaborate efforts taken to maintain that the Access Card is not an ID card, the most obvious being the positive reverberations of the title 'Access' rather than 'ID'. Prime Minister Howard, for example, claimed 'it will not be compulsory to have the card, but by the same token, it will not be possible to access many services which are normally accessed by people unless one is in possession of the card' (Howard 2006b). The proposal that the scheme is voluntary and therefore not an identity system is unsustainable if one considers the significant negative discrimination and exclusion that would accrue from not having a card (cf. Stalder and Lyon 2003: 87). Critics therefore suggest that it is disingenuous to claim that the card is not a national identity card (Australian Privacy Foundation 2007: 4).

While the government has promoted the Access Card in terms of cost-effectiveness and efficiency, there are also serious doubts that it is capable of delivering either. A major criticism of the Access Card is the significant cost of the project and the potential for those costs to continue to escalate. IT professionals suggest the complexity of the project means probable cost blow outs and deadline problems. This is particularly likely given the vague details of the Access Card project (Riley 2006a). The Australian Chamber of Commerce and Industry has suggested that the cost of the Access Card could be as high as A$750 per person or around A$15 billion in total (not including flow-on costs to business) (Johnston 2006). The projected savings claimed to result from the project are also disputed. Even consultants KPMG noted that the projected $1.6 billion to $3 billion to be saved in fraud reduction represented less than 0.3 per cent of programme costs over 10 years (*Canberra Times* 2007). As the Australian Privacy Foundation (2007: 7) remarked, in terms of fiscal return the 'money would be better off in a bank!'.

It is also possible that estimates of savings to be accrued by preventing welfare fraud are seriously over-estimated. President of the National Welfare Rights Network, Michael Raper, noted that the introduction of the Access Card would have little impact on social security fraud as most cases related to reckless or intentional failure to declare income rather than identity fraud. Moreover, as Raper stated, 'social security fraud in Australia is actually miniscule at less than half of one per cent of the 6.5 million recipients' (Pendleton 2006). Business interests, through the Australian Chamber of Commerce, have also voiced concern about the compliance costs they will potentially occur with the implementation of the Access Card (Dearne 2006). Rhetoric in terms of enhanced service delivery and efficiency for consumers is also contested. Indeed the recent history of implementing new healthcare technologies indicates very mixed results for end users (Hopkins 2007).

The efficacy of the Access Card in preventing identity theft and fraud has also been questioned. The main argument advanced is that a centralised database would tend to make identity theft and fraud more likely due to its vulnerability to hacking, corruption and manipulation. The Federal Government Attorney General acknowledged this point in 2005 in rejecting the idea of a national ID card stating that it 'could increase the risk of fraud because only one document would need to be counterfeited to establish identity' (Johnston 2006). This argument is strengthened by an Australian National Audit Office report in 2006 which found that the databases of key government agencies were vulnerable to sabotage and the theft of information (Nicholson 2006). Such risks would potentially be intensified if data were to be further centralised. A mass biometric identification database may therefore increase vulnerability rather than enhance security.

Other concerns surround the security of the personal data to be collected for the Access Card project. Concerns relating to the integrity and security of personal data are exacerbated by recent controversies surrounding existing criminal justice and welfare databases. Victoria's Law Enforcement Assistance Programme (LEAP) has been the subject of sustained criticism following the leaking of confidential files in 2005 (Dearne 2005). Similar concerns have surrounded the sizeable Centrelink database, when internal checks revealed 790 cases of 'inappropriate access' to welfare recipients records since 2004 (Shanahan and Karvelas 2006).

Such incidents have fueled skepticism in relation to the capacity of the government to secure data and manage it within appropriate privacy frameworks. A number of high profile incidents in relation to the Access Card have suggested to some commentators that the project is progressing with little concern for privacy. In May 2006, the head of the Government's Access Card taskforce, James Kelaher, resigned citing concerns about the implementation of the card including privacy issues (Grattan 2006). Suspicion has also been aroused by the Government's reluctance to release a Privacy Impact Assessment undertaken in 2006, first by claiming it was incomplete, later by claiming it was outdated and irrelevant and finally by claiming that the report was cabinet-in-confidence (Johnston 2007).

Another major objection to the Access Card project is the lack of clarity as to its aims and the consequent potential for 'function creep'. The trend towards the centralization of databases and the expansion of uses in the Australian context is already evident. The Australian Medical Association noted that in early pilot projects with HealthConnect, a smart health card project, the desire to accumulate vast stores of data and link it together was so great that the original point (improving health services) vanished altogether (AMA 2006: 6). The AMA has also expressed concerns in relation to function creep in the Access Card project. As their submission suggests, 'dangers of function creep relate predominantly to the use of the consumer identifier contained in the card and the significant capacity to link vast amounts of data through that identifier where restrictions (technical, legislative or policy) do not exist or are inadequate' (AMA 2006: 6). Similarly, arguments against potential function creep have been made by Bill Rowlings, Chief Executive of Civil Liberties Australia, who stated that 'the notion that the proposed card will be confined to social services and health in the long run is nonsense' (Dearne 2006).

Function creep may not only occur through the merging of government databases but may also incorporate the private sector. As Lyon notes, one of the factors differentiating current identification schemes from prior ones is the integration of state and commercial data thus merging national interests in individual identities with consumer ones (Lyon 2006: 74). Data might be made available to private companies such as supermarket retailers and banks. This might occur in emergency situations, but the Minister overseeing the project also noted that it might be used to restrict welfare payments to the purchase of certain commodities (Riley 2006b). A personal area of card's chip does suggest commercial potential. Expansion of this beyond emergency situations is foreseeable. The Government, for example, suggested people could use this information for personal use, for example to store their weekly shopping lists (Crawford 2006).

Graham and Wood (2003: 229) note of digital surveillance systems that, despite the image of technological neutrality they project, such systems are 'likely to be strongly biased by the political, economic and social conditions that shape the principles embedded in their design and implementation'. Thus, despite the language of efficiency and security, data mining and risk profiling enabled by the accelerated capacity of a centralized database is likely to entrench and deepen existing categories of exclusion. This is particularly concerning given the substantial portions of government revenue already being spent to 'strengthen information sharing and expand data matching activities between agencies'. The child care sector is being singled out for the application of risk profiling techniques, while pilot studies are being conducted to test the potential use of data mining (Australian Government 2006).

Data mining and risk profiling techniques are situated within a broader context in which the quest for security underpins a constant quest for more comprehensive 'risk knowledge'. While Ericson and Haggerty (1997) noted the need for risk knowledge in relation to police surveillance this might be extended more broadly (Lyon 2006: 73). The expanding informational capacity of Australian government databases therefore facilitates the assemblage of risk profiles through the collection of aggregate data about targeted populations. Large scale databases, such as the Access Card 'register', expand the potential categories and codes of risk (O'Malley 2006). Increasingly, such aggregate techniques of categorization bear little rela-tionship to any 'objective' measure of individual risk. This move towards pre-emptive surveillance (Marx 1988; Feeley and Simon 1994), based upon categorical rather than individualized suspicion, is exacerbated by the expanding computing and searching capacity of the Access Card database.

That such pre-emptive surveillance might be conducted through the Access Card database seems highly likely given the 'state of exception' (Agamben 2005) that has guided counter-terrorist initiatives post-9/11. That the Access Card was to form part of the armoury for security and law enforcement agencies has been a persistent though less dominant narrative in the public discourse surrounding the Access Card. Thus, Prime Minister John Howard stated that it was within the context of national security that the identity issue was to be revisited, commenting that 'twenty years ago when the Australia Card was knocked over, we didn't know of Osama bin Laden, we hadn't had 11th September and we didn't live in such a glob-alised world economy' (Howard 2006b).

The notion that the Access Card might combat terrorism provides a rationale for engaging the database for risk profiling and pre-emptive surveillance techniques for which there is already some precedent. The presumption of 'guilt by suspicion' in Australian measures to suppress the financing of terrorism for example indicates just such pre-emptive surveillance (McCulloch and Carlton 2006). Law enforce-ment agencies, most specifically the Australian Federal Police (AFP) and the Australian Security Intelligence Organization (ASIO), already have access to the Department of Human Services (DHS) database and those of other Commonwealth agencies (SCFPA 2007: 41). Moreover, data from the Access Card register is to be made available to police and intelligence agencies in relation to general crime and terrorism (Riley and Kearney 2006). That a national biometric database will signif-icantly amplify the capacity and reach of law enforcement was intimated in recent Senate hearings into the Access Card legislation, although ASIO seems reluctant to confirm this (SCFPA 2007: 12).

The potential that data might be utilised for ethnic profiling has been an under-standable concern in the post-9/11 context. In Australia, as in other jurisdictions, the Muslim community has suffered considerable discrimination, vilification and negative stereotyping in the wake of 9/11 (Poynting and Noble 2004; Poynting and

Mason 2006). The Chair of Federation of Ethnic Communities Councils of Australia testified before a Senate Hearing that 'the Australian Muslim community has been feeling the pressure of undue emphasis on their particular communities. We feel that, if there are no safeguards around the use of information on this card, those communities will end being, unjustly, further profiled' (SCFPA 2007: 47). Other submissions to the Government have questioned why information on ethnicity, place of birth and residency status are to be included as part of the data stored on the card (AMA 2006). The acting Victorian Privacy Commissioner Helen Versey also noted that 'if you are collecting racial origin information, then you have to ask why it is being collected. In general, the anti-discrimination principle is that you shouldn't collect this kind of information if you want to employ someone, because there is the potential for it to be misused to discriminate against them' (Stafford 2007).

As Stalder and Lyon (2003: 89) note, 'however well-intentioned the installation of advanced ID cards, the resulting classifications will produce categories of suspicion that will capture innocent persons in their net. It is not only those who have done wrong who have something to fear'. The totalitarian potential of ID card systems is evident where they have been engaged by authoritarian regimes with chilling impacts, as in the cases of Rwanda (Longman 2001) and South Africa (Breckenridge 2005). This awareness is acute in some ethnic communities. As the Chair of the Federation of Ethnic Communities of Australia noted, 'we need to be aware that people have fled repressive regimes, they have been victims, their families and they themselves have been affected by those repressive regimes and they would be very fearful about what could happen to that information' (SCFPA 2007: 48–49). Discrimination may also result from those unable to register for the Access Card due to the documentation requirements. This would particularly impact upon refugees without travel documents (SCFPA 2007: 51) and upon Indigenous Australians, especially those in remote communities and those unable to provide a 'legal name' (Aboriginal and Torres Strait Islander Social Justice Commissioner 2007).

Devils, symbols and resistance

The proposed Access Card database emerges within a particular context of risk calculation and security governance. Through data mining and risk profiling the database has the potential to significantly strengthen and deepen the capacity of the Australian State to validate and establish 'legitimate identities'. Writing shortly after 9/11, David Lyon noted that 'for all its apparent weakness in a globalizing world, the nation-state is capable of quickly tightening its grip on internal control' (Lyon 2003: 37–38). The Access Card project is one means through which such control is tightened. The project powerfully projects the symbol of an omnipotent sovereign state that can rapidly establish the identities of insiders and outsiders, legitimate and illegitimate claimants and criminal and non-criminal. This power is both symbolic and material, as categories and codes potentially deepen and extend extant categories of exclusion and inclusion.

Unsurprisingly perhaps, the 'Access Card' has been accompanied by the recitation of the banal formulation that those with nothing to hide have nothing to fear. While it may be true that the project may entail real bureaucratic efficiencies, we also need to recognize the significant symbolic resonance of the project. The Access Card encapsulates powerful imagery of reinvigorated state power. It betokens a state with immense informational capacity to deliver efficient medical and social services to those categorized as citizens, while simultaneously effectively excluding threats from both beyond and within the nation-state. The Access Card then, as with other technologies of identification such as biometric passports (Wilson 2006), has important symbolic functions.

One way in which such symbolic politics is enacted is through the mobilization of a series of 'folk devils' to use Cohen's (2002) famous formulation. The particular 'folk devil' identified via the Access Card is the 'welfare cheat', a figure familiar to the Australian public through existent criminalized stereotypes frequently portrayed in the media (Putnis 2001). Importantly the Access Card simultaneously inscribes the notion of an administratively strong and competent state secure against fraud. Moreover, the Access Card rhetorically weaves together a series of internal and external threats into a 'security continuum'. Internal economic threats of welfare cheats and criminals are fused with external threats of illegal immigrants and terrorists (Wilson 2006). The Access Card project consequently dovetails with identity management projects aimed at border control. 'Legitimate identities' are therefore regulated, symbolically at least, internally and externally.

The trend towards the 'securitization of identity' represented by the Access Card positions Australia within a broader trend, as evidenced by the range of ID card schemes discussed in this collection. A crucial question therefore remains. Does Australian political culture, with its unique history of the defeated Australia Card proposal, shape the ID card debate and project trajectory in peculiar ways? My tentative answer to this question is yes. It remains tentative as the Access Card project is currently stalled and the details of the project remain vague. Therefore comparisons with the protests that attended the Australia Card project in the 1980s may be invalid, as significant public support only mobilized at a late stage of that project when all details were publicly revealed.[2] Australians may yet demonstrate considerable resistance to the Access Card project.

And there is evidence of opposition to the Access Card project, both through opposition political parties and NGOs. The Australian Labour Party (ALP), the main opposition party, has claimed that it 'won't proceed with the card in its current form' (Dearne 2007). Similarly, both Australia's minor political parties, the Democrats and the Greens, have come out against the proposal with Democrat Senator Natasha Stott Despoja launching an internet campaign against the card (Peatling 2007). In the state of Victoria, a member of the Victorian Liberal Party (in Australia conservatives) launched an Access Card No Way campaign with an accompanying website (www.accesscardnoway.net). More recently The PIAC (Public Interest Advocacy Centre) and the Australian Privacy Foundation are also pursuing campaigns against the Access Card. State-based civil liberties organizations such as Liberty Victoria and the New South Wales Council of Civil Liberties have also contributed to public debate.

Despite emergent resistance, some commentators have suggested that public reaction to the proposal remains muted and disinterested. In early 2006, one journalist opined the Access Card proposal had 'generated only modest reaction from interest groups and little apparent concern among voters'. It was, he claimed, 'as good an indicator as you will find in Australia of how far the political winds have changed since September 11, 2001' (Riley 2006a). Such comments, however, underplay the resistance to the Access Card and overplay the influence of 9/11. For example, polling suggests public support for an ID card reached a peak of 70 per cent just after 9/11. Recent polls however suggest 65 per cent of respondents are opposed to the idea (Johnston 2007). And as Lyon and Bennett note in their introduction to this volume, the diffusion of identity card schemes cannot be explained through exclusive reference to 9/11.

Lack of overt resistance (which should not be equated with approval) may also be attributable to the changing character of public debate. In the Australian case, while 9/11 may have provided a trigger, it is possible that transformations in local political culture can account for the perceived acquiescence to the ID card concept among portions of the Australian public. Critics of the conservative Howard Government have observed a marked truncation of public debate in recent years (Marr 2007; Hamilton and Maddison 2007). Writer David Marr has described Howard as 'the most unscrupulous corrupter of public debate in Australia since the Cold War's worst days back in the 1950s' (Marr 2007: 4). The as yet limited public discussion on the Access Card may also reflect a decline in public participation in democratic processes more broadly (Maddison 2007). Recent research has demonstrated that Australians have become increasingly disengaged from politics and are 'turning inward' away from public issues (Walter and Strangio 2007). This is occurring (and partially resulting from) a government that has accumulated unprecedented executive power and exhibited a strong urge to silence dissent (Hamilton and Maddison 2007).

Conclusion

The trajectory of the Access Card proposal within Australian political culture is a complex one. The ghost of the Australia Card proposal still exerts its influence in subtle, yet significant ways. The positive nomenclature 'Access Card', the elaborate strategy of avoiding calling the proposal an ID card and the significant expenditure on public relations all indicate the legacy of political sensitivity that still resonates around mass identification schemes in Australia. This is again signaled by the fact that, with a Federal election looming, the Access Card legislation has been shelved. As of writing, the first of three pieces of legislation to facilitate the Access Card had stalled, having been sent back by an all-party Senate Committee for revision. This suggests that this is not a project the government wants on the election agenda. It also indicates that the final implementation of the Access Card is not yet inevitable.

The Access Card project reflects global trends towards national identity schemes. However, these are intertwined with domestic political forces that have shaped the project in particular ways. The reassertion of a national identity card scheme has been actively pursued by a government that has placed 'national security' at the centre of its policy agenda (Weiss *et al.* 2007). Moreover, it is one manifestation of a broader trend towards centralism in Australian politics (Van Onselen and Errington 2005). Nevertheless, an identity card scheme is still a potentially volatile political issue in Australia. Its eventual implementation is far from a foregone conclusion, and the full implications of the political legacy of the Australia Card in shaping resistance to a national identity scheme and shaping policy remain to be seen.

Notes

1 This chapter was completed before the Access Card was shelved in December 2007. I would like to thank Colin Bennett, David Lyon and Roger Clarke for their comments on this chapter. I would also like to thank the Surveillance Project, Queen's University, Kingston, for generously facilitating my participation in the National ID Card Workshop.
2 I am grateful to Roger Clarke for alerting me to this point.

Bibliography

Abbot, T. (2004) *Medicare smartcard launched.* Press release ABB123/04, 28 July. Online. Available: www.health.gov.au/internet/ministers/publishing.nsf/Content (accessed 6 October 2006).

ABC (Australian Broadcasting Corporation) (2004) 'The World Today – Dodson labels Indigenous welfare reforms discriminatory', 11 November. Online. Available: http://www.abc.net.au/worldtoday/content/2004/s1241280.htm (accessed 6 October 2006).

ABC (Australian Broadcasting Corporation) Insiders Transcript (2005) 'Beattie puts forward case for Australia Card', 17 July. Online. Available: http://www/abc.net.au/insiders/content/2005/s1415860.html (accessed 20 December 2006).

ABC (Australian Broadcasting Corporation) Stateline Queensland (Broadcast 30 July 2004) 'Big Brother Transcript'. Online. Available: http://www.abc.net.au/stateline/qld/content/2004/s1165710.htm (accessed 10 March 2007).

Aboriginal and Torres Strait Islander Social Justice Commissioner (2007) 'Submission on behalf of the Human Rights and Equal Opportunity Commission to the Senate Finance and Public Administration Committee on the Inquiry into Human Services (Enhanced Service Delivery) Bill 2007', 1 March. Sydney: Human Rights and Equal Opportunity Commission.

Agamben, G. (2005) *State of Exception*, Chicago: University of Chicago Press.

Agar, J. (2001) 'Modern horrors: British identity and identity cards', in J. Caplan and J. Torpey (eds) *Documenting Individual Identity: The Development of State Practices in the Modern World*, Princeton: Princeton University Press.

Australian Government (1985) *Reform of the Australian Taxation System*, Canberra: Australian Government Printing Service.

Australian Government (2006) 'Budget 2006–07: Budget Paper No: 2, Part 2: Expense measures'. Online. Available: http://www.budget.gov.au/2006–07/bp2_expense-12.htm (accessed 15 March 2007).

Australian Medical Association (AMA) (2006) 'Response to Discussion Paper No. 1 Access Card Consumer and Privacy Taskforce Health and Social Services Access Card', July.

Australian Privacy Foundation (APF) (2007) 'Submission on the Access Card Proposal, and Associated Legislation', 28 February. Online. Available: http://www.privacy.org.au (accessed 10 June 2007).

Bajkowski, J. (2005) 'Biometrics to work for the dole?', *Computerworld* 21 March. Online. Available: http://www.cio.com.au/index.php?id=1164473060&eid=-601 (accessed 30 November 2007).

Beattie, P. (2005) 'Smart Licence on the Cards. Ministerial Media Statement', 29 December. Online. Available: http://statements.cabinet.qld.gov.au/MMS (accessed 10 March 2007).

Breckenridge, K. (2005) 'Verwoerd's Bureau of proof: total information in the making of apartheid', *History Workshop Journal* 59(1): 83–108.

Burrell, S. (2006) 'Identity crisis', *Sydney Morning Herald* 29 April.

Canberra Times (2007) 'Fears card will access all areas', *Canberra Times* 13 March, p. 11.

Clarke, R. (1987) 'Just Another Piece of Plastic for your Wallet: The Australia Card Scheme'. Online. Available: http://www.anu.edu.au/people/Roger.Clarke/DV/OzCard. html (accessed 25 July 2007).

Cohen, S. (2002) *Folk Devils and Moral Panics*, 3rd ed. London: Routledge.

Cole, S. and Pontell, H. (2006) 'Don't be low hanging fruit identity theft as moral panic', in T. Monahan (ed.) *Surveillance and Society: Technological Politics and Power in Everyday Life*, New York: Routledge, pp. 125–47.

Council of Australian Governments (COAG) (2005) 'Council of Australian Governments', Special meeting on counter-terrorism, 27 September. *Communiqué* Online. Available: http://www.coag.gov.au/meetings/270905/index.htm (accessed 12 April 2007).

Crawford, M. (2006) 'Users to own one-third of storage capacity', *Computerworld* 11 September, 24.

Cunneen, C. (2001) *Conflict, Politics and Crime: Aboriginal Communities and the Police*, Sydney: Allen and Unwin.

Davidson, A. (1991) *The Invisible State: The Formation of the Australian State 1788–1901*, Cambridge: Cambridge University Press.

Davies, S. (1992) *Big Brother: Australia's growing web of surveillance*, Sydney: Simon & Schuster.

Davis, M. (2001) 'The flames of New York', *New Left Review* 12: 34–50.

Dearne, K. (2005) 'Access card rebellion', *Australian IT*, 24 August. Online. Available: http://www.australianit.news.com.au/story/0,24897,20049175-15306,00.html (accessed 14 April 2006).

Dearne, K. (2006) 'Libs, Business rebel on Access Card', *Australian* 31August, 8.

Dearne, K. (2007) 'Labour would scrap Access Card scheme if it wins the election', *Australian* 27 March, 6.

Department of Immigration and Multicultural and Indigenous Affairs (DIMIA) (2004) *Biometric Initiatives*, Fact Sheet 84, 30 September. Online. Available: http://www.immi.gov.au (accessed 3 June 2005).

Ericson, R. and Haggerty, K. (1997) *Policing the Risk Society*, Toronto: University of Toronto Press.

Feeley, M. and Simon, J. (1994) 'Actuarial justice: the emerging new criminal law', in D. Nelken (ed.) *The Futures of Criminology*, London: Sage, pp. 173–201.

Finnane, M. (1994) *Police and Government: Histories of Policing in Australia*, Melbourne: Oxford University Press.

Graham, S. and Wood, D. (2003) 'Digitizing surveillance: categorization, space, inequality', *Critical Social Policy* 23(2): 227–48.

Grattan, M (2006) 'Smartcard chief resigns', *The Age* 9 May. Online. Available: http://www.theage.com.au/news/national/smartcard-chief-resigns/2006/05/08/1146940479804.html (accessed 14 December 2006).

Greenleaf, G. (1986) 'The deceptive history of the Australia Card', *Australian Quarterly* 58(4): 407–25.

Greenleaf, G. (2006) 'Australian ID Taskforce Report: A sheep in wolf's clothing', submission to the Consumer and Privacy Taskforce, 11 November. Online. Available: http://www.bakercyberlawcentre.org/privacy/id_card/ID_Taskforce.pdf (accessed 20 December).

Hamilton, C. and Maddison, S. (2007) *Silencing Dissent: How the Australian government is controlling public opinion and stifling debate*, Sydney: Allen & Unwin.

Heagney, K. (2001) 'CrimTrac to keep DNA at fingertips', *Canberra Times* 21 June, 5.

Hopkins, H. (2007) 'Experience justifies suspicion of Access Card', *Australian* 10 March, p. 28.

Howard, J. (2006a) *Government to proceed with Access Card,* Prime Minister of Australia Media Release, 26 April. Online. Available: http://www.pm.gov.au/news/media_releases/media_Release1905.html (accessed 15 October 2006).

Howard, J. (2006b) *Transcript of the Prime Minister the Hon John Howard PM Joint Press Conference with, the Attorney-General, the Hon Philip Ruddock MP, and the Minister for Human Services, the Hon Joe Hockey MP,* Prime Minister of Australia Media Release, 26 April. Online. Available: http://www.pm.gov.au/news/media_releases/media_Release1906.html (accessed 15 October 2006).

Johnston, A. (2006) 'Why "Australia Card Mark II" is still a dumb idea', 27 January *Australian Policy Online.* Online. Available: http://www.apo.org.au (accessed 25 July 2007).

Johnston, A. (2007) *The Access Card – Fallacies and Facts*, Presentation at PIAC Public Forum, 9 November, Sydney. Online. Available: http://www.privacy.org.au/Papers/PublicForum-Cbra-070312.pdf (accessed 4 June 2007).

Jordan, R. (2006) 'Identity Cards', *E-Brief,* February. Canberra: Parliament of Australia, Parliamentary Library. Online. Available: http://www.aph.gov.au/library/intguide/LAW/IdentityCards.htm (accessed 22 October 2006).

Kissane, K. (2007) 'Access for whom?', *The Age* 9 February, 15.

Longman, T. (2001) 'Identity cards, ethnic self-perception, and genocide in Rwanda', in J. Caplan and J. Torpey (eds) *Documenting Individual Identity: The Development of State Practices in the Modern World*, Princeton: Princeton University Press, pp. 345–57.

Lozusic, R. (2003) 'Fraud and identity theft', Briefing Paper 8/2003, Sydney: Parliament of New South Wales.

Lyon, D. (2003) *Surveillance after September 11*, London: Polity.

Lyon, D. (2006) 'The border is everywhere: ID cards, surveillance and the other', in E. Zuriek and M. Salter (eds) *Global Surveillance and Policing: Borders, Security, Identity,* Cullompton: Willan, pp. 66–82.

Maddison, S. (2007) 'Redefining democracy', in C. Hamilton and S. Maddison (eds) *Silencing Dissent: How the Australian government is controlling public opinion and stifling debate*, Sydney: Allen & Unwin.

Marr, D. (2007) 'His Master's Voice: the corruption of public debate under Howard', *Quarterly Essay* 26, Melbourne: Black Inc.

Marx, G. (1988) *Undercover: Police Surveillance in America*, Berkeley: University of California Press.

McCulloch, J. (2004a) 'National (in) security politics in Australia: Fear and the federal election', *Alternative Law Journal* 29(2): 87–91.

McCulloch, J. (2004b) 'Blue armies, khaki police and the Cavalry on the New American Frontier', *Critical Criminology* 12(3): 309–26.

McCulloch, J. and B. Carlton (2006) 'Preempting justice: suppression of financing of terrorism and the "War on Terror"', *Current Issues in Criminal Justice* 17(3): 397–412.

Nicholson, B. (2006) 'State computers vulnerable to sabotage and data theft', *Age* 14 June, 9.

Office of Access Card (2007) 'Myth busters'. Online. Available: www.accesscard.gov.au/mythbusters.html (accessed 13 April 2007).

O'Malley, P. (2006) 'Risk, ethics and airport security', *Canadian Journal of Criminology and Criminal Justice* 48(3): 413–21.

Peatling, S. (2007) 'Campaign against data card', *Sydney Morning Herald* 10 March, 4.

Pendleton, M. (2006) 'Budget 2006: be afraid. Be very afraid. Vibewire.net', 9 May. Online. Available: http://www.vibewire.net/3/node/4800 (accessed 24 January 2007).

Pickering, S. (2005). *Refugees and State Crime*, Sydney: Federation Press.

Poynting, S. and Mason, V. (2006) 'Tolerance, freedom, justice and peace?: Britain, Australia and anti-Muslim racism since 11 September 2001', *Journal of Intercultural Studies* 27(4): 365–91.

Poynting, S. and Noble, G. (2004) *Living with Racism: The experience and reporting by Arab and Muslim Australians of discrimination, abuse and violence since 11 September 2001.* Report to the Human Rights and Equal Opportunity Commission, Sydney: Centre for Culture Research University of Western Sydney.

Putnis, P. (2001) 'Popular discourses and images of poverty and welfare in the news media', in R. Fincher and P. Saunders (eds) *Creating Unequal Futures? Rethinking Poverty, Inequality and Disadvantage*, Sydney: Allen and Unwin.

Riley, J. (2004) 'National ID cards urged in terror war', *Australian* 15 October, 4.

Riley, J. (2005) 'Privacy concerns on photo ID card Bill', *Australian* 29 March, 27.

Riley, J. (2006) 'Smartcard heading for fall', *Australian IT* 2 May. Online. Available: http://www.australianit.news.com.au (accessed 5 September 2006).

Riley, J. (2006) 'Commercial access on the cards', *Australian IT* 12 May. Online. Available: http://www.australianit.news.com.au (accessed 8 October 2006).

Riley, J. and Kearney, S. (2006) 'Police to get Access Card data', *Australian IT* 28 April. Online. Available: http://www.australianit.news.com.au (accessed 8 October 2006).

Ruddock, P. (2006) 'A safe and secure Australia: an update on counter-terrorism'. Transcript of speech given at Manly Pacific Hotel, Sydney, 21 January. Online. Available: http://parlinfoweb.aph.gov.au/piweb/Repository1/Media/pressrel/XVJ160.pdf (accessed 12 August 2006).

Senate (Commonwealth of Australia) Standing Committee on Finance and Public Administration (SCFPA) (2007) *Human Services (Enhanced Services Delivery) Bill 2007 [Provisions]*, Canberra: Commonwealth of Australia.

Senate (Commonwealth of Australia) Standing Committee on Finance and Public Administration (SCFPA) (2007) *Reference: Human Services (Enhanced Services Delivery) Bill 2007 [Provisions]*, Hearings, Melbourne, Monday 5 March, Canberra: Commonwealth of Australia.

Shanahan, D. and Karvelas, P. (2006) 'Welfare spies sacked', *Australian IT,* 23 August.

Online. Available: http://www.australianit.news.com.au/story/0,24897,20224186-15306,00.html (accessed 23 October 2006).

Stafford, A. (2007) 'Race quiz concern on smartcard', *The Age* 25 January, 14.

Stalder, F. and Lyon, D. (2003) 'Electronic Identity Cards and Social Classification', in D. Lyon (ed.) *Surveillance as Social Sorting: Privacy, risk, and digital discrimination*, London: Routledge.

Summers, J. (2006) 'The federal system', in A. Parkin, J. Summers and D. Woodward (eds) *Government, Politics, Power and Policy in Australia,* 8th ed. Sydney: Pearson.

Valverde, M. (2001) 'Governing security, governing through security', in R. Daniels, P. Macklen and K. Roach (eds) *The Security of Freedom: Essays on Canada's Anti-Terrorism Bill*, Toronto: University of Toronto Press, pp. 83–92.

Van Onselen, P. and Errington, W. (2005) 'Howard's demolition job on federalism', *On Line Opinion: Australia's e-journal of social and political debate,* 7 June. Online. Available: http://www.onlineopinion.com.au (accessed 15 August 2007).

Walter, J. and Strangio, P. (2007) *No, Prime Minister: Reclaiming Politics from Leaders*, Sydney: UNSW Press.

Weiss, L., Thurbon, E. and Mathews, J. (2007) *National Insecurity: The Howard Government's Betrayal of Australia*, Sydney: Allen and Unwin.

Wilson, D. (2006) 'Biometrics, borders and the ideal suspect', in S. Pickering and L. Weber (eds) *Borders, Mobility and Technologies of Control*, Dordrecht: Springer, pp. 87–109.

Wilson, D. (2007) 'Australian biometrics and global surveillance', *International Criminal Justice Review* 14(3): 207–19.

Wilson, D. and Weber, L. (2008) 'Surveillance, risk and pre-emption on the Australian border', *Surveillance and Society* 5(2): 124–41.

Woodhead, B. (2006) 'Canberra Planning Smartcard Manual', *Australian IT* 15 August, 30.

12 The INES biometric card and the politics of national identity assignment in France

Pierre Piazza and Laurent Laniel

Thanks to historical and sociological research, the material aspects of the 'manufacturing' of individual identities by the French national authorities are well-known at present.[1] Indeed, building on Michel Foucault's initial reflection that the state aspires to prescribe behaviours conforming with the order that it is endeavouring to impose through governmental techniques which strengthen its grip on individual behaviours (Foucault 1975, 2004), research has shown that the rise of carding[2] techniques has done much to improve our understanding of the various logics at play – control,[3] distinction,[4] codification (Bourdieu 1993) and stigmatization[5] – in the construction and consolidation of the modern state in connection with the emergence of the individual in Western society (Elias 1991). Such logics are manifested by the constant improvement of several types of bureaucratic knowledge and know-how in carding matters. They inform us of the changing nature of the concerns (law enforcement, social policy,[6] health policy,[7] etc.), strategies (ranging from official orders to softer, more symbolic forms of power imposition) and justification discourses through which state authorities have increased their prerogatives significantly by becoming involved ever more extensively in the definition and material shaping of people's identity. At present, these state logics undeniably are undergoing a major shift due to the introduction of biometrics in identity documents. Indeed, the generalized move toward biometrization of ID 'papers' results in the emergence of new issues, including the hardening of the control systems applied to international travelers (Rosecrance *et al.* 2002: 56 *et passim*), the definition of radically new criteria of dangerousness (Bigo 2004),[8] the transformation of the relations of the state with private security operators (Ocqueteau 2004), and the protection, at a global level, of the information stored in ever more extensive computer databases (Ceyhan 2007: 46).

By contrast, although part and parcel of the power politics that lie at the core of identity assignment processes, resistance to such state undertakings remain mostly obscure. There are two main reasons for this lack of knowledge. First, archive-based research does not always allow adequate analysis of the perceptions, practices and circumventing strategies of the people on whom identification techniques were applied.[9] Second, many of the issues surrounding recent biometric identification methods have yet to be studied in detail.[10] Yet it is indispensable to examine resistance closely since each carding process should be viewed as a special type of power struggle between actors that have the power to materially define, codify and fix an official identity and others who, being the targets of such identity assignment, are led to dispute its validity periodically. The forms that these protests take are all-important since they strongly influence the shape of carding systems, the specific 'carding path' followed by each state and the type of power politics that emerge between state authorities and the individuals targeted by identification enterprises (Poirmeur 2006). Resistances may have different motives and be rooted in politics, law, ethics or culture. And they may be expressed in a large variety of ways, from individual circumvention or diversion strategies aimed at avoiding state imposi-tions to collective protest movements using sophisticated types of rhetoric and action. However, it is always crucial to understand their historical genesis since the configuration of past power politics strongly impacts present-day power struggles.

This chapter is an effort to start filling the gaps in research by examining one of the main systems that the French government is presently striving to implement in order to better identify citizens – the biometric identity card project, INES (Secured Electronic National Identity). While this requires reviewing the eventful history of carding in France in order to elicit the project's novel features, due attention must also be paid to the forms of resistance that it has triggered, so as to better grasp how they have contributed to shaping the project's own history. All in all, the INES pro-ject is a fine illustration of the fact that carding, far from being a powerful instrument that a 'Big Brother' state, bent on opaque and ferocious designs, forces upon an obey-ing, helpless and amorphous mass of citizens, is better analyzed as the complex out-come of a struggle between political power and the social body that it wishes to rule.

Carding the French: An eventful history

In a little more than a century, France went from a situation where no specific piece of paper had the 'monopoly of self-denomination' (Offerlé 1993: 49) to the institu-tion of the first 'Identity Card of the French' (*carte d'identité de Français*) in one department only in 1921, then to the establishment by the Vichy regime of another 'Identity Card of the French' in 1940, which failed to be distributed everywhere in France, and finally to the 'National Identity Card' (*carte nationale d'identité*) in 1955, which would be computerized gradually starting in 1987. This expansion of carding has been underpinned by a double logic – materializing a belonging com-mon to citizens recognized as equals; and discriminating against some French peo-ple viewed as suspects or enemies of the nation.

The first card

Starting in 1870, the development of bertillonnage and dactyloscopy (Kaluszynski 1987; Piazza 2000, 2005b; About 2004) made it possible for the authorities to think methodically about the role of description, photographs and fingerprints as well as the connection that must exist between these identifiers and the information kept and classified in state records. At first, these techniques were used to identify with more certainty some categories of the population viewed as dangerous or marginal – recidivist offenders, nomads (Asséo 2002; Piazza 2002), and foreigners (Noiriel

1991). However, the entire French population would soon be subjected to carding. By a circular of 12 September, 1921, Police Prefect, Robert Leullier, instituted the first 'Identity Card of the French', which citizens residing in Paris and the Seine Department could request. This card became the sole and uniform ID paper issued to French citizens by the Paris police prefecture and a reference document to which all other ID papers for citizens had to conform.

Leullier thought that the reform was a step forward, since it remedied the diversity of existing identification practices for nationals, who until then could use a wide range of documents issued by myriad authorities, none of which was more important than the others, as proof of their identity.[11] Leullier added that the card was established 'in the public's own interest' (Valbelle 1921), since it would make it unnecessary to have two witnesses to prove one's identity – as was required for administrative procedures at that time. But if this formality was to be done away with, the card had to offer strong guarantees as to its authenticity. Hence, the Paris police resorted to the Bertillon system. On each card, the individual's description had to be drafted with utmost precision and the dimensions of the photograph were carefully set in order to facilitate the owner's identification. In addition, the card bore the fingerprint of its owner. The prefecture would file all the forms filled by those requesting the card, thereby setting up a 'centralized record [that] will make it possible to check whether card number X was indeed issued to individual Y, with a view to avoiding substitutions' (Leullier 1921).

Some of the press supported the card, depicting it as indispensable to put an end to the problems created by the need for witnesses (*La République française* 1921; *La Presse* 1921a). Some journalists even wanted to out-Herod Herod. For instance, newspaper *La Presse* (1921b) explained that the fingerprint could be useful to identify possible criminals, but Leullier denied that this was his intention.

Yet the card also attracted suspicion. Discontent focused on fingerprinting, which assimilated citizens with criminals. Both the right and the left adamantly rejected the notion that citizens could be identified thanks to techniques used by the Criminal Record Office against offenders. The communist daily *L'Humanité* (1921) equated the new card to 'some sort of criminal record', while the conservative *L'Intransigeant* (1921) compared it with a Bertillon card that would soon become compulsory for all.

While the problem was all but ignored when the interior ministry (henceforth: the Interior) had imposed an identity card on foreign residents of France in 1917, public opinion discovered in 1921 that Leullier's ID card threatened individual freedom. Leullier would eventually bow to the protest by making 'his' card noncompulsory. The first Identity Card of the French, which was invented to rationalize administrative identification procedures, thereby failed to fulfil its objective since other documents could still prove citizens' identity.

Vichy

In the context of the suspension of democracy and enhanced technocratization of power, the Vichy regime (1940–1944) launched its own ID project, which entailed, for the first time ever, a close partnership between the Interior and state statistics services.

The law establishing an 'Identity Card of the French' compulsory for all citizens aged 16 and above was published on 27 October, 1940 (*J.O.* 1940: 5740–5741). Issuance of the card started in 12 departments in 1943. Vichy thereby hoped to preserve the illusion of national unity (while France was occupied and its territory divided up into several zones)[12] and presented the card as proof of its determination to modernize a state it said had been perverted by the previous regime (*Le Cri du peuple* 1940). In fact, although the Vichy carding drive was indeed 'novel', it cashed in on the knowledge and know-how accumulated during the Third Republic.

With a view to forestalling problems arising from the wide range of documents by which the French could still prove who they were, the model of the Vichy compulsory card was unique, its dimensions, the type of paper used and the location of the rubrics it contained were precisely defined by a multitude of Interior-issued documents – decrees, circulars, orders. For practical reasons, the mayors were summoned to help deliver the card to citizens by drafting requests and recording them, but under the supervision of prefectures, which were the only institutions allowed to manufacture the card. Likewise, by subjecting the different steps of the distribution process to prefectorial control, Vichy endeavoured to standardize state identification practices and to ensure that they were carried out in accordance with the uniform rules designed by the central authority.

To make the card more secure, the police resorted once more to Bertillon's inventions and to fingerprinting. The Interior wanted to set up a central record with a copy of each card actually issued, but eventually this turned out to be impossible. In addition, the ministry called on statistics services which invented, from the data of the registers of births, marriages and deaths, a 13-digit identification number that made it possible to accurately characterize individuals during their entire lifetime.[13] That number was embossed on each card, written down on each request form filed by the prefectures and recorded in a central repertory established by the statistics services. The Interior thought that this was an efficient means to identify each requester unequivocally, carry out identity checks rapidly, detect attempts by one individual to obtain several cards, and identify counterfeit cards.

The symbol of a new regime embodied in a strong state committed to the emergence of a new order, the Vichy card also served for the more down-to-earth task of 'cleansing' the national community, which Vichy planned to 'regenerate' by excluding the 'metics' (*métèques*) that had 'debased' it. The procedures for issuing the cards (starting in 1943) proved crucial for the segregation policy launched by Vichy as early as 1940. For instance, the meticulous checks implemented by the prefectures allowed the Interior to ascertain how each requester had acquired their French nationality, and then to write this information down on the card. The stamping of the word 'Jew' on identity cards served to materialize a type of sub-citizenship. This measure, which was demanded by the German authorities and the Vichy institutions specializing in hunting Jews, was taken special care of by the Interior. Furthermore, in 1942, the ministry started distribution of customs-made punching machines intended to impede any tampering with the 'Jew' mention on the cards (Piazza 2004: 224–226). In an effort to 'steer the evolution of the race by reasoned legislative action on the individuals conforming it' (CAEF n.d.), the statistics services even imagined a system to distinguish between 'good' and 'bad' French people by means of an Individual Descriptive Book (*carnet signalétique individuel*) that would have made it possible to record myriad personal data (education, physical abilities, professional skills, morality, etc.) about its holders.

However, several obstacles would come in the way of the rationalized carding of all French people by the Vichy police. The sheer scope of the identification work to be carried out, and the division of the country into several zones complicating the transmission of official documents, made it difficult to distribute the card throughout France. Then there were material problems such as the lack of paper and chemicals needed to manufacture the card and the photographs. The carding project also attracted the hostility of many citizens. According to Interior reports mentioning 'psychological resistance', the card caused concern because of the amount of data it contained, and because it was perceived as yet another obligation forced upon the people and as 'a type of pre-mobilization' orchestrated by the Germans. Finally, the acts of resistance of some civil servants and, especially after the institution of the Compulsory Work Service (STO) in 1943, the gradual professionalization and expansion of the counterfeiting of papers by Resistance movements would also frustrate governmental carding ambitions (Noguères 1984; Wieviorka 1995).

After the Second World War

At Liberation, any type of distinction between citizens was banned. As a result, the cards bearing the word 'Jew' were withdrawn and the rubric on the method of acquisition of French nationality was deleted. On 22 October 1955, a decree by the interior ministry instituted a 'National Identity Card' and explained that this was done 'in a perfectly liberal spirit' (*Le Parisien* 1955).

This new card was based on a single model for the whole of France and issued by the prefectures only. It was optional and entailed the creation of not *one* central record but *several* departmental records. In addition, the Interior removed from the card any element that might have lent it a repressive nature. The mention 'distinguishing marks' and a front-on photograph replaced the detailed description and the photograph of the right profile that reminded of criminal identification procedures on the Vichy card. The 1955 decree required a print of the left index finger on both the card and the request form, but the Interior eventually waived this requirement in 1974, arguing that it was 'undeniably a constraint for the public' (Intérieur 1974). While the Interior officially distanced itself from Vichy with the National Identity Card, one of its unofficial objectives was the control of the French Moslems of Algeria. A 'confidential' circular by the Interior on 7 December 1955 instituted a specific form of prefectorial control on these citizens on grounds that possible suspects among them could try to take on false identities.[14]

It was not until the 1970s and an increase in the fear of crime that significant change emerged – the computerization of the National Identity Card, which gave rise to a major national debate and even became, for the first time, a bone of contention between the main political parties. The proposed reform allowed conservatives to show their determination to fight some threats: crime, illegal immigration and terrorism. By opposing the reform, the left could claim to be defending individual freedom against generalized police surveillance. As a result, the computerized card was the subject of diametrically opposed policies for years. The first model was made official on 31 July 1980 by a decree of the interior minister of a conservative government (*J.O.* 1980: 1953). In October 1981 – that is, just four months after the election as president of France of François Mitterand, a socialist – an order by the new interior minister stopped distribution of the card (*J.O.* 1981: 9065). After the conservative victory at the legislative election of March 1986, a new 'Secured National Identity Card' was issued by the Chirac government in the Hauts-de-Seine Department only as of April 1988. However, following the re-election of Mitterand in May 1988, generalization of the card would be 'frozen', and then would start again in the aftermath of the conservatives' landslide at the March 1993 legislative elections.

This new card, which is still in use in 2007 but remains optional, has several specific features. Physical production is restricted to two centers only in order to guarantee total standardization of its shape and contents. Several techniques are used to impede imitations and tampering (security paper, UV-sensitive elements, lamination, etc.). In addition to physically 'tamper-proofing' the card, the Interior has set up a 'National Management Record' that is systematically consulted through a computer terminal in order to ensure that no-one obtains more than one card. Finally, the ministry has 'hardened' attribution requirements in an effort to enhance the security of the issuing phases, but at the detriment of the principle of equality between citizens. The obligation to show two recent proofs of place of residence to issuing authorities in order to obtain the card has intensified the marginalization of homeless citizens (Bresson 1995). Another measure – considering every request as a first request – affects other categories of citizens, including those born in France of foreign or naturalized parents and those married to a foreigner. For several thousands of such people, the authorities have demanded a certificate of nationality in addition to the birth certificate with filiations required for all. This practice is strongly resented by these citizens, indignant to be subjected to 'routine state xenophobia' (Maschino 2002) and treated as second-rate citizens.

The French police carding system has become significantly more sophisticated in recent years. Yet a major fault remains – the weakness of the controls applied 'upstream' of the issuance of the card. In spite of everything, it is still fairly easy to obtain an authentic secured card by providing birth documents that do not reflect the real identity of the requester.

The INES project: Old wine in new bottle?

The INES project comes after the *Titre fondateur* project launched by socialist Interior Minister Daniel Vaillant in 2000–2001. The *Titre fondateur*, which was included in the Pluri-annual Action Plan for the Prefectures 2002–2004, attracted much criticism (CNIL 2004: 82–84).[15]

The INES project was mentioned for the first time in September 2003 by Interior Minister Nicolas Sarkozy in his closing address to the fourth Worldwide Forum on e-Democracy at Issy-les-Moulineaux near Paris. Sarkozy presented the project as 'one of the priorities of the Interior' and pledged that it would be operational by 2006. After pilot-experiments were carried out in Gironde Department, the project was taken up by Sarkozy's successor at the Interior, Dominique de Villepin, who in January 2005 requested the Forum des droits sur l'Internet (FDI 2005)[16] to organize a national debate so that citizens' opinions could be taken into account before the authorities would design the final version of INES. That version was officially approved by Prime Minister Jean-Pierre Raffarin at the inter-ministerial meeting that adopted the INES Programme on 11 April 2005. The Programme was then to become a Bill to be subjected to the approval of both the National Commission on Computers and Liberties (CNIL)[17] and the State Council[18] before it would be debated at Parliament and voted into law (Foucart 2005a).

The nature of the new carding system

INES is truly a 'revolutionary' system for identifying nationals. Indeed, with a cost estimated at €205 million a year (€25 million a year more than the current system), the project involves charging citizens for a biometric card (the state stopped charging for ID cards in 1998) that would become compulsory within five years of initial issuing. The optional nature of the French ID card was decided under the Third Republic, maintained at Liberation and never questioned by any government thereafter.

As far as the centralization of the information on card owners is concerned, INES is a significant step forward, although centralization has always been a major objective of efficiency-driven French police forces. For the first time, the INES card is to be connected to several central records of nominative data managed by the authorities, namely:

- A register of births, deaths and marriages, which the Interior intends to set up from the National Register of Identification of Natural Persons (RNIPP, which contains names, surnames, filiations, addresses, etc.) managed by the National Institute of Statistics and Economic Studies (INSEE)
- A record containing the fingerprints of card owners
- A record containing the digitalized facial photographs of card owners
- A record of passport owners.[19]

Also novel is the fact that the biometric data contained in the card is to be saved in a microchip. According to the Interior's 'The INES Program' (Intérieur 2005), the data held in the chip is to be distributed among five distinct 'blocks', unconnected to one another:

- An 'identity block' containing information including the two fingerprints and the digitalized photograph of the card's owner, which may be accessed by duly authorized officials only
- An 'authentication block' proving the card's authenticity
- A 'certified identification block' allowing owners to access public and private e-procedures
- An 'electronic signature block' allowing owners to electronically sign authentic documents (e-administration)
- A 'personal portfolio block' allowing owners to save additional data on the card (a driver's license number, for instance).

Finally, the biometric data saved in the Radio Frequency Identification (RFID) chip included in the INES card may be accessed remotely without contact during automated control procedures.[20]

Legitimization discourse

As far as identity assignment is concerned, the INES project is in many respects an undeniable break from the past. Conversely, the discursive strategies implemented by the authorities in order to justify the need for INES are clearly inherited from past rhetorical efforts aimed at convincing citizens to agree with a document intended first and foremost to meet the needs of the state (Piazza 2004: 141–145).

The authorities systematically stress the usefulness of the biometric ID card. Far from a dangerous police tool, it is described as just a 'convenient instrument' thanks to which citizens will find it easy to prove their identity and their French nationality in a world defined by increasingly complex social relations. In this view, INES is supposed to allow citizens to prove their uniqueness in an undisputable way, and to bring them the satisfaction of it being recognized at all times, while eliminating the disadvantages of identity usurpation. At certain periods of the past, some supported the idea of turning the ID card into a fully fledged 'certificate of respectability'.[21] This notion is not altogether absent in the INES project. Since owners will have the option of saving many personal details in the 'portfolio block' of their cards' chips, and since it will be possible to use the card for authentication purposes on both governmental and commercial websites, what filters through is the notion that the biometric card will make it easy for everyone to prove their own 'transparency' to demonstrate that they have nothing to hide about themselves and that their way of life is in no way reproachable.

In addition to selling the advantages of INES for the citizens themselves, the state also presents the card as indispensable to improve the efficiency of law enforcement. In this case, the legitimization of the INES project is in line with arguments deployed in the 1970s, when the authorities used to link the need to computerize the National Identity Card with the fight against illegal immigration and terrorism. The new biometric card is also said to make it impossible for foreigners to falsely claim French nationality. This, in turn, is supposed to help fight against state benefits fraud, tax evasion, etc., which cost 'several hundred million euro', according to Interior guesstimates (Intérieur 2005). As the prime minister himself insisted on his office's website, 'this is a major security problem for our territory and our fellow citizens, and an especially important issue in the fight against irregular immigration' (Villepin 2005c). Additionally, because the biometric card addresses identity fraud the authorities present it as an anti-terrorist weapon. The Interior has thus claimed that identity fraud 'is associated with all types of serious crime, from terrorism to drug trafficking and the trade in human beings' (Canepa 2005). Such fraud is depicted as a major threat to state security since terrorists 'take advantage of the holes in our present systems in order to evade checks' (Villepin 2005b).

However, while the present government has been content with recycling justifications that were formalized years ago, it has connected them to a new type of argument in an effort to convince the public that the INES project makes sense – the need to abide by international obligations, which, it is alleged, force France to implement a biometric carding system.

The decision-making process

Before INES, no consultation of the public about national carding systems had ever been organized by French authorities. Carding systems had always been established and ruled by decrees, orders, and circulars issued by the Interior. Parliament began to deal with the issue at a late stage and only through rare and brief exchanges between deputies at the occasion of debates on the different laws governing ID checks that were voted in the 1980s. In carding matters, democratic debates were always initiated and carried out by the press, which either stigmatized the authoritarian nature of carding procedures for French nationals, or conversely presented them as absolute security necessities. When the first plans for computerizing the national ID card emerged in the late 1970s, these arguments gradually overlapped with the right/left political divide. At the same period, new players began to participate in the heated debates triggered by computerization plans, including the CNIL, trade unions, and human rights NGOs.

Against this background, Interior Minister Villepin's decision to ask the FDI to organize a national public consultation on the INES project is literally unheard of in France. Between 1 February and 7 June 2005, the quasi-governmental organization set up an online forum where every specific detail of INES was discussed. With a total of 3,060 messages posted by participants, the Forum was a great success. Moreover, the six live debates orchestrated in the cities of Bordeaux, Lille, Lyon, Marseille, Paris, and Rennes between 8 March and 16 June 2005, were attended by a total of 600 people. Finally, the FDI commissioned an opinion poll on INES which involved a 950-people representative sample of the French population. These initiatives undeniably have contributed to improve public knowledge about INES while providing an opportunity for many people to express their views, including civil servants, elected officials, experts, NGO leaders, and common citizens.

Another initiative has also helped raise awareness of INES among the general public. Of its own authority, the CNIL decided to hold a series of hearings on the INES project in order to be better prepared when the Interior eventually would request its opinion officially. The hearings took place between February and May 2005 and enabled the CNIL to consult with people from many different walks of life (scholars, police officers, magistrates, and activists) and all testimonies were posted online (CNIL 2005). Finally, for the first time in France, legislators set up an information-gathering commission dealing specifically and exclusively with ID issues. The 'Information Commission of the Senate Commission on Legislation on the New Generation of Identity Documents and Documentary Fraud' headed by Senators Charles Guéné and Jean-René Lecerf of the majority UMP party has started thinking seriously about the use of biometric ID documents and especially the INES project. The commission's report published in June 2005 (Lecerf 2005) is a significant contribution to the democratic debate on INES.

Resistance stalls project

The INES project has attracted harsh criticism since its inception. This explains why Nicolas Sarkozy, who was appointed interior minister for the second time at that period, decided to temporarily suspend the implementation of INES. Here is how Sarkozy (2005) justified the freeze:

> This project has evolved a great deal in the last months. It is going to have a profound, durable impact on the daily lives of French people. While decisions at the European level force us to implement a biometric passport in the short term, it is not the case as far as the electronic ID card is concerned. Therefore, I do not wish to launch into it without taking the time needed to ponder all of its consequences. The point is not to back-pedal on some necessary changes but to correctly ascertain what direction we want to take, under what conditions and at what price.

The opposition: Varied forms, multiple actors

The FDI-organized debates provided project detractors with ample opportunity for expression. The FDI final report (2005) has reflected the scope of public condemnation, which was also largely commented on in the main newspapers – *Le Monde*: 'Criticism rains on biometric ID project' (Foucart 2005c); *Libération*: 'FDI tells Interior of French fears' (Tourancheau 2005b); *Le Figaro*: 'Interior embarrassed by biometrics' (Tabet and Leclerc 2005); *L'Humanité*: 'Electronic ID: try again!' (Mouloud 2005).

The rise of other forms of opposition also appears to have influenced Sarkozy's decision. INES was vehemently denounced by defenders of individual liberties. For instance, a 'Group for the withdrawal of the INES project' was set up in the spring of 2005. This partnership involving five non-governmental organizations and trade unions launched a website (http://www.ines.sgdg.org) intended to raise public awareness of what it called '*the dangers of INES*'. The website contains a detailed description of the French biometric ID card project as well as information on a range of initiatives from several European governments aiming to include biometric data in travel and identity documents. In May 2005, the Group launched a petition against INES, mocking it as 'Inepte, Nocif, Effrayant, Scélérat' (literally: Inept, Harmful, Scary, Nefarious). As of 8 February, 2007, 6,871 individuals and 71 associations and groups had signed this petition. Additionally, prominent individuals in the Group have explained why they oppose INES at Senate and CNIL hearings.

'Pièces et main d'oeuvre' (PMO),[22] a group of individual critics of 'freedom destroying' CC-TV, nanotechnologies and biometrics also has manifested its hostility to INES. PMO is said to have orchestrated the June 2005 'Libertys' hoax (Foucart 2005b; Le Hir and Cabret 2005). A fake four-page leaflet bearing the logo of the Isère General Council (governing assembly of the Isère Department) was slipped in thousands of mailboxes in Grenoble. To better denounce INES, the well-imitated, official-looking leaflet sang the praises of an imaginary new biometric 'life card' and urged Isère dwellers to request it at once. Meanwhile, INES was the target of a biting denunciation campaign at the hands of several key internet activists like Samizdat and Indymedia, while others, e.g. Collectif contre la biométrie,[23] Brigades des Clowns,[24] stigmatized the biometric card as 'law-and-order oriented'.

Yet, resistance to INES is not restricted to activists. Opposition also comes from institutional players. In June 2005, four Communist deputies and senators issued a statement against INES, while the Socialist Party denounced it on its website.[25] The CNIL, although it has not been officially consulted, has also been reluctant about INES. Its vice-chairman, François Giquel, voiced doubts on the real intentions behind the interior ministry's biometric ID plan by asking: 'Does the INES project consist in identifying owners of a document or does it consist in identifying unknown individuals from a criminal police perspective?' (Tourancheau 2005a). CNIL Chairman Alex Türk (2005) made it a point to stress that if the CNIL were called to give an opinion on INES it would do so 'in terms of proportionality' by taking into account four criteria: centralization of nominative data; individuals' traceability; presence of a security imperative; and individual consent. This amounts to a thinly-veiled warning that the CNIL resents a project that it deems is not in sync with its own doctrine on citizen identification. This doctrine had already been made quite clear to the Interior when INES was initially floated in 2003:

> In its deliberation of October 21st, 1986 the Commission gave a favorable opinion on the recording of individuals' fingerprints when they request an ID card, but it did so after duly noting that no manual, mechanical or automated centralized record of fingerprints would be created at national level, and that the fingerprints stored in the departmental records would not be digitalized. Furthermore, the Commission specified its doctrine during its deliberation of

April 24, 2003 on the immigration bill by stating that it is warranted to use biometric systems in order to make sure of a person's identity as long as the biometric datum is kept on a medium reserved exclusively for the use of the person concerned, by contrast, due to the characteristics of the selected physical element of identification [i.e. digitalized fingerprints] and of the possible uses to which the databases that could thereby be created may lend themselves, the storage and processing of fingerprint data must be justified by compelling security or public order necessities. In this respect, it must be stressed that the initial decree of October 22nd, 1955 states that 'an ID card certifying the identity of its owner' is created but does not mention any public order purpose … As a result, the reasons given [by the Interior] do not appear to be sufficient in view of the potential dangers inherent to the creation of a national database containing the fingerprints of all ID card owners. There could be ground already for the Commission to express its reservations on principle to the interior ministry by stating again what it stated in 1986 and especially in 2003. In any case, the purposes of the storage of the fingerprints and therefore of the checking of both the card and the data stored in the microchip that it contains should be clearly specified, since the creation of centralized databases interconnected by an identifier represents a fundamental change in how identity has been thought of in France until now.

(CNIL 2003)

Another form of institutional opposition has focused on the design of the INES project itself. The interunion committee of INSEE and all major national trade-unions – CGT, CFDT, CGT-FO, SUD and CFTC – have rejected a measure by which INSEE would be required to certify, through the RNIPP, the birth and marriages documents shown by citizens requesting the biometric card.[26] According to the unions, this type of activity does not fall within INSEE's competence and could lead to it becoming a 'police auxiliary'. Meanwhile, the Association of the Mayors of France (AMF) has condemned the Interior's proposal of issuing the biometric card in a few hundred French towns only. AMF has said that, if implemented, this option would force many citizens to travel long distances to obtain the card and therefore would lead to new territorial inequalities within France. AMF also has expressed concern about the financial cost of the INES project for the town councils since the central government would pay only for the technical, not labour, expenditures required to issue the new card (Crouzillacq 2005).

New opposition discourses

In addition to these opponents who condemn specific aspects of INES, others have found fault more generally with the efficiency of the biometric technology selected by the authorities. Supported by expert opinion,[27] many have questioned the infallibility of the high-tech card, concluding that as far as the security of identification procedures is concerned, the 'benefits' that may result from implementing INES would be minor compared to the considerable financial cost of the system.

Moreover, the methods used by the Interior to promote its project were criticized. The ministry was suspected of turning the national consultation organized by the FDI into a decoy essentially intended to legitimize pre-existing governmental options. Many of the participants in the FDI internet debate complained that the INES project was approved by Prime Minister Raffarin in April 2005 while the online consultation supposed to guide governmental choices was scheduled to end in June.

Some of the arguments used to sell INES as a security imperative were denounced as unconvincing. For instance, the Interior argued that more compelling individual identification procedures were indispensable to curb documentary fraud. Yet the scope of such fraud has never been assessed seriously in France. The only statistics ever quoted by the Interior in this respect applied to foreign countries, like the USA and the UK, where official citizen identification systems differ widely from those existing in France.[28] The ministry also failed to convince doubters when it insisted that the biometric ID card is an important anti-terrorist tool. The FDI final report thus asked: 'Will such a system really make it possible to identify first-time terrorists? How would it keep someone determined to commit a terrorist attack from obtaining an ID card quite legally?' (FDI 2005: 6). Finally, the contention that France had to conform to supranational norms on identification was often perceived as a 'clever' attempt to justify a project liable to attract much resistance. While Interior Minister Villepin declared that the biometric ID card would be issued before the end of 2006 'in accordance with our European commitments and as agreed with our American friends' (*J.O.* 2005), INES detractors have repeated ceaselessly that the E.U. Council Regulation of 13 December, 2004 on the introduction of biometrics into passports had nothing to do with national ID cards – Article 1 (3) of the regulation reads:

> This Regulation applies to passports and travel documents issued by Member States. It does not apply to identity cards issued by Member States to their nationals or to temporary passports and travel documents having a validity of 12 months or less.
>
> (E.U. 2004: L 385/2)

Additionally, INES opponents have argued that the standards of the International Civil Aviation Organization (ICAO)[29] on biometric identification only made it compulsory to use a digitalized photograph, not fingerprints, in identity documents. For instance, Meryem Marzouki (2005) of IRIS has criticized the official legitimization discourse of INES in the following terms: to present as an obligation forced upon the country the implementation of international or regional political decisions to which France has contributed, sometimes as a leading force, amounts to what some non-governmental organizations have termed 'political laundering.'

However, most of the blame put on INES ultimately has revolved around a major fear: the colonization of the intimate sphere by governmental power, which is accused of developing increasingly intrusive and tyrannical methods of intervention leading to an intensification of social control. In this respect, the fears triggered by INES are in keeping with those that exacerbated in 1921, when the Identity Card of the French project was denounced as an extension of police records to honest citizens, considerably restricting individual freedom, and again in the 1980s by opponents to the computerization of the National Identity Card.

However, in the case of INES, the concerns traditionally articulated along the lines of 'security imperatives vs. protection of the private sphere' (Guerrier 2004: 21–23) have shifted. New fears have emerged because of the technologies now available, of the nature of usable identifiers – which 'fix' individual identity more than ever before – and of the fact that identification drives have become increasingly internationalized. These fears are not only about centralized, potentially inter-connectable, mega-records of biometric data, but above all about the rise of a logic of individual traceability[30] potentially leading to a significant expansion of the control prerogatives assigned to police organizations while radically threatening the anonymity of public space and right to oblivion.

Epilogue

At the time of writing (July 2007), the future of the INES project is shrouded in mystery. No official statement about it has been made since its suspension in June 2005, nor since the presidential election of May 2007. Unofficial 'rumors' about the French biometric ID card system have filtered through from the Interior, but have been contradictory. At first, that is, before the presidential election, it was said that the INES project was being re-designed into a new version that would be more likely to be adopted. Yet since the election of Nicolas Sarkozy as president, a well-informed source has indicated that the project would be presented again to parliament in its original form (i.e. not re-designed) in 2008.

Whatever the case, it may be deduced that the INES project is not a priority for the new government, for if it was Sarkozy would most probably have taken advantage of his post-electoral 'state of grace' period[31] and majority in parliament to see it voted into law quickly. Instead, it seems that the new president prefers to use the 'state of grace' to promote other, more sweeping, and even structural, measures like reforming universities, social security, the tax system, labour laws, and criminal justice.

It may also be speculated that the new leader perceives INES as strategically risky. Indeed, the biometric ID card could be an issue around which a presently extremely weak and divided left-wing opposition may unite, just when Sarkozy is endeavouring to divide it further by co-opting some of its prominent members into his new government. As was mentioned earlier, the Left has been opposed to the carding projects promoted by the Conservatives since the 1970s. Pushing INES through parliament at this time could jeopardize the support that the new president is striving to muster up across the board for 'his' reforms. An additional factor is that the legislative elections of June 2007 were not as favourable as the new president expected (his UMP party lost seats to the socialists, although the UMP retains the majority at the national assembly). It would nonetheless be very surprising if the INES project did not resurface in 2008 or later. Indeed although it is not crucial,

INES nonetheless seems to fit in well with the tough stance against crime and terrorism that Sarkozy has taken. And of course, there is considerable industrial potential in the biometric ID card.

Notes

1 Kaluszynski (1981), Noiriel (1988), Berlière and Lévy (2001), Denis (2003), Genèses (1993, 2004), Piazza (2005a), EHESS (2004), Université Toulouse 1 (2005), Spire (2005), Crettiez and Piazza (2006).
2 We use the term 'carding' to refer to the process by which the identity of individuals is codified and written down on official papers carried by individuals, these papers being connected to records held by state authorities.
3 On the gradual transition from a police surveillance activity relying on face-to-face recognition procedures to the indirect, remote, methods for controlling individuals that emerged with the development of the nation-state, see Noiriel (2005).
4 In order to be 'imagined as both inherently limited and sovereign' (Anderson 1999: 6), the national community must take on concrete dimensions, which the state helps bring into effective and visible existence. This is achieved especially through carding procedures, which by establishing a clear distinction between citizens and foreigners facilitate the embedding in daily social practice of a nation-state logic underpinned by inclusion and exclusion imperatives, as most chapters in this volume illustrate.
5 See especially Goffman's *Stigma* (1975), which touches on the question of the connection between 'personal identity' and 'identity documents'.
6 Breckenridge's chapter (Chapter 3) on the South African HANIS system in this volume is an illustration.
7 See Maas's chapter (Chapter 16) on the European Health Insurance Card in this volume.
8 Also see Stanton's chapter (Chapter 15) on the biometric RFID passport in this volume.
9 This is not to say that such analysis is downright impossible; see especially Denis (2004) and the papers published in a recent issue of the journal *Politix* (2006) on 'Impostures'.
10 On the reactions triggered by the use of biometrics in schools, see Craipeau *et al.* (2003).
11 Identity, good character, residence, and birth certificates, family record books, military cards, hunting licences, railway cards, etc.
12 Nonetheless, Vichy often had to deal with the occupant, which deemed the card to be necessary to preserve order and keep the population under police surveillance.
13 This is the forerunner of the Social Security number presently used in France.
14 This circular may be consulted at the Centre des archives contemporaines (CAC, at Fontainebleau) under reference number 860 580 art.7.
15 With the Titre fondateur, the Interior hoped to rationalise bureaucratic practices so that citizens may obtain safer ID and travel documents through a single and simplified procedure. In addition, each French citizen was to be ascribed a single identification number (printed on both ID and travel documents) allowing them to carry out administrative procedures on the internet, since the number was to serve '*as both a signature for online exchanges with the state and a personal access key to administrative data*' (Fumaroli 2002).
16 The Internet Rights Forum is a quasi-governmental organisation set up by the prime minister in December 2000 in order to organise debates on the legal and social issues arising from the internet and new technologies.
17 Founded by the law of 6 January, 1978, the CNIL is an independent administrative authority protecting privacy and personal data.
18 The Conseil d'État (or State Council) is France's highest administrative court; its main role is to give opinions on the legality of governmental bills, decrees and ordinances.
19 In the mid-term, the Interior would like to merge procedures for obtaining the biometric ID card and the biometric passport.

20 On use of RFID technology for identification purposes, see Stanton (Chapter 15) in this volume.
21 By writing owners' criminal records down on the cards (Ceccaldi 1917), or by describing the state of owners military obligations (Bayle 1922: 29).
22 See http://pmo.erreur404.org/PMOtotale.htm
23 In November 2005, some members of this group destroyed biometric terminals in a high-school near Paris. They were sentenced by court to suspended prison and a heavy fine on 17 February 2006.
24 Inspired from the British movement CIRCA (Clandestine Insurgent Rebel Clown Army), several 'clown brigades' have emerged in France since 2005.
25 See http://www.parti-socialiste.fr/tic/spip_tic/rubrique.php3 ?id_rubrique=41
26 See the leaflet issued on 7 June 2005. Online. Available: http://cgtinsee.free.fr/ dossiers/libertes/ines/Tract%20Intersyndical%20INES%20INSEE%207%20juin%20 2005.pdf
27 Especially Philippe Wolf (2003), head of training at the Central Direction of Information Systems Security of the prime minister's office, who exposed the numerous weaknesses of biometric technology in his paper 'On Biometric Authentication'.
28 On the difficulty to assess fraud, see Ceyhan (2005: 7–8).
29 On ICAO, see Stanton (Chapter 15) in this volume.
30 On traceability, see e.g. Torny (1999), Bonditti (2005). Many critics have stressed that inclusion of a contact-free chip within the INES card would allow to read chip data from a remote location without the consent or knowledge of the card carrier.
31 In France, *l'état de grace* is the name given to the period following an election, especially a presidential election, during which the newly elected official enjoys exceptional popularity ratings. It may last for several months and has often been taken advantage of by new incumbents to promote measures previously thought of as unpopular or otherwise politically risky.

Bibliography

About, I. (2004) 'Les fondations d'un système national d'identification policière en France (1893–1914). Anthropométrie, signalements, fichiers', *Genèses* 54: March.

Anderson, B. (1999) *Imagined Communities: Reflections on the Origin and Spread of Nationalism*, revised edn., London: Verso.

Asséo, H. (2002) 'La gendarmerie et l'identification des 'nomades' (1870–1914)', in Luc J.-N. (ed.) *Gendarmerie, État et société au xixe*, Paris: Publications de la Sorbonne.

Bayle (Colonel, government commissioner at the first Paris War Council) (1922) 'Words pronounced at the session of the Société générale des prisons of December 1921', *Revue pénitentiaire et de droit pénal* 1–3: January–March.

Berlière, J.-M. and Lévy, R. (2001) 'Les techniques de contrôle et leurs mutations', in Blanc-Chaléard, M.C. *et al.* (eds) *Police et migrants. France 1667–1939*, Rennes: Presses universitaires de Rennes.

Bigo, D. (2004) 'La logique du visa Schengen comme mise à distance des étrangers et les projets de recours à la biométrie', international symposium *L'identification des personnes. Genèse d'un travail d'État*, Paris: EHESS, 30 September/1 October.

Bonditti, P. (2005) 'Biométrie et maîtrise des flux: vers une 'géo-technopolis du vivant-en-mobilité'?' *Cultures et Conflits* 58.

Bourdieu, P. (1993) 'Esprit d'État. Genèse et structure du champ bureaucratique', *Actes de la recherche en sciences sociales* 96–7: March.

Bresson, M. (1995) 'Sans-adresse-fixe. Sans-domicile-fixe. Réflexion sur une sociologie des assistés', *Revue française des affaires sociales* 2–3: April–September.

CAEF (Centre for Economic and Financial Archives) (n.d.) *Note confidentielle*, B55358.

Canepa, D. (General secretary of the interior ministry) (2005) Message on the Forum des droits sur l'Internet, 1 February. Online. Available: http://www.foruminternet.org/forums/read.php?f=16&i=2&t=2

Ceccaldi, P. (deputy) (1917) 'Bill to make effective the institution of an identity card, Chambre des deputes', document parlementaire, *J.O.* 2895: 19 January.

Ceyhan, A. (2005) 'Comment prouver l'identité d'un individu? La preuve par les nouvelles technologies', *Revue de la Gendarmerie nationale* 217: December.

Ceyhan, A. (2007) 'Enjeux d'identification et de surveillance à l'heure de la biométrie', *Cultures et conflits* 64: February.

CNIL (Commission nationale informatique et libertés) (2003) 'Procès-verbal de la réunion du mardi 9 décembre 2003 (adopté le jeudi 12 février 2004)', Paris: CNIL.

CNIL (Commission nationale informatique et libertés) (2004) *24e rapport d'activité 2003*, Paris: La documentation française.

CNIL (Commission nationale informatique et libertés) (2005) *Carte d'identité électronique: la CNIL au cœur d'un débat de société majeur*, 18 February. Online. Available: http://www.cnil.fr/index.php?id=1772&news[uid]=235&cHash=4bcd24b58e

Craipeau, S., Dubey, G. and Guchet, X. (2003) *La biométrie: usages et représentations*, report on behalf of the Groupe des Écoles des Télécommunications.

Crettiez, X. and Piazza, P. (eds) (2006) *Du papier à la biométrie. Identifier les individus*, Paris: Les presses de Science Po.

Crouzillacq, P. (2005) 'Les maires de France s'opposent au projet de carte d'identité électronique', 10 June. Online. Available: http://www.01net.com/outils/imprimer.php?article=280984 (accessed 25 July 2005).

Denis, V. (2003) *Individu, identité et identification en France, 1715–1815*, PhD thesis (history), Université Paris-1 (Denis, V. (2008) *Une histoire de l'identité en France. 1715–1815*, Paris: Champvallon).

Denis, V. (2004) 'Papiers d'identité et respectabilité. L'exemple des indigents dans la France d'Ancien Régime', paper at the symposium *L'identification des personnes. Genèse d'un travail d'État*, Paris: EHESS, 30 September/1 October.

EHESS (2004) *L'identification des personnes. Genèse d'un travail d'État*, Symposium, Paris: EHESS, 30 September/1 October.

Elias, N. (1991) *La société des individus*, Paris: Fayard.

EU (European Union) (2004) 'Council Regulation (EC) No 2252/2004 of 13 December 2004 on standards for security features and biometrics in passports and travel documents issued by Member States', *Official Journal of the European Union*, 29 December. Online. Available: http://eur-lex.europa.eu/LexUriServ/site/en/oj/2004/l_385/l_38520041229en00010006.pdf (accessed 7 February 2007).

FDI (Forum des droits sur l'Internet) (2005) *Rapport. Projet de carte nationale d'identité électronique*, 16 June. Online. Available: http://www.foruminternet.org/telechargement/documents/rapp-cnie-20050616.pdf (accessed 20 June 2005).

Foucart, S. (2005a) 'Feu vert pour la carte d'identité électronique', *Le Monde*, 13 April.

Foucart, S. (2005b) 'Libertys: Aucun problème si l'on a rien à se reprocher', *Le Monde*, 11 June.

Foucart, S. (2005c) 'Vent de critiques sur le projet de carte d'identité biométrique', *Le Monde*, 16 June.

Foucault, M. (1975) *Surveiller et punir*, Paris: Gallimard-Seuil.

Foucault, M. (2004) *Sécurité, territoire, population. Cours au collège de France (1977–1978)*, Paris: Gallimard-Seuil.

France Soir (2005) Interview with Dominique de Villepin (Interior minister), 12 April.

Fumaroli, S. (2002) 'La France prépare une carte d'identité électronique', *01net*, 11 February. Online. Available: http://www.01net.com/article/176211.html?rub=/

Genèses (1993) 'L'identification' *Genèses* 13: Fall.

Genèses (2004) 'Vos papiers!' *Genèses* 54: March.

Goffman, E. (1963) *Stigma. Notes on the Management of Spoiled Identity*, Englewood Cliffs: Prentice-Hall.

Guerrier, C. (2004) 'Les cartes d'identité et la biométrie: l'enjeu sécuritaire', *revue mensuelle du JurisClasseur-Communication-Commerce électronique*, May.

Intérieur (Interior Ministry) (1974) Circulaire no. 74-555 du 24 octobre 1974, *Archives de la préfecture de Police de Paris* DB 109: 24 October.

Intérieur (Interior Ministry) (General Secretariat, Direction of the INES Program) (2005) *Le programme INES*, 31 January. Online. Available: http://209.85.135.104/search?q=cache%3AwJNU0zZcU0kJ%3Ahttp://www.foruminternet.org/telechargement/forum/pres-prog-ines-20050201.pdf (accessed December 2005).

J.O. (Official Gazette) (1940) 20 November.

J.O. (Official Gazette) (1980) 2 August.

J.O. (Official Gazette) (1981) 10 October.

J.O. (Official Gazette) (2005) 'Réponse du ministre de l'Intérieur à une question parlementaire posée par le député UMP Thierry Mariani', No. 0068, Paris, 22 March.

Kaluszynski, M. (1981) 'Alphonse Bertillon, savant et policier. L'anthropométrie ou le début du fichage', MA thesis (History), Université Paris-7.

Kaluszynski, M. (1987) 'Alphonse Bertillon et l'anthropométrie', in Vigier P. and Faure, A. (eds) (1987) *Maintien de l'ordre et polices en France et en Europe au XIXe siècle*, Paris: Créaphis.

La Presse (1921a) 'Un métier disparaît. C'est celui du témoin complaisant', 3 September.

La Presse (1921b) 'Le Bertillonnage pour tous!', 7 September.

La République française (1921) 'Témoins patentés', 4 September.

Lecerf, J-R. (2005) 'Identité intelligente et respect des libertés', Senate Information Report, *J.O.* 439: 29 June. Online. Available: http://www.senat.fr/rap/r04-439/r04-439.html (accessed 22 July 2006).

Le Cri du peuple (1940) '"Carte de Français", c'est autrement sérieux que la "carte d'électeur"', 26 November.

Le Hir, P. and Cabret, N. (2005) 'Des activistes grenoblois contre les "nécrotechnologies"', *Le Monde*, 16 June.

Le Parisien (1955) 'À partir du 1er janvier, une nouvelle carte d'identité', 28 October.

Leullier, R. (1921) 'Depuis quatre mois qu'il exerce ses fonctions, M. Robert Leullier, Préfet de police, a réalisé immédiatement des réformes pratiques', Leullier interviewed in the daily *Excelsior*, 4 September.

L'Humanité. (1921) 'La carte d'identité', 13 September.

L'Intransigeant (1921) 'Veut-on nous imposer l'anthropométrie?', 8 September.

Marzouki, M. (2005) 'La loi informatique et libertés de 1978 à 2004: du scandale pour les libertés à une culture de la sécurité', paper presented at the symposium *Informatique: servitude ou libertés?* organized by CNIL, Paris, 7–8 November. Online. Available: http://www-polytic.lip6.fr/article.php3?id_article=95 (accessed 6 February 2007).

Maschino, M. (2002) 'Êtes-vous sûr d'être Français?', *Le Monde diplomatique*, June.

Mouloud, L. (2005) 'Identité électronique: il faut revoir la copie!', *L'Humanité*, 17 June.

Noguères, H. (1984) 'Sous la résistance, sécurité et faux papiers', *Historia* 448: March.

Noiriel, G. (1988) *Le creuset français. Histoire de l'immigration, XIXe-XXe siècle*, Paris: Seuil.

Noiriel, G. (1991) *La Tyrannie du national. Le droit d'asile en Europe, 1793–1993*, Paris: Calmann-Lévy.

Noiriel, G. (2005) 'Les pratiques policières d'identification des migrants et leurs enjeux pour l'histoire des relations de pouvoir. Contribution à une réflexion en "longue durée"', in *Piazza* 2005a.

Ocqueteau, F. (2004) *Polices entre État et marché*, Paris: Les presses de Science Po.

Offerlé, M. (1993) 'L'électeur et ses papiers. Enquête sur les cartes et listes électorales (1838–1939)', *Genèses* 13: Fall.

Piazza, P. (2000) 'La fabrique "bertillonienne" de l'identité. Entre violence physique et symbolique', *Labyrinthe* 6.

Piazza, P. (2002) 'Au cœur de la construction de l'État moderne. L'invention du carnet anthropométrique des nomades', *Les Cahiers de la Sécurité intérieure* 48: second quarter.

Piazza, P. (2004) *Histoire de la carte nationale d'identité*, Paris: Odile Jacob.

Piazza, P. (2005a) 'Police et identification. Enjeux, pratiques, techniques', *Les Cahiers de la sécurité* 56: first quarter.

Piazza, P. (2005b) 'Alphonse Bertillon face à la dactyloscopie. Nouvelle technologie policière d'identification et trajectoire bureaucratique', *Les Cahiers de la sécurité* 56: first quarter.

Poirmeur, Y. (2006) 'Entre logique d'identification et résistance identitaire', X. Crettiez and P. Piazza (eds) *Du papier à la biométrie. Identifier les individus*, Paris: Les presses de Science Po.

Politix (2006) 'Impostures' 74: June.

Rosecrance, R., Badie, B. and Hassner, P. (2002) *Débat sur l'État virtuel*, Paris: Les presses de Science.

Sarkozy, N. (2005) 'Discours devant les Préfets prononcé au ministère de l'Intérieur', 25 June, Paris.

Spire, A. (2005) *Étrangers à la carte. L'administration de l'immigration en France (1945–1975)*, Paris: Grasset.

Tabet, M.-C. and Leclerc, J.-M. (2005) 'La biométrie embarrasse l'Intérieur' *Le Figaro*, 17 June.

Torny, D. (1999) 'La traçabilité comme technique de gouvernement des hommes et des choses', *Les Cahiers de la sécurité intérieure* 38: first quarter.

Tourancheau, P. (2005a) 'La nouvelle carte d'identité met la puce à l'oreille de la CNIL', *Libération*, 21 April.

Tourancheau, P. (2005b) 'Le Forum des droits sur l'Internet a relayé auprès de l'Intérieur les inquiétudes des Français', *Libération*, 17 June.

Türk, A. (2005) Speech at the sixth Worldwide Forum on Electronic Democracy (eGov), Issy-les-Moulineaux, 29 September.

Université Toulouse-1. (2005) *Nomination, état civil, identité*, symposium, 5/6 April.

Valbelle, R. (1921) 'Dans tous les commissariats de police de Paris, on a commencé à établir les nouvelles cartes d'identité', *Excelsior*, 15 September.

Villepin, D. (Interior minister) (2005a) 'Letter to the president of the Forum des droits sur l'Internet to request the organisation of an online debate on the INES project', 6 January. Online. Available: http://www.foruminternet.org//telechargement/forum/lttre-mission-cnie.pdf (accessed 7 February 2007).

Villepin, D. (2005b) Assemblée nationale, *J.O*, 22 March.

Villepin, D. (Prime minister) (2005c) words written on the French government's internet portal. Online. Available: http://www.premier-ministre.gouv.fr/mobile.php3?id_article=52305

Wieviorka, O. (1995) *Une certaine idée de la résistance. Défense de la France, 1940–1949*, Paris: Seuil.

Wolf, P. (2003) 'De l'authentification biométrique', *Sécurité Informatique* 46: October. Online. Available: http://www.sg.cnrs.fr/FSD/securite-systemes/revues-pdf/num46.pdf (accessed 7 February 2007).

List of French acronyms used in this chapter

AMF: *Association des Maires de France* (Association of the Mayors of France)

CAC: *Centre des Archives Contemporaines* (Center for Contemporary Archives)

CAEF: *Centre des archives économiques et financières* (Center for Economic and Financial Archives)

CFDT: *Confédération Française Démocratique du Travail* (Democratic French Labour Con-federation)

CFTC: *Confédération Française des Travailleurs Chrétiens* (French Confederation of Christian Workers)

CGT: *Confédération Générale du Travail* (General Labour Confederation)

CGT-FO: *Confédération Générale du Travail-Force Ouvrière* (General Labour Confederation-Workers' Force)

CNIL: *Commission Nationale de l'Informatique et des Libertés* (National Commission on Computers and Liberties)

FDI: *Forum des Droits sur l'Internet* (Internet Rights Forum)

INES: *Identité Nationale Électronique Sécurisée* (Secured Electronic National Identity)

INSEE: *Institut National de la Statistique et des Études Économiques* (National Institute of Statistics and Economic Studies)

IRIS: *Imaginons un Réseau Internet Solidaire* (Let's Imagine a Solidarity-based Internet Network)

J.O.: *Journal Officiel* (Official Gazette)

RNIPP: *Registre National d'Identification des Personnes Physiques* (National Register of Identification of Physical Persons)

STO: *Service du Travail Obligatoire* (Compulsory Work Service)

SUD: *Solidaires, Unitaires, Démocratiques* (Interdependent, Unitarian, Democratic – labour union)

UMP: *Union pour un Mouvement Populaire* (Union for a People's Movement – political party)

13 The United States Real ID Act and the securitization of identity

Kelly Gates

In May 2005, George Bush signed into law the 'Emergency Supplemental Appropriations Act for Defense, the Global War on Terror, and Tsunami Relief'. Attached to the must-pass Bill was the 'Real ID Act of 2005', a piece of federal policy mandating 'improved security for drivers' licences and personal identification cards in the USA, as recommended by the 9/11 Commission. The Real ID Act specifically mandated that, to be accepted as legitimate identification, documents by US federal agencies, driver's licences and other cards issued by the State Department of Motor Vehicle (DMV) offices would have to incorporate a standard set of features, including specific textual information about the identity of the bearer, a digital photograph of the individual's face and tamper-resistant, machine-readable technology. The policy included requirements for more rigorous verification of identity at the time of document issuance – specifically by requiring DMVs to verify the authenticity of breeder documents, such as birth certificates and green cards. It also mandated information sharing practices among state DMV offices. The states would have three years from the Act's signing to implement the requirements (by May 2008), after which only Real ID compliant driver's licences and other identification documents would be accepted by federal agencies and authorities, including federal aviation security.

Passage of the Real ID Act sparked considerable controversy and debate among civil libertarians, policy-makers, DMV officials, and 'security experts'. Some critics interpreted the policy as a means of circumventing widespread political opposition to a national ID in the USA, by transforming DMV offices into national identification registration centres and transforming state driver's licences into *de facto* national ID cards. The Act placed considerable burden on the states to implement Real ID-compliant identification document procedures, raising fundamental issues at the heart of the US federalist system. State and DMV representatives immediately expressed concern about the policy, with some states refusing to comply with the mandates outright. (At the time of writing, 17 states had passed anti-Real ID Act legislation and other states were considering similar measures.) State opposition has stemmed largely from the enormous projected costs of implementing the Act's requirements; the US Homeland Security Department (DHS) estimated costs as high as US$23 billion. The DHS indicated that states could allot a portion of their DHS grants to implementing the Real ID Act requirements, but critics countered that this funding strategy would divert money away from other important security programmes. In short, the benefits of the proposed changes were heavily disputed from the start, with civil libertarians and security experts alike maintaining that the new requirements would add considerable administrative burden to drivers' licensing, infringe on citizens' privacy rights, and essentially create a national ID system while doing virtually nothing to improve security.[1]

Like the other contributions to this volume, this chapter adds a different dimension to critiques of the Real ID Act by placing the policy within a broader analysis of state identification practices. Rather than focusing on the Act's privacy implications or arguing that it represents an ineffectual means of providing security from terrorism (although I largely agree with the critics on both of these points), my aim in this chapter is to historicize and contextualize the Real ID Act as part of a larger movement toward intensified forms of identity documentation occurring along with the social and political–economic transformations associated with the so-called Information Revolution. I examine the Real ID Act *vis-à-vis* three inter-related dimensions of these transformations: the ongoing challenges associated with the bureaucratic rationalization of 'official identity'; the access control imperatives associated with the accelerated commodification of information and expansion of proprietary information networks over the last several decades; and the recent prioritization of governmental strategies for the 'securitization of identity' – Nikolas Rose's (1999) term for the proliferation of sites where individuals are made responsible for establishing their official identity as a condition of access to the rights and responsibilities of citizenship.

Although implementation of the Real ID Act clearly faces an uphill political battle, the policy is representative of a set of tendencies that are by no means dependent on any single piece of legislation. Real ID is part of a set of governmental strategies designed to further integrate information technologies into the administrative capacities of the state in order to significantly augment those capacities and make them interoperable with governing functions now carried out by the private sector. IT systems are being designed to automate surveillance practices, and this turn to automated surveillance, rather than representing a direct response to the threat of international terrorism, instead 'represents a continuation, albeit at an accelerated pace, of trends that were already strongly present in all advanced industrial societies' before 9/11 (Lyon 2003: 65).

A fundamental part of these continuing and accelerating trends has been the privatization and outsourcing of government functions. ID administration is no exception. Private contractors have assumed a central role in the implementation of new identification systems, including the new system requirements outlined in the Real ID Act. Here, I focus on the role of Digimarc, a company that has contracts with 37 state DMV offices to provide document issuance services and technologies. A quick perusal of Digimarc's website after the passage of the Real ID Act revealed the extent of how the company was positioning itself at the centre of the procedural overhauls. More than simply providing necessary information technology upgrades, Digimarc would function as a Real ID consultant to DMVs, providing everything from the manufacturing of the new cards to background checking services and training of DMV personnel on the new document verification procedures. However, despite its potentially profitable role in these changes to ID document issuance in the USA, Digimarc remained largely missing from the critiques and public debates about legitimacy of the Real ID Act and other related policy decisions designed to expand and improve upon identification systems.

The problem of identification

In order to fully understand the significance of the Real ID Act, it is necessary to consider a set of underlying questions at the heart of the 'problem of identification'. How can we make sense of the persistent impulse to identify individuals with recourse to official records? Why have modern societies been so intensely focused on developing official forms of identification? What compelled the move from face-to-face forms of recognition to bureaucratic forms of official identity verification? How did certain kinds of identification documents come to authoritatively represent the official identity of the individual? And what are the consistent problems that have plagued efforts to devise more efficient and fully functioning identification systems? Most of these questions have not been adequately addressed, either in the debates about the Real ID Act, or in sociological analyses of surveillance and identification.

A short answer to the first question is that the verification of official identity helps to establish a relationship of trust between individuals and the institutions with which they interact in their daily lives. Trust is 'involved in a fundamental way with the institutions of modernity', and 'is vested, not in individuals, but in abstract capacities' (Giddens 1990: 26). Modern societies are characterized, according to Anthony Giddens, by the disembedding or 'lifting out' of social relations from their local contexts and their subsequent re-embedding in dispersed time-space locations. Identity credentials function as what Giddens calls 'symbolic tokens', or media of interchange that enable the re-embedding of social relations in order to produce workable conditions of trust – 'the reappropriation or recasting of disembedded social relations so as to pin them down (however partially or transitorily)' (Giddens 1990: 79).[2]

Put more simply, the scale of modern society is such that institutions cannot possibly know each individual on a personal basis, and thus they require some form of confirmation that establishes that individuals are who they claim to be. Individuals themselves must establish their consistent identity over time and across distance for their own well-being. If a person moves from one residence to another, she must maintain a consistent identity in the move, taking identifying information with her. Certainly there may be aspects of her identity that she may want to leave behind, and in fact modern bureaucratic identification systems, and especially networked, database-driven systems, make it much more difficult for individuals to redefine themselves in new contexts. But for many people there are real and compelling needs for official forms of identity, for a stable attachment to earned credentials and other aspects of identity. It is perhaps one's money and property that is most significant, but other dimensions of our identities are also important, such as employment history, health records, citizenship status, etc. A stabilized identification scheme helps one function as a modern individual, and without a means of verifying our official identities, we quickly run into problems in daily life, when we go to cash a check, apply for a job, get pulled over for speeding, or attempt to cross a national border.

Despite the utter necessity of official forms of identification in modern societies, 'official identity' should not be viewed as natural or self-evident. As Craig Robertson (2007) has argued, official identification is an under-theorized practice of modern society. Making sense of this practice requires unpacking the relationship between identification and identity rather than taking this relationship as given. What exactly constitutes an 'official identity' and how do administrative identification systems go about capturing or representing it? As a number of historians have shown, the relationship between individual identity and official forms of state identification took shape at a particular historical moment. According to Robertson, US society came to place trust in documents to accurately identify individuals between the middle of the nineteenth century and the interwar period of the 1930s. The historical transformations of this period, roughly from the Civil War to the Depression Era, contributed to and relied on state practices for the official documentation of individual identity – the development of an *ad hoc* bureaucratic apparatus of identity verification, or what Robertson refers to as a 'documentary regime of identification'. As societies grew in size, mobility and anonymity, the introduction of official forms of authentication and verification into informal, *ad hoc* types of face-to-face recognition became an increasingly pressing social necessity.

These new documentary forms of official recognition made authoritative claims to truth about individual identities. However, rather than merely documenting or representing already existing stabilized identities, the emerging documentary regime of identification in fact constituted 'official identities' in the act of documenting them. The official identity represented on identification documents became intelligible through the development of a bureaucratic state apparatus of official identity verification. Indeed, the most powerful rhetorical device of identification documents was their claim to transparency as direct reflections of existing identities. In reality, the official forms of identification cobbled together a set of existing and already mediated markers of identity – such as names, addresses, signatures, and photographs – to create a stabilized form of identity that could be verified via the very bureaucratic state apparatus that constituted those identities.

This process of creating a document and archive-oriented regime of official identification also occurred in other parts of the Western world. In her analysis of the personal name as a component in the apparatus of identification in nineteenth century France, Germany and England, Jane Caplan (2001: 50) examined 'some of the processes by which mechanisms of 'identity' were made available for the purposes of identification in a particular historical context'. New systems for administering standardized identity documents involved the introduction of official techniques of verification into existing practices of trust and face-to-face recognition. The identity document came to stand in for a bureaucratic encounter with the state, whereby the individual's claim to identity would be verified through a new form of official recognition. According to Caplan, the identity document came to function as 'the portable token of an originary act of bureaucratic recognition of the "authentic object" – an "accurate description" of the bearer recognized and signed by an accredited official, and available for repeated acts of probative ratification' (Caplan 2001: 51). The authority of identification documents derived from the context in which they were issued, and specifically the credentials and bureaucratic location of the issuing agent, which had to be inserted into and read off of the document (Robertson 2007). The document became 'official' by taking a standardized form, including a set of identifying information, and by incorporating signs of the issuing authority. A 'regime of verification' took shape that set standards for the specific ways an identity would be defined, as well as 'the evidence needed to verify that identity, and the authorities who could ultimately determine an individual's (official) identity' (Robertson 2007: 13).

Since the mid-nineteenth century, a considerable amount of administrative bureaucracy has been developed, in *ad hoc* and discontinuous fashion, to address the problem of identification. Although states have consistently held out the promise (and threat) of perfectly functioning identification systems, these systems have been fraught with administrative difficulties. Persistent challenges, leading to constant improvements in identification systems, have included human error in the administration of identification systems, the scale of the administrative apparatus necessary for effectively functioning systems, document forgery and the problem of binding identities definitively to bodies. At the heart of these problems is the fundamentally unstable and mediated nature of identity. The administrative problems that plague the ongoing development of official identification procedures are in fact evidence of the fundamentally mediated nature of 'official identity' and the always unstable and imperfect relationship between identity and identification. And new technical systems and procedures can never fully solve the problem of identification, primarily because official identification involves verifying an object that does not exist *a priori*, but is in fact constituted in the act of verification.

Informationalized capitalism and network access control

Certainly the intense preoccupation with establishing bureaucratic identification systems, and the corresponding internal contradictions of such systems, have been with us for some time. However, there is a sense in which, over the last several decades, the sites at which individuals are asked to verify their identities have proliferated. The development of biometric technologies, the turn to machine-readable identification documents, the expansion of databases that house personal information about individuals, the adoption of new policies for official identification systems like the Real ID Act – all of these developments point to an intensification of the problem of identification in the present historical context. Why have modern societies become so obsessed with documenting individual identity? More specifically, what recent developments might help explain why policy-makers in the USA are advocating new requirements for the verification of individuals applying for driver's licences at state DMV offices?

The intensification of the problem of identification has arisen out of a number of interrelated developments associated with the 'Information Revolution', or what is more accurately understood, in political–economic terms, as a transition to 'cybernetic' or 'informationalized capitalism' (Robins and Webster 1999; Schiller 2007). At its core, informationalized capitalism involves the commodification of information, that is, the production of information by wage labor for market exchange (Schiller 2007). Understood in terms of this process of commodification, the 'Information Revolution' in fact seems less like a 'revolution' and more like the continuation of processes of capitalist accumulation underway over a much longer historical period. According to Robins and Webster (1999), the 'Information Revolution' is not best viewed as the result of technological innovation, as is common in popular discourse and among IT enthusiasts. Rather, it is more adequately understood as 'a matter of differential (and unequal) access to, and control over, information resources' (Robins and Webster 1999: 91). Viewing technological development as a matter of shifts in the availability of and access to information foregrounds its thoroughly political dimensions. New information technologies are not designed to bring about revolutionary change so much as to serve an existing and long-standing set of political–economic priorities.

Robins and Webster place the origins of the 'Information Revolution' not in the turn to computerization, but more than half a century earlier in the industrial project of Scientific Management and its more generalized application for the rationalization of other areas of social life throughout the twentieth century. Namely, principles of scientific management were applied not only in the workplace, but also to the consumer and political spheres in order to bring consumption practices in line with productive capacity and to control the political process (Robins and Webster 1999). The historical development of identification systems is part and parcel of the historical development of information technologies as mechanisms for surveillance and social management. It is significant that Taylor and his contemporaries developed the principles of Scientific Management during the same period in which identification systems were more thoroughly rationalized and a documentary regime of identification took shape. What is new about the present context, according to Robins and Webster, is the scale at which these principles are applied, as well as the increasing reliance on information and communication technologies for the combined efforts of planning and control.

What is also noteworthy about the present context, although perhaps not entirely new, is a 'protracted episode of accelerated information commodification' that began roughly at the beginning of the 1970s (Schiller 2007: 36). This acceleration was precipitated, according to Dan Schiller (2007), by the generation of surplus productive capacity in a wide range of industries, especially in the USA but also in Europe and Japan, and a subsequent period of profit slowdown and stagnation. Corporate and political elites began organizing a response to this economic crisis that would enable the development of new profit sites; as Schiller (2007: 36) explains, 'this was not the first time that overproduction and competition engendered efforts by elites to rejuvenate the market system, but the pivotal role accorded to information and communications as a solution was unprecedented'.

It should come as little surprise that along with this acceleration in the commodification of information has come not only a major overhaul and expansion in intellectual property law, but also a more intense regime of identification for controlling access to information. It is through this historical lens that we should view the current rise of security consciousness and the intensified interest in improving upon identification systems. Although it seems on its surface to be a response to a newly intensified threat of terrorism, in fact security discourse has merely subsumed the threat and fear of terrorism into its logic. The rise of security consciousness corresponds to the intensified commodification of information and to the corresponding imperative of public and private institutions to monitor and control access to information networks, and to the spaces and resources of value in the information society.

The securitization of identity

The logic of access control occurring along with the commodification of information also must be considered in relation to a related development: the rise of the political ethos of neoliberalism or 'advanced liberalism' (Nikolas Rose 1999). In his theoretical diagnosis of 'advanced liberalism', Nikolas Rose points to a pronounced 'individualization of security' occurring along with the dismantling of the welfare state – that is, the tendency to place responsibility on individuals, families, and organizations for their own security and risk management. In a general trend that accelerated during the 1980s and 1990s, social welfare programmes designed to provide some measure of economic security for individuals and families became subject to criticism, and were replaced or modified to a significant extent by entrepreneurial models of self-motivation and self-reliance. At the same time, the developed world has seen the emergence of post-disciplinary control strategies, an array of ideas, diagrams, and technologies for applying increasingly specialized knowledge and techniques to govern populations in the face of seemingly more complex problems and risky social, political, and economic contexts. Rose divides these 'control strategies' roughly into two groups: those designed to tie individuals into 'circuits of inclusion' and those designed to exclude and otherwise administer those problem identities deemed threatening and uncivilized.

The process of sorting individuals according to their appropriate location in these circuits of inclusion and exclusion has enlisted technologies for the 'securitization of identity', networks or assemblages for 'securing the obligatory access points for active citizenship' (Rose 1999: 241), or conversely, denying access to certain individuals at those same points of interface. The 'active citizenship' of advanced liberalism is realized not primarily in voting or participating in an idealized political public sphere, Rose maintains, but through employment, consumption, and other practices, including financial and other transactions, virtually all of which require the verification of legitimate identity. The individualization of security has compelled individuals to adopt increasingly defensive postures with regard to their personal property, resources, and identities, providing a social context in which an intensified securitization of identity appears necessary. The rise of this security-conscious governmental rationality represents another important dimension for understanding the current preoccupation with new identification systems. Such systems are envisioned not only to exclude problem identities from the rights and responsibilities of citizenship, but to facilitate the active involvement of 'legitimate' subjects in their own self-government. Carrying a verifiable – that is, *machine-readable* – identification document is becoming a condition for the exercise of freedom.

The Real ID Act and the problem of identification

The Real ID Act presents an opportunity to examine in detail the manifestation of the 'problem of identification' in the US context in these times. In what specific ways does the Real ID Act relate to the 'securitization of identity' and the access control imperatives arising as a result of the transition to informationalized capitalism? How does the Act address the bureaucratic problems historically associated with identification systems, and how do the solutions it proposes resemble or diverge from those promised by earlier identification systems? In particular, how are information technologies envisioned as solutions to ongoing problems with bureaucratic identification systems, such as lack of trust in documents and the objectivity of verification techniques?

The substance of the Real ID Act is in Section 202 outlining the 'minimum document requirements and issuance standards for federal recognition' of new driver's licences and other identification documents. This section first stipulates that only documents that meet the new requirements will be accepted by a federal agency for any official purpose. The section is then divided into 'minimum document requirements', 'minimum issuance standards' and 'other requirements'. Real ID documents will be required to contain, at a minimum, the bearer's full legal name, date of birth, gender, driver's licence or identification card number, address of principal residence, and signature. In addition, Real IDs must contain a digital photograph of the person, as well as 'physical security features designed to prevent tampering, counterfeiting, or duplication of the document for fraudulent purposes', and 'a common machine-readable technology' that stores all of the identifying information visible on the card.

The minimum issuance standards subsection of the Real ID Act outlines what the States must require from individuals applying for a driver's licence or other DMV-issued identification card. At a minimum, individuals must present: (1) a photo-identity document or an ID document that contains both the person's full name and date of birth (e.g. a birth certificate would be acceptable); (2) documentation showing date of birth; (3) proof of social security account number or verification that the person is not eligible for such a number; and (4) documentation showing full name and the address of the principal residence. Additional 'special requirements' indicate that applicants must provide 'evidence of lawful status', in other words, documents that show that they are US citizens or nationals, or that they are lawfully in the USA. Only temporary driver's licences and identification cards can be issued to applicants with non-immigrant visas, pending applications for asylum, pending or approved applications for temporary protected status in the USA, or other types of official-yet-precarious legal status. The third part of the minimum issuance standards subsection defines required procedures for the verification of documents presented by ID applicants: States 'shall verify, with the issuing agency, the issuance, validity, and completeness of each document'. The only foreign document that States may accept are official passports, and States must agree to 'routinely utilize the automated system known as Systematic Alien Verification for Entitlements' to verify the legal status of non-US citizens applying for driver's licences or other IDs.

The Act stipulates the adoption of a number of additional procedures in the document issuance process. States must 'employ technology to capture digital images of identity source documents' in order to retain images of these documents in electronic databases in 'transferable format'. In addition, each applicant must be subjected to a 'mandatory facial image capture'. Although the Act does not stipulate what States must do with those facial images, it does indicate that states must refuse to issue a driver's licence to anyone holding one from another state; thus the policy may read as anticipating the use of facial recognition technology – already integrated into numerous DMV systems – to search facial images against other State's driver's licence databases. States must maintain motor vehicle databases that contain all of the data fields printed on driver's licences and ID cards, along with drivers' driving histories. States must also 'ensure the physical security of locations where drivers' licences and identification cards are produced', and 'subject all persons authorized to manufacture or produce driver's licences and identification cards to appropriate security clearance requirements'.

The Real ID Act outlines a desired policy outcome rather than actually existing administrative system. As much of the response from civil libertarians and individual states indicates, the requirements will not be easy to implement, and certainly not within the three-year timeframe mandated by the Act. Nevertheless, it is important to make sense of the underlying rationale for the proposed changes, some of which have already taken place on an *ad hoc* and voluntary basis (e.g. most driver's licences already include machine-readable technology and digital photographs).

The framing logic of the Real ID Act centres on the 'securitization of identity', especially in terms of developing more rigorous procedures to ensure that individuals 'are who they claim to be'. Toward that end, the Real ID Act requirements aim to codify a process already underway: the delegation of identity verification to automated systems. The digital photo requirement facilitates this process; using digital images not only enables their easier reproduction and storage in a database, but also makes them more readily accessible for automated searches. Mandating machine-readable technology on the card is a way of lending the document the symbolic authority of the 'high-tech', but machine-readable documents also have the practical advantage of being able to communicate with information networks, where conventional documents relied on static, analogue content alone for their authority. Machine-readability eliminates the need for humans to read the document, de-skilling and otherwise taking humans 'out of the loop' of responsibility for reading and authorizing identification documents. New document technology also provides a means of automatically connecting those documents (and their bearers) to database records. This provides the basis for a new form of identity verification, or at least a new way of connecting identities to archives – a significant and necessary move in order to integrate identification systems into information networks and effectively control access to those networks.

The Real ID issuance standards aim to automate, and make more secure, the process of determining the legitimacy of an individual's claim to the identity represented on an identification document. As Robertson (2007), Caplan (2001) and Stalder and Lyon (2003) have shown, this process has always relied on an 'originary act of bureaucratic recognition' (Caplan) that paradoxically depends on other 'breeder' or 'seed' documents that themselves are representations of an individual's identity, rather than the identity as such. This perpetual reliance on documents demonstrates the fundamentally mediated and constructed nature of official identity. What is often the first originary document, the birth certificate, is the least verifiable, because agencies have not kept consistent records and because the documents take so many different forms. Likewise, the range of documents for proving legal status is quite variable, making their definitive verification exceedingly challenging. The reliability of this process of verifying identity with perpetual recourse to additional documents of questionable authority 'is defined by the weakest link in this chain of references' (Stalder and Lyon 2003: 84).

Real ID attempts to circumvent the problem of seed document validity in two primary ways: requiring DMVs to verify the validity of seed documents with their issuing agencies, and storing digital copies of the documents along with other identifying information in individual database records for future reference and verifiability in case an identity is called into question. Like the digital photograph requirement, digitization is intended to render the documents more open to reproduction, distribution and analysis. DMVs are encouraged to use database searches as a means of verifying the legitimacy of documents presented by applicants. However, as the ACLU has noted, often no such databases exist, and 'many verification databases that do exist ... are incomplete, inaccurate and so far unable to perform the functions required by Real ID' (ACLU 2007).

The fundamental problem underlying the seed document verification requirement is not so much incomplete, inaccurate databases, however, but again, the fundamentally unstable and mediated nature of 'official identity'. Not only will the verification of seed documents add a considerable administrative burden to DMV offices and lengthen waiting times for receipt of the new *de facto* national ID cards. More importantly, it will make receiving such documents impossible for a significant number of individuals whose identities are simply not verifiable with recourse to a final, objective, authoritative document. These individuals in turn become members of a particular 'class' of individuals by nature of their lack of official documentation – i.e. an 'undocumented' class. As Taha Mehmood argues of India's Multipurpose National Identity Card (see Chapter 7), new and seemingly more sophisticated identification card schemes in fact often have the effect of further complicating distinctions between 'legible' and 'illegible' people, rather than settling those categories once and for all.

Other requirements of the Real ID Act are similarly aimed at the 'securitization of identity', such as ensuring the physical security of driver's licence production facilities and subjecting DMV and other employees to security clearances. However, these requirements do little to address the fundamental problems associated with bureaucratic identification systems – namely, establishing a factual, original basis of identity with perpetual recourse to documents and bureaucratic authority. The policy does not explicitly address what verification procedures should be used to determine whether seed documents describe the persons presenting them, i.e. the problem of how to bind those identification documents definitely to bodies (Egelman and Cranor 2005). Nor does the Real ID Act stipulate how new *machine-readable* ID documents will be articulated to specific bodies. Biometric technologies are being envisioned to address this problem; however, as I have argued elsewhere, biometrics – while ostensibly targeting the 'body itself' – in fact add another layer of mediation to the already mediated process of identification.

Clearly, if the larger aim of the Real ID Act is to produce a perfectly functioning national ID card system in the USA, then it is an imperfect and incomplete piece of legislation. Of course, it is not the explicit purpose of the Real ID Act to institute a complete and perfectly functioning national identification system. Federal officials have emphasized repeatedly that the Act does not mandate a national ID. Such a system would surely meet formidable resistance in the USA, with its strong bi-partisan libertarian coalition and general opposition to the idea of centralized government registration. (An effectively functioning national ID system would also threaten to reduce the critical mass of low-wage laborers from the south – an undesirable outcome for the US economy, regardless how effective anti-immigrant rhetoric can be in winning elections.) But despite its shortcomings, the Real ID Act represents an important articulation of the bureaucratic rationalization of 'official identity' and the intensified 'securitization of identity' that has accompanied not only the emergence of international terrorism as a more salient problem, but also the more enduring access–control imperatives associated with the accelerated commodification of information that has underpinned the transition to an 'Information Society'.

Outsourcing ID administration

The US Real ID Act must also be examined *vis-à-vis* the political–economic logic of privatization that has shaped strategies of government in the USA and other industrialized countries since the economic crises of the 1970s.[3] As David Lyon and Colin Bennett point out in Chapter 1 of this volume, states cannot fulfil their visions for ID card schemes alone, but depend on high-tech corporations, as well as technologies and international standards organizations, for guidance and assistance. The logic of privatization underpins this 'Card Cartel' and has shaped the administration of new, IT-intensive identification systems to the extent that private-sector actors have been fully integrated into formerly state-run systems, from drivers' licensing to passport issuance. Thus the private sector has captured large US federal outlays for domestic security: US$41 billion in fiscal year 2004, up from US$33 billion the year before, and US$21 billion the fiscal year that ended just after 9/11 (Uchitelle and Markoff 2004). There is nothing special about the Real ID Act in this regard: under the pretence of state security provision, it translates into another federal handout to private contractors, including companies like Digimarc and L-1 Identity Solutions, which together cover most of the state DMV offices with contracts to provide card administration and production services.

Companies that produce and market photographic technologies have been involved in the production of driver's licences and identification documents since they began incorporating photographs in the late 1950s. Recently, however, more than merely providing cameras and document production equipment, companies have provided a much wider range of ID document production and archive services to DMV offices and other government agencies that issue identification cards. In the 1990s, Polaroid, for example, was billing itself as 'the world's leading supplier of identification systems, including large-scale systems for government' with systems in 25 states and more than 60 international government and commercial entities worldwide (PR Newswire 1997). Digimarc, a company marketing digital watermark and copyright protection technologies, acquired Polaroid's ID Systems business in December 2001, adding ID systems to its 'brand protection' and 'brand management' products. The new company, re-named Digimarc ID Systems, became the producer of driver's licences for 37 US states, business that generated 'in excess of $50 million in annual revenues' (Digimarc 2001).

Although the Real ID Act says nothing about private contractors in the rules it mandates for the states, companies like Digimarc assumed a central role in helping states comply with the new requirements. A March 2007 issue of the online newsletter, *SecureIDNews*, noted that Digimarc was well-positioned to help states comply: 'The fact that the Oregon-based company is already in more than two-thirds of US state driver licence offices certainly gives it a leg up' (*SecureIDNews* 2007). The article also noted that Digimarc 'has been heavily involved in Washington, D.C.', testifying before Congress on border crossings and security.

Digimarc's enthusiasm for the new federal ID guidelines was apparent at its website. In addition to claiming to be the 'trusted partner' of government agencies and standard promotional literature explaining its 'complete solution for the secure ID Lifecycle', the website included an 'information portal' dedicated to explaining 'Digimarc Solutions for REAL ID'. The Digimarc information portal had links to a company White Paper summarizing the Department of Homeland Security's 'Real ID Notice of Proposed Rulemaking' (accessible only to authorized site visitors) and a link to Real ID regulations at the DHS website. The main page of the portal also displayed a statement of Digimarc's ability to support US states as they seek efficiency and security in driver licence issuance, to help them achieve Real ID compliance, to offer cost-effective solutions that enhance customer service and to 'protect citizens from identity theft, fraud and terrorism'. The main page then listed a series of links to Digimarc's 'solution offerings', including 'applicant data verification', 'document authentication with scanning and archiving', 'effective systems for interstate and interagency communication', 'secure data storage', 'expertise in business logic and workflow', 'quality portrait capture and storage', 'fraudulent document recognition training', 'secure central issuance production facilities', 'machine-readable security features', and 'expert card design services' (http://www.digimarc.com/govt/realid.asp).

It should come as little surprise that policies like the Real ID Act represent such a potentially enormous windfall for companies like Digimarc. It is also unsurprising, yet telling, that Digimarc's two main service offerings are identification systems and digital copyright projection. These two IT 'services' are absolutely essential to the commodification of information at the centre of informationalized capitalism. As an IT company with a mission to provide technologies for secure access control of information, Digimarc is indeed well placed to help states comply with the US Real ID Act. Yet the company is virtually absent from public debates about the legitimacy of this controversial piece of legislation. This glaring absence should be a telling wake-up call about the effects that privatization of government services has had on a social right that is absolutely essential to a functioning democracy: access to information.[4]

Conclusion

The burning question at the heart of the debate over the Real ID Act is whether the policy would essentially create a national identification system in the USA, and whether that is a desired outcome for democratic government. Many state officials and proponents of Real ID are adamant that the answer to the first question is 'no'. They insist that the Real ID Act was a response to specific recommendations from the 9/11 Commission, that the policy would not *require* citizens to carry a Real ID, that Real ID-compliant documents would continue to be issued by the states not the federal government, and that nothing in the Act required states to transmit information on licence holders to the federal government. Others have defended the national ID-like qualities of Real ID as beneficial for security and even democracy. In a co-authored op-ed piece in *The New York Times* (Carter and Baker 2005), former Democratic US president Jimmy Carter and former Republican secretary of state James Baker together argued the benefits of standardized, government-issued IDs as a way of increasing voter participation. They recommended that the new Real ID cards be used as standardized voter ID cards as part of their recommended voting system reforms, and suggested that critics of government-issued IDs often overlook their larger benefits for the poor and minorities (i.e. when they are issued for free, which is not the case for driver's licences in the USA). As Carter and Baker's recommendations suggest, the argument that Real ID is not *really* a national form of identification is a dubious one, based on too narrow a definition of such a system.

I have argued in this chapter that the Real ID Act should be connected to a broader set of political–economic tendencies, and a longer history of institutional interest in identification systems, than we find in most public debates over national ID cards. The establishment of a totalizing programme for the 'securitization of identity' is by no means complete or inevitable, nor would such a system likely result from a single piece of legislation.[5] But regardless of whether Real ID advanced a national form of identification or whether the policy is more accurately viewed as outlining a limited, voluntary, decentralized and *ad hoc* state-run system, Real ID is clearly another incarnation in the ongoing drive for bigger and better identification systems in the USA, this time aimed at enabling institutional actors to control access to proprietary information networks and to the spaces and resources of value in the so-called information age. The specific improvements to ID systems outlined in the Real ID Act were aimed at resolving a set of long-standing problems associated with identification systems: binding identities definitively to bodies; eradicating human error in the administration of identification systems; eliminating the production of fraudulent documents; and managing the enormous scale of identification systems. However, even were these problems to be decisively solved by drawing on the powerful potential of new information technologies, individual identity would remain a mediated construct, an object that does not exist *a priori* but is produced in the act of documenting it. No amount of technological development can transform national identity from a mediated process to an already accomplished fact. Unfortunately, this will not stop the ID enthusiasts from trying. They are convinced that the security of the nation is in the cards.

Notes

1 There is bipartisan opposition to the Real ID Act in the USA, and to the idea of a national ID card in general. The American Civil Liberties Union's thorough and ongoing critique of the Real ID Act can be found online at http://realnightmare.org. The conservative Cato Institute published a critique of the Real ID Act in Jim Harper (2002). For a critique of the Real ID Act as ineffectual for security, see Egelman and Cranor (2005).
2 On the problem of trust, identity and anonymity in modern societies, see also Erving Goffman (1967).
3 On the economic crisis of the 1970s, see David Harvey (2005) and Dan Schiller (2007).
4 On the importance of access to non-trivial, contextualized social information as a condition of a functioning democracy, see for example, Herbert I. Schiller (1996), especially the Introduction and Chapter 3 on 'Data deprivation'. For arguments about access to information as a social right, see also the arguments of UNESCO and the Non-Aligned Movement (NAM) for a 'New World Information and Communication Order' (NWICO) in the 1970s and 1980s (e.g. Kaarle Nordenstreng 1984). See also Dan Schiller (2007), especially Chapter 3 on the accelerated commodification of information.
5 In July 2007, the US Senate defeated a Republican-backed spending Bill that would have allocated US$300 million to states to help them implement the Real ID Act, further calling into question the legitimacy of the policy as an 'unfunded mandate' (Broache 2007).

Bibliography

American Civil Liberties Union (ACLU) (2007) 'New federal regulations get an 'F' in addressing issues with the Real ID Act', March. Online. Available: http://www.realnightmare.org/resources/106/ (accessed 20 March 2007).
Belluck, P. (2006) 'Mandate for ID meets resistance from states', *The New York Times*, 6 May. Online. Available: http://www.nytimes.com (accessed 6 May 2006).
Broache, A. (2007) 'Senate rejects extra $300 million for Real ID', *CNET News.com.*, 27 July. Online. Available: http://news.com.com/Senate+rejects+extra+300+million+for+Real+ED/2100-7348_3-619220.html (accessed 2 August 2007).

Caplan, J. (2001) '"This or that particular person": Protocols of identification in nineteenth-century Europe', in J. Caplan and J. Torpey (eds) *Documenting Individual Identity*, Princeton: Princeton University Press, pp. 49–66.

Carter, J. and Baker, J.A. III (2005) 'Voting reform is in the cards', *The New York Times*, 23 September. Online. Available: http://www.nytimes.com/2005/09/23/opinion/23carter.html (accessed 24 September 2005).

Digimarc (2001) 'Digimarc completes acquisition of Polaroid ID Systems', 21 September. Online. Available: http://www.digimarc.com/ (accessed 20 March 2007).

Egelman, S. and Cranor, L.F. (2005) 'The Real ID Act: Fixing identity with duct tape', *I/S: A Journal of Law and Policy for the Information Society* 2: 149–83.

Giddens, A. (1990) *The Consequences of Modernity*. Stanford: Stanford University Press.

Goffman, E. (1967) *Interaction Ritual: Essays on Face-to-face Behaviour*. Garden City: Anchor Books.

Harper, J. (2002) *Identity Crisis: How Identification is Overused and Misunderstood*, Washington, DC: Cato Institute.

Harvey, D. (2005) *A Brief History of Neoliberalism*, New York: Oxford University Press.

Lyon, D. (2003) *Surveillance after September 11*, Malden: Polity.

McGray, D. (2006) 'A card we should all carry', *The New York Times*, 21 February, A19.

Nordenstreng, K. (1984) *The Mass Media Declaration of UNESCO*, Norwood: Ablex.

PR Newswire (1997) 'Polaroid and West Virginia agree to issue world's first driver's licences, using facial recognition technology', *PR Newswire*. Online. Available: Lexis Nexis Academic Database (accessed 5 December 2003).

Robertson, C. (2007) 'A documentary regime of verification: The emergence of the US passport and the archival problematization of identity', unpublished manuscript.

Robins, K. and Webster, F. (1999) *Times of the Technoculture: From the Information Society to the Virtual Life*, New York: Routledge.

Rose, N. (1999) *Powers of Freedom: Reframing Political Thought*, New York: Cambridge University Press.

Schiller, D. (2007) *How to Think about Information*, Urbana: University of Illinois Press.

Schiller, H.I. (1996) *Information Inequality: The Deepening Social Crisis in America*, New York: Routledge.

SecureIDNews (2007) 'States prepare for Real ID in advance of pending driver licence mandates', *SecureIDNews*, 9 March. Online. Available: http://www.secureidnews.com/library/2007/03/09/states-prepare-for-real-id-in-advance-of-pending-driver-licence-mandates/ (accessed 20 March 2007).

Stalder, F. and Lyon, D. (2003) 'Electronic identity cards and social classification', in D. Lyon (ed.) *Surveillance as Social Sorting: Privacy, Risk, and Digital Discrimination*. New York: Routledge, pp. 77–93.

Uchitelle, L. and Markoff, J. (2004) 'Terrorbusters Inc.: the rise of the homeland security-industrial complex', *The New York Times*, 25 October, Sect. 3, pp. 1, 8, 12.

United States REAL ID Act of 2005. Public Law 109-13. 109th Congress. Online. Available: http://www.epic.org/privacy/id_cards/real_id_act.pdf (accessed 15 November 2006).

Visionics (2000) 'West Virginia DMV adopts Polaroid's second generation ID system enabled by FaceIt®', 28 February. Online. Available: www.shareholder.com/identix/ReleaseDetail.cfm?ReleaseID=53281 (accessed 10 December 2003).

Zureik, E. and Hindle, K. (2004) 'Governance, security, and technology: The case of biometrics', *Studies in Political Economy* 73: 113–37.

14 Towards a National ID Card for Canada?

External drivers and internal complexities[1]

Andrew Clement, Krista Boa,
Simon Davies and Gus Hosein

Introduction

Canada is one of the very few industrialized countries that does not have nor is actively considering a National ID Card.[2] This is not because Canada has been immune from the multiple forces that have propelled other countries further along this route, most notably the 'War on Terror', with its imperative to better secure borders and air travel. Nor does it mean there has been no activity at the national level around identity documentation and management. Indeed, far from it. Following the events of 9/11, Canada was among the first countries to discuss officially a national biometric ID card, and when this did not proceed, the federal government continued with several other initiatives aimed at strengthening border documents and managing citizen identity records that may well provide the ingredients for a national ID scheme in the future. Canada's now slower pace gives it an opportunity for a suitably thorough debate of the complex issues, drawing on the recent and often troubled experiences of ID card development in the Anglo-American countries that Canada usually takes as its most direct comparators.[3]

To provide the basis for such a debate, this chapter examines the current (mid-2007) state of development of ID cards and identity policies in Canada. It seeks to understand why Canada is not actively developing a National ID Card and if its current identity initiatives, whether by design or happenstance, may be laying the groundwork for a future deployment. Is there a stealthy advance in this direction likely or already underway as some suggest? Does Canada face extraordinary obstacles in developing ID cards and policy? Has the Canadian government adopted a careful 'wait and see' approach that will enable it to learn from others' experience, and thereby develop an identity policy framework that earns the support of its citizens better than its comparators have done?

We will address these broad questions by first reviewing the short, truncated, but revealing debate over the development of a national biometric ID card that took place in 2003. We then turn to various federal identity initiatives that, while falling short of a full National ID Card, reflect many of the policy drivers and technical capabilities commonly associated with such developments. Specifically, we examine the Canada–US Smart Border Declaration with its Action Plan, its successor, the Security and Prosperity Partnership of North America and the Western Hemisphere Travel Initiative. These have provided powerful imperatives that constitute the principal policy drivers in the identity arena, but are facing implementation difficulties. We then look at the progress of the Canadian biometric passport, the document that figures most frequently in these 'smart border' initiatives and is closest in function, technology and institutional apparatus to a National ID Card. Due to a combination of largely organizational factors it too has been slow in coming when compared with other countries. The last federal initiative we analyse is the government-wide identity management discussion coordinated by Treasury Board Secretariat currently underway. It seeks to provide a common understanding of an approach to ID management issues in all the major federal departments and agencies that manage the identity records of Canadians. While much of its work is oriented to everyday governmental activities, it also addresses issues that would underpin any National ID Card. We conclude by returning to the central guiding questions and offer informed speculation about where ID cards and identity policies may and should be heading.

The abbreviated National ID Card debate in Canada

Public discussion of national identity issues was virtually non-existent in Canada until the terrorist attacks of 9/11. However, in its immediate aftermath media attention suddenly focused on the potential for a National ID scheme to help prevent a re-occurrence. Within a week, pollsters got to work, and according to Canada's 'national' newspaper the *Globe and Mail*, found that 80 per cent of Canadians would submit themselves 'to providing fingerprints for a national identity card that would be carried on [their] person at all times to show police or security officials on request'.[4]

A year later, the federal Minister of Citizenship and Immigration Denis Coderre proposed that Canada develop a National ID Card. During the period when the Parliamentary Standing Committee on Citizenship and Immigration considered the Coderre proposal, they observed there were a variety of poorly understood rationales in circulation:

- the need to combat terrorism (e.g. the UK government argued that a third of all terrorists use multiple identities)
- the need to combat fraud (e.g. to ensure that only those who are entitled to government services may actually receive them)
- the need to combat identity theft (e.g. the growing concern about fraudulent use of identities to open accounts in other people's names)
- the need to manage borders (e.g. the implementation of biometric visa schemes to combat illegal immigration)
- the need to support the private sector with an adequate regime of identification (e.g. the Industry Canada principles of authentication to guide industry adoption of identification services)
- the need to aid the development of electronic government services (e.g. to

enable citizens to gain access to government services on-line will require some form of authentication in order to file taxes, etc.)

> (Government of Canada. Standing Committee on Citizenship and Immigration 2003)

These may all be valid reasons to reconsider existing policies, but it is daunting to consider them all within a single policy, since the varied rationales call for different techniques and policy solutions. After holding public hearings, receiving briefs, interviewing experts and visiting other countries where National ID Cards were under development, the Committee found that the need for such a card had not been adequately demonstrated and that more study was needed. In order to arrive at a definite response to the issue of a National Identity Card, the Committee specified a set of 37 questions that would have to be answered. Its Interim Report in October 2003 concluded with a clear call for the need for an informed public debate:

> It is clear that this is a very significant policy issue that could have wide implications for privacy, security and fiscal accountability. Indeed, it has been suggested that it could affect fundamental values underlying Canadian society. A broad public review is therefore essential. The general public must be made more aware of all aspects of the issue, and we must hear what ordinary citizens have to say about the timeliness of a national identity card.
>
> (Government of Canada. Standing Committee on Citizenship and Immigration 2003)

A few months later, the Liberal Government announced that it would not be pursuing further a National ID Card and relieved the Parliamentary Committee of its ID card duties before it could issue its Final Report (Webb 2007: 95). Apart from a brief flurry of speculation in February 2006 (*Globe and Mail* 2006), when the new Minister of Public Safety was reported as suggesting that a National ID Card was 'inevitable' (CTV.ca News 2006) and a national poll conducted in July 2007 found that 72 per cent of Canadians agreed with 'implementing a National identification card for all Canadians' (Angus Reid Global Monitor 2007), there has been no public mention of a National ID Card since.

However, the idea of a national biometric identification system did not end there. Within a month of the official end of the Coderre ID Card proposal and on the eve of his April 2004 visit with United States President George Bush, then Prime Minister Paul Martin announced *Canada's National Security Policy* (Government of Canada, Privy Council Office 2004). This policy reiterated a commitment to the *Canada–US Smart Border Declaration* and for the first time set a timetable and initial budget for 'a biometrically enabled smart chip passport' (Foreign Affairs and International Trade Canada 2001, 2007). While the ambitious target date of early 2005 has long since passed, the biometric passport and other federal identity initiatives have proceeded largely behind the scenes, in effect replacing the National ID Card as the focus of governmental attention, and keeping the issues out of the public spotlight. While these initiatives raise many of the same public policy concerns as National ID Cards, they have not been subjected to the 'broad public review' that the Parliamentary Committee called for. It is to these various federal identity initiatives that we now turn.

Major federal ID policy drivers and initiatives in Canada

There are three main policy initiatives relevant to developing national level identity documents in Canada, all aimed at establishing a 'smart border' between Canada and the USA:

1   The Canada–US Smart Border Declaration and 32-point Action Plan
2   The Security and Prosperity Partnership of North America (SPP)
3   The Western Hemisphere Travel Initiative (WHTI).

The term 'smart border' implies increasing the degree of automation and technologization of border crossing documents and practices. The need to increase use of information and communications technologies, and notably biometrics, to enhance border security is deeply embedded in all three initiatives.

While the Smart Border Declaration and the successor SPP[5] are much more comprehensive and far reaching in subject matter than simply articulating identity policy, border security and identity documents do form a significant part of their mandates. Of the three, the WHTI is the most focused on identity documents and dictates changes to what is acceptable documentation to enter the USA. Both the Smart Borders Declaration and the SPP are multilateral policy initiatives, while the WHTI is unilateral, originating in the USA, but having direct implications for Canadians.

The Canada–US Smart Border Declaration and 32-point Action Plan

The Smart Border Declaration and its associated 32-point Action Plan is a formal agreement between Canada and the USA, signed in December 2001 to ensure: 'the secure flow of people, the secure flow of goods, a secure infrastructure, and the coordination and sharing of information in the enforcement of these objectives' (Foreign Affairs and International Trade Canada 2001). Regular status reports and updates were issued by the Canadian and US governments until December 2004. Since this time, there has been relative silence from both governments with respect to this agreement, presumably replaced by the SPP.

Identity, identification and information sharing, including personal information, form a significant part of the agreement, in addition to points relating to increased harmonization of the technologies used. The 'secure flow of people' element comprises 13 points in the Action Plan and focuses most directly on identity issues.

Some of the points of the Action Plan have direct implications for Canadian identity documents. The first point in the Action Plan, for instance, focuses on biometric identifiers. The 2004 Status Report highlights the progress made toward using biometrics for particular identity documents. It explains that agreements have been reached to develop common standards and to adopt interoperable and compatible technologies. In addition, both countries agree to work with the International Civil Aviation Organization (ICAO) on international standards for biometric travel documents. The report also states that Canada will begin issuing biometric passports by mid-2005, which as we discuss further below has not occurred. The report also explains that the NEXUS frequent traveler programme will be expanded. These points all relate to increasing the use of biometric identifiers for travel and border crossing (Foreign Affairs and International Trade Canada 2004).

The second Action Plan point focuses specifically on permanent resident cards, stipulating the need to 'develop and deploy a secure card for permanent residents that includes a biometric identifier' (Foreign Affairs and International Trade Canada 2003). While a new, more secure permanent resident card was issued in 2002 and required for re-entry to Canada by 2004, this card so far does not contain biometric data, although it was designed with the capacity to store biometric images.

The NEXUS frequent travel (or 'trusted traveler') card programme is discussed in two points of the Action Plan – 'Biometric Identifiers' and the 'Single Alternative Inspection System'. NEXUS is a joint programme between Canadian Border Services Agency, Canada Customs, Citizenship and Immigration Canada and US Customs and Border Protection (Foreign Affairs and International Trade Canada 2004). It is a voluntary programme to expedite border crossing between Canada and the USA, by pre-screening travelers through a risk assessment process. Those who qualify for the programme receive a card, containing digitized facial and iris images, that allows them to be used with self-serve kiosks in airports or express lanes at land border crossings (Canada Border Services Agency 2007b). Membership in the NEXUS programme must be renewed every five years, at which time another risk assessment is conducted.

Security and Prosperity Partnership of North America

The Security and Prosperity Partnership (SPP) was initiated in March 2005 between the USA, Canada, and Mexico, by their respective leaders. The SPP:

> provides a framework to advance collaboration with Canada's neighbours in areas as diverse as security, trade facilitation, transportation, the environment and public health. This partnership has increased institutional contacts between the three governments to respond to a shared vision of a stronger, more secure and more prosperous region.
>
> (Department of Finance Canada 2006)

Unlike the Smart Borders Declaration, the SPP is not a formal written agreement, but described instead as a 'framework' or a 'dialogue' between the three countries, making it very difficult to learn what is discussed, let alone assess critically. Critics charge that the SPP is aimed at promoting North American integration and designed deliberately to avoid any kind of legislative oversight and public scrutiny, to achieve integration through a process of 'evolution by stealth'.[6] US leadership in the SPP is much clearer and more directly articulated than in the Smart Border Declaration. The US SPP website explains that this 'is a White House-led initiative among the United States and the two nations it borders – Canada and Mexico – to increase security and to enhance prosperity among the three countries through greater cooperation' (SPP.gov no date). Furthermore, the SPP describes even more extensive concerted action than the Smart Border Declaration and there are concerns that the SPP is too secretive, too focused on big business needs, and will have ramifications for sovereignty (Council of Canadians 2006). Of the five main areas under the SPP, 'North American Smart, Secure Border' (Government of Canada, Office of the Prime Minister 2006) is the most relevant to issues of identity and again invokes the rhetoric of 'smart borders' to create 'a border strategy to build smart and secure borders that rely on technology, information sharing and biometrics' (Department of Finance Canada 2006). Canada allocated funds specifically to meet SPP goals in the 2006 Federal Government Budget.

> [The] budget will invest $303 million over two years on a range of initiatives. Key among these is the border strategy aimed at efficient and secure movement of low-risk trade and travelers to and within North America, while protecting Canadians from threats, including terrorism.
>
> (Department of Finance Canada 2006)

One of the SPP priorities, supported by the allocation of $25 million over the fiscal years 2006–2007, is expanding the NEXUS programme. This is noteworthy in that all applicants become subject to risk assessments in both Canada and the USA, requiring an unusual level of personal information sharing between countries (Department of Finance Canada 2006).

Western Hemisphere Travel Initiative

The Western Hemisphere Travel Initiative (WHTI) is part of the US Intelligence Reform and Terrorism Prevention Act of 2004. The WHTI puts forward new requirements for all individuals entering the USA (including US citizens). Everyone must now present a passport or some other secure identity and citizenship document. These new requirements come into effect for different ports of entry (air, land, and sea) at different times. Given that until 2007, Canadians were free to enter the USA simply with proof of citizenship (often a birth certificate) and photo-ID, the key question is what documents other than the passport, if any, will be accepted by the US government.

The WHTI requirements came into effect for air travel in January 2007. Canadians must now carry a passport or a NEXUS card 'when used at a NEXUS kiosk at designated airports' (Canada Border Services Agency, 27 July 2007a). The deadline for WHTI compliance at land and sea ports of entry has been extended from 1 January 2008 to 1 June 2009, in the Fiscal Year 2007 Homeland Security Appropriations Act.

Given that alternative documents are being accepted at airports, it seems likely that alternative documents will also be accepted at sea and land ports of entry, particularly given the extension of the deadline for compliance. However, what might be deemed acceptable to the Department of Homeland Security (DHS) is not yet clear. One option, in addition to the NEXUS programme, is some form of an upgraded driver's licence that contains citizenship information. By July 2007, DHS had pre-approved the pilot use of RFID-enabled Washington State driver's licences as an alternative to showing a US passport or PASS[7] card at border crossings between Washington and Canada.[8] Ontario and British Columbia are similarly looking at options for implementing new 'secure' licences, which could be deemed acceptable travel documents for crossing the US border (Ferguson *et al.* 2007). In a press conference Dalton McGuinty, Premier of Ontario, indicated that the only additional information needed for the driver's licence to be used as a travel document is 'encrypted citizenship information' (CBC Radio Hourly News 2007). DHS continues to press for its People Access Security Service (PASS) card standard, despite evidence that its long-range wireless technology would create an increased security risk (Electronic Privacy Information Centre 2006). However, details of what will be acceptable for land and sea border crossing are still in flux, and not likely to be resolved in time for the Summer 2008 deadline. Headline news stories about many month delays in issuing passports, frequent policy changes (e.g. around age limits, and 'proof' of application) and even public apologies by senior officials give the impression of policy and programme disarray.[9]

In all three policy initiatives, the USA appears to be driving changes to identity documents, not only within their own country but also in Canada. With the SPP this 'harmonization' process expands to include Mexico. Once the USA finally settles on which documents will be acceptable for crossing its borders and demonstrates their workability, it will have direct implications for Canadian identity and travel documents. Until this point, other governments will be reluctant to commit themselves to their own standards for ID documentation. While these changes are presented as a 'harmonization' of multiple standards, it is clear that in many cases US interests are the dominating ones, raising significant concerns about sovereignty and adequate policy transparency and deliberation.

We expect to see even greater fluctuation and uncertainty in this domain before final results emerge. The public discussion in Canada of these proposed border security measures has mainly focused on the potential disruption they may cause for cross-border travel, which will be felt most directly by communities near the border where citizens of both countries are accustomed to crossing easily, without need for a passport. There has been much less public discussion or analysis of the longer-term implications for national sovereignty and civil liberties.

Biometric passport

The first formal announcement of a pending Canadian biometric passport came with the Smart Border Declaration in 2001. Since then it has been mentioned in each of the subsequent policy statements discussed above, but beyond this there is remarkably, and disturbingly, very little public information available. In 2002, Passport Canada began issuing passports with a new, more tamper-resistant design, but without biometric encoding. It required digitally produced photos, and famously, prohibited applicants from smiling in these photos, presumably to ease automated facial recognition. These images are scanned and used in printing the passport, but there is no machine-readable digital storage of the image on the passport itself.

In 2004, Passport Canada sought approval from the federal Office of the Privacy Commissioner (OPC) to use its recently tested facial-recognition technology in processing passport applications (Bronskil 2004). A summary of the resulting Privacy Impact Assessment (PIA) identifies 10 areas of concern/risk[10] and lists 18 recommendations by the OPC for bringing the use of facial recognition into compliance with privacy standards. Passport Canada agreed in principle with most of the recommendations, but on the first two, concerning establishing a legislative/regulatory framework and lawful authority, it dissented.[11] Nor so far is there any substantive public information about how it will meet the recommendations agreed to in principle.

On 1 September 2004 and again 15 June 2006, the federal Parliament amended Section 8 of the Passport Order, the Act that governs the passport in Canada, to read:

8.1 (1) The Passport Office may convert any information submitted by an applicant into a digital biometric format for the purpose of inserting that information into a passport or for other uses that fall within the mandate of the Passport Office.

(2) The Passport Office may convert an applicant's photograph into a biometric template for the purpose of verifying the applicant's identity, including nationality, and entitlement to obtain or remain in possession of a passport.

(Government of Canada 2004, 2006)

In July 2006, Passport Canada issued a public Notice of Proposed Procurement inviting vendors to submit bids for 'a high volume Facial Recognition Solution (FRS) that will verify and process digital images of passport applicant's picture as part of the passport application process' (MERX 2006). The bidding period closed 28 September 2006. However, the Notice of Potential Procurement was re-issued in July 2007, revealing that no progress has been made to date. A news report that same month based on an access to information request indicates that Passport Canada, which functions on a cost recovery basis, lacks the funds to proceed with upgrading the Canadian passport to include biometrics (Bronskil 2007).

A further likely cause for delay is the difficulty in the timely linking of the passport issuing process with the recording of vital statistics, notably deaths, which is normally handled by provincial authorities. To address this problem, which is faced by other agencies that manage citizen identities, several departments at the federal and provincial level have initiated a pilot project on the National Routing System (NRS):[12]

... a secure electronic communications environment permitting provinces, territories and federal departments to exchange vital event information. It allows provincial and territorial vital event registrars to validate birth information that is essential to authenticate identity and to notify federal departments of deaths in order to manage changes to program entitlements in a timely manner.

(Menic and Turner 2006)

However, no department has yet taken on the operational mandate, and the consequent funding requirements.

Although the biometric passport is far behind its original schedule, there are still signs of activity in this direction. However, the federal government has chosen neither to inform nor consult the public about what is planned. The serious issues concerning rationales, privacy, security, function creep, costs, oversight, governance, information sharing (e.g. with the USA) and national sovereignty have not been addressed openly. This raises questions about what exactly is being planned and strongly suggests that the government fears the reactions of Canadians, either for what it is planning, or out of embarrassment for the inadequacy of its preparations. Not only does this call into question the legitimacy of the exercise, it undermines the public support that will be needed to make the deployment successful.

Treasury Board Secretariat identity management discussions

While the initiatives discussed above are the ones in Canada most directly relevant to national identity documents, issues around the handling of individual identity are widespread throughout the federal government. Typically these are referred to under the broad rubric of 'identity management', which includes such elements as ID cards, access controls, privilege management, and data-sharing, etc. To facilitate the development of government-wide identity management policies and systems, the Treasury Board Secretariat (TBS) established an inter-departmental working group in the expectation that a common understanding of identity could provide gains in economic, social and international arenas.

The TBS project's first stage objectives were two-fold:

1   To map the current state of identity management of individuals requesting programmes and services from the Government of Canada
2   To identify opportunities that will enable the transformation of identity management in Canada with service improvement and greater trust.[13]

It conducted a series of workshops that included participation from 11 federal government departments to investigate systematically the programmes and services that require that the identity and/or entitlement of individuals be determined before granting access to these programmes and services. The study found that these determination processes rely on a wide range of identifiers and documents (11 identifiers and 55 documents for the 29 programmes and 71 services studied), which have different degrees of reliability, different issuing processes and are from different jurisdictions (federal, provincial and territorial).[14] This shows that identity management currently is far from systematic, and means that re-designing the information systems to enable timely, accurate authentication and identification processes will be slow and expensive.

Accessing programmes and service entitlements relies heavily on identity documents, particularly foundation documents such as birth certificates. Furthermore, while the driver's licence is provincial, since it is the only widely issued government document containing a photo, it is broadly used in circumstances, federal, provincial and municipal, where accessing a programme or service requires photo-ID as a proof of identity. TBS concludes that as a result, 'identity management is an inter-jurisdictional concern'.[15] This drastically increases the challenges to developing a national (or even federal) identity management policy.

Since completing its Phase I Mapping Report, the interdepartmental working group has shifted its focus toward developing a framework that can guide identity management policy and identity systems building. It takes an important step in doing this by noting that whereas identity has long been understood as a component of security and privacy, it is better treated as a distinct 'discipline' with its own goals, practices and processes. Essential to this is the definition of identity, which it articulates as:

> *Identity*: a reference or designation used to distinguish a unique and particular individual (organization or device).
>
> (Bouma 2006)

This clearly reflects a government-centred identity perspective, consistent with the government-only make-up of the committee and its central objective of 'Making sure we are dealing with the right person'. However, from the point of view of individuals encountering a government agency, who overwhelmingly are legitimate and law-abiding, this is not their central concern. They already know they are the person they claim to be, so the key identity question for them is whether they will be recognized by the agency as an entitled subject or more generally enabled to proceed with the requested transaction.

This lack of an person-centred view of identity documentation and performance represents a serious shortcoming in a framework that explicitly recognizes that the 'uncertainty of identity has now become a significant risk factor for governments, with potentially adverse impacts on the clients they serve and the citizens to whom they are accountable'. At the very least, it raises questions about the need for a broader definition of identity, one that figures centrally the perspective of the identity-subject in which status judgements are intrinsic.

The interdepartmental working group also considered in general terms how to implement government identity initiatives. Based on a review of principles developed in Canada as well as internationally, they proposed 11 broad principles to guide their efforts. While the TBS formulation is valuable in many ways, it again reflects an exclusively internal government process and consequentially the perspective is dangerously narrow. So far, this second phase of TBS-led work has been made public only through oral presentations accompanied by PowerPoint 'decks' with no official reports released yet.

In all these federal policy and identity system initiatives discussed above, we see a remarkable lack of transparency. Far from heeding the Parliamentary Committee's advice about addressing key questions and involving the public in a deliberative process, the federal government has been proceeding with national identity initiatives apparently willfully disregarding its Parliamentarians' advice. It has so far not clearly specified the purposes for them, the necessity for new systems rather than improving existing means, the financial costs (for start up and on-going administration, liability and cost sharing arrangements), the handling of personal information, and the security of identity documents, devices and databases, among other matters of public concern. There is however, still time to correct this lapse before new ID systems are implemented.

Complex dynamics

While Canada has not officially embarked on a National ID Card scheme, there are clear signs that important changes are afoot in terms of new national identity documentation and management measures. These appear largely in response to persistent strong pressure from the USA to 'secure' the common border and introduce biometrics as a key technology. We have highlighted the major federal initiatives and drivers in this direction – the Smart Border Declaration, the Security and Prosperity Partnership of North America, the Western Hemisphere Travel Initiative, as well as the planning by Passport Canada for a biometric passport. In each case, the publicly available material is confined to relatively vague statements of intent, but with scant detail about the many policy and civil liberties issues they provoke.

Of the several pressures to develop a National ID Card in Canada, the most prominent and persistent is the demand by the USA for a higher degree of document 'security' for crossing its common border. As reflected in the uni-, bi-, and tri-lateral initiatives since 2001, the USA has consistently expressed its demand for biometric identification techniques. This insistence that Canada conform to its security standards, rather than negotiate them in a reciprocal manner, is not unusual. Such national asymmetry follows a well-established pattern (Clarkson *et al.* 2005: 168–194) but has been exacerbated in the post-9/11 period as the Bush Administration has assumed an unusually aggressive and refractory posture in its international dealings. In particular, as Maureen Webb points out in *Illusions of Security: Global Surveillance and Democracy in the Post-9/11 World*, its adoption of a 'pre-emptive' model of security involves asserting US hegemony in new arenas beyond its borders even as it undermines the basis for real security (Webb 2007).

We have also seen the Government of Canada engaged, somewhat independently of these external pressures, in a government-wide identity management discussion coordinated by Treasury Board Secretariat. This seeks to provide a common understanding of ID management issues in many of federal departments and agencies that manage the identity records of Canadians. The TBS discussion has usefully highlighted 'identity' as a distinct area of focus, overlapping with, but not subsumed by, such other areas as privacy, security and information management. They have further articulated a preliminary conception of identity, overarching goals and a set of broad principles for guiding government ID management initiatives. However, publicly visible results are sketchy and the linkages between the internal and external identity initiatives remain obscure. Indeed the multiplicity of objectives, actors and sociomaterial contingencies make for a complex and even contradictory developmental trajectory.

To return to the questions with which we began the chapter, we can see several factors that might account for why Canada has not (yet) embarked on a National ID Card venture in spite of the strong pressures:

Technical immaturity

While there has been steady pressure to implement biometrics in ID documents, whether in the passport or cheaper border crossing alternatives, this technology is still very much in the development stage, with many practical obstacles to achieving an integrated functional system. Given that the USA is leading the way here and will likely define the *de facto* standards, there is little Canada can do until the USA has established a clear course of action.

Technical ineffectiveness

Once such a system is functioning technically, it is highly unlikely to be effective in the most prominently stated goal – protection against terrorist attack (Schneier 2003; Clement *et al.* 2002). In addition, given the lack of success so far in other jurisdictions, notably the UK and the USA, to achieve jurisdictional biometric ID schemes, even federal officials who favour this approach may be understandably wary to commit their government to an unproven, complex and expensive scheme.

Border ambiguities

Reflecting the geographic scale of Canada and the USA as well as their long history of close relations, the demarcation between the two has been characterized, generally proudly, as the world's 'longest undefended border' (Wikipedia 2007). This is seen in the heavy flow of people and goods across the border[16] facilitated by documentary requirements considerably lighter than usual for international borders. The progressive tightening of economic integration, notably in cross border shopping, but especially in just-in-time industrial supply chains, poses a serious challenge to the Bush Administration in its attempts to 'secure the border'. A very extensive infrastructure of documentation, surveillance and screening must be put in place before full implementation can be achieved. Even apparently ordinary measures, such as closer inspection of truck contents and requiring passports for international travel, have provoked sharp reactions by corporations, individuals and political leaders in the border states and provinces. So, ironically, US pursuit of its 'security' agenda is running foul of the long-standing trend of greater economic integration (the 'prosperity' agenda) (Clarkson *et al.* 2005: 168–194) and is 'hardening' the border even as it attempts to project its hegemony further into Canadian sovereignty.

Jurisdictional fragmentation

The political structure of Canada as a federation, in which 10 provinces and 3 territories maintain jurisdiction over many aspects of government operations in relation to citizens means that developing National ID schemes requires negotiations among the 14 governmental units. As in the case of the National Routing System pilot and the TBS consultations over identity management, there is much practical work to be done in creating inter-operable systems. The question of who provides the funding for what also gets worked out in these multi-jurisdictional negotiations. While the federal government would be the main beneficiary of an integrated identity management scheme, much of the cost would be borne by the provinces as they issue most of the foundation documents as well as the driver's licences. Only if the federal government were willing to put up the very large sums needed to implement such a scheme would we expect negotiations to proceed quickly.

Political wariness

National ID schemes are not widely popular in North America and governments promoting them incur significant political risks. US Homeland Security Secretary Michael Chertoff has claimed publicly that opposition to a National ID Card is so strong that Americans would never stand for it. 'Their heads would explode' (*Canadian Press* 2007). In Canada, the reaction may not be as extreme, but there are still political risks, especially in that since June 2004, Canada has had minority federal governments, first lead by the Liberal Party and then by the Conservative Party. As is usual in such politically uncertain times, governments concentrate public attention and funding on those areas where they are likely to get popular advantage and win a majority position in the next election. Far from there being no public clamour for National ID Cards or biometric passports, these initiatives raise a host of thorny issues and are very likely to court popular opposition. Until a majority government is formed, these restraints will likely remain.

Each of these factors: technological over-reach; an historically porous international border; Canada's federal structure with fragmented jurisdictions; and political uncertainties, individually and in combination contribute to making Canada's situation distinctive, if not unique, in relation to other leading industrial countries in terms of development of a National ID Card. They go a long way to accounting for why Canada is among the few such countries to not have or be developing a National ID scheme, and also why the related activities underway are so halting and shrouded with ambiguity.

Future prospects?

While there are few public signs that a National ID Card for Canada is imminent, the situation is in flux and may shift suddenly. Certainly the inhibiting factors discussed above by no means guarantee that the current stasis will last long. Eventually the technical problems will be worked out and unless there is a major change in political will in the USA, it will establish durable standards and the rest of the infrastructure needed for routine identity authentication at its borders. Then the pressure on Canada to follow suit will rise considerably, even if the effectiveness of ID technologies as an anti-terrorism measure remains imaginary. With a majority government federally willing to take bigger political risks and play a stronger hand in negotiations with the provinces, ID management and documentation systems can also move faster domestically.

On the other hand, some of the pressures may lessen. If the fear of a terrorist threat is allowed to subside and the severe limits of identity technologies as means for assuring security become more widely recognized, there will be less of an apparent imperative to enrol everyone in biometric ID schemes. A new US Administration in January 2009 less aggressive in imposing untried technological solutions of dubious merit would likewise lower the heat.

On balance however, it would be foolhardy to predict that Canada would remain an international outlier indefinitely. More likely is a haphazard series of incremental steps towards some form of National ID scheme. In this probable scenario, the various current ID-related activities we have documented here will have laid much of the groundwork for such an infrastructure. So while the slower than expected pace has given valuable time for a public debate, its absence is not an encouraging sign. Among all the various behind the scenes activities there has been no serious attempt to consult with the public about these developments – ones that arguably touch core concerns about the relationship between Canadian citizens and their government. Since 2003, when the Parliamentary Standing Committee that considered a biometric National ID Card issued its report posing a host of specific questions and calling for a broad public review, the federal government has moved in the opposite direction from the recommendations it solicited and received. While the border crossing documents currently being developed do not constitute a full National ID Card system, they do raise many of the same issues that concerned the Committee and deserve similar public examination. Why delay further opening an informed public debate that can help Canadians shape national identity policies that will serve them well for the decades to come?

Acknowledgements

We appreciate the research funding support provided by the Initiative for the New Economy (INE) programme of the Social Science and Humanities Research Council (SSHRC) and the Contributions Programme of the federal Office of the Privacy Commissioner (OPC). We are also grateful to Colin Bennett, David Lyon and Lucy Suchman for their helpful editorial advice, and to Joe Cox and Charleen Davidson of the FIS Inforum for their assistance in the final preparation.

Notes

1 This chapter draws heavily upon the results of the research project 'CAN ID? Visions for Canada: Identity Policy Projections and Policy Alternatives', which examined the current state of identity policy development across the various relevant federal and provincial programmes with a view to highlighting the feasible and attractive identity policy options. The research was conducted jointly by the authors, researchers based at the University of Toronto's Faculty of Information Studies and the London School of Economics' Department of Information Systems, with funding from the federal Office of Privacy Commissioner and SSHRC. Online. Available: http://www.fis.utoronto.ca/research/iprp/publications/PDFs/CANID/CANIDreportv2gaJul3.pdf

2 Canada, like Britain, had National ID Cards during wartime, but these were terminated soon after hostilities ended (see Thompson's Chapter 9, in this volume). Canada is home to more than 300 'First Nations', which with their 'Indian Card' have a form of imposed National ID Card (see Brown's Chapter 4, in this volume.) The USA is also not officially developing a National ID Card *per se*, but as Kelly Gates argues (Chapter 13), their Real ID Act can be viewed as a *de facto* National ID.

3 For example, the Parliamentary Standing Committee that was charged to look into the case for a National Identity Card for Canada, when they questioned why so few countries do not have identity cards, remarked, 'The relationship between the individual and the state in Canada, the U.S., the U.K. and Australia was also discussed as a commonality that distinguishes our countries from those with a long-standing tradition of National identity card systems'.

4 Ipsos-Reid/CTV/*Globe and Mail* poll conducted 17–20 September, 2001 (*n* = 1,000), reported 6 October, 2001 in the *Globe and Mail*.

5 It appears that the SPP supersedes or replaces the Smart Borders Declaration because the most recent Smart Borders Status Report was released in December 2004 and the SPP was announced in March 2005.

6 Council of Canadians, 2006. Citizen's Guide to the Security and Prosperity Partnership (SPP) See: http://www.canadians.org/integratethis/backgrounders/guide/ABCs.html. Interestingly, even the North American Competitiveness Council, comprised of 30 chief executives from Canada, the USA and Mexico, which advises the three leaders, argued in a progress report that elected politicians need active input if the public is to understand and support measures for harmonizing security and consumer regulations. 'In particular, the leaders should consider ways to ensure that legislatures of the three countries remain fully informed about progress and actively engaged in the process of improving the region's competitiveness'. *National Post*, 21 August, 2007 Online. Available: http://www.canada.com/nationalpost/news/story.html?-id=8775f9c1-60aa-4c68-a242-e418cfa0547f

7 PASS (People Access Security Service (PASS) card), which the US Department of Homeland Security (DHS) is developing as an alternative to passports.

8 See, 'Washington driver's licenses to carry EPC Gen 2 inlays' by Mary Catherine O'Connor, 30 July, 2007, *RFID Journal*. Online. Available: http://www.rfidjournal.com/article/articleview/3514/1/1/ (accessed 8 August 2007). Interestingly, this article makes no mention of citizenship information being recorded on the card, presumably because the Real-ID Act restricts licence issuing to US citizens only.

9 For instance, 'Travelers face frustrating passport delays', *USA Today*, 31 May, 2007. Online. Available: http://www.usatoday.com/travel/news/2007-05-31-passport-woes_N.htm. 'Passport delays draws an apology', *Boston Globe*, 23 July, 2007. Online. Available: http://www.boston.com/news/nation/articles/2007/07/23/passport_backlog_draws_an_apology. 'Minister Day announces progress on WHTI with the United States and increased security cooperation with Mexico', *Public Safety Canada Press Release*, 23 February, 2007. Online. Available: http://www.securitepublique.gc.ca/-media/nr/2007/nr20070223-1-en.asp

10 The six areas of 'concern' draw from EPIC's privacy analysis of facial recognition technology: Storage, Vulnerability, Confidence, Authenticity, Linking and Ubiquity. The four other areas of 'risk' mentioned are: Function creep, Third party access, Centralized retention and Individuals' loss of control.

11 A summary of the Facial Recognition Project PIA is available on the Passport Canada website: http://www.ppt.gc.ca/publications/facial_recognition.aspx?lang=e. Access to Information (ATI) requests to obtain the full PIA and that for the biometric passport itself are pending.

12 Now referred to as the Inter-jurisdictional Information Sharing Exchange (IJIE) programme.

13 Identity Management: Mapping the Continuum: Phase 1, March 31, 2005, p. 8. File Name: BTEP IdM Final Report. Version 0.0.2, obtained through Access to Information (ATI) from Treasury Board Secretariat.

14 The inter-relationships between programmes and documents are presented in a matrix in the accompanying document. File name: IDM ID-DOC Interrelationships, which is an appendix to the report.

15 See Note 14.

16 For example, according to Canadian officials 'the trade across the Ambassador bridge at Windsor/Detroit (16,000 trucks/day) reflects the greatest amount of trade at any single crossing point on the face of the earth'. See: http://ias.berkeley.edu/canada/Sanford-NewNorth1002.htm

Bibliography

Angus Reid Global Monitor (2007) 'Canadians Open to National ID Card', 1 August. Online. Available: http://www.angusreid.com/polls/index.cfm/fuseaction-/viewItem/itemID/16691 (accessed 19 November 2007).

Bouma, T. (2006) 'Identity: setting the larger context and achieve the right outcomes', presentation at CACR Workshop, Toronto, 3 November. Online. Available: http://www.cacr.math.uwaterloo.ca/conferences/2006/psw/agenda.html (accessed 19 November 2007).

Bronskil, J. (2004) 'Plan to match Canadian passport photos with terrorist watch lists in works', *Canadian Press*, 29 August.

Bronskil, J. (2007) 'Passport Canada pleads for cash', *Canadian Press,* 15 July.

Canada Border Services Agency (2007a) 'Travel Documents for Entering the United States', 27 July. Online. Available: http://www.cbsa-asfc.gc.ca/whti-ivho/gov-gouv-eng.html (accessed 19 November 2007).

Canada Border Services Agency (2007b) 'About Nexus', 16 October. Online. Available: http://www.cbsa-asfc.gc.ca/prog/nexus/about-sujet-eng.html (accessed 19 November 2007).

Canadian Press (2007) 'Information Needed on Travellers: Security Chief', 26 September. Online. Available: http://www.ctv.ca/servlet/ArticleNews/story/CTVNews/20070926/traveller_information_070926?s_name=&no_ads= (accessed 19 November 2007).

CBC Radio Hourly News (2007) 26 February. Online. Available: http://www.cbc.ca/news/ (accessed 19 November 2007).

Clarkson, S., with Davidson Ladly, S., Merwart, M. and Thorne, C. (2005) 'The primitive realities of North-American transnational governance', in E. Grande and L.W. Pauly (eds) *Complex Sovereignty: Reconstituting Political Authority in the Twenty-first Century*, Toronto: University of Toronto Press.

Clement, A., Guerra, R., Johnson, J. and Stalder, F. (2002) 'National Identification Schemes (NIDS): A remedy against terrorist attack?', in K. Brunnstein and J. Berleur (eds) *Proceedings of the Sixth Conference on Human Choice and Computers* HCC6, IFIP World Computer Congress, Dordrecht: Kluwer. Online. Available: http://www3.

fis.utoronto.ca/research/iprp/publications/IFIP_NIDS_final_reprint.pdf (accessed 19 November 2007).

Council of Canadians (2006) 'Citizen's Guide to the Security and Prosperity Partnership (SPP)'. Online. Available: http://www.canadians.org/integratethis/back-grounders/guide/ABCs.html (accessed 19 November 2007).

CTV.ca News (2006) 'Day puts National ID Card back on the agenda', 17 February. Online. Available: http://www.ctv.ca/servlet/ArticleNews/story/CTVNews/2006-0217/id_card_060217?s_name=&no_ads= (accessed 19 November 2007).

Department of Finance Canada (2006) 'Canadian Budget 2006', 2 May. Online. Available: http://www.fin.gc.ca/budget06/bp/bpc3de.htm (accessed 19 November 2007).

Electronic Privacy Information Centre (2006) 'Homeland Security PASS Card: Leave Home Without It', August. Online. Available: http://www.epic.org/privacy/surveil-lance/spotlight/0806/ (accessed 19 November 2007).

Ferguson, R., Benzi, R., and Harper, T. (2007) 'Ontario cautioned on drivers' licenses', *Toronto Star,* 23 February. Online. Available: http://www.thestar.com/News/arti-cle/184971 (accessed 19 November 2007).

Foreign Affairs and International Trade Canada (2001) 'Building a Smart Border for the 21st Century on the Foundation of a North American Zone of Confidence', 12 December. Online. Available: http://www.dfait-maeci.gc.ca/anti-terrorism/declaration-en.asp (accessed 19 November 2007).

Foreign Affairs and International Trade Canada (2003) 'The Secure Flow of People', 2 February. Online. Available: http://www.dfait-maeci.gc.ca/anti-terrorism/actionplan-en.asp (accessed 19 November 2007).

Foreign Affairs and International Trade Canada (2004) 'Smart Border Action Plan Status Report', 17 December. Online. Available: http://geo.international.gc.ca/can-am/main/border/status-en.asp (accessed 19 November 2007).

Foreign Affairs and International Trade Canada (2007) '32-point Action Plan', 1 October. Online. Available: http://geo.international.gc.ca/can-am/main/border/32_point_action-en.asp (accessed 19 November 2007).

Globe and Mail (2006) 'Day Proposes National ID card', 17 February. Online. Available: http://www.theglobeandmail.com/servlet/story/RTGAM.20060217.wstockwell0217/BNStory/National/home (accessed 19 November 2007).

Government of Canada (2004) *Canada Gazette*, 22 September, Vol. 138, No. 19. Online. Available: http://canadagazette.gc.ca/partII/2004/20040922/html/si113-e.html (accessed 19 November 2007).

Government of Canada (2006) *Canada Gazette*, 28 June, Vol. 140, No. 13. Online. Available: http://canadagazette.gc.ca/partII/2006/20060628/html/si95-e.html (accessed 19 November 2007).

Government of Canada. Office of the Prime Minister (2006) 'Leaders' Joint Statement', 31 March. Online. Available: http://www.pm.gc.ca/eng/media.asp?category=1&id=1085 (accessed 19 November 2007).

Government of Canada. Privy Council Office (2004) 'Securing an Open Society: Canada's National Security Policy', April. Online. Available: http://www.pcobcp.gc.ca/default.asp?Language=E-&Page=informationresources&Sub=publications&Doc=natsecurnat/natsecurnat_e.htm (accessed 19 November 2007).

Government of Canada. Standing Committee on Citizenship and Immigration (2003) 'National Identity Card for Canada?: Interim Report of the Standing Committee on Citizenship and Immigration', October. Online. Available: http://www.oipc.bc.ca/pdfs/public/cimmrp06-e.pdf (accessed 19 November 2007).

Menic, J. and Turner, M. (June 2006) 'National Routing System for Vital Events'. Online. Available: http://www.unece.org/stats/documents/ece/ces/sem.54/3.e.pdf (accessed 19 November 2007).

MERX (2006) 'Facial Recognition System'. Online. Available: http://www.merx. com/English/SUPPLIER_Menu.Asp?WCE=Show&TAB=1&State=7&id=PW-%24EEM -006-14751&hcode=shsxpr2tIBMeERly4npDoQ%3D%3D (accessed 19 November 2007).

Schneier, B. (2003) *Beyond Fear: Thinking Sensibly in an Uncertain World*, New York: Copernicus.

SPP.gov. (n.d.) 'SPP Myths vs Facts'. Online. Available: http://www.spp.gov/ myths_vs_facts.asp (accessed 19 November 2007).

Webb, M. (2007) *Illusions of Security: Global Surveillance and Democracy in the Post-9/11 World*, San Francisco: City Lights Books.

Wikipedia (2007) 'Canada–United States border', 19 November. Online. Available: http://en.wikipedia.org/wiki/Canada%E2%80%93United_States_border (accessed 19 November 2007).

Section Four

Transnational regimes

15 ICAO and the biometric RFID passport

History and analysis

Jeffrey M. Stanton

Radio frequency identification (RFID) systems provide digital information about an object without the need to touch or view the object. RFID tags can store information about the history, provenance, contents, attributes and location of an object and can provide that information to an RFID reader system upon request. Such systems promise to move the world one step closer to the so-called 'Internet of Things'. In this vision, objects in the physical world – including human beings – will become as accessible to information systems as data already are (ITU 2005). Governments, industrial consortia and individual organizations have begun to examine and/or adopt RFID technologies as a means of identifying people, with the expectation of improvements in flexibility, efficiency and productivity that outstrip those provided by mature technologies such as magnetic stripe cards and barcodes (Engels *et al.* 2001). On 14 August, 2006, the US Department of State began issuing passports containing an RFID chip encoded with biographical and biometric information. Since 1 January, 2007, all newly issued US passports have contained this technology.

Using RFID as part of a personal identification system generally involves scanning and recording a biometrically unique feature of a person and encoding these data digitally on an RFID chip (i.e. enrolment) for later retrieval and analysis during an authentication process. The specifics of the biometric used and the security issues related to storing the biometric data on mobile media make RFID-based personal identification systems problematic from several perspectives. For example, it is often important to encrypt the biometric data using asymmetric key (public key) cryptography, but this also requires an infrastructure for security certificate issuance and maintenance that has proven difficult to administer, particularly on a large scale.

One organization with a particular interest in RFID and biometric-based personal identification systems is the International Civil Aviation Organization (ICAO) (http://www.icao.int). The ICAO is an international governmental organization – a specialized agency of the United Nations – that has historically been instrumental in the development of strategies and standards for implementing machine readable passports. The ICAO's 'Machine Readable Travel Document' (MRTD) initiative evolved from its roots in a 1986 resolution of the ICAO's internal governance body into a full fledged research programme on biometrics, RFID and anti-fraud technologies.

On the face of it, the efforts of a capable international body to develop technical standards with the potential to improve air travel safety seem laudable. Although legal scholars, such as Osieke (1979) have questioned the ICAO's authority to set and enforce international policy, the organization boasts participation by 189 nations and has a 60-year history of improving the quality and safety of the world-wide air travel infrastructure. At the same time, however, the ICAO standards are sometimes seen by politicians as a quick and inexpensive basis for new national policy (Singel 2004).

For these reasons, the ICAO seems to exert a substantial influence on the technology and adoption of RFID-based personal identification card systems, at least in the context of international travel. This chapter examines the ICAO's involvement in the development and deployment of the RFID-enabled, biometric passport to analyses of the most prominent influences on its technological policy-making processes. Guided by Hosein's (2004) discussion of policy laundering, I address the question of whether the US government used the ICAO as a shortcut around a more substantive policy-making process about the use of RFID and biometric identification in international travel documents. To accomplish this, I present a brief history of the ICAO followed by a timeline of the organization's internal deliberative process that led to the RFID and biometric passport recommendations. I then describe a parallel timeline for the US legislative process in order to examine the precedence of key events in the two processes. Results of this analysis may illuminate strategies for injecting the interests of civil libertarians into the processes by which the ICAO standards are informally adopted into national standards for personal identification.

A brief history of the ICAO

At the close of the Second World War, the USA and its allies anticipated the need for a uniform body of standards and regulations that would govern the operation of non-military aviation in the post-war period. Representatives of 55 nations convened in Chicago in 1944, to discuss the development of a body of regulatory controls that would enhance the safety, efficiency and commercial viability of international air travel. By 1947, the International Civil Aviation Organization existed as an international, non-governmental agency charged with the responsibility of achieving, 'safe, secure and sustainable development of civil aviation through cooperation amongst its member States'.[1]

The ICAO is an agency of the United Nations (UN), itself also created in the immediate post-war period. The Economic and Social Council of the UN, which was established in 1946 under the UN's original charter, nominally controls the operations of the UN's specialized agencies, functional commissions and regional commissions. As in other specialized agencies of the UN – including the International Telecommunications Union and the International Maritime Organization – the ICAO has a substantial autonomous existence independent of the auspices of the UN. For example, the ICAO has its own international headquarters in Montreal, its own operating budget, its own charter and bylaws, and even its own rules for state membership and privileges.

The ICAO's regulatory reach includes a wide variety of responsibilities such as air navigation, flight safety, environmental protection and international aviation treaties. As a nutshell example, in an effort to improve flight safety, the ICAO co-ordinated the ratification by 67 nations in 1991 of an international treaty to chemically mark all plastic explosives during manufacture (*U.N. Chronicle* 2001). Most pertinent to the present document, the ICAO has always had active involvement in the standardization of passenger travel documents. In 1968, the ICAO established an advisory panel which was charged with the responsibility of standardizing passports to a sufficient extent such that they would be machine readable. A resulting standard was issued in 1978; it focused on the use of optical character recognition to obtain essential traveler information from the passport document. Upon completion of this activity and subsequent disbanding of the original advisory panel, a new, more permanent committee was formed in 1986 called the Technical Advisory Group on Machine Readable Travel Documents, abbreviated as TAG/MRTD.

TAG/MRTD and new passport technology

TAG/MRTD comprises a group of experts from 13 of the ICAO's member states including the USA, Canada, Australia, New Zealand, 6 European Union states, Russia, India and Japan. So-called 'delegations' of experts from various government agencies (e.g. the US Department of Homeland Security) represent each of the member states at TAG/MRTD meetings. Only the leading individual (the 'member') from each delegation has the right to vote on decisions before the advisory group, but other individuals in each delegation may participate in debates, discussions and subcommittees. In addition, 'observers' from government, other non-governmental organizations (such as national and international standards organizations and aviation industry representatives) may attend TAG/MRTD meetings by invitation and may thus provide input into the committee's working activities. Observers at meetings over the past five years have included individuals from more than 20 countries including Korea, Israel, Saudi Arabia and China. These working activities are divided into three general areas: education and promotion (mainly to UN member states that are not yet compliant with existing machine readable travel document standards), document content and format and new technologies.

The new technologies working group naturally has had the greatest involvement in the analysis of RFID and biometric authentication strategies for personal identification. The most recent meeting of the group – which always convenes at the ICAO headquarters in Montreal – took place in September of 2005. In a working paper for this meeting, the new technologies group reported on the status of their work with respect to standards for biometric identification technologies that include RFID (ICAO 2005). In brief, the initial work of the group focused on a read-only technology containing a so-called 'contactless' chip. In this context, contactless is interchangeable with RFID, although the type of technology they considered was a subset of the available range of RFID technologies. The group focused on 'read-only' technologies with the expectation that a travel document whose information content was finalized at the time of manufacture and not changeable afterwards would simplify some of the security issues involved.

The new technologies working group resolved to use biometric data describing the passport holder's face as the sole basis for the chip's biometric content. The recommended implementation allows for states to adopt secondary biometrics such as fingerprints or iris scans if they wish, but digitally encoded facial features were selected as the primary and universal form of identification. One critical advantage of using facial features is that the verification processes and algorithms can be deferred to the individual countries' passport control authorities. The travel document stores an encrypted and compressed photograph of the individual, which a reader device uploads to a verification system. The verification system uses a camera to capture a facial image of the traveler in real time, and uses an algorithm to compare the stored and live versions of the individual's face. This strategy allows states to choose and update their verification systems freely and thus eliminates the need for the ICAO to lock in a particular verification algorithm or method.

The new technologies working group also resolved to recommend a contactless integrated circuit device for storage and retrieval of travel document data. The group settled upon the International Standards Organization's ISO/IEC 14443, a short read range (approximately 10 cm) radio frequency (13.56 MHz) standard for proximity cards. This package, originally published as an international standard in April 2000, is considered a relatively mature RFID technology with a wide variety of form factors and demonstrated interoperability among different vendors' product offerings. The new technologies working group specified that the traveller data stored on these RFID devices would be digitally signed and that some data stored on them would be encrypted (although not necessarily the photographic/biometric data). Both specifications generally require public key encryption, which in turn requires a 'public key infrastructure' (PKI) – that is, a set of facilities for distributing and maintaining the digital certificates, encryption keys, revocation lists and so forth which are the heart of most public key encryption systems. The working group explicitly disavowed the option of having the ICAO (or any other single agency) serve as a central authority for PKI:

> It is not feasible that the ICAO, or some other single, central organization will assign, maintain or manage secure private keys for any State. Despite many strategic alliances among participants this will not be recognized as being a trusted solution.
>
> (ICAO 2004a: 8)

Having made this commitment, the ICAO subsequently qualified their position by suggesting one aspect of the public key infrastructure that would require both centralization and single agency management. Specifically, in a 2006 'information paper' the ICAO Secretariat underscored the need for a single source repository of states' *public* keys (ICAO 2006). In a public key cryptography system, public keys are the cryptographic information elements which may be (in fact, must be) freely shared among systems that exchange encrypted information. In taking this position, the ICAO bowed to the logistical challenge of having each of 189 member states individually send their public key(s) to every one of the other 188 states. Note that the so-called 'public key directory' that the ICAO planned on implementing is just one administrative element out of many needed for a complete PKI, and an ICAO controlled public key directory does not imply fully centralized control of the cryptographic infrastructure needed for RFID passports.

In summary, then, the new technologies working group of TAG/MRTD has been instrumental in developing and publishing a set of standards that will allow the ICAO member states to issue machine readable travel documents – primarily passports but also potentially visas and other document types – that will incorporate a short range RFID chip. This RFID chip will contain biometric information about the passenger in the form of a digital photograph of the face along with encrypted material requiring the use of public key cryptography and a partially-centralized PKI to support it. Although the standards are not in a completely mature state at this writing, member states have already begun to issue machine readable RFID passports containing digital photographs. These states include the USA, Canada, UK, Australia, Singapore, Malaysia, Finland, France, Germany, and a number of other European countries.

US legislation and TAG/MRTD – A case of policy laundering?

The ICAO's primary mission – to support secure international aviation – is at heart a beneficent one. Few would disagree with the value or importance of helping to develop and maintain a transportation infrastructure that provides safe international passage for people and goods. Over its 60-year history, the ICAO boasts many notable successes such as uniform air traffic control, noise management, and airport ground signage, marking and lighting. At the same time, however, scholars such as Osieke (1979) have underlined an important tension between the ICAO and its member states. While the organizing basis of the ICAO, the so-called Chicago Convention gives the organization certain powers with respect to the regulation of international aviation, the extent of those powers has been in continuous dispute since the early days of the organization. The ICAO has some limits with respect to its ability to impose regulations, procedures and standard practices on matters occurring within the bounds of the sovereign states that comprise its membership.

For example, in 1971, India suspended over-flights by Pakistani airliners in the wake of destructive events that had occurred at Lahore airport. Pakistan filed a complaint with the ICAO alleging that India had no right to unilaterally suspend over-flights because of its status as a member of the ICAO and its concomitant acceptance of international aviation treaties. This case eventually rose to the level of the International Court of Justice, which affirmed the authority of the ICAO to mediate that particular dispute. At the same time however, the Court noted that the ICAO's jurisdiction over such matters was a reasonable matter for states to bring before the Court, thereby effectively curbing the power of the ICAO with respect to regulating sovereign states. In this light, one might conclude that the ICAO can *influence* the conduct of states through the issuance of standards, rules, and recommendations, but its power with respect to coercing states into compliance is less than absolute.

This example represents a relatively pure instance of the interests and power of a particular state – in this case India – opposed to the regulatory authority of an intergovernmental international organization. A more subtle example arises when the same international regulatory authority is used within a country to expedite or circumvent normal policy-making methods. The ICAO's personnel – particularly those who work in advisory groups, such as TAG/MRTD – are each and all representatives of their respective countries. Most of these individuals are politicians, political appointees, or representatives of particular corporate interests. As such, the workings of the ICAO are inevitably influenced by a range of specialized interests from their respective domestic constituencies. It is possible that these specialized interests use the regulatory power of the international organization to circumvent policy-making practices that might have been used by more generalized constituencies. Some have referred to such practices as *policy laundering*. First alluded to in a book on international business by Braithwaite and Drahos (2000: 68), policy laundering refers to the practice by one branch of a government (e.g. the executive branch) leveraging the power of an international organization against the normative deliberative activities of a nation (e.g. in the form of public debate and the development of laws or regulations by other branches of government).

For example, late in 2001 the Council of Europe, a non-governmental organization that coordinates international treaties for 43 European nations, approved a Cybercrime Treaty whose global adoption would force signatory nations to permit the use of advanced digital wiretapping techniques. Although the USA was ostensibly only an observer at the Council of Europe discussions, it was widely seen as the major impetus behind the treaty at a time when controversial wiretapping programmes such as FBI's so called Carnivore were running into major objections domestically. Ratification of the Cybercrime Treaty by the US Senate in 2006 thus represented an end run around the normal deliberative and legislative processes that might have prevented or severely curtailed programmes such as Carnivore.

The foregoing example provides some insight into what Putnam (1988) referred to as a 'two-level game' of international diplomacy and domestic politics. In the two-level game, central leaders who are conducting the focal policy negotiation sit simultaneously at two negotiating tables. The Level I table comprises the international forum (e.g. a treaty-making body) while the Level 2 table comprises domestic constituents (e.g. a treaty-ratifying authority, such as a congress or plebiscite). Dilemmas in the two-level game arise from the fact that in most negotiations the interests of the Level I and Level II bodies are unaligned. Putnam (1988) sensibly observes that none of the two level games that unfold in practice exhibit pure unidirectional causation. Put plainly, it is not the case that domestic interests are articulated, set into stone, and brought to the international forum for negotiation. Neither is it the case that a treaty is negotiated in a vacuum and then brought back home for an unambiguous thumbs-up or thumbs-down. Instead, there are inevitably reciprocal feedback loops in which domestic constituencies influence the negotiation process in the international body, and the course of the negotiation in the international body may in turn affect coalitions or opinions among the domestic constituencies, and so on.

With respect to the formulation of laws that affect privacy and civil liberties, Hosein (2004) describes three activities in which governments may engage in order to resolve dilemmas in the two level game: policy laundering, modelling and forum shifting. His definitions of these activities are as follows:

> Policy laundering is a practice where policymakers make use of other jurisdictions to circumvent national deliberative processes. Modeling occurs when governments... shape their laws based on laws developed in other jurisdictions. Forum shifting occurs when actors pursue rules in [IGOs] ... and, when opposition and challenges arise, shift to other IGOs or agreement structures.
>
> (Hosein 2004: 187–188)

Using these definitions, policy laundering addresses two-level game dilemmas by forcing a preferred Level I solution onto a Level II constituency through the symbolic authority or real influence of the forum where the Level I negotiation occurred. Modelling is, in essence, a process that occurs domestically, that is, primarily or solely at Level II. A prior Level I negotiation involving central leadership need not have occurred in a case of modelling. Finally, forum shifting comprises an effort to resolve a two-level dilemma through changing the venue in which Level I negotiations occur. Such shifts are undertaken by central leaders under the assumption that changes to the position or interests of the domestic constituencies (i.e. Level II) are intractable, or at least less politic than shifting the forum. At a first level of approximation, then, policy laundering involves precedence of Level I over Level II, forum shifting involves precedence of Level II over Level I, and modeling lacks clear precedence. Note that taken together, policy laundering, modeling, and forum shifting do not comprise an exhaustive array of techniques for resolving two-level game dilemmas.

Hosein (2004) has applied the notion of policy laundering to the ICAO's pursuit of an RFID-enabled biometric passport. Hosein contended that the USA was engaged in policy laundering when it passed the Enhanced Border Security and Visa Entry Reform Act of 2002. The law contains a variety of sections pertaining to immigration control. Most relevant to this chapter, this law called for the integration of a machine readable biometric method of authentication into passports over the period 2003–2006 (Section 303 of Public Law 107-173). The law made explicit reference to the adoption of standards under development by the ICAO. The law also contained an implicit threat against the 27 so-called visa waiver countries. Specifically, the law indicated that those countries that failed to adopt a machine readable biometric passport during the specified timeframe would be dropped from the visa waiver programme. Under the visa waiver programme, citizens from countries such as Australia, which have historically friendly relations with the USA, do not have to obtain a visa in advance of their entry into the USA. Citizens of countries that do not participate in the visa waiver programme must submit to the US-VISIT procedures, which, among other measures, require fingerprinting when entering and leaving the country. In effect, then, visa waiver countries were strong-armed into adoption of machine readable biometric passports by the passage of the law.

This law was originally introduced by Representative James Sensenbrenner (R-Wisconsin) in the US House of Representatives in December of 2001, a mere three months following the events of 9/11.[2] The law was passed with minimal debate, although the executive branch introduced a few months of delay in the consideration of the bill as a result of an attempt to include a reactivation of an immigration amnesty clause that had expired from an earlier law. The law was considered by the House Judiciary, House Intelligence, House International Relations, House Ways and Means, and House Transportation and Infrastructure committees, from which it was returned to the House floor and passed on a voice vote with no debate. Subsequently, the bill was considered by the Senate Committee on the Judiciary, after which it was debated on the Senate floor. Successful amendments relevant to the present chapter included a requirement that visa waiver countries report the theft of blank passports to the USA, and a one year extension to the timeframe for implementing machine-readable passports (to October 2004; the deadline was subsequently extended twice). The bill was subsequently passed unanimously in the Senate, and after approval of amendments by the House, was referred to the President, who signed the bill in May 2002. Nearly two years passed before the US government had workable plans to incorporate RFID chips into the passport. By 2004, documents from the State Department[3] suggest that US government planning for creating an RFID-enabled passport was well underway (though nowhere near completion).

It is important to note that this law was not Representative Sensenbrenner's first foray into the use of biometric identification technologies. US Congress records from the THOMAS information system show that Representative Sensenbrenner cosponsored the Immigration in the National Interest Act of 1995 (H.R. 1915, 104th Congress) and the Immigration Control and Financial Responsibility Act of 1996 (H.R. 2202, 104th Congress). The original language for these bills contained requirements that legal immigrants who wished to cross US borders to obtain US employment would be required to carry an identity card that contained biometric features. Thus, it seems certain that Representative Sensenbrenner had substantial knowledge of the use of biometrics in identification at least seven years before the introduction of the Enhanced Border Security and Visa Entry Reform Act of 2002.

As our analysis below will suggest, the 2002 passage of this law provided substantial new impetus to TAG/MRTD's new technologies working group, which held primary responsibility for the development of the biometric component of a machine readable passport. Representative Sensenbrenner's inclusion of language in the original bill requiring adoption of the ICAO's emerging standard suggests that he and his staff were, at minimum, aware of the work of TAG/MRTD prior to December of 2001. Additionally, Sensenbrenner must have had sufficient confidence in the progress of TAG/MRTD that he could argue effectively before his colleagues – primarily in the House Judiciary Committee, of which he was chair at the time of introduction of this bill, that TAG/MRTD would produce a workable standard within the timeframe specified by the bill. Thus, on the face of the matter, a tight level of integration between US policy development and the workings of an international governmental organization appears to have existed at the time of passage of the Enhanced Border Security and Visa Entry Reform Act.

Ironically, however, Representative Sensenbrenner sent a disapproving letter to the European Union (EU) on 5 April, 2005 (Zetter 2005) criticizing the EU's pursuit of including RFID in machine readable passports. In this letter, Sensenbrenner took both the ICAO and the EU to task for wasting time on RFID when simpler and more secure technologies were available. He emphasized that the Enhanced Border Security and Visa Entry Reform Act did not require RFID, but only a biometric identification technique and machine readability. At the same time, a considerable degree of analysis and debate occurred with respect to the inclusion of RFID in passports, particularly with respect to the lack of encryption of the biographical and biometric data recommended by TAG/MRTD. In particular, panelists at the 2005 Computers, Freedom and Privacy conference,[4] including cryptography expert Bruce Schneier, harshly criticized the US plans for an ICAO-compliant passport that contained an RFID chip but did not encrypt the data stored on it. The critique was based on the idea that an RFID passport can be easily 'skimmed', a process by which an unauthorized person uses an RFID reader to obtain passport holders' personal information without their consent or knowledge. Frank Moss, Deputy Assistant Secretary of State for Passport Services, gave opening remarks on this panel, and made public comments after the conference suggesting that the panelists' discussion and other information he had gleaned at the conference had changed his mind with respect to the importance of including encryption on an RFID-capable passport. One of the other pieces of evidence that reportedly swayed his opinion evidently arose from a demonstration of an RFID reader that could obtain data from a 13.56 MHz chip (supposedly limited to a 10 cm read range) at a distance of 30 feet.[5] One of the ironic aspects of these comments is that TAG-MTRD had previously suggested a method of preventing the so called 'skimming' attack that was the source of the criticism against the plans of the USA. TAG-MRTD's method, called Basic Access Control, would have required passport control agents to optically scan the physical passport document before subjecting it to an RFID scan. This optical scan, which required direct physical access to the interior pages of the document, would have created a cryptographic hash that would function as a kind of password to unlock the RFID features of the passport. Although this would have severely curtailed the skimming attack, the USA rejected the idea, apparently in a belief that no valuable information could be read from the passport and/or that other protections against skimming (e.g. metal fibres in the passport cover) would suffice.

As the foregoing discussion suggests, the implementation of a machine readable biometric passport does not appear to have proceeded smoothly. The implementation details that were left to the ICAO to implement following the passage of the Enhanced Border Security and Visa Entry Reform Act led to a range of controversies. These controversies centred on the necessity of RFID, the use of cryptographic protections, and the pace at which the USA and other countries adopted the required technologies. In the analysis below, I examine the activities and composition of the TAG/MRTD new technologies working group over the period of 1997–2005 to document how the USA and the ICAO interacted during this critical period.

TAG/MRTD and the new technologies group 1997–2005

In 1997, TAG/MRTD began a comprehensive review of Document 9303, the ICAO's general standard on machine readable travel documents, with an eye towards harmonizing all of the language to include the effects of new technologies (ICAO 2004b). At first the pace of progress was very slow – not an atypical finding for TAG/MRTD. The first revision of the standard was not released until two years later. Five years passed before a revision to Part 3 (travel document design) was issued to include consideration of newly available machine reading and security technologies. Importantly, although the inclusion of biometrics had been raised as early as 1993 (possibly in connection with the World Trade Center bombing) and formally recommended to the ICAO in 1995, it took until May 2003 for TAG/MRTD to generate an acceptable standard – the so-called 'biometric blueprint'. In the same series of 2003 updates, TAG/MRTD issued a 'normative annex' – essentially a brief outline to be filled in later – on the inclusion of contactless chips in passports (ICAO 2003).

This late and sketchy inclusion of consideration of RFID appears to be in accord with Representative Sensenbrenner's public objections to the inclusion of RFID as a response to the Enhanced Border Security and Visa Entry Reform Act. Although contactless chips were undoubtedly a topic of informal discussion in the new technologies working group, the fact that no formal mention of contactless chips appears until the 2003 TAG/MRTD meeting report suggests that the USA was not a proponent of an RFID enabled passport prior to 2003, and was thus not using the ICAO as a surreptitious method for developing this particular technology. In addition, popular press reports of official US government reactions to the inclusion of RFID subsequent to 2003 also affirm this position (Zetter 2005).

I thus focus attention on assessing the extent to which the USA could be considered to have manipulated the ICAO's deliberations as a method to advance the development of biometric passports. Prior to 2003, public documents recording the conduct and results of TAG/MRTD meetings are not publicly available, but Kefauver (2003) has summarized some of the activities of the group from 1997 to 2002. Between 1994 and 1997 TAG/MRTD did not hold a meeting. At the ninth meeting of TAG/MRTD in January 1997 the group began a review of biometric technology as part of its general revision of Document 9303. In February 1998, the group's technology focus was still on barcodes, although a 'Request for Input' document concerning biometrics was developed. In 1999 and 2000, biometric techniques were not a major agenda item; no meeting was held in 2001. At the thirteenth meeting of TAG/MRTD in February 2002, a variety of vendors conducted technology demonstrations, including demonstrations of biometric enrolment and authentication techniques. The group also generated a 'workbook' on the selection of biometric techniques: essentially a strategy guide to the major criterion issues that the group would consider in settling on a standard for a biometric passport. This workbook evolved into the so-called 'Berlin Resolution', a statement issued by the new technologies working group at a meeting in June 2002. The statement appears below:

ICAO TAG-MRTD/NTWG RESOLUTION N001 – Berlin, 28 June 2002

ICAO TAG-MRTD/NTWG endorses the use of face recognition as the globally interoperable biometric for machine assisted identity confirmation with machine readable travel documents.

ICAO TAG-MRTD/NTWG further recognizes that Member States may elect to use fingerprint and/or iris recognition as additional biometric technologies in support of machine assisted identity confirmation.

(Kefauver 2003)

One final piece of evidence concerning the ostensible use of the ICAO by the USA with respect to biometrics in passports comes from the composition of the new technologies working group. As previously mentioned, TAG/MRTD includes representatives from 13 ICAO member countries. Because the size of a delegation from a country is not specified, however, and because observers may be invited from any country or entity, the size and composition of TAG/MRTD is quite variable. This is particularly true of TAG/MRTD's working groups, which grow, shrink, and change membership in response to the varying external demands on the group. (Formally speaking, these demands are imposed by the Secretariat – the general governing body of the ICAO through a three layer bureaucracy comprising the Air Transport Bureau, the Aviation Security Branch and the Facilitation Section.) Analysis of the new technologies working group membership shows that the official US delegation generally consists of between four and ten members, all of whom represent the federal government. In comparison, Canada usually has four to six delegation members, other TAG/MRTD states have two to four delegation members, and observer countries and organizations usually have only one individual. Agencies represented in the US delegation include the Department of State and the Department of Homeland Security. Among the government delegation, however, about half of the members appear to have been selected for their technical, rather than their political expertise. Some observers from the USA also appear in TAG/MRTD rosters, generally representing segments of the aviation industry (ICAO 2003, 2004a,b, 2005).

Although I could not find rosters for the new technologies working group prior to 2003, the implication from Kefauver (2003) was that this group was relatively balanced with respect to the size of the other two working groups in TAG/MRTD. Starting with the 2003 roster, the new technologies working group swelled to 45 members, as compared with 29 members for the document content and format group and 9 for the education and promotion working group. The new technologies working group remained extraordinarily large through 2004, but shrunk back to a more typical size in 2005 when it was again equal to the content and format groups.

Discussion

To summarize the foregoing material, on the basis of public statements by US officials and the timing of legislation and the activities of TAG/MRTD, it is evident that the USA had little policy interest in promoting an RFID-enabled passport prior to 2003. That an RFID enabled passport is now standard according to the ICAO appears to have come about as a result of forces other than US influence on TAG/MRTD. Thus, it appears unlikely that the USA used policy laundering, modeling, and/or forum shifting as strategies for gaining acceptance of RFID-enabled passports by using the ICAO's leverage.

With respect to biometrics, the evidence is not as clear cut. The introduction of the idea of a biometric passport to TAG/MRTD's deliberations in the 1990s may well have been part of a US plan to push biometrics. Certainly the USA has consistently had strong representation in TAG/MRTD and in the new technologies working group. The legislative history of the Enhanced Border Security and Visa Entry Reform Act makes this interpretation problematic, however. Representative Sensenbrenner's office introduced this bill at a time when the USA was still reeling from the events of 11 September, 2001. The three month delay between these events and the introduction of the bill is consistent with the authoring of original legislation (in contrast, say, to the USA-PATRIOT act, which seems to have been authored prior to 9/11). Further, the relative lack of attention to biometrics paid by TAG/MRTD between 1994 and 2001 suggests that biometric passports were a relatively low priority issue for this group prior to 2001. The relative dearth of congressional debate concerning the Enhanced Border Security and Visa Entry Reform Act is interpretable as resulting from the general flurry of legislative activity following 9/11, rather than as an attempt to ramrod an issue that had received too little deliberation. Additionally, using the two-level game framework, policy modelling involves a precedence of the international forum's deliberations (Level I) leading to an influence process over domestic deliberations (Level II). Thus, if the classic case of policy laundering involves ratification of an international treaty whose contents had been unduly influenced by the opaque activities of an international organization, then the Enhanced Border Security and Visa Entry Reform Act does not fit the mold. This law only made reference to emerging the ICAO standards, and not to a completed treaty or international regulatory structure.

Instead, a plausible case of cause and effect is that 11 September engendered both the passage of the Enhanced Border Security and Visa Entry Reform Act *and* TAG/MRTD's close attention to biometric passports. The Berlin Resolution and the passage of the Act were nearly coincident in time. In addition, the swelling of the new technology working group appeared to follow both the Berlin Resolution and the new-found interest of the USA in increased passport security. Thus, although TAG/MRTD's activities between 2003 and 2005 may have been strongly influenced by the passage of the Enhanced Border Security and Visa Entry Reform Act and the consequent interest of the US delegation on finishing a biometric passport standard, it does not appear that the Act itself resulted from policy laundering prior to its passage in 2002.

From a theoretical standpoint, the actions of the USA and TAG/MRTD seem to match more closely the notion of 'modeling' as described by Hosein (2004). The classic instance of modelling is when a law exists in one state, and a similar law is then adopted in another state using rhetoric, such as, 'Well, they thought it was a good idea, so we should do it too, or we'll be left behind'. Thus, modelling generally focuses on imitation of an existing policy structure. But in the case of the ICAO, the detailed implementation of a biometric RFID passport remained to be completed when the Enhanced Border Security and Visa Entry Reform Act was passed. Representative Sensenbrenner 'sold' the bill to Congress and the president based on the past performance of the ICAO and the expectation that it would eventually produce a workable standard that the USA could adopt for its own passport production. In this light, the policy being emulated was a future work product of an international forum that the central leaders believed could be trusted to serve the prevalent domestic interests. Although logistically very distinct from policy laundering, this strategy is just as perfidious, because like policy laundering it circumvents the domestic deliberative process by hiding implementation details under the cloak of an opaque international deliberation.

The consistent representation of the USA on TAG/MRTD may have provided Representative Sensenbrenner with the idea that the ICAO could be used as a forum for ironing out the many details required for a next generation passport. As noted above, Sensenbrenner cosponsored bills in the 104th congress that contained language concerning the use of biometrics in identity cards – in that case pertaining to the regulation of legal immigrants. Wisconsin, Sensenbrenner's home state, is also the home to several biometrics companies, including one – Verax – that has engaged the lobbying firm American Defense International, Inc. to serve their interests in Washington, DC. So it seems likely that Representative Sensenbrenner was convinced of the efficacy of biometrics for identification technology well before the introduction of the bill leading to the Enhanced Border Security and Visa Entry Reform Act, and for that matter well before 9/11.

Further, because international compliance would eventually be required on a matter such as passports, having those details ironed out in an existing international forum also made strategic sense: For those who promoted the implementation of biometric passports standards issued by the ICAO are doubly useful because they are automatically binding on the 189 member states. Most importantly, because the legislation called for adherence to an international standard that did not exist at the time of its passage, public debate about the eventual implementation details was severely curtailed. In essence, the US government managed to hide the 'end game' of formulating the technology for next generation passports from the US public by transferring the detailed decision making into an international forum that could not as easily be scrutinized as a domestic body (for example, one cannot obtain ICAO documents through a Freedom of Information Act request).

As a result, even though policy laundering does not appear to have occurred in the case of the Enhanced Border Security and Visa Entry Reform Act, the warnings of Hosein (2004), Privacy International (2004), and others still carry weight. As the importance and influence of international governmental organizations has increased, so has the need for mechanisms that ensure public scrutiny of these organizations' activities. In the case of the ICAO and TAG/MRTD, the voluntary (or inadvertent) publication of reports, meeting rosters and meeting summaries has provided a welcome view into the operations of the group. Unfortunately, for each positive example of an international organization that invites scrutiny, there are probably a dozen or more that use opaque deliberative processes.

One positive step with respect to this problem would be to legislate – within the confines of individual democratic governments such as the USA and Canada – public disclosure of each government's involvement and activities with international governmental organizations, to the extent allowable by national security concerns. Although such disclosure is possible through mechanisms such as the Freedom of Information Act, this mechanism assumes that formal records of governmental representatives' participation in the international organizations exists and can be located by the press and advocacy groups. Relatedly, it would be possible and may be desirable to legally compel publicly owned for-profit organizations to disclose observer and advocacy activities in international organizations as part of their array of filings for investors with the Securities and Exchange Commission or the corresponding regulatory bodies in other countries. Finally, international organizations, such as the ICAO are ultimately funded by member governments and these funders can influence charter and rule changes to encourage greater deliberative transparency. Through mechanisms such as these it may be possible for members of the public to have greater access to – and more debate about – the workings of international governmental organizations that influence the standards and regulations affecting us all. Given the extent to which international forums are being used as the locale for negotiations that affect domestic constituencies, this is an important goal advocacy groups must pursue in order to ensure the free flow of policy-making information to the media and general public.

Notes

1 Quoted from the 'Strategic Objectives of the ICAO'. Online. Available: http://www. icao.int/icao/en/strategic_objectives.htm
2 Material for the discussion of the legislative history of the Enhanced Border Security and Visa Entry Reform Act of 2002 was obtained from the THOMAS record for H.R.3525. Online. Available: http://www.congress.gov/cgi-bin/bdquery/z?d107:H.R.3525
3 For example, 'Abstract of Concept of Operations for the Integration of Contactless Chip in the US Passport' was published by the Department of State on 26 April, 2004 and contained a quite extensive discussion of technical requirements, including a detailed proposal from the Government Printing Office for manufacturing the RFID-enabled passports. A PDF of this document is available at: http://www.statewatch.org/news/2004/jul/us-biometric-passport-original.pdf
4 Discussion based on a session entitled 'The Privacy Risks of New Passport Technologies', with an audio transcript of the session is available at: http://www.cfp2005.org/ Programme.html
5 I was not able to obtain a detailed description of this demonstration from available Internet or scholarly sources. Although not impossible, it is highly unlikely that a 13.56 MHz tag could be read at this distance with any type of portable equipment. Smart card chips deployed under the ISO 14443 standard work on the basis of magnetic induction in the

so-called 'near field' (high frequency and ultra-high frequency chips work on a different principle, which makes it possible for them to work at much longer distances). Doubling the read distance for a 13.56 MHz chip, from, e.g. 10 cm to 20 cm, requires an enormous increase in the strength of the local magnetic field generated by the reader device. At 13.56 MHz, the theoretical boundary between the near and far field is at about 3.6 metres, so it is difficult to conceive of a tag operating on magnetic induction that would work at a read range of 30 feet.

Bibliography

Braithwaite, J. and Drahos, P. (2000) *Global Business Regulation*, Cambridge: Cambridge University Press.

Engels, D., Foley, J., Waldrop, J., Sarma, S. and Brock, D. (2001) 'The Networked Physical World: An Automated Identification Architecture', paper presented at the WIAPP, Second IEEE Workshop on Internet Applications.

Hosein, I. (2004) 'The sources of laws: policy dynamics in a digital and terrorized world', *The Information Society* 20(3): 187–99.

ICAO (2003) 'Technical Advisory Group on Machine Readable Travel Documents Fourteenth Meeting (Technical Report No. TAG-MRTD/14)', Montreal: International Civil Aviation Organization.

ICAO (2004a) 'PKI for Machine Readable Travel Documents offering ICC Read-Only Access (Technical Report)', Montreal: International Civil Aviation Organization, Technical Advisory Group, Machine Readable Travel Documents.

ICAO (2004b) 'Work of the Technical Advisory Group on Machine Readable Travel Documents (Technical Report No. FAL/12-WP/20)', Cairo, Egypt: International Civil Aviation Organization.

ICAO (2005) 'Proposed Development of a Technical Report, PKI for Machine Readable Travel Documents, Version 2 (Working Paper No. TAG-MRTD/16; WP/10)', Montreal: International Civil Aviation Organization, Technical Advisory Group on Machine Readable Travel Documents.

ICAO (2006) 'Information Paper – Issues of the ICAO Public Key Directory (PKD). Working paper', Montreal: International Civil Aviation Organization.

ITU (2005) *Executive Summary: The Internet of Things*, Geneva: International Telecommunications Union.

Kefauver, B. (2003) 'ICAO: Structure and Process for Machine Readable Travel Documents'. Online. Available: http://www.quintessenz.at/doqs/000100002777/2003_03_07,ICAO,structure%20process_MRTD.pdf (accessed 29 December 2006).

Osieke, E. (1979) 'Unconstitutional Acts in international organisations: the law and practice of the ICAO', *The International and Comparative Law Quarterly* 28(1): 1–26.

Privacy International (2004) 'Towards an International Infrastructure for Surveillance of Movement'. Online. Available: http://www.privacyinternational.org/issues/terrorism/rpt/icaobackground.html (accessed 29 December 2006).

Putnam, R. (1988) 'Diplomacy and domestic politics: the logic of two-level games', *International Organization* 42(3): 427–60.

Singel, R. (2004) 'Passport safety, privacy face off', *Wired News*, 31 March.

U.N. Chronicle (2001) 'International instruments against terrorism', *United Nations Chronicle* Online Edition 38(3): 74(2).

Zetter, K. (2005) 'Lawmaker rips RFID passport plans', *Wired News*, 5 April. Online. Available: http://www.wired.com/politics/security/news/2005/05/67418

16 Another piece of Europe in your pocket

The European Health Insurance Card

Willem Maas

Introduction[1]

From the earliest days of European integration in the aftermath of the Second World War until the present day, European institutions have actively promoted intra-European movement (Maas 2007). The push to introduce a European Health Insurance Card (EHIC) to replace the paper forms previously needed to access health treatment during a temporary stay in another country fits within this general phenomenon. Introducing the EHIC, the Irish Prime Minister Bertie Ahern called it: 'a very tangible manifestation of an initiative by the European Union with real, practical benefits for its citizens', while Commission president Romano Prodi labelled it 'another piece of Europe in your pocket' (European Commission 2003a, 2004b). Thus, the symbolism of the European health card is not accidental: it was intended to reinforce the portability of benefits throughout EU territory. Its introduction achieves an aim expressed in the 1975 Tindemans report: the 'day that Europeans can move about within the Union, can communicate among themselves and when necessary receive medical care without national frontiers adding to the problems of distance, European Union will become for them a discernible reality' (Tindemans 1976: 28). But introducing the card also activated the Telematics for Social Security Programme, which attempts to 'speed up and simplify administrative procedures in order to improve the acquisition of entitlement and the granting and payment of social security benefits to migrant workers and other persons who have exercised their right of free movement'.[2] Furthermore, the agreements concerning the EHIC required all member states to issue national health insurance cards. Those member states previously without national cards were obliged to introduce them before the end of 2005. Finally, the Card's introduction raised the spectre of the further categorization and sorting of individuals within Europe into those granted entitlements and those not granted them, perpetuating or perhaps even creating social disparities between different categories of people. Despite its novelty as a supranational identity card, the EHIC thus exhibits similar tendencies (potentially empowering yet simultaneously classifying) as other identity cards.

By January 2006, the EHIC was recognized in all 27 EU member states plus Norway, Iceland, Liechtenstein and Switzerland. It is freely available to any individual covered by health insurance in a member state, giving access to treatment that becomes medically necessary during a temporary stay abroad. The Card proves entitlement to the same level of care covered by the health insurance scheme of the host state, at the same reimbursement level. Healthcare providers 'must therefore provide all the types of medical care and treatment that the patient's state of health necessitates to enable him to continue his stay in your country under safe medical conditions. The key is that he should not be obliged to cut short his visit in order to return to his country of residence for treatment'.[3] As this statement indicates, significant discretion surrounds the determination of what level of treatment is medically necessary. Also open to variability is the intended length of stay. Some categories of people (such as tourists from one European country visiting another) may be entitled to fewer medical benefits than other categories (such as students or employees sent by their companies to work elsewhere in Europe, so-called posted workers): for such people, 'the period can be relatively long, and the range of treatment accessible may be more extensive'.[4] As these examples indicate, the purpose of the EHIC is to facilitate free movement by ensuring the coverage of unexpected medical treatment. This is separate from the issue of planned medical treatment, going abroad for the purpose of receiving medical care. Extensive case law dating back to 1998 established the principle that EU citizens may obtain treatment in another European state without prior authorization and still be reimbursed by their own health insurance system.[5] Because of its roots in the free movement principle, the EHIC thus represents an integral part of the process of creating European citizens in which European institutions such as the Commission, Council, Parliament and Court are engaged (Maas 2007).

This chapter addresses, in turn, three central questions: the motivations for the ID scheme, its operation in practice and the lessons for other jurisdictions. The next section identifies the domestic and international motivations for the EHIC, focusing on the symbolic value of the card for European integration. The following section discusses the card's introduction and various administrative and technological issues it raises, concentrating on the difficulties of coordinating the various national and subnational systems. The final section extrapolates from the experience to date to discuss both EHIC's role in supporting European integration and its future prospects, drawing lessons for other jurisdictions and the EHIC's future.

Motivations for a supranational European health insurance card

The idea for a common European health insurance card has a long history: as early as 1978, the European health ministers meeting in the Council indicated their interest in a European health card and suggested that the Commission should devise specific proposals. In 1981, the European Parliament followed by arguing for a common European Health Card (European Parliament 2000). The Commission two years later recommended adopting an emergency health card. And in 1986, the Council supported this recommendation with a Resolution specifying that, 'in order further to protect the health of European citizens and to enhance their freedom of movement', it was 'desirable to provide for means whereby in an emergency their pre-existing or present health problems can be identified' (European Council

1986). But the Resolution was voluntary and non-binding. The 1989 Commission report on the Resolution's implementation concluded that only some countries (e.g. Germany, Luxembourg, and Portugal) had fully developed implementation measures and that technological improvements were needed. The Advanced Informatics in Medicine Project, funded by the Commission, was charged with this task (European Parliament 2000: 1).[6]

Further developments slowed, though in 1995 the member states adopted a Directive on the protection of personal data and data exchange (European Council 1995). More significant was the 1996 report of the European Parliament's Committee on the Environment, Public Health and Consumer Protection, chaired by Giacomo Leopardi. The Leopardi Report called on the Commission to develop, by January 1999, 'a European health card to be issued to every European citizen' (European Parliament 1996). The Committee's rationale is worth examining in some detail. The Report started with a recital of eleven reasons (the famous 'whereas' clauses that start every Parliamentary report or resolution) for developing the card. The first one specified: 'whereas the Treaty on European Union provides for the introduction of a citizenship of the Union, and whereas that must take the form of measures to ease the daily life of its citizens while increasing the protection of their rights and interests'.

This invocation of European citizenship is important because it demonstrates Parliament's desire to portray a European health card as an essential element of EU citizenship and thus a natural outgrowth of the Union's political development. The second reason similarly attempts to justify EHIC, adding mobility to citizenship: 'having regard to the increasing mobility of the citizens of Europe within the European Union for both business reasons and tourism'. The third asserts that 'European citizens are entitled to proper care as required by their state of health while travelling'. All three reasons – EU citizenship's promise of convenience and the protection of rights and interests, increasing mobility, and the entitlement to proper healthcare while travelling – focus on the rights of individuals. The next reason switches the emphasis to health: a health card would 'help avoid the potentially serious or fatal outcome of ineffective or dangerous treatment, especially in cases of chronic or serious disease or allergies'. The fifth reason asserts the Union's competence to take action, specifying that Article 129 of the Treaty provides that the EU institutions shall 'contribute towards ensuring a high level of human health protection'. Then the focus shifts to the operation of the card itself. The Report asserts that 'it is already technically possible to introduce a health card which could be used in all the countries of the European Union and outside its borders', and that 'it must be possible for the card to be used throughout the system, i.e. by doctors, hospitals, casualty departments and duty doctors, since, if the system is not a comprehensive one, it will be neither useful nor secure'.

This invocation of security is immediately followed by two related 'whereas' clauses. The first asserts that the 1995 data protection Directive 'provides the legal framework for the confidentiality of data entered on health cards', while the second is much longer, containing several subclauses. It starts by specifying that 'the purpose of such cards must first and foremost be to serve the citizen', continuing that 'they may perhaps be a way of reducing health costs but never a surveillance tool for public authorities of whatever nature'. This is noteworthy because it addresses head-on a key worry surrounding many identity cards, as discussed by other chapters in this volume. Yet the way in which this desire that the cards should never be a surveillance tool should be operationalized is unclear: 'the information on the card should not therefore be held in any data file, but should appear only on the card itself', and 'the citizen should therefore decide him- or herself what data should appear, and should have the right to omit certain information'. And 'it should be easy to change the information on the card, the issuing of which should not involve the cardholder in any expense'. In the context of the data protection Directive, these are perhaps laudable goals. But they do not seem particularly practical. It is unclear what happens, for example, when cardholders lose their cards: if the data was held solely on the card and not in any file, the card would need to be re-issued from scratch, which could become cumbersome if the card contained much data. The final three 'whereas' clauses of the Leopardi Report place the proposal for a European health card in the context of other cards in use in Europe and elsewhere, the confusing proliferation of identity and health cards within member states (the implication is that a single European card could eliminate this proliferation), and the interest shown by international health organizations and non-EU countries.

In the aftermath of the Leopardi Report, further work on the European health card continued slowly. A 1997 European Council Regulation established a Technical Commission on Data Processing, adhering to the principle that each member state would be responsible for managing its own part of the telematic services in accordance with EU data protection and privacy provisions, while the Administrative Commission on Social Security for Migrant Workers (discussed further below) would establish provisions for the operation of the common part of the telematic services (European Council 1997).

A more significant impetus for cooperation was provided by two cases decided by the European Court of Justice in 1998, the Decker and Kohll cases, in which the Court ruled that healthcare was subject to EU rules on the free movement of goods (Decker) and free movement of services (Kohll). In both rulings, the Court noted that, while European law 'does not detract from the powers of the Member States to organize their social security systems, they must nevertheless comply with Community law when exercising those powers' (European Court of Justice 1998a,b). Decker concerned a Luxembourg national who was told by the Luxembourg health insurance Fund that it would not reimburse him the cost of corrective spectacles he had bought in Belgium, on the ground that they had been purchased abroad without the Fund's prior authorization. The Court found that European law precludes national rules under which member state social security institutions refuse to reimburse an insured person on the ground that prior authorization is required for the purchase of any medical product abroad. Kohll concerned another Luxembourg national, who sought orthodontic treatment in Germany for his daughter. The Court ruled that European law precludes national rules under which reimbursement of the cost of dental treatment provided by an orthodontist established in another member state is subject to authorization by the insured person's social security institution. Such rules, it found, deter insured persons from approaching providers of medical services established in another member state, constituting a barrier to the freedom to provide services. The Decker and Kohll cases thus established that patients receiving healthcare in other member states were entitled to be reimbursed by their national health insurance. They, and subsequent cases, exemplify the use of European law to challenge the retention of national borders for healthcare provision, illustrating the growth of a supranational source of rights which augments European citizenship (Martinsen 2005).

In September 2000, representatives of card issuers, consumer and citizen groups, as well as the smart card industry met in Athens to decide on concrete steps for implementing a smart card charter that followed the invitation of the European Council's meeting in Feira in June (European Parliament 2001: 34). The greatest impetus was the creation of qualified electronic signature. The so-called eEurope initiative 'triggered a major industry-led smartcard initiative backed by €100m research funding' and established the smart card charter, launched under the Danish Presidency in December 2002 (European Commission 2003b: 16). But tying this charter to the EHIC did not gain the support of the member states, possibly because of the worry that e-smartcards developed for civic purposes for EU citizens would be extended to e-security: it was the potential 'surveillance of individuals by unknown agencies for nebulous ends which led to concern that the EU citizen could also be an unwitting 'suspect'' (Lodge 2004: 256).

At the Barcelona European Council meeting in March 2002, Europe's political leaders finally agreed to introduce a European Health Insurance Card, which would replace the paper forms needed for health treatment in another Member State. Under the heading 'Promoting skills and mobility in the European Union', they agreed that the card would simplify procedures without changing existing rights and obligations. At the same time, however, the leaders supported the aim of increasing the transferability of social security rights, including pensions, across the European Union. The European Commission was tasked with presenting concrete proposals before the 2003 Spring European Council meeting (European Council 2002: 33, 34).

The Commission duly complied and concluded that the European health insurance card was 'an ambitious project serving the interests of a real citizen's Europe', and that by drawing on the wealth and diversity of experience of many countries, it would be able to be brought into use 'as a simple, practical and flexible facility from 2004' (European Commission 2003a: 16). The Commission urged member states to enact two legislative changes in the proposed health card Regulation. The first was to align all the categories of insured persons, so that they would all be entitled to the same level of care. The existing legislation provided for different levels of care: everyone insured by national health insurance, with the exception of third country nationals and the members of their families, are entitled to all 'immediately necessary' care. But the broader category of 'necessary' care was available to those receiving retirement or invalidity pensions (E111 with appropriate endorsement), students (in the country of study, using E128), posted workers, seafarers, etc. (E128), transport workers (E110), unemployed persons moving to another Member

State to seek work (E119) and employed or self-employed victims of an industrial accident or occupational disease (E123). These differences were 'a complicating factor and could increase the cost, in that the cards would have to carry a means of identifying the 'category' of the insured, and the procedures for checking entitlement between social security institutions would be more involved' (European Commission 2003a: 11). The second change involved removing formalities required in addition to presentation of the form for obtaining care. In some member states, for example, the insured needed to go to the social security institution of the place of stay before approaching a care provider. Introducing EHIC provided a way to eliminate this requirement.

The introduction and operation of the EHIC

EHIC was introduced in the context of the coordination of social security for individuals moving about within the Union. There had been long-standing agreements concerning the coordination of social security, and they included very detailed provisions for emergency healthcare. Previous agreements had distinguished between 'immediately necessary care' and 'necessary care' but the Regulation removed this distinction, specifying that all insured persons would be entitled to the benefits in kind which become necessary on medical grounds during their stay in the territory of another member state (European Council 2004).

The detailed social security provisions under which EHIC fell had been developed over the years by the Administrative Commission on Social Security for Migrant Workers (often known by its French acronym CASSTM), made up of a government representative of each member state. CASSTM is aided by the Advisory Committee on Social Security for Migrant Workers, composed of representatives of governments, trade unions, and employers' organizations, which prepares opinions and proposals with a view to possible revision of the regulations. CASSTM handles all administrative questions and questions of interpretation arising from the social security Regulation and it also takes 'to foster and develop cooperation between Member States in social security matters by modernising procedures for information exchange'. It is in this vein that it developed the standard forms for the exchange of standardized data (such as E111, which EHIC's introduction rendered outdated), guides the work of the Telematics in Social Security programme, and introduced EHIC.

EHIC demonstrates insurance coverage. Because everyone insured by a social security system of any member state and eligible for care in that member state benefits from the rules on the coordination of social security, everyone so insured is automatically entitled to receive an EHIC (European Commission 2004a: 2). Thus, for example, third country national students studying in the UK and covered by the National Health Service (or studying in any other EU member state and insured by health insurance there) could request EHICs for health coverage when they travel to other EU member states.

The EHIC's design is identical in all member states and is intended to enable healthcare providers throughout the EU and EEA states to identify the card

immediately. The only personal information on the card is the cardholder's surname and first name, personal identification number and date of birth. Against
some early proposals, discussed above, the EHIC itself does not contain medical
data. There are two variants of the common design. The first consists of the
common design on the front of the card, with the back available to the issuing member state. This is the option chosen by most member states. The second is for the
common design to be placed on the back of an existing national or regional card,
an option chosen by Austria, Germany, Italy, Luxembourg, Lithuania, the
Netherlands and Liechtenstein.[7]

Because each member state is responsible for producing and distributing the
EHIC to everyone covered by health insurance in that state, the procedures for
acquiring or renewing a card differ from member state to member state. For example, residents of the UK may apply at http://www.ehic.org.uk, where they provide
their NHS number (England and Wales), CHI number (Scotland), or H&C number
(Northern Ireland). The British website is run by the Business Services Authority
and the Department of Health, whose data protection guarantee promises that they
will use the information provided only for processing the EHIC application, store it
for no more than 24 months after the expiry of the EHIC, and not transfer the data
outside the European Economic Area or 'disclose it to any third party other than the
Department for Work and Pensions (for the purpose of validating EHIC claims)
and the NHS Counter Fraud and Security Management Service and Department of
Health – International Division (in order to prevent and detect fraud and errors)'.[8]
By contrast, the equivalent website in the Netherlands (http://www.ehic.nl/) col-
lects the information on behalf of several Dutch health insurance companies (at
time of writing, 17 health insurance companies used the website; some 60 others
did not). The card is issued directly by the insurance companies after they verify
that the person requesting the card is covered. Applicants using the website are
guaranteed that they will receive their card within four working days. In France, the
EHIC must be requested from the local Caisse Primaire d'Assurance Maladie
office and can take up to 15 days to process. In Ireland, yet another national website
(http://www.ehic.ie/) facilitates the application process: applications submitted
online are processed on behalf of local health offices. Those who wish to fill out
paper application forms do so at their local health office. As these examples indicate, the issuing of cards occurs with much national variation.

Similar variation exists in terms of the EHIC's validity. Here also, because member states remain responsible for issuing the card, they may make their own rules
regarding validity. For example, an EHIC issued in Ireland is valid for up to two
years, up to five years in the UK, but only one year in France. In the Netherlands,
the insurance companies determine the validity: some companies make the card
valid for only the period requested (for example, to an applicant who requests the
card for a short trip), while others make the card valid for up to one year. In all cases,
the EHIC remains valid only as long as the holder remains insured. The example of
the Dutch insurance companies, each of which establish their own rules for validity
and none of which issue cards valid for more than one year, is one response to
possible lapse of coverage. The British website, by contrast, places the onus on

applicants to inform the NHS if they decide to remain abroad to live or work so that their coverage ceases. Because each member state retains responsibility for issuing the EHIC, the determination of eligibility rests with national authorities or the delegated regional office or private insurance companies. Each authority therefore is responsible for maintaining its own records concerning who is entitled to coverage and hence the EHIC. This means that any changes to the EHIC (e.g. due to name changes) must be submitted through the issuing authority. A common European database lists all the authorities entitled to issue the card.[9] For example, at time of writing, there is only one authority in the UK (Department for Work and Pensions) but there are 76 authorities in the Netherlands (all of the insurance companies) and 2,162 authorities in France (all of the local Caisses Primaires d'Assurance Maladie). Healthcare providers consult the common database of issuing authorities when they wish to submit a claim for healthcare provided. Each issuing authority then verifies coverage, according to its own systems, before any payments are approved.

Because member states retain responsibility for issuing and distributing the cards, there has been differential adoption of the EHIC. Some governments devoted significant resources to making citizens aware of the cards, while others did not. For example, health authorities in the UK and the Netherlands launched advertising campaigns, while there were no such campaigns elsewhere. The differential resources allocated to informing citizens paralleled earlier differences in informing citizens about the previous forms: E111 for tourists, E110 for international transporters, E119 for jobseekers and E128 for students and workers in other member states. Such differences reflect the variety of national approaches to health insurance and protection, differences which will no doubt continue to exist as long as national (or even regional) administrations retain responsibility for health insurance provision.

European integration and EHIC's future prospects

In the hope of bringing 'American-style mobility to the European employment market', the European Commission constantly works to facilitate mobility by attempting to coordinate social security systems, harmonize taxation systems, and increase information about employment opportunities (Maas 2007). Indeed, the Commission had earlier proposed a European identity number similar to the Social Security Number in the USA or the Social Insurance Number in Canada.[10] Those plans were placed on hold when the EHIC was introduced.

The EHIC in its first incarnation is simply a means of demonstrating entitlement to healthcare on the same terms as insured nationals. But the Commission expected that the card would in the future carry much more information. The 'long term intention is that the card will be issued with an electronic chip to greatly facilitate exchange of information between Member States and reduce the risk of error, fraud and abuse. There is no fixed timing for either of these future phases, which depends on the evaluation of the first roll-out of the card, and the development of technological systems that allow exchange of information without changes to the architecture of national systems' (European Commission 2004a: 2). The desire for the EHIC to carry more information is clear, but it is phrased in terms of techno-logical limitations and the need to maintain the existing architecture of national systems.

When EHIC was introduced, the European Commission's 'Frequently Asked Questions' page about the card, responding to the question of whether the card would carry personal information about the patient, asserted that the card simply concerned 'making access easier and getting reimbursements more quickly, not carrying information about health status, condition or treatments. Personal infor-mation about the card-carrier – e.g. blood type or medical records – will only be included insofar as the European health card is delivered as one side of a national card, and the national card already contains such information. Not all Member States issue national cards, and few Member States that do include personal health information' (European Commission 2004a: 2).

The desire to maintain the architecture of existing national systems (flowing from the requirement that member states retain authority and control over issuing the EHIC) coupled with the desire to have the card contain no personal health infor-mation about the holder, appear to stymie the future development of EHIC as a truly European identity card. As long as national authorities – or even subnational or other-wise delegated authorities, like the Dutch insurance companies – retain responsi-bility, the sole 'European' dimension to the card is its common design. Even the question of the number on the card seems intractable. For example, the British authorities expected that the EHIC would eventually carry the holder's NHS num-ber in England and Wales, CHI number for residents of Scotland, and Health and card number for Northern Ireland residents (United Kingdom Department of Health 2004: 2). There is little scope there for a common European number.

Despite EHIC's relative inutility as a common European identity card, observers do expect that its introduction and spread will simplify insurance coverage proce-dures, facilitate access to unplanned and perhaps also to planned medical treatment in other member states (Österle 2007; Hunt and Wallace 2006). At the same time, the mere existence of a common card – even though it is only a common design with very little information – represents another step in the gradual process to a common European healthcare space. The Kohll and Decker cases discussed above were only the first in a series of rulings of the European Court of Justice that have strength-ened patients' rights to receive cross-border care. Ongoing efforts at both European and national level ensure that European patients are no longer restricted in their choice of where to receive medical treatment or services. Instead, the newly created and enlarging European healthcare market has turned patients into pan-European consumers, forcing insurance authorities to adapt (Sieveking 2007). The EHIC is a symbolic representation of that common market.

Conclusion

The development of the European Health Insurance Card reflects the tensions sur-rounding the construction of a supranational political community in Europe. The vast majority of ID cards are national cards, issued by and recognized by national governments. As the other chapters in this volume demonstrate, national states promote ID cards for various purposes, including not only population identification and control but also as a means for individuals to demonstrate entitlement to social or other state-provided programmes. Although many programmes in the member states are regulated by European legislation, the European Union is not a state and does not fund its own social programmes. There is therefore no easily identifiable functional need for a European ID card. Consistent with the political project of constructing not only a free market area but also a common supranational political community, however, European political leaders introduced the EHIC to help develop in European citizens a feeling of identification with the Union. This aim is captured in Commission President Prodi's characterization of the Card as 'another piece of Europe in your pocket', as well as by the debates preceding its eventual introduction.

The EU is not a state, but it fulfils some functions of a state. This explains why, in the field of identity, the EU attempts to act like a state. The EHIC, like other ID cards, fits within the context of the production of identity and the differentiation and categorization of individuals into discrete classifications. EHIC is a good example of the explicit desire to create and foster identity. Because the European Union is not a state in the traditional sense (at least not yet) but does carry out some functions of a state, political leaders favoring further integration use EHIC as a means of gaining popular acceptance and legitimacy to the integration project. A major aim of European integration has been to lower barriers and remove impediments to the free movement not only of goods, services, or capital but also, especially, the free movement of people (Maas 2005, 2007). Though the introduction of the EHIC did not mean any new rights for cardholders, the symbolic value of the card is substantial. Indeed, some commentators describe EHIC as a new 'health passport' that reinfoces the ideas both of a citizens' Europe and of social Europe, thereby adding to the concrete value of European Union citizenship (Sabatakakis 2007). Cardholders are aware of existing in a common space for healthcare – just as the existence of a common currency makes consumers aware of the common economic and financial space. But EHIC is less universal than the euro. Consumers use the euro in their own as well as in other states, but the EHIC is – in many states, at least – used only for proving coverage outside the member state. The EHIC's role as another piece of Europe in the pocket of Europeans thus outweighs any other functionality it might have.

Notes

1 I thank Christin Gountouvas for research assistance and Colin Bennett and David Lyon for editorial suggestions.
2 Online. Available: http://europa.eu/scadplus/leg/en/cha/c10518.htm
3 Online. Available: http://ec.europa.eu/employment_social/healthcard/ prestataires_ en.htm#5
4 Online. Available: http://ec.europa.eu/employment_social/healthcard/prestataires_ en.htm#oxo

5 Online. Available: http://ec.europa.eu/employment_social/social_security_schemes/ healthcare/e112/ conditions_en.htm
6 For a series of papers on the AIM project and its successors, see Laires *et al.* 1995.
7 Directive 95/46/EC of the European Parliament and of the Council of 24 October, 1995 on the protection of individuals with regard to the processing of personal data and on the free movement of such data. Personal data provides that personal data should not be processed unless doing so meets the conditions of transparency, legitimate purpose, and proportionality. The website http://ec.europa.eu/justice_home/fsj/privacy/ provides full details and regular updates.
8 Online. Available: http://ec.europa.eu/employment_social/healthcard/situation_ en.htm
9 Online. Available: https://www.ehic.org.uk/ under 'terms and conditions'
10 Online. Available: http://ec.europa.eu/employment_social/cld/displayMain.do
11 See 'EU Plans to Issue 'Identity Number' for Every Citizen', *The Independent*, 5 February, 2001.

Bibliography

European Commission (2003a) 'Communication from the Commission concerning the Introduction of a European Health Insurance Card', *COM*: 73.
European Commission (2003b) 'Communication from the Commission to the Council, the European Health Insurance Card', *COM*: 66.
European Commission (2004a) 'European health insurance card: frequently asked questions', *MEMO* 4: 75.
European Commission (2004b) 'More Europe in Your Pocket – the European Health Insurance Card'. Online. Available: http://ec.europa.eu/employment_social/news/2004/ mar/healthcard_en.html
European Council (1986) 'Resolution of the Council and of the Representatives of the Governments of the Member States', meeting within the Council of 29 May, concerning the adoption of a European emergency health card. *OJC* 184: 4–7.
European Council (1995) 'Directive 95/46/EEC' of 24 October 1995 on the protection of individuals with regard to the processing of personal data and on the free movement of such data.
European Council (1997) 'Council Regulation (EC)', No. 1290/97 of 27 June, amending 'Regulation (EEC)' No. 1408/71 on the application of social security schemes to employed persons, to self-employed persons and to members of their families moving within 'Community and Regulation (EEC)' No. 574/72 laying down the procedure for implementing 'Regulation (EEC)' No. 1408/71.
European Council (2002) 'Presidency Conclusions', Barcelona European Council, 15 and 16 March, SN 100/1/02.
European Council (2004) 'Regulation (EC)' No. 631/2004 of 'European Parliament and of the Council' of 31 March 2004, amending 'Council Regulation (EEC)' No. 1408/71 on the application of social security schemes to employed persons, to self-employed persons and to members of their families moving within the Community, and Council Regulation (EEC) No. 574/72 laying down the procedure for implementing Regulation (EEC) No. 1408/71, in respect of the alignment of rights and the simplification of procedures.
European Court of Justice (1998a) 'Case C-120/95. Nicolas Decker *v* Caisse de maladie des employés privés', *ECR* I-1831.
European Court of Justice (1998b) 'Case C-158/96. Raymond Kohll *v* Union des caisses de maladie', *ECR* I-1931.

European Parliament (1996) 'Report of the Committee on the Environment, Public Health and Consumer Protection of the European Parliament on the European Health Card (Leopardi Report)', PE 215.231/fin, A4-0091/96, 26 March.

European Parliament (2000) 'A European Health Card', PE 296.701.

European Parliament (2001) 'A European Health Card – Final Study', PE 296.701/Fin.St.

Hunt, J. and Wallace, C.J. (2006) 'Citizens' rights to receive medical treatment in another EU member state', *Journal of Social Welfare and Family Law* 28(2): 217–28.

Laires, M.F., Ladeira, M.J. and Pihlkjær Christensen, J. (1995) *Health in the New Communications Age: Healthcare Telematics for the 21st Century*, Amsterdam: IOS Press.

Lodge, J. (2004) 'EU Homeland Security: Citizens or Suspects?', *Journal of European Integration* 26(3): 253–79.

Maas, W. (2005) 'Freedom of movement inside fortress Europe. Global surveillance and policing: borders, security, identity', in E. Zureik and M.B. Salter (eds) *Global Surveillance and Policing: Borders, Security, Identity*, Cullompton: Willan.

Maas, W. (2007) *Creating European Citizens*, Lanham: Rowman & Littlefield.

Martinsen, D.S. (2005) 'Towards an internal health market with the European court', *West European Politics* 28(5): 1035–56.

Österle, A. (2007) 'Healthcare across borders: Austria and its new EU neighbours', *Journal of European Social Policy* 17(2): 112–24.

Parliament, the Economic and Social Committee, and the Committee of Regions (2002) *eEurope Final Report*.

Sabatakakis, E. (2007) 'La carte Européenne d'assurance-maladie: Le nouveau passeport pour la mobilité en Europe', *Revue du Marché commun et de l'Union européenne* 504: 48–60.

Sieveking, K. (2007) 'ECJ rulings on healthcare services and their effects on the freedom of cross-border patient mobility in the EU', *European Journal of Migration and Law* 9: 25–51.

Tindemans, L. (1976) European Union Report to the European Council. *Tindemans Report*.

United Kingdom Department of Health (2004) 'Proposals for the Introduction of the European Health Insurance Card'. Online. Available: http://www.dh.gov.uk/prod_consum_dh/groups/dh_digitalassets/@dh/@en/documents/digitalasset/dh_4087422.pdf

Index